A HISTORY OF THE ARCTIC

A HISTORY OF THE
ARCTIC

NATURE, EXPLORATION AND EXPLOITATION

JOHN MCCANNON

REAKTION BOOKS

With love to Pam and Miranda

Published by
Reaktion Books Ltd
33 Great Sutton Street
London EC1V 0DX, UK
www.reaktionbooks.co.uk

First published 2012

Printed and bound by TJ International, Padstow, Cornwall

British Library Cataloguing in Publication Data
McCannon, John, 1967–
A history of the Arctic: nature, exploration and exploitation.
1. Arctic regions – History.
2. Arctic regions – Discovery and exploration – History.
3. Arctic regions – Climate.
4. Arctic regions – Environmental conditions.
5. Geopolitics – Arctic regions.
I. Title
998-DC23

ISBN 978 1 78023 018 4

Contents

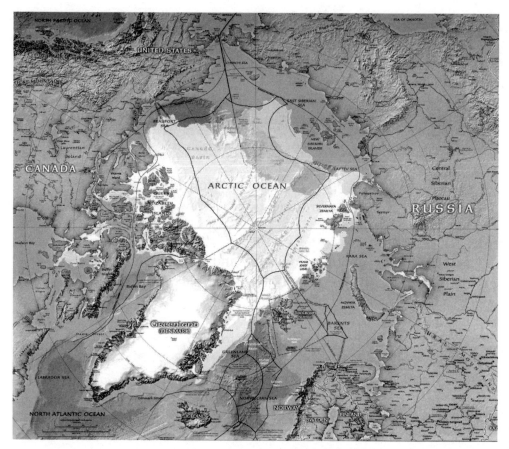

Circumpolar view of the Arctic.

I
Origins: Introduction and Environmental Overview

In July 1895, after months of allowing his research vessel, the *Fram*, to drift through the pack ice of the Arctic Ocean, Fridtjof Nansen of Norway caught sight of land for the first time in almost two years. Finally, he exclaimed, 'we again see something rising above that never-ending white line on the horizon yonder – a white line which for count-less ages has stretched over this lonely sea, and which for millennia to come shall stretch in the same way.' For the crew of the *Fram*, to be where the human eye could once more perceive topographical difference was to recover the human sense of passing time, an experience Nansen likened to starting 'a new life'. 'For the ice', by contrast, every moment was, and ever would be, 'the same'.[1]

Throughout recorded history, wilderness in many forms has served to symbolize elemental vastness and permanence. The forest primeval. The earth-rooted mountain. Boundless steppes and limitless seas. That said, perhaps no landscape has stood out in the modern mind as so quintessentially timeless as the Arctic. In the Western imagination, the polar world has featured as a realm of crystalline purity, as a grey kingdom of frozen death, and in other guises besides, but is most often seen as eternal and unchanging. Nansen described it further as 'so awfully still, with the silence that shall one day reign, when the earth again becomes desolate and empty' – making him merely one of dozens who essentialize the Arctic, even if just for poetic effect, as an ageless expanse marked solely by the inexorable encroachment of glaciers upon the land, the mesmerizing shimmer of the aurora borealis, and endless cycles of migration leading polar bears, reindeer and whales in never-varying circles over the earth and through the ocean depths.[2]

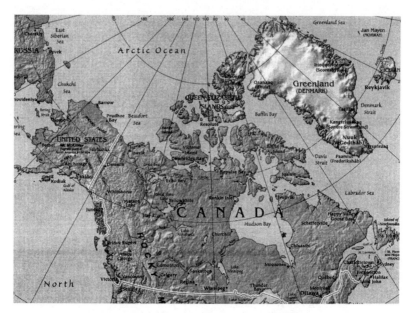

The North American Arctic and Greenland.

But the Arctic, of course, *does* change. Like all places, it moves through time, shaped by natural forces and human agency alike. Also, to those who live there or pay it close attention, it presents more faces than it is commonly thought to have. The American explorer Elisha Kent Kane cleaved to the standard view in his Grinnell expedition diaries, declaring the Arctic 'a landscape such as Milton or Dante might imagine: inorganic, desolate, mysterious . . . unfinished by the hand of its Creator' – whereas the Canadian naturalist Farley Mowat insists that 'the Arctic is not only the ice-covered cap of the world' or 'the absolute cold of the pole', but also 'two million square miles of rolling plains that, during the heat of midsummer, are thronged with life and brilliant with the colors of countless plants in full bloom'.[3]

The purpose of this book is to portray these many visages and to trace the Arctic's passage through time as fully as possible. Both tasks necessitate the weaving together of many narratives, for 'Arctic history' encompasses not just the oft-repeated chronicle of polar exploration, but processes of national development, economic organization and resource mobilization. It is the still-undervalued tale of the peoples indigenous to the Arctic and their frequently painful interactions with Euro-American outsiders and colonizers. It is bound up with the histories of science, technology, diplomacy and war. It demands an appreciation of the environment's climatological and zoological

Siberia and the Eurasian Arctic.

complexities. No book of this length can pretend to cover any of these topics encyclopaedically, but it can aim for a global *approach* by emphasizing the interrelationships that exist among them. Above all, it will strive to be guided by the insight, voiced by the respected author Barry Lopez, that, in the North, 'people's desires and aspirations [are] as much a part of the land as the wind, the solitary animals, and the bright fields of stone and tundra' – and that, at the same time, 'the land itself exist[s] quite apart from these'.[4] Both humanity and natural space are part of Arctic reality, and both will be as present as I can make them in this slim volume.

Conventions

By rule-of-thumb reckoning, the Arctic consists of 11 million square miles of sea and solid land. Delimiting this territory, however, is no straightforward task, for there exists no generally agreed-upon definition for it. The region's most distinct landmark, the North Pole, is not just invisible, but is in fact several poles. The Geographic North Pole, at 90°N – 'the' Pole in most people's minds – has the most firmly fixed location, but even it wobbles from month to month in an erratic circle about 15 feet in radius, and the North Magnetic Pole, toward which the compass points, strays more widely still: 77°N 120°W in 1985, 81°N 111°W in 2001, and 83°N 114°W in 2005. Scientists have also mapped out a

North Geomagnetic Pole and a Northern Pole of Relative Inaccessibility, the point farthest from any land mass.[5]

As for the Arctic Circle, or latitude 66°33′N, this is a cartographic abstraction that marks the southernmost point where polar day and polar night – 24 hours of uninterrupted light or darkness – occur in the northern hemisphere. Such a demarcation gives little sense of actual conditions on the ground, for certain areas enclosed by the Circle are surprisingly temperate, owing to peculiarities of wind, terrain or water, while many 'subarctic' zones are actually Arctic in their climate or ecology. For example, the second-coldest temperature known to modern science in the northern hemisphere was recorded in Oimyakon, in Russia's Sakha Republic (formerly Yakutia), 200 miles south of the Arctic Circle, while Norway's Lofoten Islands, at 68°N, but bathed by warm ocean currents, enjoy an average January temperature above 32°F. Other commonly suggested definitions – such as the northern treeline, the southern extent of iceberg drift or continuous permafrost, or the 50°F isotherm as recorded in midsummer – likewise fail to capture the region's characteristics consistently and inclusively. Wildlife and weather systems are no respecters of lines drawn on maps, and neither, for most of their history, have aboriginal populations been. Certain regions lying below the Arctic Circle, including Iceland and the Faeroes, Newfoundland and Labrador, Kamchatka and the Aleutian Islands, have played important roles in Arctic history, whether as jumping-off points for the exploration or colonization of the Arctic, or because their inhabitants based substantial parts of their economic practices on the exploitation of Arctic resources. For ease of use and the sake of flexibility, this book will take as its subject the land and waters north of 60°N, granting itself leeway to veer to the south when the topic at hand calls for doing so. It will avoid excessive technicality and use the terms 'north', 'far north', or 'high north' interchangeably with 'Arctic'; more restrictive designations, such as 'circumpolar', 'high' and 'low' Arctic – the line between which is customarily taken to be 75°N – and the names of specific places or subregions will be used where appropriate. The term 'subarctic' will refer to regions lying between the 55th and 65th parallels.

If geographical terminology requires discussion, so does that for the Arctic's inhabitants, with many well-known labels having become less politically acceptable or less ethnographically precise, and with different countries observing different protocols. Herein, the terms 'indigenous', 'native' and 'aboriginal' are treated as synonymous and as suitably applicable to any region; if the word 'primitive' is used, it refers to levels of technological development and is not meant to carry the connotations it once did of savagery or inferiority. With respect to specific groups, this book will privilege the names favoured by the groups themselves, but also make clear how they used to be known, or how they are still known popularly. In other words, it will be evident that the Sami are the people once called 'Lapps', that the Nenets appear in old chronicles as 'Samoyed', and so on. The term 'Indian' will appear mostly in quoted material or direct context, and occasionally on its own when the preferred u.s. and Canadian labels, 'Native American' and 'First Nations', fit poorly into a given sentence. In Russia, the most common umbrella terms are 'native Siberians' and 'small peoples of the North' – 'small' referring to population count, not physical size – although many of the country's northern aboriginals live west of Siberia or, like the Sakha (Yakut) and Komi, are too numerous to fall into the category of 'small'. Here as elsewhere, particular groups will be called by their own names whenever feasible. As for the non-natives who came to the Arctic or claimed dominion over it, they will be identified, if not by specific nationality, as 'European', 'Western', 'Euro-American' or 'white'.

The nomenclature presenting the most difficulty is 'Eskimo', which, like 'Indian', was applied by outsiders to people who have their own names for themselves and is rejected by some as derogatory, but nonetheless remains acceptable in certain quarters. 'Eskimo' once served as the standard ethnonym for all Inuit and Yupik peoples who inhabit the territory stretching from eastern Siberia to Greenland and share a common ethnocultural heritage. (Linguistically related to both, the Aleuts of the Bering Sea are considered distinct and do not factor into this debate.) On the other hand, the word was borrowed by Europeans from Algonquin-speaking Native Americans – who, if the traditional etymology holds true, mocked their northern neighbours as 'eaters of raw flesh' – and many consider it offensive. Since the 1977 formation of the Inuit Circumpolar Conference, and especially in Canada and Greenland, where the old usage is heavily stigmatized, the habit has been to revive indigenous names, with the term 'Inuit' most frequently employed as a collective label for the peoples once known as 'Eskimo'. However, the former has not won the same breadth of acceptance as the latter used to enjoy. One complication arises from its dual nature: Inuit serves as a general category, but also refers specifically to certain natives in the Canadian Arctic – as distinct from other 'Inuit', such as central Canada's Inuinnaq, the Inughuit of Greenland and Ellesmere Island or the Inuvialuit of Canada's western territories. A second problem centres on Alaska, where many Inupiat of the North Slope resist being classified as Inuit, and where the term excludes the Yupik. In Alaska, 'Eskimo' holds more currency as a generic label, and it is used among Russia's Yupik as well, although less readily than in the United States. Like many works on the subject, this book will follow the conventions laid out in the 'Arctic' volume of the Smithsonian Institution's *Handbook of North American Indians*, which recommends using 'Eskimo' in the Alaskan case, 'Inuit' when referring to Canada or Greenland, and more precise designations wherever possible.[6] In no case will the terms 'Indian', 'Native American' or 'First Nations' apply to Eskimo or Inuit, although the phrase 'Alaskan native' includes Eskimos, Aleuts and Native Americans.

Many languages are relevant to Arctic history, a number of which must be transliterated from non-Latin alphabets, and there is no one method of rendering foreign terms and names into English that perfectly balances consistency, academic rigour and readability. As a rule, I have favoured the last, choosing where I can the best-known and/or most visually pleasing version of a word borrowed from another tongue or orthography. Place names change over time and due to political circumstance; older names will be used in their proper context, but also identified with the newer toponyms that have replaced them. Dates are given according to the Western calendar, with distinctions between BCE (before common era) and, where necessary, CE (common era), rather than BC ('before Christ') and AD (*anno Domini*). Unless otherwise specified, all dates, including those in the sections on prehistory, are measured in calendar years rather than radiocarbon years.

The Ecosphere

In the beginning, during the volcano-charged Hadean and Archean eons (4.6 to 2.5 billion years ago), immense fountains of magma gouted upward into the northern sky. Then, for many millions of years, there was little but ocean, for it was largely in the south that the first land masses formed, broke apart and recombined into the early supercontinents. Tectonic forces periodically carried sizable fragments of land close to the Arctic Circle, but not until the cusp between the Palaeozoic and Mesozoic eras, or around 260 million years ago, did elements of what is today circumpolar territory drift into the North. The Arctic Ocean took its largely landlocked form around 50 million years ago, during the Eocene epoch, and it was at the beginning of the Pleistocene, nearly 2.6 million years ago, that the rest of the Arctic map came to look fundamentally as it does today.[7]

Only after 12,000 years ago, as the Younger Dryas, the last cold snap of the Pleistocene, came to an end, and as the great ice sheets receded from Eurasia and North America, did the Arctic's present-day ecosystem take shape. Ironically, for all the perception by outsiders of the region as primordial and permanently formed, the Arctic environment is the world's youngest; not long ago on the geological timescale, the flora, fauna and climate of the circumpolar north were startlingly different from anything imaginable today. Alaska's North Slope and the 'greensands' of Canada's Devon Island have yielded fossil evidence from 70 to 75 million years ago which indicates that, during the Cretaceous, tall trees stood in the Far North, while sinewy plesiosaurs and huge, primitive sharks patrolled the ocean depths. The north polar waters were virtually free of ice, and portions of upper Siberia, Alaska and the Canadian archipelago were carpeted with ferns, gingko, swamp cypress and dawn redwood (*Metasequoia*). As far north as 75 degrees – on land that would have drifted as high as 85°N during the Cretaceous – palaeontologists have uncovered the remains of such unexpected creatures as gliding lemurs, the hippopotamus-like *Coryphodon*, and a miscellany of dinosaur species, from the pint-sized therapod Troodon to the 4-ton, plant-eating Edmontosaurus and the Gorgosaurus, a fierce, 30-foot-long carnivore. Whether the Arctic at this stage was as temperate as the existence of such species would imply or whether the animals were better adapted than their modern descendants to cooler conditions, the region for a long time resembled the sort of fantasy adventureland more typically encountered in the pages of a Jules Verne or H. G. Wells novel.

All this changed with the advent of the Pleistocene, which repeatedly blanketed the northern hemisphere with enormous continental glaciers. Popularly but erroneously thought of as 'the' ice age, the Pleistocene was a time of successive glacial periods, each separated from the next by a warm interglacial phase, and with brief spells of gentler weather, called interstades, punctuating the glacial periods themselves. This cycle has not stopped: the Holocene epoch we live in now, far from having ended the ice age, is merely the latest interval in the long process of Quaternary glaciation – a blink of the eye in planetary terms before the inevitable return of the ice some thousands of years from now. (A sobering thought for those disposed to think about history on the grand scale, but given the pressures placed on the environment by civilization today, we will be lucky indeed to survive long enough for a new approach of the ice to be humanity's terminal crisis.) The last ice age began around 100,000 years ago, spawning the glacial masses conventionally known in North America as the Wisconsin, comprised of the Cordilleran and Laurentide ice sheets; the Devensian or Midlandian in the British Isles and Ireland; the Würm atop Europe's Alps; and the Weichselian in Fennoscandia and European Russia, made up of the Scandinavian and Barents-Kara ice sheets. Siberia east of the Taimyr Peninsula, most climatologists believe, was left relatively unglaciated. More recently, scientists have come to use the marine isotope stage (MIS) as a preferred yardstick with which to measure the Quaternary period's glacial and climatic fluctuations, with warm interglacials and interstadials represented by odd-numbered stages, and glacial advances by even-numbered stages.[8] MIS 1 corresponds with the Holocene, MIS 4 with the early onset of the Wisconsin-Weichselian glaciation. Whatever label one gives them, the late-Pleistocene ice sheets reached their maximum extent between 22,000 and 18,000 years ago, and although they began their gradual retreat thereafter, this age of mastodons, sabre-toothed cats and woolly rhinoceroses persisted for several more millennia. As described in chapter Two, hominid presence had already made itself felt in the North, many times in the subarctic during interglacials and interstades, and increasingly in the Arctic during the late Upper Palaeolithic.

Except for the Greenland interior – where the 660,000-square-mile, berg-birthing ice cap preserves the character of the Pleistocene into our own day – the Arctic terrain left behind by the glaciers' withdrawal ranges up from the northern edge of the taiga, or boreal forest, through the permafrosted shrublands and sedges of the tundra, and finally to the polar deserts of the extreme north. Commonly spoken of as 'belts', these biomes are in reality spread irregularly across the map. A sparser, more open type of woodland often sits between taiga and tundra, with the treeline meandering back and forth across the Arctic Circle, and occasionally past 70°N. Tundra, from the Finnish word for 'treeless land', is interspersed with mountains, river deltas, woods and coastlines, all capable of creating their own localized climates. Usually thought of as 'nothing but a gray sea of moss scarcely diversified by gray rocks, gray lakelets, and gray streamlets' – Jack London's description from the story 'Love of Life' – the tundra varies considerably according to moisture levels and soil quality, supporting only grasses and dwarf shrubs in the high Arctic, but larger shrubs and even trees in the lower Arctic.[9] Most barren of all are the rock- and gravel-strewn polar deserts of the islands and the high Arctic, where the ground supports little or no vegetation and in some cases lacks even the barest bit of soil to cover it. 'Desert' is no misnomer here: precipitation is minimal by comparison with farther south, although what snow does fall is whipped into massive blizzards by the fierce northern winds. Except during the summertime thaw, most of the region's moisture is locked in the ice.

The Arctic Ocean, the world's smallest, at 5,427,000 square miles, or just under 3 per cent of the earth's saltwater surface, and the shallowest, with an average depth of only 3,400 feet, is divided physically into several basins by large undersea ridges – among them the Lomonosov, Gakkel, Northwind and Mendeleyev – and oceanographically into several subregions. Centremost, or farthest north, is the high Arctic abyssal, the zone most heavily cloaked by ice year-round, and the one most poorly understood by scientists. Next are the high Arctic shallows, and then the high Arctic brackish region, where salinity and temperature vary more than they do closer to the Pole, due to the intermingling of this zone's waters with those fed into the ocean by the North's mighty rivers: the Coppermine and Mackenzie in North America, the Tanaelva that flows along the Finno-Norwegian border, and Russia's Dvina, Ob, Yenisei and Lena, to list only a few. On the outermost ring, there is the boreal littoral, bordering Eurasia's and North America's coastlines. Some scholars, particularly in Russia, argue that a 'low Arctic shallow region' exists as well, and with recent technological revolutions in undersea research such classifications, not to mention the map of the Arctic seabed, will be in flux for years to come. To the extent that the circulation of the planet's waters can be thought of as driven by an ocean 'conveyor belt' – a model that now strikes a number of oceanographers as conceptually incomplete[10] – it is at the juncture between the Arctic Ocean and the North Atlantic that this complex interplay of cold and warm currents is believed to originate and end. Add to this the role of the Greenland ice cap in generating high and low pressure cycles in the northern hemi - sphere, and the Arctic is revealed as an influential fashioner of global weather patterns.

The Arctic may support more life than is customarily thought, but its ecosystem remains one of the world's least productive. The number of species resident in the far north year-round, and even seasonally, is relatively small, and food chains tend to be short, a sparsity that begins at the microlevel. By contrast with oceans elsewhere, polar seas are colder on top than in the depths, thanks to a halocline layer that makes it difficult for warmer and saltier water to rise higher than 150 to 300 feet below the surface. Not only do low salinity and cool temperatures speed the formation of ice, but vertical stability interferes with the cycle of oceanic upwelling that pumps inorganic salts from the depths to the sunlit shallows. These phosphates, nitrates and silicates nourish the plant plankton that feed zooplankton, such as krill, and thereby start the chain which extends upward to fish like cod, char, whitefish and salmon, and further to seals, whales, bears and humans. In places where the halocline layer is weaker, or where plankton-rich water is washed in by rivers or the currents that stream north from the Atlantic and Pacific, sea life spawns in greater profusion. Among these are Lancaster and Cumberland sounds in eastern Canada; the Bering Sea, nourished by Russia's Anadyr River and the Yukon and Kuskokwim in Alaska; and the Norwegian coastline, warmed by the Gulf Stream and its northeastward continuation, the Spitsbergen Current. But for the Arctic Ocean as a whole, limitations on upwelling limit fecundity on the larger scale.

On terra firma as well, at least north of the taiga, the food chain grows out of a similarly unpromising foundation. Soil, where it exists, tends to be acidic and nutrient-poor, owing to the slender variety of saprophagic detritovores: the worms, fungi and beetles that feed on decaying plant and animal matter, facilitating the cycle of decomposition and soil enrichment. (Regarding insects, any visitor to the North whose tender dermis has been subjected to the summertime aggressions of flies and mosquitoes normally comes away convinced that the region is endowed with more than enough of them. In fact only 600 or so species make the Arctic their home, including *Boreaphilus henningianus*, which actually requires frigid temperatures to survive, and whose ice-encased remains make an excellent palaeoclimatological marker of where conditions of extreme cold have prevailed in the past.) Only with difficulty do plants establish themselves above the treeline, owing to killing temperatures, dryness comparable to that of the Gobi or Kalahari and the darkness of polar night, which can inhibit photosynthesis for betewen two and four months of the year. Another obstacle to plant growth is the permafrost covering 20 per cent of the northern hemisphere's land mass and most of its Arctic and subarctic territory. A curious substance exhibiting some of the properties of ice – it expands by crystalline formation and is able to 'colonize' deposits of conventional soil – permafrost can run to depths of 1,000 feet, as it does in northern Alaska, and even up to 5,000 feet, as in parts of Siberia. It is generally topped by a thin 'active' layer, anywhere from 2 to 15 feet thick, which thaws on a seasonal basis but allows little drainage, turning much of the summer landscape into bog and muskeg. Shrubs and some trees take root in the active layer, but nothing on the order of what unfrozen soil to the south will support. One of the North's more unusual sights is the 'drunken' forest, formed when wind and their own weight cause trees rooted in permafrost to lean during the annual thaw, only to be left with the appearance of lurching inebriates when the ground freezes again.

As a result, the majority of Arctic flora are small and hardy, starting with moss and lichen, which need not root at all, and moving on to grasses and sedge. Flowering plants, including mountain sorrel, glacier buttercups and Labrador tea, bloom and fruit during the brief summer, although they must do so quickly, whereas the simpler growths are metabolically designed to survive the winter by entering into a frozen state. The abundance of larger plants depends on latitude, elevation, and proximity to coastlines or river valleys, but the tundra sustains the growth of many shrubs, such as alder, sweetbroom, twinflower and lingonberry (also known as mountain cranberry), and the much-loved cloudberry, found as far north as the 78th parallel and yielding not just preserves but flavouring for the Finnish potable *lakkalikööri* and various types of Scandinavian *akvavit*. In turn, the shrubs protect weaker and lower-lying herbaceous grasses and flowers. Trees are more plentiful in the taiga, where a number of deciduous varieties like poplar and birch stand beside pine, fir and spruce, and where more delicate growths like ginseng and mushrooms are found closer to the ground. Near the tree-line and on it, the specimens that thrive best, along with juniper and dwarf birch, are black spruce in North America and, in Eurasia, larch, Norway spruce and cedar pine. Varieties of willow grow also, in tundra valleys sheltered from the wind. All this helps to dispel the misconception that the Arctic is devoid of life, but neither should the far north be mistaken for a land of plenty. Trees stand only ten inches to three feet high on the tundra, although they are taller on the treeline. And to measure by the standard of primary production, or the amount of biomass a terrain type generates by means of plant photosynthesis, the Arctic tundra manages a paltry annual output of 140 grams per square metre, as opposed to 600 grams for temperate grassland, 1,200 grams for deciduous forest and a whopping 2,200 grams for tropical rainforest. Primary production determines how many herbivores can be nourished by plant matter (secondary production) as well as how many omnivores and carnivores an ecosystem can feed (trophic or high-energy production).

This is a less than efficient system of exchange: even in richer ecospheres – Yosemite or the Black Forest, say – more than 90 per cent of the caloric energy generated by primary production is lost to decomposition, with less than 5 per cent passed on to herbivore consumers. In the Arctic, where the numbers start off small to begin with, the pickings are decidedly slim.

No mystery, then, that species diversification is so limited. A stunning array of bird types, including the snow goose and the fabled Arctic tern, with its yearly journey of more than 40,000 miles, migrate to and through the far north. But few overwinter in the region like the snowy owl and the raven, or the ptarmigan and the gyrfalcon – and even the number that breed there seasonally does not go much above 60 or 70. More than 3,000 species of mammal reside in the subarctic, but in the Arctic proper that number shrinks to a bare three or four dozen, not counting marine mammals. Smallest and lowest on the food chain are voles, Arctic lemmings and ground squirrels, along with marmots and hares. Fur-bearing mustelids – among them otters, weasels, martens and sables – abound in the subarctic taiga, with some, like the ermine and the wolverine, prone to roam into the higher latitudes. Canid predators, who stoop to scavenging as well, include the ever-resourceful coyote; various foxes, including the red and Arctic varieties; and subspecies of the wolf, particularly *Canis lupus arctos*, the white Arctic wolf of North America and Greenland, and the tundra wolf (*Canis lupus albus*) of Fennoscandia and Russia. Their sole feline counterparts are the Canada lynx and Eurasian lynx, shadowy hunters of the boreal woods.

Mammals larger than this have been rare in the far north since the mass extinction of ice-age megafauna like the woolly mammoth and Irish elk. The deer species and wild sheep so prevalent in today's subarctic woods and mountains can also be found in the Arctic if the terrain provides enough vegetation. These include the Dall sheep, the elk (*Cervus canadensis*, or wapiti) and the monarch of the boreal forest, the moose (*Alces alces*) who, 7 feet tall at the shoulder and crowned with a 6-foot spread of palmate antlers, is the North's largest herbivore. The brown bear (*Ursus arctos*) inhabits the entire Arctic margin of Eurasia, from Norway to Chukotka, while its grizzly cousins in North America are happy to roam the northernmost parts of Alaska and western Canada. Four other mammals perhaps embody the Arctic most fully: the musk ox, reindeer, walrus and polar bear. The first is a relic from the Pleistocene, originating more than a million years ago in Asia from the genus *Ovibos*, then crossing to North America between 200,000 and 90,000 years ago.

Rangifer tarandus – the reindeer in Eurasia, the caribou in North America.
Crucial for centuries to indigenous peoples throughout the circumpolar
north as a source of food, toolmaking materials, and transport.

Although small numbers have been transplanted to Alaska, Siberia and
Scandinavia, the musk ox's real home is Greenland and the islands of
Canada's high Arctic, where it is known to the natives as *oomingaaq*,
or 'animal with skin like a beard'. It is famous for its pungent smell –
produced not by musk, but by the urine of males in rut – and the
circular, back-to-the-centre defensive posture adopted by herds under
threat to protect their young. Some see it as epitomizing the unflinching
stoicism required for survival in the North, with one essayist noting
how 'the winter face of a musk ox, its unperturbed eye glistening in a halo
of snow-crusted hair, looks at you over a cataract of time, an image that
has endured through all the pulsations of ice.'[11]

In contrast to the musk ox, which migrates only short distances, the
reindeer, or *Rangifer tarandus* – known in North America as the caribou, the Mikmaq word for 'shoveller', for the way its hooves dig in the
snow for food – is one of the Arctic's great travellers. Many of its subspecies have survived into the historical period, both in North America
and Eurasia, and several are mighty seasonal wanderers, setting out twice
every year on journeys that cover hundreds of miles. In the spring, herds
numbering in the thousands head north to their calving grounds in the
tundra, where fresh herbiage is exposed by the melting of the snow, and
where relief can be found from the suffocating clouds of biting insects

Marine mammals – walruses, sea cows and the narwhal – as depicted in
Emil Hanselmann's *Naturgeschichte des Tierreichs* ('A Natural History of
the Animal Kingdom', 1868).

brought to life by the Arctic summer. In autumn, mating along the way,
they return to the treeline, where enough plants and mosses grow to
keep them alive through the winter. The sight of 50,000 and more of
these swift, proud beasts coursing across the land ranks as one of the
most heart-stirring spectacles the Arctic has to offer. In Alaska and
Canada, native peoples came to follow and hunt the caribou – the
Eskimo and Inuit gave its name to the constellation we know as the Big
Dipper or the Plough – but never tamed it. Things turned out differently
in Europe and Asia, where a number of groups learned to domesticate
the reindeer, causing great ecological transformation.

The gargantua of the order *Pinnipedia* (which also includes sea lions
and seals), the tusked and mustachioed walrus is equally at home on
icy shores and on the sunless floor of the ocean. Like mammalian
submarines, walruses cruise the seabed at depths of up to 300 feet, their
whiskers allowing them to navigate the darkness and locate clams, crabs
and oysters. More ungainly out of the water than in it, walruses use
their trademark tusks, which are 2 to 3 feet long and sported by males
and females alike, to drag themselves onto the ice and to move across it;
indeed, their scientific name, *Odobenus rosmarus*, translates literally as
'tooth-walking horse of the sea'. The tusks serve a defensive purpose

as well – both against predators and other walruses, particularly when mating bulls compete over harems – but they have also attracted centuries of unwelcome attention from human hunters. Nor is ivory the only thing humans have wanted from the walrus. Like seals, walruses have provided native populations with meat and oil for their lamps. Walrus hide, tough and waterproof, served as a perfect external skin when building kayaks, and it could be braided into thongs and ropes nearly as strong as steel cable. Small wonder that Atlantic and Pacific herds alike are only a fraction today of what they used to be in the distant past.

'Stepfather' to the Ket of Siberia, 'God's dog' to the Sami and Nanuq to the Inuit, who also call him 'the ever-wandering one' (*pihoqahiak*), the polar bear is the Arctic's undisputed apex predator, and the beneficiary of a supremely successful and rapid process of natural selection. Once relegated to its own genus, *Thalarctos*, the polar bear was restored in 1971 to the genus *Ursus*, with brown and black bears. Science has shown since then how recently in evolutionary terms the polar bear branched off from its cousins, and how close its genetic relationship to them still is, despite key anatomical and behavioural differences. Fossil analysis and mitochondrial sequencing indicate that the line leading to *Ursus maritimus* diverged from that of brown bears a mere 150,000 years ago,

A female polar bear surveying the northern landscape. The Arctic's apex predator – but for how much longer in this era of global warming?

and several matings between polar bears and north-ranging grizzlies, producing fertile 'grolar' and 'pizzly' offspring, have been documented. And yet how can one blame those who once saw the polar bear as fundamentally unlike other ursines? The obvious difference in colouration aside, brown bears hibernate during the winter, while male polar bears hunt year-round, and even pregnant females in their winter dens enter a state of 'carnivore lethargy', experiencing a less dramatic drop in body temperature and heartrate than that associated with full hibernation. Polar bears feed almost exclusively on meat and fish, giving them sharper canines and more jagged molars than their omnivorous kin. Moreover, the brown bear's huskiness contrasts with the streamlined build of the polar bear, which is designed for aquatic endurance and grace. Rivalled in size only by the Kodiak bear of Alaska, the male polar bear typically weighs 600 to 1,700 pounds but can reach a full ton, and measures 8 feet or more from nose to tail. Both males and females are powerful swimmers and accomplished, patient stalkers of prey, capable of both absolute stillness and sprints of up to 25 miles per hour on paw pads specially evolved to provide traction on ice. Except during the spring mating or when rearing cubs, a task that falls solely to the mother, polar bears live solitary lives, hunting far and wide on the ice and in the water, preying on seals, fish and the occasional walrus or beluga whale. Often they are accompanied only by the seabirds and scavengers who follow in their trail to feed on the carrion they leave behind. Most notably, the Arctic fox tracks the polar bear far out onto the winter ice, a self-appointed jester dining on the scraps discarded by the North's pale king.

The workings of all ecospheres turn on the change of the seasons, but in few places do summer and winter extremes create such radically distinct worlds. Beneath the warming rays of the midnight sun, the Arctic experiences a riotous explosion of life as spring turns into summer. During these months of fertility that the Inuit call *upinngaaq*, acres of wildflowers bloom, with the dainty blue of alpine forget-me-nots and the pale yellow of mountain avens contrasting with the vibrant hues of purple saxifrage and Arctic poppies. Rodents emerge from their burrows to skitter through the sedge and the heath, and foxes, owls, ptarmigans and weasels throw off their winter white, camouflaged for the next few months in drabber hues. Cubs, calves and other newborns learn the ways of survival as the weather warms, while grizzlies feast on the runs of salmon and char that surge up the northern rivers to spawn. At sea, especially along the coastlines and the edge of the ice, efflorescing masses of phytoplankton revitalize the waters, causing them to boil with shrimp, fish and the larger creatures that prey on them. Bowhead and northern right whales, along with their smaller cousins, the narwhal and beluga, are joined by other cetaceans who spend the cooler seasons farther to the south: humpbacks and orca, as well as sei, fin, minke and grey whales. Thousands of walruses and millions of seals – fur seals and harp seals, hooded and bearded seals, and *Pusa (Phoca) hispida*, the ubiquitous ringed seal – congregate on shorelines and ice floes to give birth, to raise their calves and pups and, in the case of most seal species, to mate for the following year. Multitudes of birds, migratory and native, flock to the Arctic's coasts and marshes to build summer nests and cliffside rookeries. For weeks on end, the northern skies fill with the squawks and cries of sandhill cranes and Arctic loons, kittiwakes and gulls, puffins and fulmars, and dovekies, murres and tundra swans.

But all too fleeting is this season of warmth, a fact made apparent by the ever-present reality of the ice, which governs the movements and habits of Arctic fauna whatever the time of year. The ice shelters prey from predator, helping fish to hide from seabirds, or lesser whales to outmanoeuvre the orca. In the form of drifting floes, it provides much-needed havens and nurseries to seals and walruses whose search for feeding grounds takes them far from shore. Solid ice serves as an insulating sheet, protecting undersea life from the full blast of winter temperatures above, and also as a turnpike conveying caribou, musk oxen and polar bears to where their cold-season needs drive them. Leads, or navigable cracks that open and close in the ice, block the progress of some creatures and offer added mobility to others, while Arctic oases called polynyas, where the sea water remains free of ice year-round, attract bustling concentrations of marine life. In stark contrast to the polynyas are savssats, autumn and early winter bands of ice that form rapidly across the mouths of fjords and inlets. Savssats pose a special danger to sea mammals like beluga and narwhals, for if they grow too wide to be swum under in the space of one breath, the animals are trapped, doomed to drown or beach themselves as the water freezes over. They also become easy prey for human hunters. It was a rapid freeze of this type that led to the famous stranding of three grey whales near Point Barrow, Alaska, in October 1988. As dramatized in the motion picture *Big Miracle* (2012), Soviet icebreaker crews, American scientists and oilmen, and local Inupiat, in a triumph of environmentalist enthusiasm over Cold War animosity, carried out Operation Breakthrough, saving two of the unfortunate creatures.

The ice metamorphizes throughout the year, ensuring that the Arctic's natural contours change with the unpredictability and hypnotic beauty of a kaleidoscope, never the same from one moment to the next. The sea ice north of Siberia tends to drift east to west, while above North America it rotates in the clockwise Beaufort Gyre, over 1,200 miles in diameter. Wind and currents cause the ice to form pressure ridges and irregular surfaces when it freezes, and to break apart and recoalesce without warning. By about May, much of the polar ice pack is less stable, with numerous 'rotten' patches appearing, and new ice is only about 3 to 5 feet thick. If this first-year ice survives the summer – an increasingly less certain prospect in this new century of global warming – it becomes second-year ice, and eventually multi-year, or pack, ice: a permanent part of the polar seascape, anywhere from 10 to 15 feet thick, and up to 50 feet thick in the case of long-lived palaeocrystic ice. Larger formations progress through the northern seas as well, particularly the 10,000 or so icebergs calved every spring and summer by the Greenland ice cap and glaciers in Norway and Canada. (Bergs in the North Pacific are few in number and tend to be restricted to Alaska's and Canada's subarctic coasts.) Icebergs range in size from 'growlers' and 'bergy bits' – the International Ice Patrol's designations for ice blocks 3 to 16 feet high and 16 to 50 feet in length – to the true behemoths, such as ice islands and tabular bergs whose volume is measured in hundreds of cubic miles. Most are carried south by the Greenland and Canadian currents, with nearly 400 per year travelling far enough south to pose a danger to Atlantic shipping. A few end up drifting in the Arctic basin, sojourning a while with the pack ice, sometimes merging with it.

Colder weather returns in the autumn, firming up the ice and foreshadowing the harsher conditions yet to come. Temperatures drop, then plummet. The twilight grows longer each day until, around October or November, the full weight of polar night descends, not to lift again until late the following January or February. (For visitors and even native inhabitants, the winter darkness noticeably depresses moods and may be the cause of so-called 'Arctic hysteria' – observed occasionally among indigenes like the Sami and Eskimo-Inuit and thought by some scientists to result from seasonally based deficiencies of vitamin D or calcium.) Migratory instincts assert themselves, causing throngs of birds and animals to leave the polar realm behind, as do bodily and behavioural changes in the creatures who stay.

It is the winter, of course, that tests this ecosystem to its limits, forcing adaptations of all kinds. Those with winter plumes or coats of white regain them. Herbivores like moose and reindeer retreat to zones more abundant in plant life; predators like the wolf follow in their tracks. Their senses atwitch for any sign of canids, falcons or snowy owls, Arctic hares forage in the open for wind-exposed plants. Voles and lemmings, while not hibernating, confine themselves as much as possible to lairs and burrows beneath the snow. With the serenity of a Zen master, the polar bear stands hours of silent watch over *aglus*, the ice holes where seals must surface to breathe. The Arctic fox scavenges off these open-ice kills, but also sets up an ingenious system of caches to guarantee itself a steady supply of nourishment throughout the season.

For such animals, whose winter-survival strategy is to increase food intake, a high degree of mobility is a must: migratory foraging is often the only way to stay alive, and many Arctic creatures are, in the words of biologist Maxwell Dunbar, 'desperate for space'.[12] That said, most polar species seek instead, or in addition, to decrease their dependence on food energy. This may mean relying on better insulation – few animals fail to grow a thicker, denser pelt or put on an extra layer of fat or blubber as the autumn gives way to winter – it may mean some sort of metabolic adjustment, or it may mean both. Many fish and some insects take advantage of special glycoproteins to keep their bodily fluids from freezing solid and to restrict the damage done to their organs by the extreme chill. Whether or not they can be said to hibernate in the truest sense of the word, grizzlies, female polar bears, ground squirrels and others slow down their bodily functions considerably, in some cases to the point of near-torpor; the squirrels and their fellow rodents lose up to 40 per cent of their body weight in the process. Mosses, lichens and certain insects go beyond that, entering a state of almost utter lifelessness until the next spring's warmth reawakens them. The larch, one of the few evergreens to shed its needles over the winter, does so to minimize the surface area it exposes to the cold.

These are lives lived on the margin, no matter how well evolution has suited them to their environment. It may not be in the Arctic that nature is reddest in tooth and claw, but weather and scarcity lend an extra intensity to the struggle for existence there. Large-scale displacements of entire species to the south, then back to the North, in response to even relatively slight stimuli, are not uncommon, and neither are episodes of near-extinction followed by rapid recovery. Many botanists and zoologists speak of this ecosystem as uniquely fragile and easily stressed. Others point to its elasticity and to the capacity of Arctic life forms to persevere – at least as species, if not individuals – in the face of recurring hardship and periodic disaster. Few on either side, however, would deny that the latter holds true only if the hardships and disasters are the product of ecological processes. The Arctic ecosystem is more finely calibrated than most, able to operate only within the narrow range of tolerances set for it by nature. For it to function as designed is difficult enough. Any outside pressure is nigh unbearable.

And yet such pressure, in the form of human presence, has borne down on the Arctic for many thousands of years, and has made itself infinitely more burdensome since the 1500s CE – in other words, since the irruption of Euro-Americans into the far north. Even populations native to the Arctic have had destabilizing effects on its ecological equilibrium, despite small numbers, low levels of technological development and a willingness to adapt to the environment. But it took the arrival of foreign mariners and empire-builders, acting on mercantile and political ambitions all out of proportion to the place, to put the equation truly in peril of fatal imbalance. It has been this way for the last five centuries, which have shown clearly that Arctic flora and fauna, already straining to survive the natural conditions to which they are adapted, are too easily taxed beyond their capacity if forced to cope at the same time with any but the most minimal human-caused impact. So it remains today, as our actions push the region to the brink of a momentous, if not calamitous, set of transformations. How we have reached such a point is the subject of the chapters to come.

2

Encounters: Prehistory and Early History to 1500 CE

Long ago, in the time before time, the world was fashioned from the bones of Ymir, the frost giant born in the fog-choked pit known to the old Norse as Ginungagap. Or perhaps it was formed, as the Mansi of western Siberia say, from the clumps of earth dredged up by two loons diving to the bed of a vast lake. The creator may have been a giant beaver, as the Inuvialuit of the Mackenzie Delta teach, but to take the word of most Inuit and Eskimo (and of the Koyukon, Tlingit and others), it was the Great Raven who made the world. Many speak of how Raven, in mid-flight, let slip from his talons a huge rock whose broken shards became the islands and continents – although certain Chukchi clans find it amusing to regard the land and waters as the droppings and urine that passed through Raven's belly. Human beings are the children of the Khanty god Numi Torum, or of the Tungus god Buga, who breathed life into them after mixing iron, fire, water and soil. If the Tanana River people of Alaska have it right, Raven transformed two pine cones into the first man and woman, but if one believes the Siberian Koryak, this boreal Adam and Eve were the offspring of deer. Perhaps the human race was birthed by the Finnish sky goddess Ilmatar, or perhaps it simply rose out of holes in the ground, as the Netsilik Inuit of central Canada once maintained.

We know a great deal about the creation myths of the world's northern peoples and the way they once conceived of their place in the cosmos. Their actual origins remain more of a mystery, owing to the nearly complete absence of documentary sources and the inscrutability of much of the physical evidence unearthed in these bleak climes. The broad brushstrokes of the picture seem clear. The outmigration from Africa of anatomically modern humans, starting around 100,000 years ago, eventually led to the colonization of Eurasia's northern zones, with hunter-gatherer communities reaching the Arctic Circle as early as 40,000 to 28,000 years ago, and no later than 12,000 BCE. From northeast Siberia, Asiatic travellers crossed the Bering land bridge to North America, most likely at some point between 14,000 and 12,000 BCE.

Not that this process was linear, for periods of glaciation drove Pleistocene humans back to the temperate south, and smaller fluctuations in climate had their own effects on where people could or wished to live. New discoveries surface constantly, radiocarbon dates are calibrated with greater precision, and innovative methodologies, uniting the efforts of scientists across disparate disciplines, from geology to genetics, yield fresh insights. All the same, it remains difficult to determine when and where prehistoric northerners emerged, in which directions they dispersed, or whether specific peoples were ancestral to others. We can say with confidence that most of the groups presently indigenous to the Eurasian Arctic were in place or moving northward between 1000 BCE and 1000 CE, and that Palaeoeskimo cultures had spread from the Bering Strait and Alaska to eastern Canada and Greenland by no later than 2500 BCE. And yet many gaps in this story remain.

By comparison, the European nations' early Arctic encounters are more easily mapped out. Populations in Scandinavia and Russia grew steadily during the Bronze and Iron ages, and the ancient Greeks and Romans had a dim, if somewhat fanciful, awareness of the regions that lay to the far north. The Middle Ages witnessed more than a few ventures into the Arctic, carried out by sea and over land by Vikings, Slavs and others. These, however, were temporary forays or failed endeavours, or efforts at expansion blocked by some natural obstacle or human foe. Also, after about 1200, a major cooling cycle lasting several centuries set in, making further northward movement more difficult and in some cases reversing what had gone before. Sustained contact between Europe and the larger Arctic world would have to wait until the sixteenth century.

The Pleistocene North: Earliest Habitations

At 61°12′N, approximately 90 miles south of the Siberian city of Yakutsk, lies Diring Yuriak, a high, sandy terrace on the banks of the Lena River. Here, in 1982, the Soviet archaeologist Yuri Mochanov stumbled upon the remnants of a series of Stone Age camps, from which several thousand artefacts have since been retrieved. These objects are thought by some to have been manufactured during the Lower Palaeolithic, sometime between 300,000 and 260,000 years ago. If this estimate is correct, Diring Yuriak is by far the first place on earth where hominids can be said to have lived north of the 60th parallel.

Unfortunately, this is a large and unanswerable 'if', and while it might seem tempting to begin a human history of the North here, Diring Yuriak is more useful as a cautionary tale about how risky it can be to make definitive pronouncements about Arctic archaeology. Debates still rage over how old the Diring artefacts really are, and evidence is similarly inconclusive for most subarctic sites claimed as points of human settlement before 200,000 years ago. Human beings are persuasively proven to have reached the 50th parallel during the Lower Palaeolithic, and there are sure signs that Neanderthals settled in subarctic Scandinavia and Siberia by no later than 100,000 years ago. But none of this makes for a satisfying start. It leaves us quite some distance from the Arctic itself, and the fact that all these ancient wanderers were archaic humans gives us only an indirect connection to the region's present-day reality.

Occupation of the Arctic by *Homo sapiens sapiens* was a long time coming, and scholars even now disagree as to when it can be verified beyond doubt. Modern humans emerged in Africa around 200,000 years ago; small groups moved with relative ease into the Middle East 100,000 years after that, and additional waves of migration between 70,000 and 50,000 years ago populated Asia's lower latitudes out to China and points south, including Australia. Not until around 45,000 years ago did modern humans begin to enter chillier environs like Europe, Central Asia and Siberia. This round of settlement appears to have gone faster than previously imagined by archaeologists, with Upper Palaeolithic tribes reaching the 50th parallel not long after 40,000 BCE. Soon they were following antelope, woolly rhinoceros, steppe bison and mammoths across the grasslands of southern Siberia, out to the Altai Mountains and Amur River, and up to 55°N. Between 40,000 and 30,000 BCE, the Russian-Siberian subarctic was penetrated at many points, including multiple sites along the Yenisei River and Lake Baikal. The Weichselian ice bore down more heavily on Fennoscandia and the British Isles, which meant less northward headway in Europe than in the east. Still, by around 35,000 years ago, representatives of the Aurignacian culture, the toolmaking tradition associated with the advent of modern humans in Europe, had advanced to at least 50°N in places like France, Germany, Moravia and Crimea.

Two factors prompted these high-latitude peregrinations. First, the global climate had been growing milder since 60,000 years ago, the approximate starting date for the interstadial corresponding to marine isotope stage (MIS) 3. To many prehistoric groups, this was not an automatically welcome development, because temperature by itself mattered less than the correct distribution of flora and fauna in determining where prehistoric people chose to live. For those who hunted large grazing mammals, the most congenial settings were open, relatively arid steppes with enough shrubs and trees to support their prey and provide fuel for fire. Increased warmth and moisture caused forest and woodlands to spring up in such places, shifting the grasslands farther to the north, and as steppe creatures relocated, the hunters who relied on them for food did so as well – a pattern repeated more than once. Second, Stone Age humans, starting around 50,000 years ago, acquired the capacity to manufacture tools more skilfully and to coordinate complex efforts more effectively. These new advantages allowed Upper Palaeolithic communities to hunt and gather food more efficiently, sew warmer and more water-resistant clothing and build winter dwellings that offered more protection. Physically less able than their older cousins to withstand low temperatures, modern humans, using technology to overcome that deficit, travelled farther north than any Neanderthal or archaic human is known to have done.

So far, in fact, that *Homo sapiens sapiens* is now widely acknowledged to have crossed the Arctic Circle at least 28,000 to 32,000 years ago, and possibly earlier. Conventional wisdom once held that the land north of 65° had remained inviolate until after the glacial maximum of 20,000 BCE. However, artefacts dating to 28–29,000 years ago, plus a mammoth-bone hut of newer construction, have been unearthed at Byzovaya, in Russia's Pechora basin, only 60 miles south of the Arctic Circle. And to Byzovaya's northeast, in the foothills of the Polar Urals, lies Mamontovaya Kurya, at 66°34′. Archaeologists digging here have made a case since 2001 that the site was inhabited between 35,000 and an astonishing 40,000 years ago. But apart from lingering questions about the date, no skeletal remains have been recovered, leaving some confusion about whether the Mamontovaya artefacts were made by *Homo sapiens sapiens* or an archaic subspecies like *neanderthalensis*. If the former is the case, and so long as the dating holds true, Mamontovaya Kurya is the earliest known point of modern human occupation above the Arctic Circle. (Even the latter would constitute a significant find, for with the possible exception of those who lived at Diring Yuriak, no archaic humans are thought to have reached 60°N or higher.) Second place would then go to the Yana Rhinoceros Horn Site (RHS), an east Siberian riverside camp that lies on the 71st parallel, not far from the shores of the Laptev Sea. This site contains bones from mammoths, reindeer and other animals, as well as artefacts dating to 28,000 years ago, including the eponymous rhino horn, carved into the foreshaft of an atlatl, or spear-throwing stick. But there are no signs of permanent shelter, and the best guess is that Yana RHS (and probably Byzovaya and Mamontovaya Kurya) served as a temporary seasonal stopover, not a long-term settlement. The Yana River's location east of the Verkho-yansk Mountains places the RHS site in the northwest corner of Beringia, the transition zone between Siberia and Alaska, and its discovery in 1993 fueled much initial speculation about whether the Yana's north-land hunters might have been the forebears of the first Americans. But while they were geographically well-positioned to have crossed the Bering land bridge, it seems unlikely that they did so. Their tools bear no archaeological resemblance to any found in the New World, and interstadial warming is believed to have submerged many portions of the land bridge at this time.

If climate change allowed humans into the high north, it pushed them out again not long after. Around 28,000 years ago, the Pleistocene glaciers began their slow final advance, and the weather harshened over the next several millennia. This drawn-out crescendo climaxed between 22,000 and 18,000 years ago, in the episode known as the Last Glacial Maximum (LGM), when the ice sheets swelled to their fullest extent. The Alps disappeared under the Würm glaciation, and the Devensian-Weichselian ice, more than 2 miles thick in places, engulfed Fenno-scandia, Russia out to the Ural Mountains and down to the 53rd parallel, and nearly all of what is now Great Britain. Northern France, the Low Countries and Central and Eastern Europe were reduced to tundra, as was much of Siberia. In Europe, the glacial maximum forced popula-tions to relocate to warmer havens in the south. Resettlement patterns were more complicated in Siberia, which, with the exception of localized glaciation in the Taimyr Peninsula and the mountain ranges of the far northeast, remained more or less ice-free. Between 45 and 55°N, the centuries preceding the LGM were actually a time of bounty for Siberian hunter-gatherers, as cooler temperatures converted forest back into the steppelands and shrub tundra their prey found so hospitable. Nothing of the sort was true above 60°N, though, and the frigid weather eventu-ally caught up to those in the lower latitudes as well. Even if the bitter cold could be endured bodily, its effects on the vegetation that provided fuel for fire were too deleterious to overcome; mammoths and other megafauna might be able to survive as the open lands changed into sparser grass tundra, but humans could not. From 22,000 to 20,000 years ago, and perhaps later, the retreat from Siberia and the East European plain was almost total, certainly from territory north of 50 degrees. Across the entirety of Eurasia, the Arctic and subarctic lay empty of human presence.

By 18,000 to 16,000 BCE, depending on region, the worst of the LGM was over, although it took until 10,000 BCE for the glaciers to recede completely. The unpredictable but generally milder weather of the late-glacial period (c. 16/15,000–11,000 BCE) accelerated the thaw, especially during the Bølling and Allerød interstadials, which overlapped with the late-glacial between 12,700 and 10,800 BCE. The ice made a brief recovery during the Younger Dryas – a sudden cold spike that lasted from 10,800 to 9600 BCE – before renewed warming brought the Pleistocene to its end. In late-glacial Europe, dwarf willow, then birch, pine and poplar, began to replace the tundra covering the middle parts of the continent, and people emerged from their refuges in the south. Especially during the two interstadials, the reindeer hunters of the Magdalenian and Ahrensburg-Bromme cultures reoccupied northern France, Germany, and southern Scandinavia up to and beyond the 55th parallel, and their Epigravettian contemporaries reached subarctic latitudes in the eastern Baltic and European Russia. Still, the slow withdrawal of the ice sheets, combined with the chilling effect of the Dryas, delayed any push toward Europe's uppermost reaches until the final years of the Palaeolithic.

It was in Siberia, then, that the recolonization of the North proceeded most rapidly. It took little added warmth to turn grass tundra back into shrub tundra and even steppe. So, after about 18,000 BCE, humans living in Siberia's western lowlands, on the southern extent of the Yenisei, and southeast of Lake Baikal began to fan out along the river basins into the subarctic, although they remained for the most part below the 60th parallel. Compared to the earlier communities of the MIS 3 interstadial, those of late-glacial Siberia tended to be smaller and more itinerant, and those who headed north were transient hunter-gatherers. Among some of these, the most distinctive feature was their use of microblade tools, fashioned by chipping tiny slivers from easily transported stone cores and using them as blades, barbs and edges for a variety of implements – as opposed to the more common unifacial and bifacial methods of knapping flakes off one or both sides of a stone until a usable blade or point was left. This multi-purpose toolmaking method arose in Mongolia and northern China as far back as 30,000 years ago, and was well suited to a high-mobility lifestyle.

The microblade type of greatest interest to Arctic history appears to have originated near Lake Baikal at around 19,000 BCE, in the vicinity of Studenoe, but is named after a site 1,200 miles to the northeast, where tools made in this style were first found by archaeologists. This was Dyuktai Cave, nestled partway up a limestone cliff that rises over the Aldan River at 59°18′N, where hunters of mammoths and bison may have lived as far back as 17–16,000 BCE (although most scholars are more comfortable with estimates of 16,000 to 13,000 BCE). Identified formally in 1964, the Dyuktai microblade culture is now believed to have spread widely throughout eastern Siberia, from the Angara River in the west to the Pacific coast in the east, and as far south as the Amur basin. What makes the Dyuktai intriguing is the fact that tools made in their style have been traced not only to the Siberian Arctic, but to Alaska and Canada as well, and near-consensus has it that representatives of their culture were the first humans to cross the Bering land bridge into North America.

Such northward roaming was the product of its times – or, put another way, the consequence of late-glacial warming. The mass forestation touched off by rising temperatures and higher levels of moisture directly threatened mammoths and other megafauna of the steppe and tundra, including musk oxen, steppe bison and the woolly rhino, and it was no boon to the reindeer, which was now firmly established throughout Eurasia as a staple source of food and toolmaking materials. As changes in climate gradually but surely drove these creatures to the higher latitudes – and in most cases to eventual extinction – the humans who depended on them were forced to adapt as well. With the bow and arrow now appearing alongside the spear and spear-thrower, many readjusted their hunting practices, targeting elk and moose with greater frequency, and in some cases learning to pursue woodland species like deer and wild boar or to net and trap birds and small mammals, such as rodents, lapines and the occasional fox. Harpoons and fish-spears dating to 15,000 years ago have been unearthed along Siberian riverbanks, and other fishing techniques are thought to have emerged by 12,000 years ago. There was, of course, an alternative strategy for survival: following one's traditional prey and seeking new homes in the higher north.

Accordingly, artefacts bearing Dyuktai characteristics have been found at the 71st parallel on the coastal plain of Yakutia, along the Berelekh River, a tributary of the Indigirka. Thought until recently to be the first place above the Arctic Circle ever occupied by human beings, the Berelekh encampment sits within reach of Russia's northeast frontier, and although its inhabitants would not have thought about it in such terms, it was clearly a way-station on the road to the Americas. Its age, widely agreed to be at least 14,500 years old, with some dating it to 17,000 years ago, is frequently used as a chronological anchor point in calculating when the Bering land bridge was traversed. Whether other Dyuktai sites of equal or greater antiquity await discovery in Russia's far northeast remains to be seen.

Whatever the case, the Dyuktai dominated eastern Siberia for some time, although certain areas – such as the Ushki Lakes of volcano-studded Kamchatka, first occupied around 13,000 years ago, as well as the uplands of western Chukotka and the basin of the Upper Kolyma – appear to have been settled by unrelated peoples who did not use micro-blades. Sometime around 11,000 years ago, the Dyuktai were superseded by the Sumnagin people, who emerged along the banks of the Lena River and did even more than their predecessors to populate Siberia's northern fringe. By 8400 BCE, the Sumnagin had entered Yakutia's Arctic tundra, where they learned to subsist on reindeer, and they settled as far north as Zhokhov, now one of the New Siberian Islands, then a peninsula jutting into the Arctic Ocean. This was a fascinating habitation, marking the first human occupation of 75°N or higher known to science, and is discussed at greater length below. From the mouth of the Lena, some Sumnagin tribes travelled west to make their home in the remote Taimyr Peninsula, the northernmost part of the Eurasian land mass. Others drifted eastward to Chukotka, and the Siberian Arctic has never been empty since.

Nor has the North American Arctic, which was settled via the Bering land bridge, most probably between 14,000 and 12,000 BCE, and perhaps slightly before that. Few topics have provoked as much dispute among prehistorians as the riddle of how the Americas were peopled, but the plethora of alternative theories notwithstanding, it is beyond question that the trans-Bering migration of Asiatic nomads was crucial to that process. Whether, as the traditional model suggests, these boreal wayfarers were the *first* Americans, or whether they begat *all* early Americans, from the Seward Peninsula to Tierra del Fuego, are questions outside the scope of this book. A Bering-only explanation still seems likeliest; at the least, those who made the crossing are central to the indigenous heritage of North and South America alike.

The Bering land bridge was both more and less than it is generally taken to be. On one hand, it is popularly misunderstood as a simple cause-way between continents, an image reinforced by schoolbook and en-cyclopaedia depictions of headlong winter dashes over narrow spits of land and frost-nipped refugees glancing apprehensively over their shoul-ders toward Russia. ('What could be chasing them?' I recall wondering as I pored over one such illustration in my first-grade history text, concluding in a Cold War schoolboy way that it must be the KGB.) The bridge was in fact a belt of land twice the size of Texas, with an average north–south width of 600 miles. Dry winds from the south and the temperature-moderating influence of the Pacific are thought to have kept it largely unglaciated. It was the centrepiece of the large ecozone known as Beringia, a name coined by the Swedish botanist Eric Hultén in 1937 and now used to denote the 2,500-mile span encompassed by Siberia's Verkhoyansk Mountains and Canada's Mackenzie River. On the other hand, the bridge was a most undependable viaduct, subject to partial or complete flooding during temperate intervals – precisely the times when human beings were likeliest to be living at high enough latitudes to take advantage of it. The bridge sank beneath the waves for good between 10,000 and 9000 BCE, leaving, in the end, surprisingly few moments when it could have been navigated. For those seeking to uphold the thesis that the Americas were populated exclusively by way of the Bering Strait, the fact that the Wisconsin glaciers – the Cordil-leran and Laurentide ice sheets – blocked transit from Alaska to the rest of North America for 10,000 years, starting around 22,000 BCE, adds extra complexity to the equation.

A scholarly minority, recently emboldened by the discoveries at Yana RHS, or in some cases by work done at the Yukon's Bluefish Caves (where bones ranging from 40,000 to 28,000 years old bear marks that a few scholars think were left by man-made tools, but that most see as the product of natural abrasion), has long maintained that a crossing took place around 30,000 years ago: the tail end of the MIS 3 interstadial, when the climate might have cooled down enough to restabilize the bridge after millennia of warm weather, but not so much as to make human presence this far north unrealistic. However, not all are con-vinced that the bridge was passable at this time, and more troubling is the complete lack of evidence for any habitation in the New World even remotely close to this old. If one excludes this pre-LGM possibility, the theoretical window of opportunity for a crossing opens up at around 16,000 BCE, when the glacial maximum was over, the land bridge had regained its structual integrity, and Dyuktai hunters were at least arguably present in northeast Siberia. The strictest readings of the evidence put the crossing at about 12,000 BCE. These rely solely on archaeological dates universally accepted as secure beyond doubt: 12,500 BCE for Berelekh, as the oldest post-LGM site in Russian Beringia, and 12,000–11,700 BCE for Swan Point, in central Alaska's Tanana Valley, as the earliest site in North America. They also presume the bridge to have been environmentally unwelcoming until 15,000 or 16,000 years ago, when central Beringia underwent a transformation from herbaceous tundra to more biologically productive shrub tundra. More expansive theories, based on what is archaeologically plausible, as opposed to provable, push the date back somewhat. This may involve accepting dates of occupation that, although taken seriously, are unverified – such as 15–14,000 BCE for Berelekh or 13,000 BCE for the Bluefish Caves – or envisioning other points of Dyuktai habitation, possibly older and farther to the east than Berelekh, that have yet to be unearthed or have vanished for good beneath the sea. A migration date of 15,000 or 16,000 years ago is hypothetical but not unreasonably speculative.

As to whether a Bering-only model explains further migration into the Americas, the central question has to do with whether new arrivals in Alaska could have penetrated or sidestepped the Wisconsin ice in time to account for the earliest verifiable dates of human presence below the U.S.–Canadian border. The dominant orthodoxy once held that the first Americans to live south of the glaciers were the Clovis people, whose oldest sites date to 11,500 BCE, late enough to be explained by a southward descent of Beringian forerunners through the ice-free corridor that opened up between the Cordilleran and Laurentide sheets between 12,700 and 11,500 BCE. Since the 1980s, however, this comfortable assumption has crumbled under a burgeoning mass of evidence that human beings colonized the continental United States and even Latin America before the glaciers separated. Although the academic mainstream has yet to accept the oldest dates for most sites claimed as 'pre-Clovis', a few have gained sufficient credibility to force major rethinking about how the New World was first settled, with Monte Verde in Chile being of greatest importance. Occupied 14,600 years ago – a date embraced by a majority of scholars since the late 1990s – Monte Verde is too old to have been founded by anyone relying on the ice-free corridor for their passage south, and it verges on being too old to have been founded by anyone who traversed the Bering after the glacial maximum.

Hence the readiness of some to turn to the notion of a Bering migration circa 30,000 years ago, or to propose multiple crossings of the bridge: one before the LGM, and one or more afterwards. But aside from the gaping holes this leaves in the archaeological record, DNA-based studies, as they grow in sophistication, tend to argue in favour of a single foundational migration from Siberia.[1] Others have mooted theories about boat travel, both across the Pacific and even the Atlantic, with one model suggesting that Solutrean mariners from southwestern Europe landed on North America's eastern seaboard between 15,000 and 18,000 years ago. Voyages of this sort are possible in the abstract, but would have required a much higher degree of open-water or ice-edge seafaring skill than there is proof for this far back in time. A few have wondered whether narrow passages could have opened up between the Cordilleran and Laurentide sheets in advance of the ice-free corridor. However, no trace of any such pathways has been found, and even had they existed, they would have been such forbidding, bog-ridden places that one cannot imagine beasts or humans willingly entering them.

If there is any continued hope of attributing all ancient settlement of the Americas to those who trekked across the Bering, it most likely lies in recent conjectures that Alaska's panhandle and the British Columbian shoreline deglaciated more quickly than territory farther inland. A model attracting much attention postulates that a coastal byway could have grown wide enough by 13,000 BCE, even 15,000 BCE, to convey animal and human travellers all the way from Alaska to the west coast of the United States. Such a route would have offered trans-Bering pioneers immediate access to the wider New World, and if one grants that they crossed over from Asia soon enough – closer to 14,000 than to 12,000 BCE – and that they moved at a brisk pace, they could feasibly have colonized the Americas in time to account for the earliest legitimate dates for human habitation, whether in the North or the South. Later migrations through the ice-free corridor, once it materialized, would have added even greater variety to the New World's rapidly diversifying population. Of course, future archaeological findings may yet reveal that the earliest Americans in fact crossed the land bridge more than once, or that they arrived by more than one route, with places like Monte Verde and other sites purporting to be of pre-Clovis vintage belonging to patterns of settlement that have nothing to do with Beringia. But even if this turns out to be so, the Bering migration remains a momentous occasion in world history, and if those who accomplished it are not the ancestors of all earliest Americans, they are provably ancestral to most.

Be that as it may, Beringia itself became an effervescent cauldron of cultures, although with the bulk of it lost beneath the waves, there is much that will never be learned about how its people lived and interacted. As long as the land bridge stood intact, technology transfer continued between Siberia and Alaska. The obsidian tools found at Swan Point and neighbouring digs in the Tanana Valley bear all the marks of the Dyuktai microblade industry, as do tools found at other sites throughout Alaska and in the upper layers of Canada's Bluefish Caves. The influence of non-Dyuktai cultures forming in Kamchatka and Chukotka may also have been felt on the American side of the strait. Throughout late-glacial Alaska and northwest Canada, a multitude of microblade and non-microblade toolmaking styles emerged, including the Denali complex (or, as some have begun to call it, the Dyuktai-Denali complex), the Nenana Valley or Chindadn complex, the Mesa culture of the Brooks Range and northern Yukon, and the Sluiceway-Tuluaq complex of northwest Alaska. Archaeologists have long struggled to classify the jumble of artefact assemblages unearthed from this period, most often assigning them to the vaguely defined American Palaeo-arctic tradition, although some scholars have come to prefer the term Beringian or East Beringian.

Things grew even more complicated after 11,000 BCE, during the time of the Younger Dryas. In the first known intermingling of the Palaeoarctic and Palaeoindian traditions, hunters from the North American Plains followed herds of steppe bison back up the now-open corridor through the Wisconsin glaciers, appearing in the northern Yukon and in Alaska as far as the Tanana Valley and the Brooks Range. Also during these years, southeast Alaska was occupied for the first time. Groups living here adapted microblade tools to a maritime economy and may have been in contact with the denizens of Kamchatka and Chukotka across the Bering. As in Siberia, the peoples of eastern Beringia modified their hunting and gathering practices to cope with changing climate and the dwindling availability of megafauna prey. They turned more to the exploitation of fish, fowl, Dall sheep and members of the deer family, especially caribou, and they learned over time to domesticate the dog.

Beringia was forever transfigured between 10,000 and 9000 BCE when, in a reversal of the normal pattern for cooling periods like the Younger Dryas, the ocean waters rose and swallowed the land bridge whole. This was no localized cataclysm, but one of many signs that an old age was ending. Global warming, halted temporarily by the Dryas, now resumed, and on a greater scale. Throughout the hemisphere, the contours of land and sea alike were altered beyond recognition. The megafauna of the Pleistocene were dying out or already dead, with the mammoth, for instance, all but extinct by 11,500–10,000 BCE. (Isolated herds survived until the remarkably late date of 2000 BCE by taking refuge in hard-to-reach places like the Taimyr Peninsula and Wrangel and St Paul islands. They subsequently evolved into a dwarf subspecies, only 6 feet tall at the shoulder, requiring less nutritional sustenance than normal-sized mammoths.)

For changes in the weather and terrain, humans of the Stone Age bore no responsibility, as we do in our own day, but for the extinctions they deserve some of the blame. How much, though, has long been a matter of contention. Since the 1960s, proponents of the famed 'Pleistocene overkill' thesis have equated the human predations of this era to a 'blitzkrieg', especially in North America. Such metaphors are overdone, but contrary to romanticized visions of ancient natives living in Edenic harmony with nature, Palaeolithic peoples indeed slaughtered colossal numbers of grazing animals, typically more in a single kill than they could butcher or eat. As anthropologist Tim Ingold has observed, the physical risks and unpredictability inherent in big-game hunting made it sensible to bring down as many beasts as possible whenever one could, making 'the rationality of conservation totally alien to a predatory subsistence economy'.[2] Furthermore, the low reproduction rates characteristic of most megafauna meant that even minimal culling by human hunters – 'guerrilla warfare' as opposed to 'blitzkrieg', in the words of one archaeologist – could put herds at risk within a generation or two. Conversely, greater awareness of the vulnerability of megafauna herbivores to changing botanical conditions, not to mention the fact that many North American species perished before the arrival of humans in the New World, has convinced most scholars that the impact of climate change on the Pleistocene's now-departed giants outweighed the impact of human activity. Spearpoints did their grisly share of the work, but the world as a whole was changing, and that mattered all the more.

When the Holocene did dawn, the transition was anything but uniformly gentle. In some places, rising seas inundated low-lying land; in others, terrain long bowed under by the weight of now-dissipating glaciers lifted up tens if not hundreds of feet. Weather patterns shifted,

leading to forestation, desertification and other ecological transmogri-
fications, and plants and animals were distributed anew. In some areas,
the changes created immediately favourable conditions for new modes
of subsistence, such as herding or even agriculture, placing the peoples
living there on a fast track from the Stone Age to the ages of metal.

For the Arctic, the Holocene meant above all a greater capacity to
support human settlement – and more settlers were in fact on their way.
Some were crowded out of more desirable ecozones by accelerating population growth. Others had their skills and folkways rendered obsolete
by alterations to their habitat. Many were refugees, fleeing environmental shocks and stresses. Over the millennia to come, these and others
who came to the North taught themselves to carve out a new existence
wherever the tundra, the taiga and the cold, grey shores permitted.

Arctic Societies in Prehistoric Europe

On the north coast of Norway's Finnmark county, keeping silent watch
over Jiepmaluokta, the 'bay of seals', are 3,000 petroglyphs, carved into
the rock with chisels of quartz and filled in with paint made from red
ochre. The earliest of these date to 4200 BCE, and they were added to
over many generations, until at least 500 BCE, and some say for a thousand
years after that. They depict fertility rituals and the worship of bears,
marriages and moments from everyday life, and perhaps the investiture
of chieftains and shamans. They form part of the larger Alta complex,
so named after the town nearby, and have been preserved as a UNESCO
World Heritage Site since 1985. As with so many of the prehistoric
monuments scattered throughout Europe's far north, we cannot know
with certainty who created the Alta petroglyphs. Were they the children
of the Komsa, reindeer- and seal-hunters in these parts from an earlier
era? Are they the ancestors of the Sami, whose origins remain a mystery
with political ramifications still felt today? We are also left to wonder
about the glyphs' function. Their purpose may have been religious or
aesthetic, or it may have been a marking of territory, an assertion of
identity. They appear related to other rock paintings found as far away
as northwestern Russia, implying an extensive network of interaction
along the Arctic coast, and the numerous scenes of sea fishing and
reindeer hunts speak eloquently, if wordlessly, about the economic
practices that structured human activity in Europe's ancient north.

The passing of the Younger Dryas radically reshaped the environment and landscape in which these people dwelled. As during the Bølling

and Allerød interstadials, a new explosion of tree growth rolled the tundra back to the continent's Arctic fringe, with swathes of oak and elm enshrouding Europe up to southern Fennoscandia by 6000 BCE, and miles of boreal forest and taiga spreading beyond that to the treeline. Also as before, animals adapted for colder weather, particularly the reindeer, made their way back to the North. Less foreseeable was what happened to Europe itself, whose map during the early Holocene was unrecognizable to modern eyes. Not only were the British Isles still connected to the mainland, but much of the present-day North Sea was dry land, linking Denmark with Sweden to the north and with England to the west, while the Baltic Sea existed only as a cold freshwater lake, sealed off to the east by a dam of ice. Weakened by rising temperatures, the ice dam gave way soon after 9600 BCE, and the consequent flooding united the waters of the North and Baltic seas. At the same time, new highlands were formed throughout the region, as ground that had carried the burden of the Devensian-Weichselian ice sheets for thousands of years quite literally sprang up once that burden was removed. Between the rising waters and the rising land, it was not until 7200 BCE or so that northern Europe's topography came to look as it does today.

This meant highly unsettled conditions for the region's late Palaeolithic and early Mesolithic inhabitants.[3] Still present from the late Pleistocene were hunting clans of the Ahrensburg-Bromme cultures who, since before the Younger Dryas, had preyed on the reindeer herds then ranging seasonally between northern Germany and Sweden. The two groups were related, with the Ahrensburg confining themselves to Germany and the Bromme residing throughout Denmark and southern Sweden, where they augmented their diet with moose and beaver. Both, like a growing number of hunter-gatherers, had added bows and arrows to their arsenals, boosting their efficiency as slayers of beasts.

For Europe, though, the classic 'age of the reindeer' – the late-glacial *âge du renne* identified in the 1870s by the French palaeontologist Édouard Lartet – ended with the Holocene, with reindeer-based lifestyles now consigned to the Arctic and near-arctic margins. Such places were occupied as early as 9000 BCE in Scandinavia, and some centuries later in Finland and European Russia. Leading the way were the Fosna-Hensbacka people, a northern offshoot of the Ahrensburg-Bromme culture. The Hensbacka populated Sweden's western coast, while the Fosna settled southern Norway and the Atlantic coast to 65°N. Cousins of the Fosna, the Komsa culture – named after a low-lying mountain near the aforementioned town of Alta – continued this line of migration, driving into the Arctic and rounding the northernmost tip of Norway. From there the Komsa went east: their sites have been found as far as Finland's Utsjoki River and the Russian port of Murmansk, and they are thought to have been related to the Arctic Palaeolithic culture which inhabited the Kola Peninsula and the shores of the White Sea.

Although they began as reindeer hunters, these groups blended old traditions with new practices suited to coastal settings. They started with beachcombing: feeding on shellfish, stealing eggs from rookeries, and scavenging bones, blubber and flesh from whales that periodically washed up dead on the shore. They became skilled at fishing from boats and extracting salmon and rainbow smelt from the mouths of rivers. Between 6000 and 3000 BCE, they learned to hunt sea mammals – one of humankind's hallmark adaptations to Arctic environments. Until the Neolithic or the Bronze Age, the harvesting of large whales was beyond their abilities. For now, they relied principally on ringed and bearded seals, and to a lesser extent the walrus; eventually, they were able to land narwhals and beluga as well. Like others throughout the Mesolithic and Neolithic north, the Komsa and their neighbours lived in skin tents during the spring and summer, then crowded into more durable quarters during the winter. Large pit-dwellings, dating from 8000 BCE onwards and grouped into sizable villages, have been discovered throughout Fennoscandia and northern Russia. Covered above ground by a frame and roof, such excavations, waist-to-shoulder-deep, took advantage of the earth's insulating effect to provide extra protection from the cold.

The Komsa and its related cultures survived for several thousand years. At the same time, new groups appeared alongside them and to the south. In subarctic Scandinavia, the Maglemose and Kongemose cultures, circa 8000–6000 BCE and 6500–4500 BCE respectively, developed a mixed economy based on woodland hunting, mainly of deer and wild pig, and coastal fishing. Their major settlements, such as Skateholm, in Sweden's Scania region, tended to lie below the 60th parallel, but the remains of the fish and animals killed there indicate that these were winter encampments and that the Maglemose and Kongemose roved farther to the north during the warmer seasons. Possibly akin to the Maglemose but extending farther into the Arctic were the Kunda people, who flourished from 8000 BCE until the end of the Mesolithic. Originating in present-day Estonia, the Kunda spread into southern Finland and Karelia, establishing themselves on the shores of lakes Ladoga and Onega, and following river valleys deeper into northwest Russia – perhaps as far east as the Pechora Basin. On this eastern flank, they encountered the Shigir culture, which inhabited the subarctic forests on both sides of the Ural Mountains. That the Shigir and Kunda exchanged tools or toolmaking techniques is clear from the artefacts both left behind.

Many see in the Maglemose, Kunda and Shigir cultures the first successful adaptations to subarctic Eurasia's boreal forest. In characteristically Mesolithic style, the hunting of moose, boar and the wild oxen known as aurochs was combined with fishing, trapping and foraging for berries, fruit and mushrooms. Dogs were domesticated, and the wide assortment of tools, wonderfully preserved in the peat bogs of the North, permitted economic versatility. Slate axes and bone daggers of fine workmanship have been recovered from gravesites such as Oleneostrovsky Mogilnik. The Lake Sindor encampment of Vis, most likely settled by Kunda people between 7000 and 6000 BCE, has turned up the remains of nets, fish traps and hunting bows, along with the fragments of a sled and what may be the world's oldest extant pair of skis. The canoe became more commonplace, and pottery, once thought to have been manufactured no earlier than the Neolithic, is now known to have been produced in Sweden and Finland as far back as 4500 BCE.

Whether on the tundra or in the forest, the Neolithic offered the Arctic little that was groundbreaking by way of technological or economic advancement. It did, however, bring in-migration and other changes to the population. In southern Scandinavia, the Kongemose were followed by a profusion of Neolithic groups customarily identified by the way they shaped and decorated their pottery. In the Baltic and Russian subarctic, the Kunda were succeeded by Finland's Sperrings culture and the Narva people (c. 5300–1750 BCE), while, closer to the Urals, the Shigir gave way to the Gorbunovo. The Arctic itself experienced significant population growth, due to overcrowding in Scandinavia, Russia's Volga and Oka regions, and even western Siberia. By 3000 BCE, newer cultures, named simply after the locales they settled in, were forming in the far north: the labyrinth-building Karelians, who ranged from Lake Ladoga to the Arctic coast; the Kargopol, who preferred the forests around Lake Onega; and the fishers and sealers of the Kola Peninsula and the White Sea. Above the Gorbunovo, on the frontier between European Russia and Siberia, lived the Ches-Tyi-Iag people of the North Sosva River. Three hundred miles north of Norway, the Svalbard archipelago – often called Spitsbergen, after its largest island – came to be inhabited by 2000 BCE. Trade linked most of these peoples, with amber, green slate, quartz and other goods, raw and crafted, making their way back and forth between Norway's western shores and the Ural

Mountains. Such commerce became even more extensive during the ages of metal.

Despite an abundance of tantalizing clues, the world view and life-ways of these Mesolithic and Neolithic northerners remain opaque to us. Many burial sites from these years have been uncovered, none more spectacular than Oleneostrovsky Mogilnik, or Deer Island Cemetery, a tiny island in the middle of Lake Onega. Here, throughout the seventh millennium BCE, the tribes living in the surrounding woods laid their dead to rest in no fewer than 500 graves, almost 200 of which have been excavated since the cemetery's discovery in the 1930s. The Stalin-era scholars who first worked on the site dated it to about 2000 BCE and analysed it strictly in Marxian terms. Two major excavations, carried out in the 1980s and '90s, affirmed that the remains were several thousand years older, but disagreed fundamentally on how to interpret them. The first team argued that the positioning of the bodies – some buried upright, others set apart – and the distribution of bear-tooth and beaver-tooth pendants, as well as small figurines carved in the shapes of moose and vipers, were signs of a socially stratified, village-based community with divisions drawn sharply along gender and clan-based lines. By contrast, the second group concluded that Oleneostrovsky Mogilnik was sacred ground shared in common by widely scattered bands of forest-dwelling, relatively egalitarian hunter-gatherers. Similar debates are played out over dozens of sites throughout the North, and all that seems certain is that this era witnessed some degree of class and gender differentiation and – as confirmed by the growing quantity of beads, amulets and objects fashioned from amber, antler and stone – an expanding capacity for creative self-expression.

And, of course, a more elaborate set of spiritual and ritual practices. The custom of entombing the dead on islands was widespread in this region and is thought to reflect a desire to prevent restless spirits from disturbing the living. Less apparent is the purpose of the hundreds of rock carvings and standing stones that dot the shores and islands of Europe's Arctic coast. Large as Norway's Alta complex may be, it is but one of the region's many petroglyph assemblages, with equally striking specimens found throughout the frontier that joins Fennoscandia to northwestern Russia. At Old Zalavruga, where the river Vyg flows into the White Sea, depictions of bear, moose and lizards grace the seaside cliffs, as does an enigmatic, 6,000-year-old image of a man – a harpooner, perhaps, or maybe a shaman – gesturing to a beluga whale. Sigils in the same style are inscribed on the shores of the Kola Peninsula's Lake

Kanozero, well above the Arctic Circle, and in other places besides. On hilltops north of Lake Onega and on the spruce-covered archipelagos of the White Sea, granite labyrinths spiral and twist in indecipherable configurations, some of them more than 40 feet in diameter. Often in their proximity loom the rock compositions now called *seida*, a Sami term, and these have numerous counterparts throughout Scandinavia, in the megaliths raised by Sweden's and Norway's Neolithic inhabitants. Unlike better-known prehistoric constructions like Newgrange and Stonehenge, these stones and mazes appear to serve no astronomical function, and few of them are burial markers. Scholars and poets alike, then, have given themselves free rein to imagine what ceremonies took place here, under the aurora-lit nights of a long-dead age. The painter and semi-professional archaeologist Nicholas Roerich, one of many artists and littérateurs in *fin-de-siècle* Russia who were caught up in popular fascination with Finno-Ugric and Slavic paganism, wrote lyrically about these spaces as 'mute witnesses to immemorial rites . . . where enchantresses brewed poison from the heads of serpents and where the splendid northern sagas live on'.[4] These may have been altars for blood sacrifice and the propitiation of gods whose names will never be known, and it may be that shamanic magic was worked here to summon fish and whales to their summer feeding grounds. But if an aura of the numinous still radiates from these spaces, it reveals little of what made them sacred to their creators.

Bronze and iron tools were never as common in the Arctic as they were in the south, but neither were they unknown. They came up via trade with the south, they circulated along the network of exchange that operated between northern Scandinavia and the Urals and they were manufactured on site, with smelting ovens appearing in Karelia and elsewhere no later than the 700s BCE. On an ethnographic basis as well, the Bronze and Iron Ages brought Europe's north closer to the present day. Among the groups now arriving in the lower latitudes were those who, over time, founded the Fennoscandian states. The Germanic tribes that engendered the Swedes, Danes and Norwegians entered Scandinavia no later than the first millennium BCE; the *Suiones* and *Dani* were known to Roman authors including Tacitus and Jordanes during the first five centuries of the common era. The Slavs are conventionally thought to have emerged between the Vistula River and the Carpathian Mountains by the 500s CE, with eastern subgroups moving into Russia during the 600s and 700s. The Suomi, or Finns, are the offspring of Finno-Ugric settlers who migrated to northern Europe from western Siberia or the near side of the Ural Mountains at some undetermined date.

It is similarly hard to pinpoint the origins of the European Arctic's oldest living indigenes, whose languages belong to the Finno-Ugric family tree. These are the Sami, long known as the Lapps, and the Komi, referred to in older days as Zyrians and Permians. The territory of the former spans the northernmost reaches of Norway, Sweden and Finland, and extends into Russia; the Komi live farther to the east, out to the Arctic and subarctic Urals, along the Pechora and Kama basins. The earliest solid evidence that Finno-Ugric tongues were spoken in these lands surfaces only at around 2000–1500 BCE, but it may be that the Sami and Komi descended physically and culturally from the Stone Age peoples already living in northern Scandinavia and adopted the new languages rather than arriving with them. (Some also make this argument regarding the Finns.) Especially in the case of the Sami, there has been a concerted effort to push back the date of their ethnogenesis, or to win wider acceptance for the idea that the region's older cultures, such as the Komsa or the archaic tribes of Karelia and the White Sea, were proto-Sami. Speaking of Scandinavia's Mesolithic and Neolithic inhabitants, Norway's Sami Parliament states that 'while we do not know whether they were Sami, we do assume that the Sami culture emerged and developed from the[m].'[5] Sami archaeologists have laid claim to ancient artefacts and ruins that non-Sami scholars are inclined to label 'prehistoric Norwegian' – or Swedish, Finnish or generically 'Stone Age'. Such assertions, however, have as much to do with modern struggles for minority rights and self-determination as with understanding the past, and are exceedingly difficult to prove. Whatever their relationship to the ancients preceding them, the safest assumption is that the Sami as they are today – and the Komi – came into being sometime between 2000 and 1 BCE. It is generally believed that the Sami, not the Finns, are the *Phinnoi* and *Fenni* alluded to by Greek and Roman commentators such as Ptolemy and Tacitus. As for the moniker 'Lapp', given to the Sami by outsiders, it is thought to derive from a Scandinavian term for 'patched clothing' or perhaps 'moose dung'. It was popularized in the thirteenth century by the Danish historian Saxo Grammaticus, but is nowadays considered derogatory.

Although the Sami and Komi hunted and fished, their defining characteristic was the shift that many of them made during the Middle Ages to the herding of reindeer, a change that required a new, semi-nomadic lifestyle. In the case of the Sami, clans called *siida* clustered together in large winter camps, living in turf houses. In spring, families dispersed to calving grounds not far from the treeline, building lighter, wood-framed shelters and subsisting on caches of meat and cheese left behind from the previous autumn. Summer was the time for lodging in leather tents and following the deer to the tundra; autumn brought the herd back to the spring dwellings. After the October rut, selected deer were slaughtered and the caches replenished for next year. The first heavy snow signalled time to return to winter camp. Unlike some of Siberia's reindeer herders, neither the Sami nor the Komi rode reindeer like horses, although both harnessed them to sleds.

The later Middle Ages brought greater social stratification and more fixed settlement. Wealthy herders among the Sami – *finnekonger*, or 'Lappish kings', as the Norse called them – acted as chieftains of a sort, and in the wake of the fourteenth-century Black Death many Sami repopulated the coastal fishing villages left empty by the disease. This distinction between 'sea Sami' and 'mountain' or 'inland Sami' widened further over the coming centuries. The Komi, the most commercially savvy of Eurasia's reindeer people, were managing their herds on an almost industrial basis by the early modern period. Those on the edge of the Urals formed their own polity, the Principality of Great Perm, which reached the peak of its power in the 1300s and 1400s. For as long as they could, the Sami and Komi kept up their pagan ways, rooted in polytheistic shamanism. Totemic veneration of the bear was central to Sami religious life, as were daily appeals to the forest god, who governed the movements and well-being of all animals. Sami shamans, called *noiadi*, wielded magic drums and interceded with spirits and deities to heal the sick and bring good fortune to their people. They remained active in some areas through the 1600s and 1700s.

The Middle Ages were also a time of more frequent contact between Europe's Arctic peoples and the embryonic kingdoms forming to the south. By the 900s CE, Norse hunters and whalers were often in the far north, as were merchants and trappers from Russia's city-states, starting in the tenth and eleventh centuries. Such encroachments did little to improve the natives' lot. Benefits that came from trade were offset by competition with outsiders for scarce economic resources. Once the Scandinavians Christianized, they forced the cross upon the pagan Sami, and the Komi were among the first northern peoples the Orthodox Russians strove to convert. As Europe's states extended their political authority northward, the Sami and Komi found themselves drawn into webs of taxation and service obligations, sometimes to more than one

Sami shaman with ritual drum, as shown in an engraving by Odvart von Lode
for Knud Leem's ethnographic study *Beskrivelse over Finnmarkens Lapper*
('A Description of Finnmark's Lapps', 1767).

ruler, if they were unlucky enough to live on contested land or if their
migratory routes took them across territorial boundaries. They would
struggle to preserve their old ways and their former independence –
but time's passage diminished the little autonomy left to them.

Siberia and its Northern Natives

On the grass-and-gravel beachfront of Yttygran, a low-lying isle off the shores of Russia's Chukchi Peninsula, one of the polar world's most unusual shrines sprawls majestically but eerily over a length of more than 1,000 feet. This is Whale Alley, an arched walkway lined with the meticulously emplaced skulls and jawbones of almost 60 bowhead whales, leading to a hilltop circle of standing stones.

Groundwater contamination has made it difficult to radiocarbon-date Whale Alley, but since the opening up of scientific studies there in the mid-1970s, its excavators have maintained that it was constructed in the 1200s or 1300s, most likely by the Punuk, a Bering culture of long duration. Here sea hunters may have celebrated successful kills with feasts of thanksgiving or inducted young men into some sort of mystery cult or fraternal society. Whatever its function, Whale Alley remains the most elaborate ritual centre ever discovered in the Arctic, and it testifies to the growing sophistication of Siberia's native cultures in the years before Russian conquest.

Unlike in Scandinavia, an unbroken line of human habitation continued in the Siberian Arctic from the Pleistocene to the Holocene. In the east were the Dyuktai, the likeliest ancestors of the first Americans, as well as the Sumnagin, who settled the northern coast between 9000 and 6000 BCE, from the Taimyr Peninsula to Chukotka. With sea levels not yet risen to where they are today, the Sumnagin also reached sites in the high Arctic that the ocean has since separated from the mainland. Among these is Zhokhov, a basalt isle bisected by the 76th parallel and buffeted by fierce polar gales. Zhokhov's settlers, present at about 6400 BCE, developed a hunting-and-fishing economy different from anything else known in the Arctic. Apart from being possibly the first humans to live above 75°N, they appear to have been the first to use dogsleds. They fished, using barbed hooks carved from bone, and created needle-shaped arrowheads out of flint and obsidian, quite distinct from the bifacial projectile points manufactured by most Sumnagin groups. Most unusually, the mainstay of the Zhokhov people's diet was the polar bear, which in other Arctic communities has never been more than an ancillary source of food.

Most of Siberia's Stone Age northerners arranged their economic lives along less adventuresome lines. Traditionally, native Siberians, both prehistoric and historical, have been classified according to their modes of subsistence, both because of Marxism's influence over the social sciences during Russia's Soviet period and as a way to make sense of the dizzying array of cultures that have lived in the region. The standard typology, devised by Soviet scholars and still used in modified form today, includes forest hunting and fishing, sedentary fishing along large rivers and coastlines, Arctic sea-mammal hunting and two industries that grew out of deer hunting: reindeer herding combined with taiga hunting, and tundra pastoralism based exclusively, or nearly so, on the reindeer.[6] Variations on each of these fed and clothed communities throughout the subcontinent. Sealing and whaling were the most perilous, especially when done offshore. Reindeer herding was the newest and, after a short time, the most widespread. The domestication of reindeer is thought to have been practised earliest in the Altai and Sayan uplands of southern Siberia sometime around 1000 BCE, although there is disagreement as to whether it originated there and spread to other locales by a process of cultural diffusion, or arose in various parts of Siberia independently. However they came to adopt the habit, the tending of reindeer sent Siberian natives on an annual cycle of seasonal journeying, and dwellings were designed for maximum mobility; well into the modern era, *chumy* and *yarangi*, the Nenets and Chukchi names for the all-season herder's tent, dotted the northern landscape. The deer provided nourishment – 'our food walks on its own four feet', the Chuvantsy of the far northeast liked to say – as well as hides for tents and clothing, sinew for binding and sewing, and bone and antler for carving. No later than the 600s CE, their musclepower was harnessed for sled haulage, and some groups rode them like horses, with and without saddles.

A fruitful season of deer breeding or a successful hunt, whether on land or at sea, was regarded as the gift of gods and unseen forces. The religions of ancient Siberia were animistic; worshippers lived in awe and fear of spirits around them, and came to believe that select individuals possessed the ability to fall into trance and intercede with the spirits or combat them when necessary. These primitive theurgists were called by many names, although we know them today as shamans, a word from the language of the Evenki, whose rituals were recorded in the seventeenth century by the Russian archpriest Avvakum, exiled to Siberia for heresy. Although the global applicability of the term 'shaman' is acknowledged by all but a few scholarly purists (if one can speak of a Shinto 'priest' or a Shaolin 'monk', one can fairly speak of a Yanomamo or Hopi shaman), Siberia and Central Asia are the true cradles of shamanism, and it was from those places that the phenomenon spread outwards, including to the circumpolar north. 'Global' should not be taken to mean 'generic', for while shamanism is perceived by many to be a universal wisdom tradition practised more or less identically around the world, there is a great deal of diversity as to how shamans were called to their vocation, whether they enjoyed leadership or marginal status among their people, and what ceremonial regalia they used. The drum was near-ubiquitous, but masks, headdresses and other paraphernalia differed from place to place, and Siberia's shamans entered their states of trance in a number of ways. One favourite means, aside from the rhythm of drumbeats and chanting, was the ingestion of *Amanita muscaria* or the fly-agaric mushroom, a known hallucinogen. The powers shamans were thought to command likewise varied among the North's many ethnicities. These ranged from healing, exorcism and the transformation of the self into animal form to appeasing long-dead ancestors and petitioning the gods for happy fates and material plenty.

The Neolithic and Bronze Age cultures of Siberia were many and diverse, even on the northern fringe, but there is no saying for certain how much of their legacy has been passed on to the present. In the northern zones of western Siberia, peoples like the Ust-Polui may have intermixed with Finno-Ugric newcomers to give rise to the natives who now reside there. In central and eastern Siberia, the societies clustered along Lake Baikal, the Amur basin and north-flowing rivers like the Lena and Aldan may have contributed to the bloodlines and cultural-technological development of those who yet remain in Yakutia and Chukotka. Systems of exchange are known to have connected these regions: the hunters of Lake Ymyiakhtakh crafted their tools from white jade that came from the distant Vitim River, while the Siktiakh people inhabiting the Lena's Arctic lowlands traded as far south as the Amur and the Pacific coast to obtain metal objects such as copper needles, as well as raw ore to smelt for themselves. The Ymyiakhtakh (*c.* 3000–1 BCE) have been proposed as possible ancestors of still-surviving ethnicities like the Yukagir, Chukchi and Koryak – although others have wondered whether they, or perhaps the Syalakh and Belkachi (*c.* 4500–3200 BCE and 3000–1900 BCE, respectively), are the source of the Arctic Small Tool tradition (ASTt) that played such a role in populating the North American Arctic.

In the event, archaeologists generally agree that the majority of today's indigenous Siberians emerged in or moved into their present homelands during the Bronze and Iron ages, roughly from 2000 BCE to the first millennium CE. There were Komi in western Siberia, along the north Urals and lower Ob, and nearby lived their fellow Ugrians, the Khanty and Mansi, who may have descended partly from the older

Ust-Polui. For the Khanty and Mansi, the Ob and its tributaries formed the heart of their physical existence and the *axis mundi* of their spiritual geography; Khanty shamans taught that the river flowed from the heavenly realm ruled by the sky god Numi Torum to the underworld, passing through the earthly plane inhabited by humankind. Fine archers and crafters of birchbark boats, most Khanty and Mansi fished and hunted, but some lived farther to the north and acquired the art of reindeer herding from more recently arrived neighbours to the east. Among these were the Samoyed groups who came north sometime around the first century CE, filling up the land between the Ob and the Yenisei. Except when referring to the language family, the term 'Samoyed' has been rejected as academically obsolete, and although most Russian scholars dispute the etymology, many believe it to be a slur originating from a Russian coinage meaning 'self-eater' and implying cannibalistic practices. The Samoyed-speakers of the Yamal ('end of the earth') and Gydan peninsulas, where the Ob empties into the Kara Sea, were the Nenets, some of them hunters of walrus and seal, most of them herders of reindeer. The Enets settled the lower Yenisei and the Taz, while the Nganasan (formerly called Tavgi) made their homes in the Taimyr Peninsula. Others living along the Yenisei include the Selkup and Ket. The latter are distinguished by the fact that their language is the first in Eurasia to be definitively linked not just with Eskimo-Aleut tongues, but also with those of the New World's Native Americans – in this case with the Na-Dene language family, whose speakers include the Tlingit and Athabaskan groups like the Gwich'in, Koyukon and Dene.

Beyond the Yenisei, the uplands of central and eastern Siberia came to be dominated by two groups. More numerous, and the second to appear, were the Sakha, better known as the Yakut, the name given to them by their neighbours. Turkic herders of horses and cattle, the Yakut left the steppes to move north along the Lena River, but were less nomadic than the reindeer people among whom they settled. They had readier access to iron tools, lived not in tents but in huts called *yurta* (not to be confused with the Mongol yurt) and organized their clans into a more unified social system – reflected in the complexity of their hierarchy of gods, governed by the 'great chief', Ulun Toyon. Preceding them, and shunted to the north and east by their arrival, were the Tungus-speaking Evenki and Eveny. In the second millennium BCE, the Evenki and Eveny quit their ancestral lands in northeast China, first to settle the Amur basin and Lake Baikal and then, around 1 CE, to roam the 2 million square miles that sprawl between the Central Siberian

Plateau and the Pacific shore. The Evenki took up residence principally to the west, between the Tunguska-Yenisei river network and the Lena, while the Eveny established themselves farther to the east. Those who remained in the forest hunted moose and used canoes to navigate the local waterways; the Eveny who settled on the shores of the Sea of Okhotsk led a sedentary maritime lifestyle. However, most Evenki and Eveny, whether they lived in the shadow of the Verkhoyansk Mountains or along the Kolyma and Indigirka rivers, relied on the reindeer – a gift to humankind from the sky god Hövki – for sustenance and transport. Not only did they harness their deer to sleds, they rode them like horses, wielding lassos like *vaqueros* of the tundra. As noted above, it is the Evenki who gave us the word 'shaman'.

Moving up the Okhotsk coastline, or across the Verkhoyansk and Chersky mountains, eastern Siberia gives way to the far northeast, which consists of Chukotka – the size of Norway and Sweden combined – Kamchatka and all else that remains of western Beringia. This territory has hosted human settlements since the Palaeolithic, and even faraway Wrangel Island was inhabited by 2000–1500 BCE. Despite the absence of the land bridge, northeastern Siberia continued to serve as a conduit between Asia and North America, and although scholars still guess at the first steps in the process, the emergence of the Palaeoeskimo and Eskimo cultures, discussed further on in this chapter, involved a number of the peoples who lived here. The microblade-manufacturing techniques later adopted by North America's first Palaeoeskimos, the Arctic Small Tool tradition, were brought to Siberia's northeast from the middle latitudes during the early years of the third millennium BCE. As for the Eskimos, anthropologists generally agree that they sprang from Alaska's Norton tradition and the Old Bering Sea cultures, both of whose ancestors appear to have left the Amur and Okhotsk regions to colonize the Chukchi coast and the islands offshore. From Russia's Cape Dezhnev and the Gulf of Anadyr, and from Sivuqaq, or St Lawrence Island, these groups spread gradually to Alaska. The Old Bering cultures developed distinct identities from the 200s BCE onwards, although ethnographers today know them by the names of their settlements: the Birnirk, for example, who reached their zenith around 500–700 CE, and the Punuk, who flourished between 800 and 1400. Adept hunters of seals, walruses and whales, Old Bering societies had at their disposal powerful recurve bows, large whaleboats and toggle harpoons – an advanced design whose detachable head kept one's prey from shaking the point loose once it was lodged in the flesh – and it is to the Punuk

Chukchi warrior from northeasternmost Siberia, armed with spear and shield and clothed in metal armour. Sketched as part of the fieldwork carried out by Waldemar Bogoras (Vladimir Bogoraz-Tan) for the Jesup North Pacific Expedition (1897–1902).

that Whale Alley and the much-studied whale-butchering site of Masik, on Chukotka's Mechigmen Bay, are thought to belong. Vestiges of the Old Bering cultures are evident among North America's Eskimo and Inuit and in Russia as well, among the Siberian (or Asiatic) Eskimos, also referred to as Yupik, the same name used by their closest Eskimo relatives in Alaska.

Sharing Siberia's northeast are a miscellany of peoples classified as Palaeoasiatic: a language family whose members are largely unrelated, but which provides a home for small groups who would otherwise remain uncategorizable. Although their numbers are much reduced today, the most widely distributed of the northeast's Palaeoasiatics were the Yukagir, 'whose campfires', notes one prehistorian, 'were once as many as stars in the sky'.[7] The Yukagir worshipped the spirits of moose and reindeer, and were among the few northern natives to develop their own written script: a system of pictograms that allowed clans speaking different dialects to communicate with each other. Interspersed among them were their less populous kin, the Chuvantsy, as well as Eveny, Yakut and others.

Of those others, the most numerous and, at least in Russian eyes, the most exotically primitive, were the Chukchi, along with the Koryak, who are cousins by language. The antiquity of both groups is debated; some maintain that they appeared as early as 2000 BCE, rooted, perhaps, in the Ymyiakhtakh people of the late Neolithic, while others argue for a more recent origin, around 1 CE. Among both, specific communities earned their keep in different ways, depending on whether they lived along the beaches enfolded by Chukotka's cliffs and bays or on the tundra flats further inland. The Chukchi and Koryak of the coast fed on seals, walruses and grey whales (with Siberian Eskimos specializing more in the hunting of bowheads), while those of the inland herded reindeer. Russian ethnographers categorized maritime and interior Chukchi as if they were separate ethnicities, following the same protocol for the Koryak, and such distinctions came naturally to the natives themselves; a creation myth recounted by the reindeer Koryak jeeringly describes the Koryak seal-hunters of the seaside as having been formed out of reindeer excrement. Skilled weaponsmiths who fashioned armour out of seal and walrus hides splinted with bone, Chukchi and Koryak bands warred on each other, as well as on their neighbours, and when the Russians sought to impose their will on Siberia's easternmost reaches it was the Chukchi and Koryak who put up the stoutest and longest-lived resistance.

Ensconced in Kamchatka on the dividing line between Arctic and subarctic, the Itelmen (known to the Russians as Kamchadal) birded, hunted and, from the skin boats they call *baidars*, fished. While their language is genetically related to Chukchi and Koryak, the Itelmen may be considerably older, with some theorizing that they descend from the Palaeolithic settlers of the Ushki Lakes. To Kamchatka's south, on the Pacific islands and along the Okhotsk shore, down to the mouth of the Amur, there reside a number of groups who, while geographically distant from the Arctic, have traditionally been classified as 'northern'.

Numbered in this category are Tungus-speakers like the Nanai, Orochi and Ulchi, as well as the Palaeoasiatic Nivkhi (Gilyaks) of Sakhalin Island and the Ainu, whose range extends south to Japan. While not technically 'Arctic', these groups enter into the Arctic narrative on occasion, and will appear in later chapters where appropriate.

Indigenous Peoples of the North American Arctic

Blank eyes stare out from a mask carved from sea-stained driftwood, daring the viewer to enter a phantom world of spirits and lost ancestors. Undulating whales hang suspended in the air, as if cradled by the waters of an unseen but eternal ocean. And then there are the polar bears, solemn and inscrutable, sometimes depicted as flying, perhaps to symbolize the shaman's self-transformation and mystical journey to the realm of spirits.

Such are the figurines and miniatures left to us by the Dorset, a Palaeoeskimo culture that inhabited the Canadian and Greenland Arctic from 500 BCE to the centuries following 1000 CE. The Dorset remain in many ways unfathomable, but on one point there is near unanimity: of all the art produced in the ancient North American Arctic, theirs was the most stunning, unmatched for fineness of detail and power of expression. And also for existential profundity, with many Dorset pieces radiating a disquieting sense of gloom. These may have been shamans' implements, and because the making of them reached its peak late in the culture's history, when the Dorset were threatened by ecological crisis, some suspect, as the Canadian Museum of Civilization puts it, that they 'reflected attempts to control an increasingly unpredictable environment through religious and magical means'.[8] Whatever fears haunted the minds of Dorset artists, they were soon justified. Although some of their folkways were taken up by those who followed them, the Dorset faded away as a distinct culture at some point between 1200 and 1500 CE, their place taken by the forerunners of the modern Eskimo and Inuit peoples.

But this was no overnight development. For much of the early Holocene, the only part of the New World north capable of sustaining human life was eastern Beringia, due to the length of time it took for the Cordilleran and Laurentide glaciers to melt away. Over the several millennia that followed the crossing of the Bering land bridge, Alaska and Canada west of the Rockies were populated by the melange of hunting and fishing cultures traditionally categorized as Palaeoarctic, along with a scattering of Palaeoindians who drifted north from the Great Plains or up the Pacific coast. How to classify and interpret Palaeoarctic artefacts remains a subject of perpetual debate, and the question of how closely, or even whether, these groups are related to the Eskimo-Inuit peoples and Native Americans of the present day is still clouded.

Only around 6000 to 5000 BCE did post-Palaeoarctic cultures begin to fill up the continent's higher latitudes more broadly, the result of two parallel developments. From the south, as the ice sheets vanished, Palaeoindians moved into the subarctic portions of Canada and Alaska and into the lower Arctic as well. Perhaps as early as 7000 BCE, and certainly by 4000 BCE, those known as the Maritime Archaic settled in the east, from Maine and Quebec up to Labrador and Newfoundland. They are thought to have given birth to the Beothuks and the Algonquian-speaking Innu, known as the Naskapi in the north and the Montagnais in the south and east, and in neither case to be confused with the Inuit. By no later than 5000 BCE, the elk-, moose- and caribou-hunting peoples of the Shield Archaic appeared west of Hudson Bay, spreading out from the shoreline and into the woods and barrens of Nunavut and the Northwest Territories, while those of the Northern Archaic reached the Alaskan interior around 4000 BCE, looping back to parts of the Yukon and Northwest Territories by 3000 BCE. Together these were the forerunners of Canada's Cree nations and the Athabaskan speakers of northwest Canada and Alaska, including the Chipewyan, Tutchone, Gwich'in, Tanana, Koyukon and Dene. Among the other aboriginals of southern Alaska and the Pacific subarctic, the most prominent are the Eyak, Tlingit, Tsimshian and Haida, the last often credited with having invented the practice of carving totem poles.

Meanwhile, Beringian cultures thrived and diversified, some of them gradually evolving into today's Aleuts, Eskimos and Inuit. Exactly when cannot be said. The Inuit Tapiriit Kanatami, an influential Canadian NGO, argues that southwestern Alaska was 'the first Inuit territory' as early as 6500 BCE, but that presumes an unbroken chain of kinship which not all archaeologists or ethnographers are prepared to take for granted.[9] An Aleutian lineage can be traced with confidence to about 2000 BCE, but some speculate that it stretches back to the maritime peoples who lived in southern Alaska during the sixth and fifth millennia BCE. In particular, the seafarers of Anangula, near Umnak Island, may have been proto-Aleut. The Anangula were among the first to hunt sea mammals in North America, and the practice spread throughout the Aleutians and the Kodiak region – where the Ocean Bay people (*c.* 5000–2000 BCE) slew whales by smearing their spearheads with a poison made from monkshood – and eventually to all of coastal Alaska.

Whatever their parentage, the Aleuts, also called Unangan, created village-based societies, the biggest of which supported populations of over 1,000, quartering 50 and more at a time in sturdy longhouses. They fished, sealed and hunted walruses, otters and seabirds, and took to the water in *iqyaks*, as they called kayaks, to pursue migrating whales offshore. The Aleuts are ethnolinguistically related to the Eskimo and Inuit but, unlike their far-ranging kin, never broke out of the North Pacific sphere.

True outward journeying began sometime between 3000 and 2000 BCE, with the rise of the Palaeoeskimo cultures – or, as many Inuit prefer to call them, Sivullirmiut ('first inhabitants').[10] The earliest of these belonged to the Arctic Small Tool tradition, whose type site, dating to about 2500 BCE, is located near Cape Denbigh, on Alaska's Seward Peninsula, but which most likely grew out of an influx of new arrivals from Neolithic Siberia after 3000 BCE. ASTt peoples manufactured a unique, double-pointed style of microblade, and it may have been they who introduced the bow and arrow to the New World. They spread into the Brooks Range and through most of Alaska, and some, with little hesitation, hurled themselves along the 3,000-mile arc that runs from the Bering to the Atlantic. Two landmark discoveries in 1948 brought to light the remarkable speed with which this happened. That year, U.S. archaeologist Louis Giddings, working in Alaska, defined the Denbigh Flint Complex, while a quarter of the world away in northwest Greenland, Denmark's Eigil Knuth uncovered the remains of a culture only slightly younger, which he called Independence I after the fjord whose shores they occupied. Comparison of the Denbigh and Independence tools showed them to be unmistakably related, and in the years since, archaeologists have identified a variety of ASTt peoples who emerged in Alaska and made their way eastward.

This wave of migration brought the Independence I, Saqqaq and Pre-Dorset cultures to eastern Canada and Greenland by approximately 2500 BCE, although prehistorians are undecided as to whether they travelled as a single group and then split apart, or journeyed separately. All three survived until about 500 BCE. The Independence I people pushed up to the high-Arctic islands of the Canadian archipelago, including Devon and Ellesmere, and on to northwest Greenland. The first human beings to travel so far north, they camped seasonally within

400 miles of the Pole, and a few rounded the top of Greenland and settled halfway down the island's eastern coast. A later ASTt culture, Independence II, succeeded them from 500 to 100 BCE. The Saqqaq, who may have been an offshoot of Independence I, occupied the west coast of Greenland south of the 70th parallel, near the imposing Ilulissat glacier of Disko Bay, where more glaciers are spawned than anywhere else in the northern hemisphere. The Pre-Dorset tucked themselves into the low Arctic portions of central and eastern Canada, especially Melville Peninsula, southern Baffin Island and other territories ringing Foxe Basin and northern Hudson Bay; some reached Labrador and Newfoundland after 1900 BCE, while others, by the 1300s BCE, drifted back to the west. In the east, the Pre-Dorset encountered the Palaeoindians of the Maritime Archaic, although whether they fought, traded or ignored each other is difficult to say. Those who inhabited the high Arctic preyed mainly on the musk ox, while those to the south depended more on caribou. All of them fished, sealed and birded. They possessed technology of a high level, including bows and arrows, barbed tridents for spearing char and other fish, toggle harpoons and atlatl throwing sticks with which to propel darts and spears.

All of this lends mystery to the next transition: the emergence around 500 BCE of the Dorset, who were identified by Canadian archaeologist Diamond Jenness in 1925. Unlike the Arctic Small Tool peoples, the Dorset did not migrate to the east but originated there, on Cape Dorset and other parts of Foxe Basin – evidently as an outgrowth of the Pre-Dorset, but with a much-altered toolkit. Gone, for example, were the bow, the atlatl and the stone drill, and the Dorset were not skilled in the making or handling of boats larger than kayaks. Some have held them up as an example of technological regression, but they are better seen as having adapted to changing environmental circumstances. Starting around 500 BCE, a severe cooling trend set in, increasing the extent and durability of coastal pack ice, and the Dorset responded by mastering the art of hunting seals and walruses by foot. Even narwhals and beluga could be killed from the ice, especially with the help of kayakers. The Dorset worked up close with toggle harpoons. For surer footing they attached crampons to their boots and, to transport meat back home, they used man-hauled sleds shod with runners of bone or ivory. Depending on where they lived, the Dorset also hunted caribou or musk oxen, relying on spearwork to finish off their prey, and supplemented their diet with fish and small mammals. They were able craftsmen, with their quartz microblades, jade chisels, soapstone lamps and stone-and-turf winter houses. And, of course, their spectacular art.

The Dorset experienced Early and Late periods, divided at around 600 CE, with some scholars proposing a Middle period from about 100 CE to 600 CE. From Foxe Basin they expanded north to Ellesmere and Greenland, west as far as Victoria Island and south to Newfoundland. After the 600s CE, gradual warming spelled slow doom: the freer of ice the ocean shores became, the more inaccessible the Dorsets' traditional prey. During these later centuries, many Dorset communities relocated to the colder north to preserve their sealing way of life or abandoned their coastal homes to take up hunting in the interior. The saturnine character of Late Dorset art is commonly interpreted as a reaction to these new stresses.

Pressure on the Dorset worsened around 1000 CE, with the arrival of the Thule – the direct ancestors of today's Eskimo and Inuit – from Alaska. Even if the Thule did not war on the Dorset or knowingly compete with them for food, the newcomers were supremely skilled sea hunters, and by ranging far out from shore they intercepted and decimated seal herds and whale pods long before they migrated within reach of the Dorset. The Dorset entered a terminal stage, although how and when it ended has never been determined. Small pockets may have held on as late as the 1300s and 1400s in Quebec and the Labrador interior, but the rest appear to have died out by the 1200s. No one knows whether the Dorset were eradicated or assimilated into the Thule by intermarriage, but their legacy survives in several ways. Most scholars believe that, with machete-like knives designed for the purpose, they built the first of the snow-block huts that Westerners associate with the term 'igloo' (Inuit use the word *iglu* to describe many kinds of shelters). They seem to have been the first to mark the landscape with the stone cairns the Inuit call *inuksuit* (sing. *inukshuk*), erected to guide travellers through the wilderness and, as Farley Mowat puts it, to defy 'a loneliness which is immeasurable'.[11] The Dorset may also live on in folk memory. Across much of Canada, Inuit oral tradition – as related to ethnographers like Franz Boas in the 1880s, Knud Rasmussen in the 1920s and Jørgen Meldgaard in the 1950s – speaks consistently of the Tuniit, a tribe already present when the Inuit came into their new lands. The tales describe the Tuniit as a strong but gentle people, 'timid and easily put to flight'.[12] It is widely, though not universally, supposed that they are the Dorset, hazily remembered by the newcomers who displaced them.

If the Thule begat the Eskimo and Inuit, who begat the Thule? It is now generally accepted that they were the product of ethnic and cultural-technological intermingling among some combination of Asiatic peoples in Beringia between 1 and 1000 CE. This consensus did not form quickly, for while most Euro-Americans from the sixteenth century onwards subscribed to one Asiatic-origins theory or another, a vocal and not easily dismissed minority, including the Danish geographer Hans Steensby and the eminent Franz Boas, remained convinced until the early 1900s that the Eskimo were cold-adapted Indians who had ventured up from North America's subarctic forests. Only during the Fifth Thule Expedition of 1921–4 did Knud Rasmussen and Therkel Mathiassen strike the final blow in favour of the thesis that now holds sway. The Thule owe much of their pedigree to the Norton complex, a cluster of Alaskan cultures – the Choris (c. 1000–500 BCE), Norton (c. 500 BCE–800 CE) and Ipiutak (c. 1–800 CE) – rooted in the ASTt peoples who remained in Beringia after 2500 BCE. They also descend in part from the Old Bering Sea cultures, the maritime hunters who dominated the waters and islands between Chukotka and Alaska from the 200s BCE through the first millennium CE. The Thule were fully established on the shorelines of Alaska by 900 CE, if not the 800s. By 1000 CE, in a migratory odyssey that rivals the Polynesian voyages and the Africa-wide treks of the Bantu, the Thule had spread across most of the North American Arctic, forming the cultural continuum that to this day stretches unbroken from Beringia to Greenland.

Both through borrowing and invention, the Thule developed the most successful hunting economy seen to that date in the high north. Their tools included the spear and toggle harpoon, the bow and arrow, snow goggles and pottery, and they appear to have invented the ulu, the all-purpose 'woman's knife' whose axehead- or moon-shaped blade, set perpendicularly to the handle, could be used for everything from butchering and skinning to carving sod bricks and trimming hair. Although ore was scarce, available only through trade or from rare meteoric deposits, the Thule knew the arts of copper- and ironsmithing long before European contact. On land, their proficiency as dogsledders offered them unparalleled mobility, both as explorer-settlers and trackers of prey. Like other Beringians, and like the Palaeoeskimos before them, they were expert kayakers, but they set themselves apart by their use of a newer kind of boat: the longer and broader umiak, which had a larger carrying capacity and made coastal net-fishing feasible. Most of all, the deployment of kayaks and umiaks in tandem transformed whale hunting into a more lethal enterprise than before. Instead of harvesting only lesser whales, or waiting for brief spring and autumn opportunities to catch larger cetaceans close to shore or in narrow ice leads, Thule boatmen were able to pursue whales like the bowhead far out to sea, even to their distant summer feeding grounds. Darting ahead, kayakers fatigued their prey by tagging it with harpoons attached to floats made from inflated skins. With the whale thus exhausted, the umiak would close in for the kill as the master harpooner, armed with a heavy lance, used the slower but more stable boat as a platform from which to administer the *coup de grâce*. The Thule became as adept at sealing and walrus-hunting as they were at whaling.

The Thule's eastward expansion proceeded in stages, aided by the warm period that environmental scientists call the medieval climatic optimum. Their first push, circa 1000 CE, took them along the coast past the Mackenzie River and into the Canadian archipelago, to Banks, Victoria and Devon islands, as well as to north Baffin Island and the southern shores of Ellesmere. Between 1000 and 1200, they reached northwest Greenland, settled all of Baffin Island and moved into Foxe Basin, Southampton Island and north Hudson Bay. In the next three centuries, they inhabited Greenland and the Hudson Bay region more thoroughly and ventured south to Newfoundland and Labrador. With the passage of time came cultural differentiation, especially as the climatic optimum waned and cooler weather forced new adaptations. In Alaska, numerous Eskimo peoples derived from the Thule, their Western-given names changing with ethnographic and political fashions. Among these are the Inupiat of the Arctic north and northwest, the Yupik of the west and southwest (close kin of Siberia's Asiatic Eskimos), and groups like the Sugpiat, Koniag and Chugach in the south. Taking a simplified view of Canada, major subdivisions in the west and centre include the Inuvialuit of the Mackenzie Delta, the Copper Inuit, the bands of Caribou Inuit living in the Barren Grounds and groups west of Hudson Bay such as the Central Inuit, Netsilik and Iglulit. In Canada's east live the Labrador Inuit, Ungava Inuit, Baffin Island Inuit and others. On Ellesmere Island and in northwest Greenland, one meets the world's northernmost people, the Inughuit, once called the Polar Eskimo. To their east and south are the native Greenlanders or Kalaallit, a related but distinct group. Where Eskimo-Inuit territory abutted that of First Nations or Native Americans, the outcome varied, with trade and violence equally possible.

Although Westerners are prone to overgeneralize about the Eskimo and Inuit, the degree of homogeneity among them is indeed high,

Alaskan Eskimo from Nunivak Island, off the Yukon and Kuskokwim deltas, wearing a ceremonial mask. Photographed in 1927 by Edward S. Curtis.

especially by comparison with the northern peoples of Eurasia. When the Danish colonial administrator Henrik Rink noted that 'the different branches of this race exhibit the most striking uniformity in their language, habits, and mode of life', he did not overshoot by far, even if the mutual intelligibility of dialects diminishes with distance, or if local variations cause different groups to hunt different beasts.[13] With entire ethnic subgroups sometimes numbering only in the hundreds, individual communities tended to run small. Most economies were mixed and seasonal, with bands typically camping together over the winter and early spring and then scattering during the summer and early autumn to hunt and fish in family-based parties of around a dozen. To take one example, the Netsilik hunted seals communally, out on the ice, in the season called *ukiuq* (early November to early March). Families went their own way in the spring, trading winter quarters built from peat and sod for skin tents called *tupiq*. They spent the summer inland, fishing the rivers and hunting caribou, driving them into shallow water or pounds constructed of wood or stone. Autumn was time to exploit the salmon run, and then, as the ice thickened once again, bands reunited on the coast to set up their winter camps. Details changed from place to place. Hunting the *agviq*, or bowhead, was crucial to the Inupiat of Alaska's north coast, where success in whaling is still celebrated biennially during the midwinter 'messenger feast', or Kivgiq. Elsewhere, musk oxen or walruses might matter more to a group's livelihood. As in the Eurasian Arctic, secondary sources of nutrition included birds, eggs, shellfish and small mammals. Some Eskimo and Inuit devised traps for polar bears, with sliding doors of stone.

As discussed further in chapter Three, the Eskimo and Inuit fashioned clothing, tools, sleds and boats with an ingenuity all the more remarkable for the dearth of wood and metal ore above the treeline. Many groups traded, both with other Inuit and with Native American and First Nations neighbours. The waterways that most facilitated exchange were the Bering Sea, the straits and channels of the Canadian archipelago, Hudson Bay, the corridor separating Canada from Greenland, and rivers linking coastlines with the interior, such as the Yukon–Kuskokwim and Mackenzie. In ways not uncommon among hunter-gatherers, especially in the North, labour among the Eskimos and Inuit was sharply divided along gender lines. Kayaking, sledding and the hunting of large prey belonged to the masculine sphere. When women hunted, it was for small game like birds and foxes, and when they fished, it was from rivers or from the umiak, known in many communities as the woman's boat. Women assumed near-total responsibility for childcare, cooking and maintaining tents and igloos, which they often built themselves. They tended the oil lamps and cut peat or gathered caribou dung as fuel for fires, and it often fell to them to haul seal or deer meat back to the camp, using small sleds pulled by forehead straps. Because survival in the high north was impossible without well-made and properly maintained gear, women were particularly valued for skill in sewing and the preparation of hides and skins.

Like most circumpolar peoples, the Eskimo and Inuit were animists, relying on shamans for spiritual guidance. Whereas in some societies shamans occupied ambiguous status, feared as well as respected, or seen as afflicted rather than blessed by their talents, those of Arctic North America and Greenland tended to be figures of charisma and authority, often drawn from the ranks of the best hunters. Thought to possess the gifts of healing, weather prediction, exorcism and shapeshifting, typically into the form of a polar bear, the *angakok* (pl. *angakut*), the most widespread term for the Eskimo-Inuit shaman, also heard confessions and assigned penance for violating taboos. The essence present in all things was known as *inua*, and the spirits with whom *angakut* held converse had many names. The most helpful were *tornait* or *tornrait*, which Christian missionaries later tried to identify with demons or the Devil himself. Certain myths travelled the breadth of the continent, including numerous tales of Raven, the trickster god, and of the sky deity to whom hunters appealed before setting out after prey. Darkest were the legends of the Sea Woman, whose most famous incarnation is Sedna but who also bears the names Nuliajuk, Niqlik and Takanakapsaluk. Married against her will to a malevolent bird spirit, Sedna is stolen away by her father in his kayak, but cast overboard by him when the spirit, in angry pursuit, calls up a torrential storm. When she grabs hold of the kayak to clamber back on, her father slashes at her hand with his paddle, severing her fingers – each of which becomes a monster of the sea, such as the Greenland shark – and consigning her to a sombre immortality in the watery abyss. This unhappy episode, combined with the fact that humankind's sins float to the bottom of the ocean to choke her, inclines Sedna somewhat to bad temper. The Netsilik recognized her as 'Mother of the Sea' – but also as 'the Most Dangerous and Terrible of All Spirits'.[14]

As an Iglulik shaman once confided to Knud Rasmussen, 'We do not believe. We fear.'[15] This stark awareness of the ever-present reality of peril and death helped to shape some of the Eskimos' and Inuit's more distinctive social practices, which were shared by Siberia's Eskimos and to a degree by other northeastern Siberians like the Chukchi and Koryak. Infanticide was documented as late as the early twentieth century, as was senilicide – the abandonment or willing suicide of the infirm and elderly – and both are assumed to have been a normal part of life in earlier times. On the other hand, a shared sense of vulnerability encouraged genuine communalism, with food and gear lent out at need and theft barely heard of. Crimes of violence resulted not from tensions over property but from passion, blood feud or the rough justice that condoned the murder of someone considered unbearably noxious to the entire community. The aspect of Eskimo-Inuit life that most raised eyebrows among Westerners, the custom of sexual sharing, has, since coming to light in the Victorian era, earned northern natives an overblown reputation as lascivious beyond the norm. Men indeed had wife-friends whose spouses' companionship they might enjoy under specific circumstances, generally when taking shelter at a friend's dwelling while the husband was away hunting, and white explorers and scholars, whether prudishly or with amusement, always proved quick to comment on what they saw as frolicsome randiness among the Eskimo. But spouses were not swapped indiscriminately, and the practice, far from allowing orgiastic licence, provided a way to forge extra personal and protective bonds in an environment where the long-term survival of family members was far from assured.

Two macroscopic developments altered the lives of the Thule and their Eskimo-Inuit scions during the European Middle Ages. One was ecological: after 1200, the warm climatic optimum that had permitted the Thule to penetrate so far into the highest Arctic came to an end. This cooling trend eventually triggered the Little Ice Age of 1500–1850, but already by 1300 it was clogging northern waterways with heavier ice and driving many fauna, including whales, farther to the south. This change, coming just as the Thule were splintering into separate cultures, accelerated the process of diffraction and, for some, caused certain technologies and hunting methods to be forgotten. The medieval period also brought the Thule and post-Thule peoples into contact with European outsiders. A few encountered the Viking voyagers of Eric the Red's and Leif Ericson's generations. Between the 1000s and the 1400s, Greenland Inuit interacted for several centuries with the Norse settlement there. Briefly interrupted by that colony's demise, contact resumed in the 1500s as exploration and colonization brought Europeans to North America to stay. While the foreigners' impact was limited until the 1800s by their inability to overwinter so far north, their presence, whether intermittent or constant, became an increasingly intrusive fact of existence for Inuit and Eskimo peoples from the Middle Ages onwards.

European States and the Arctic to 1500

Monarchs throughout history have always loved their menageries. There is nothing remarkable, then, in the fact that Egypt's Ptolemy II, who ruled from 285 to 241 BCE, and Seiwa, a ninth-century emperor of Japan, were avid collectors of the most exotic beasts they could bring into their possession. The true surprise comes in hearing that both rulers, in their palace courts of Alexandria and Heian, were the proud owners of full-grown polar bears: gifts or plunder from the frigid, frightening lands that lay to the farthest north, beyond the ken of civilized men and women.

Long before southerners sailed the Arctic's waters or set foot on its ice fields and tundras, they knew of it, if only vaguely, and coveted the rare commodities locked away there. In the fifth century BCE, Herodotus recorded in the fourth book of his *Histories* rumours of a northern country where 'an altogether unsupportable cold' prevailed for eight months out of the year, and the Western world's direct encounters with the Arctic are considered to have begun a century later, with the voyage of Pytheas. A geographer from the Greek colony of Massalia (now Marseilles), Pytheas headed west through the Pillars of Hercules in 330 BCE, then sailed north in search of amber and tin. Continuing for six days past the British Isles, he drifted into the pack ice, which he called *mare concretum*, and sighted a land where 'the sun rose again a short time after it had set'. This is thought by some to have been Iceland or Greenland, and by others to have been the coast of Norway. Pytheas affixed to it the fabled name of Thule, synonymous ever since with the Atlantic high north.

Whether Pytheas indeed reached the Arctic waters – the geographer Strabo, among others, questioned his veracity – a dual perception of the region took hold among the Greeks and Romans, even though it lay outside the bounds of their *oikoumene*, or known world. On the one hand, they saw the North as a menacing wilderness, whence came strange beasts and fierce barbarians. But beyond this realm of savagery and ice, they believed, was a happier, more welcoming north: Hyperborea, where the breezes were gentle, the waters warm and open and the land fertile. Like the Atlantis myth, this blissful vision exerted a strong pull on the popular imagination, and up to the eve of the twentieth century it fuelled many speculations, both scientific and fantastical, about an ice-free polar ocean at the top of the world. The Romans had no first-hand way to verify Hyperborea's existence, or much of anything else about the Arctic, although authors such as Tacitus, in their efforts to learn more about the barbarian tribes beyond the Rhine and Danube, gleaned a few kernels of information about northern peoples like the Sami. Somehow, the Romans contrived to bring polar bears to the Eternal City, where, in special basins built for the emperors' games, these ursine gladiators battled seals and other creatures for the entertainment of the masses.

It was the Middle Ages that brought Europe and the Arctic truly into each other's worlds. Commerce and state-formation played the starring roles, supported by Christian missionizing and the natural impulse to see the far side of the horizon. The earliest stages of this process remain in shadow. Most historians assume that the first Europeans to venture into the far north were anonymous hunters and sailors more concerned with keeping their traplines and fishing grounds secret than with their place in the annals of exploration. Moreover, the documents we do have – the Norse Eddas and Icelandic sagas, Russia's first chronicles and the Irish sea-adventure tales called *immrama* – are, as the explorer Fridtjof Nansen observes, composed 'in the light of historical romances founded upon legend' and not invariably reliable.[16] It is diverting, for example, to imagine the Apostle Andrew evangelizing in the north Russian town of Novgorod, as the Primary Chronicle claims he did, or to picture St Brendan of sixth-century Ireland in his tiny currach, floating past Jan Mayen Island and Iceland on the way to the 'Isles of the Blessed' that some insist were Newfoundland. But it would be rash to wager too much on the truth of such tales.

Important thresholds were crossed in the ninth and tenth centuries as Viking raiders and colonizers, impelled by wanderlust, overpopulation and stiff-necked unwillingness to submit to centralizing monarchs, swept through the North. Some were freebooters and merchants, harvesting or trading with natives like the Sami for furs, ivory and other goods from the Scandinavian Arctic and Bjarmaland, as the Vikings called Russia's White Sea coast. One of the first Europeans to venture to such high latitudes, and perhaps the first to reach Bjarmaland, was the Norse hunter Ottar (also spelled Ohthere) who, in 890 or thereabouts, rounded the crest of Norway and the Kola Peninsula, sailing until he reached the estuary of what was probably the North Dvina. Later, guesting at the court of Alfred the Great of England, Ottar boasted of the quantities of tusks, walrus hides, bearskins and marten and seal pelts – and the thirty score of 'Rayne Deere' – he had obtained from the 'Fynnes' and Bjarmians, by which he most likely meant the Sami and the Komi of Perm. The Norse king Eirik Bloodaxe led an expedition there in 920, and in 1026 the adventurer Tore Hund, posing as a trader, attempted to steal the crowned idol consecrated to the Permian god Jomali.

Many of the Vikings' movements reshaped Europe's political landscape by creating new states, as in Ireland, Normandy and the Danelaw in England. Two other such places were Iceland and Russia. Unverified tradition has it that Irish and Scottish monks inhabited Iceland's shores as early as the 700s, but the nation proper was founded around 870 by Ingólfur Arnarson and other Vikings fleeing the stern rule of Harald Fairhair, the first king of a united Norway. (The Faeroe Islands, halfway between Norway and Iceland, provided another haven for similarly disaffected Vikings.) Once settled around Reykjavík, or the 'bay of smokes', so named after the local hot springs, the Icelanders appointed no monarch but, starting in 930, entrusted government to a semi-parliamentary council called the Althing, elected by well-off landowners. The island's population swelled with Viking émigrés, and it remained autonomous until 1262, when civil strife caused a near-collapse and compelled it to accept Norwegian overlordship. In the meantime, Iceland served as the launch pad for the Norse colonization of Greenland. Over in the east, Swedish Vikings known as Varangians streamed through present-day Finland, Russia and Ukraine to the empire of Byzantium, trading with the emperor when they could, pillaging his lands during less amicable periods and eventually serving him as the fiercest mercenaries to be found in Constantinople. Amid the lakes and forests of northern Russia, they built the cities of Staraya Ladoga (Aldeigja) and Novgorod (Holmgard) in the 750s and 850s respectively. From there they blazed the famed 'Varangian Road to the Greeks', a system of river routes, portages and outposts that linked the northern towns with the Dnieper River and the Black Sea. In this way, and by assimilating into the local Finno-Ugric and Slavic populations, the Vikings contributed to the consolidation of Kievan Rus', the earliest Russian state. Russia's Primary Chronicle tells a colourful tale of how, in 862, the Varangian prince Rurik accepted an invitation from warring Slavic tribes to govern them and thus re-establish order in the land – but while Russia's dynastic history conventionally dates from this moment, Rurik is a mythical figure cut from the same cloth as Romulus or King Arthur, and his story is best seen as a tidy encapsulation of a slower, more prosaic process of economic and cultural amalgamation.

By the 900s, nearly all the European states we now think of as Arctic nations had come into being: Norway under the dynasty founded by Harald Fairhair and his son Eirik Bloodaxe; Kievan Rus' under the grand princes said to descend from Rurik; Sweden under the heirs of Erik the Victorious, who united the lands of Svealand and Götaland (land of Beowulf's Geats); and Denmark under the family of Harald Bluetooth. Only Finland failed to materialize, with most of that territory coming under Swedish rule after the 1323 treaty of Nöteburg and remaining there till the early 1800s. During most of the Middle Ages, the hold these regimes had on their Arctic lands was tenuous. Economic incentives to master the North might be multiplying, but the region remained difficult to access, much less control, especially for polities handicapped by the frailties and discords common to feudal states. If the Arctic seemed physically remote and forbidding, it seemed conceptually so as well. Adam of Bremen, a German monk of the eleventh century, marvelled in his *Description of the Northern Islands* at the wizardry he witnessed among the Sami of Karelia, whose shamans told fortunes and intoned 'songs with powerful words in a murmuring voice to persuade great whales to come close to shore'. Where Adam saw mystery, Denmark's Saxo Grammaticus, writing around the year 1200, saw Stygian desolation. Norway he described as a 'rock-strewn desert' and Iceland as the scene of 'happenings beyond credibility'; in the Scandinavian forests, evil spirits and grotesque man-beasts lurked. Even the Vikings and Finns, in their mythologies, betrayed a similar uneasiness about the extreme north. In that direction, say the Norse legends, lie Hel, the underworld, and Niflheim, the fog-choked land of death where the dragon of destruction gnaws at the roots of the world-tree Yggdrasil. In the *Kalevala*, Finland's national epic, the northland of Pohjola, understood to be home to the Sami, is depicted as a 'death-realm' of 'ever-silent waters' and 'darksome plains'.

Still, there was wealth to be had in the North, and land to claim, and pagans to bring to Christ. In high medieval Europe, the most sustained campaigns of Arctic colonization were directed at northwestern Russia and its environs and, farther to the west, the Atlantic islands, including Iceland and Greenland. In Russia, the pioneering entity was Novgorod, transformed between the ninth and twelfth centuries from a Viking stronghold to a thriving commercial metropolis whose form of local government, while not democratic in the modern sense, was more representative than anything else on offer in Russia, or indeed in most of Europe. Always the most independent-minded of old Russia's city-states, Novgorod asserted its autonomy even more after the mid-1200s, when the Golden Horde's conquest of Russia shattered the Kievan principality. Relatively unburdened by the 'Mongol yoke' that weighed on Russia's shoulders until the mid-1400s, Novgorod expanded its already extensive trade network to the point of becoming a provisional member of the Hanseatic League.

Also expanding was Novgorod's territorial sway, which grew steadily and impressively after the 900s. In the west, the Novgorodians annexed the city of Pskov and enough of the Baltic region to gain access to the Gulf of Finland, but it was in the north and northeast that they made their largest acquisitions. By the early 1100s, Novgorod controlled a number of forts in the lands above lakes Ladoga and Onega, all the way to the White Sea and the mouth of the North Dvina. Novgorodian merchants and hunters pressed east towards the Urals, following river valleys to the Pechora basin. After many battles in the 1200s and 1300s, which pitted Russian *ushkuiniki*, or sea raiders, against the Swedes and Norwegians, much of Karelia and the Kola Peninsula fell to Novgorod.

Novgorodians also moved along the Arctic coast, proceeding from the White Sea into the Barents Sea and even slipping through the Kara Gates past the northern tip of the Urals to the mouth of the Ob River – the Russians' first foothold, however tiny, in Siberia proper. They had knowledge of Novaya Zemlya as early as the 1000s. Their empire amounted to several hundred thousand square miles.

Many commodities drew Novgorod to the North: amber and honey in the forests; gyrfalcons, sent to hunt in noble courts throughout Europe; whale and seal oil; and ivory, taken from walruses and occasionally narwhals. Valued above all, though, was the 'soft gold' of fur, with squirrel, fox, marten and sable in high demand throughout Europe and beyond, and sealskins and bearskins fetching welcome profits as well. Resource extraction on the Arctic frontier brought the Novgorodians and, with time, other Russians, into contact with natives who dwelled 'far in the midnight lands', as the Primary Chronicle put it. The first of these collisions were with the Sami of Karelia and the Kola Peninsula, and the Komi, whom the Russians knew as Zyrians and, closer to the Urals, as Permians. Further eastward progress brought Russians into the herding and hunting grounds of the 'Yugrians' – the Khanty and Mansi, or at least their immediate ancestors – and the westernmost 'Samoyeds', or Nentsy. The resulting interactions involved the usual borderland mix of trade, bloodshed and competition over resources; in the 1300s and 1400s, the Russians tried systematically to Christianize and subjugate native groups, starting with the Komi. Once they reached the Arctic, a number of Russians went near-native themselves. Chief among these were the Pomors, or 'sea people', the descendants of the Novgorodians and other outsiders who colonized the White Sea coast and the North Dvina and Onega river basins. Ethnically Slavic with a distinct frontier culture and more than a little native admixture, the Pomors in some respects resemble a cold-climate, maritime analogue to the Cossacks of the Russian and Ukrainian south. Until the founding of Arkhangelsk, the Pomors' principal town was Kholmogory on the North Dvina, which grew out of an earlier settlement in the 1300s.

While the Russians drove to the east, the Vikings moved farther to the west. During the tenth and eleventh centuries, places like the Faeroes – brought under Norwegian rule in 1035 – and Iceland became integral parts of Scandinavia's cultural and economic spheres, even if the latter remained politically independent for some time to come. Scandinavia's kingdoms themselves were tamer places now, constrained by the laws of the Crown and, increasingly, those of the Christian god. New frontiers beckoned, and thus began the colonization of Greenland and the first Western voyages to America, the stories of which come to us from the texts known as the Vinland Sagas. In 982, one Eirik Thorvaldsson, better known to English-speakers as Eric the Red, was banished from Iceland for wrongful killings, a history of which had already caused his expulsion from Norway. As he passed three years of exile on the southern tip of Greenland, Eric decided that the island had potential as a home for those who felt pent-up in an Iceland growing more crowded and hierarchical. Indeed, he had little trouble persuading more than 500 fellow pioneers to return with him to Greenland in 986. At the site of Eric's first camp, near what is now Julianehåb, they built the so-called Eastern Settlement; as more colonists responded to Eric's call, a second outpost, the Western Settlement, went up almost 200 miles to the north, where Greenland's capital, Godthåb (Nuuk), stands today. At its largest the Greenland colony supported between 3,000 and 6,000 people, with 300 farms to feed them – raising sheep, goats and a species of miniature cattle – and sixteen churches, plus a cathedral, to tend to their religious needs. To round out their food supply, the Greenland Norse fished and hunted seals and walruses, but their survival depended on trade with the homeland. When Norse ships came calling, the colonists exchanged furs, walrus tusks and falcons for what they could not grow or make themselves. By about 1100, they traded and sometimes fought with their native neighbours, the Thule, whom they called Skraelings.

Famously, if fleetingly, the Vikings brought a piece of the Americas into their domain, becoming the first Europeans verifiably to reach the shores of the New World. In the year 1001, Eric's son Leif sailed with a crew of 35 toward the *ubygdir*, or 'uninhabited land', that lay to Greenland's west. The Vinland Saga catalogues the places they visited: Helluland, the country of flat rocks, thought to be Baffin Island; Markland, or the forest land, probably Labrador; and the renowned Vinland, or wine-land, in the vicinity of Newfoundland's L'Anse aux Meadows. (The berries which gave Vinland its name, commonly trans-lated as 'grapes', were actually 'wineberries', or mountain cranberries.) The following spring, Ericson returned to Greenland, and although he never went back to Vinland, his siblings and in-laws did so more than once, attempting to maintain a self-sufficient settlement there. Their short-lived efforts were hindered by hostile interactions with the natives. During one famous skirmish, Leif's redoubtable sister Freydis, despite being pregnant, startled the Vikings' attackers into retreat by ripping her dress open to the waist and slapping her defiantly exposed breasts with the flat of a sword taken up from a fallen comrade. The Vikings abandoned Vinland in 1014, erasing all the long-term potential Leif's voyage might otherwise have had and delaying for almost half a millennium the onset of regular Euro-American contact.

Like Iceland, Greenland submitted in the mid-1200s to the rule of Norway's king, Haakon the Old – a far cry from Eric the Red's dream of autonomy – and a royal monopoly channelled the island's trade through the Norwegian port of Bergen. This tighter tie, though, would be severed before too long. The cooling of the climate after 1200 struck a double blow against the Greenland Norse: colder weather killed their livestock and caused their farms to fail, and ice build-up made it difficult to maintain naval communications with Norway. Norway's involvement with Hanseatic trade reduced Greenland to an economic afterthought – as did the rise of Russia as Europe's premier source of furs and the greater availability of elephant ivory from Africa and Asia – and internal crises in Scandinavia marginalized it further. The Black Death hammered Norway hard in 1349, killing one in three people in Bergen and distracting the city from its duty of supplying the Greenland settlements. The joining together of Norway, Sweden and Denmark under one crown in the 1380s, followed by the transfer of Norway's capital to Copenhagen, made it all the easier for Greenland to be forgotten. The colony flickered out of existence during the late 1300s or 1400s, although when or how has never been determined. That the settlers suffered severe malnutrition is evident from skeletal remains, which show their average height to have shrunk alarmingly, with many adults less than 5 feet tall. But was it starvation that finished them, or were they massacred by the Skraelings? Perhaps some were absorbed into the native population through intermarriage. Whatever the case, this slow, gloomy decline left Greenland empty of foreign presence for many years – although the Scandinavians never relinquished their claim on the island and took it up again in the 1700s.

Greenland's misfortunes notwithstanding, the fourteenth and fifteenth centuries brought greater centralization to Scandinavia and Russia and strengthened their hold on their northernmost territories. The thrones of Norway and Sweden were united in 1319 by Magnus Eriksson. After the 1380s, the century-and-a-quarter Kalmar Union joined that state with Denmark's under one crown, which also claimed suzerainty over Greenland, Iceland, the Faeroes and Österland, or

Swedish-ruled Finland. The Union dissolved in violence after the 1520s, and came close to falling apart a number of times before that, but it kept alive a set of monarchies which never lost their desire to assert authority over the Arctic. The number of encounters between northern natives and Scandinavian outsiders increased during the late medieval years. By the 1500s, many Sami would be forced to pay tribute to the kings of the south.

In Russia, authority over the North passed into the hands of the rising state of Muscovy, which, during the 1300s and 1400s, gathered to itself most of the Kievan princes' former territory and extended its own reach to the Urals. By the 1480s, Ivan III, known as the Great, had formally renounced Mongol rule and brought to heel rivals like Novgorod, whose Arctic possessions Muscovy thus inherited. As before, the demand for furs and ivory drove exploitation of these new acquisitions, but, as the example of the Pomors shows, frontier settlement for its own sake took place, in many cases as a way to live free of rent-gouging landowners or the tsar's tax collectors. In its own way, the Orthodox Church built up Russia's presence in the North. Beginning with the twelfth-century opening of the Monastery of the Archangel Michael on the North Dvina, monks came to the region seeking seclusion and to test their faith in the crucible of the elements. Few places better suited to that purpose can be imagined than strongholds of piety like the Solovetsky Monastery, founded in 1429 on a remote group of islands in the White Sea (and fated centuries later to become the USSR's first forced-labour camp), or the St Cyril-Belozersk Monastery. Russian churchmen also arrived to stamp out ways they saw as heathen. The most famous of Russia's early ministries to the native northerners was that of Stepan Khrap of Ustiug, canonized as Stephen of Perm, who set out in 1383 to bring Christianity to the Zyrians, or northern Komi. Like the prophet Elijah challenging the priests of Baal to match their god's wonder-working powers against Jehovah's, Stephen was fond of inviting shamans to jump into fires with him or to swim with him in icy waters as a way of testing whose deity would lend more divine assistance. In the 1400s, Russian clergy needed no such stratagems, for they had the armed might of the state to baptize by force, as Bishop Ioann of Moscow did the Komi of the Kama basin. Also at this time, the Muscovites began to draft Komi warriors to serve in their campaigns against the Yugrians and other peoples of the Urals. All this marked an early chapter in what would become a long and sadly familiar story to non-Russian natives, especially after the 1500s, when the Muscovite state entered Siberia in force.

However, with the year 1500 approaching, other nations were poised to have an impact on the Arctic. For a long time there had already been little to stop the whalers and fishermen of various countries from availing themselves of the Arctic's bounty when the opportunity presented. Basque sailors, for instance, who had followed whales from the Bay of Biscay to Arctic waters in the 1200s, hunted off the Greenland coast in the 1300s, whatever the kings of Norway might have to say about it. (Some speculate that the Basques reached the coast of Newfoundland as early as the 1370s, beating Columbus to the New World by more than a century.) But most important now was the dawning of Europe's age of exploration. After the 1480s, sea routes around Africa to Cathay and the Indies lay open to the Portuguese, and Christopher Columbus's unexpected landfall in the Caribbean delivered much of the Americas into Spanish hands after 1492. With the fabled wealth of the east at stake, it was inevitable that those countries with access to the Orient would seek more expeditious ways of getting there, and that those without, such as the English, French and Dutch, would be eager to find their own approaches. It occurred to mariners throughout Europe that Asia might be reached from the Atlantic by navigating the Arctic seas, either along Eurasia's northern coast or through waters north of the lands that Columbus had brought to their attention.

So began the search for the Northeast and Northwest Passages, a quest that spurred much of the Arctic adventuring of the next 400 years. The hunt for the latter was launched by a trio of explorers at the cusp of the fifteenth and sixteenth centuries, beginning with John Cabot, or Giovanni Caboto, a Venetian captain in the service of England's Henry VII. Cabot reached the straightforwardly named Newfoundland in the summer of 1497; attempting another such voyage the following year, he and his crew perished. In 1500, the Portuguese government dispatched João Fernando to scout the waters of Greenland, but he found no clear route to the northwest. Neither did Gaspar Corte-Real, who sailed the same year, also for Portugal, both to Greenland and Newfoundland, returning to Lisbon with five dozen Beothuk captives. Like Cabot, Corte-Real and his brother Miguel died upon returning to the New World.

Still, the process, once begun, would not be halted. Many more expeditions headed northwest during the sixteenth century, amassing invaluable data for Europe's mapmakers and seeding northern North America with its first European colonies. A parallel effort sent European explorers to the northeast, past the Scandinavian coast and into the chilly waters north of Russia, with merchants, hunters and whalers in their wake. As in so many far-flung parts of the world, the impact of Western expansionism would be felt in the Arctic all during the early modern era, in terms both human and environmental.

3
Incursions: 1500 to 1800

There is an irony of Hegelian proportions in the fact that a yearning for luxuries from the lushest and warmest parts of the earth – jade and silks from China, pepper and nutmeg from Java and the Moluccas, cinnamon and cardamom from Ceylon and Malaya – caused the Europeans to pit their skills and courage against some of its coldest and bleakest places. But if human events are propelled by world-historical forces, as the German sage once taught, the combination of avarice and ambition that motivated the Columbian age of exploration – and with it the search for Arctic passages to Asia – qualifies as such a force. The maxim 'God, gold and glory', Cortés's pithy summary of why one explores, does as much to explain the first Western probings of Cumberland Sound and Hudson Bay or the opening of searoads to Spitsbergen and Novaya Zemlya as it does the triumphal march of the conquistadors through the desert Southwest and the Andes' peaks and valleys.

Other desires, too, made themselves felt in the Arctic from the sixteenth to the eighteenth centuries. Early modern state formation and the building of empires gave governments more reason to impose their will on peripheral and overseas territories. Religious conflict in Europe lent urgency to Catholic and Protestant efforts to Christianize native populations, and the Orthodox Russians did not lag behind in converting the unbaptized. The Arctic held treasures of its own, making it more than a simple conduit between one ocean and another: if European ships began by searching for routes through the mazy waters of west Greenland and the Canadian archipelago, or along the ice-crusted coastline of Fennoscandia and northwest Russia, they turned soon enough to fishing, sealing and whaling, all with a rapacity unprecedented in northern waters. The French and English established their colonies and companies in Canada, bringing massive quantities of furs back to Europe, while the Russians, taking possession of Siberia and Alaska, did the same. The Kingdom of Denmark and Norway renewed the old Norse claim to Greenland and, like its neighbour Sweden, tightened its grip on its northern frontier. As a consequence Arctic natives became the subjects of states fundamentally alien to them, and even those beyond the reach of 'civilization' saw their economies disrupted by the mercantile dealings of foreigners.

Also during these years, all aspects of existence in the Arctic were affected by a hemisphere-wide environmental trend: the so-called Little Ice Age that lasted from the early 1500s to the mid-1800s. As noted in chapter Two, the long cool-down preceding this event had already altered the migratory patterns of Arctic animals and the distribution of the human presence there. The effects of this cooling became even more pronounced after 1500, limiting population growth in the North and delaying for many peoples the transition from nomadism to more settled forms of existence. At the same time, the colder climate slowed the pace at which Europeans gained access to the remoter parts of the North. While this era witnessed numerous incursions, nothing yet approached the full-scale onslaught that the Arctic would face in later and warmer centuries.

The North American Arctic and Greenland in the Sixteenth and Seventeenth Centuries

For the Eskimo and Inuit peoples, the line separating history from prehistory runs through the sixteenth century, when the Thule culture broke apart into the subgroups listed in the previous chapter. Heavier ice build-up in this chillier era, plus the departure of several whale species for waters farther south, caused certain skills to atrophy and a measure of vitality and confidence to be lost. Some have wondered whether Westerners might have held Arctic natives in higher regard had their initial encounters been with the Thule, rather than their descendants – but seeing what little good high cultural achievement did to shield peoples like the Aztecs and Incas from ill-treatment at European hands, one suspects that the answer would have been 'no'.

However that may be, the Eskimo and Inuit continued in most respects to live as the Thule had, their folkways standing as a premier example of what anthropologists call 'enskilled living'. Ingenuity and aptitude, applied to the smallest details of life and labour, went a long way towards overcoming the harsh ecosystem and a lack of natural resources that other peoples would have found debilitating. Masters of mobility in the high Arctic, the Eskimo and Inuit covered ground in the *komatik*, or dogsled, cunningly constructed from lengths of driftwood, bone or ivory, and lashed together with sealskin thongs. The best material for the harness was narwhal hide, which kept its shape and pliability no matter how wet or cold. On the water, they handled kayaks with a grace that outsiders found astonishing. As George Tyson, assistant navigator on the 1871 *Polaris* expedition, observed, kayaks were 'invaluable to the Esquimaux', who had the years of practice, starting soon after birth, to use them well – but the white man, he believed, 'might almost as well launch out on an ostrich feather and think to keep afloat, as in these unballasted little sealskin shells'.[1] Although, contrary to popular belief, Inuit languages do not contain an unusual number of words for snow (that distinction belongs more to Sami dialects), patient observation gave Eskimos and Inuit a keen sensitivity to the workings of wind, current and ice. They were intimately familiar with their surroundings, charting by the stars and making maps, some of them carved in three dimensions out of wood, without any tutelage from Euro-Americans. The explorer Robert McClure called them 'born hydrographers', and Franz Boas marvelled

Greenland Inuit in their kayaks. Premodern expertise at a pitch of perfection.

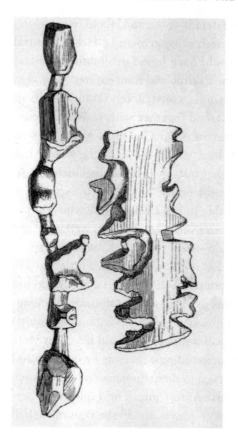

Arctic knowledge through time, 1: Driftwood maps carved by Inuit on Greenland's eastern coast during the 1800s. Indentations in the wood correspond with painstaking exactitude to coastal contours.

at their 'remarkable' knowledge of coastlines that extended over 'linear distances as much as a thousand miles'.[2]

Eskimos and Inuit wasted no material if something useful could be made from it. Bone, ivory and antlers were shaped into tools of all types and sharpened into points and edges, and whalebones were used to build everything from kayak frames to the roofs of houses. In a land so badly supplied with the kind of wood that could be carved long and straight, tusks from narwhals and walruses served as tent poles, spear shafts, struts and braces. Whale and seal blubber could be eaten or rendered into oil for burning in lamps, as was caribou fat. Even intestines had their purposes: scraped and stretched, they became translucent enough to serve as window-hole coverings, and they could be fashioned into waterproof sheeting and cloaks. Another waterproof material was salmon skin, used for making bags and pouches.

Furs and hides were desired for many reasons. Tents, sleeping bags and the shells of kayaks were made from them, as were the warmest and finest clothes known in the Arctic until the age of Gore-Tex. In its classic form, the full-season Eskimo-Inuit attire consisted of a double-layered set of anorak and trousers, made of sealskin or caribou hide and sometimes dogskin, depending on time and place; the anorak's hood was typically lined with wolf or wolverine fur, which best resisted the build-up of frozen water vapour from the wearer's exhalations. The outfit's inner layer placed the hair or fur directly against the wearer's skin, while the external layer turned it outward. Mitts and hide boots (*mukluks* in Yupik, *kamiit* in Inuit), worn directly over hareskin linings, completed the ensemble, which, all together, weighed less than ten pounds. Tailored precisely to the wearer's measurements, and painstakingly stitched and maintained – work that fell to the women – the outfit kept out cold air and was as water-resistant as any non-synthetic gear could be.

In such ways and others, the Eskimo and Inuit contended with exceptional 'dexterity' and 'sagacity', to borrow the assessment of Danish geographer Henrik Rink, against the rigours of their environment.[3] But if it is wrong to ignore their strengths and talents, it is as wrong to overidealize their supposed noble savagery. Hardships were many at the best of times, and one turn of the weather or a single sickness burning through the community, or through a herd of caribou the community depended on, could spell starvation or ruin. Thus arose the infanticide, senilicide and other draconian practices described in chapter Two. To live communally did not mean living free of conflict, either with one's neighbours or within one's group: Eskimo-Inuit groups are known to have warred with each other, with the Athabaskan peoples of Alaska and northwest Canada and with Newfoundland's Beothuk. Nor did they live as lightly on the land as is commonly supposed. The Arcadian vision Euro-Americans often have of native peoples existing in a state of pre-lapsarian harmony with nature has always been overblown. As the environmental historian Clive Ponting notes, 'gatherers and hunters, by no means passive in their acceptance of ecosystems, alter the environment considerably and cause damage.'[4] Where they were still able to take whales, the Eskimos and Inuit, like their counterparts in the Eurasian north, killed more than was strictly necessary to feed themselves, multiplying the harm by targeting the more easily slain females and young. And even before they obtained Western firearms, or before trade with Westerners motivated them to hunt for profit rather than sustenance, they wiped out, in a number of places, local populations of auks, otters, seals, wolves and musk oxen. These were survival-oriented pragmatists, not utopian conservationists, and the logic of the hunt in such unforgiving conditions was to maximize each opportunity to take prey, not knowing when or whether the next chance would present itself.

That said, they did not despoil the land and waters with the greed and shortsightedness shown by the Europeans now arriving on the scene. If the Viking settlement in North America had been a false start, and the colonization of Greenland a tragic sputtering-out, the French, Dutch, English and others who came to the northern New World in the 1500s and 1600s had larger and longer-term purposes in mind. Early reconnoitring for a northwest passage had begun at the turn of the fifteenth and sixteenth centuries, with the voyages of Cabot, Fernando and the Corte-Real brothers. It continued with coastal surveys by Portugal's João Fagundes, who reached Nova Scotia's Cape Breton in 1520–21, Giovanni da Verrazano, who sailed for France in 1524, and Robert Thorne, who mapped part of Labrador for Henry VIII in 1527. In 1534, the Breton mariner Jacques Cartier, who had sailed under Verrazano ten years before, made his own North American journey on behalf of France, searching for a route to Asia and hoping to unearth deposits of precious metals to rival the rich mines that the Spanish were exploiting in the south. He found neither of these during this voyage or the second and third he made in 1535–6 and 1541–2, but he charted Newfoundland and the St Lawrence seaway as far west as present-day Montreal, and he established France's claim to 'the Country of the Canadas' – a name based on the Iroquois word *ƙanata*, meaning 'settlement' or 'village'. Sadly, the gold and diamonds he thought he had found during his third voyage turned out to be pyrite and quartz; for some time afterwards, *diamants du Canada* served as a stock expression for anything counterfeit.

Cartier likened Canada to the land given by God to Cain in his exile, and Henry VIII's enthusiasm for passage-seeking dimmed over time. For half a century, then, European voyages to Greenland and the New World's northern waters were made by whalers, walrus hunters and fishermen. Prior to 1580, an average of 400 ships per year, from Portugal, France, England and elsewhere, fished for cod off Newfoundland, and the Basques dominated whaling off Labrador during the middle third of the century. These tended to be short annual forays with little impact on the Americas themselves, although those who preferred to clean and salt their fish on land before returning home, like the English, traded with the natives and set precedents for greater involvement with the New World.

Active exploration resumed in the late 1500s, pushing farther to the north. The Dano-Norwegian kingdom sent out voyages of rediscovery to Greenland in 1578–9 and 1581, hoping to find the lost Norse colony, but although Mogens Heinson sighted the island's southeastern coast, none of the Danish ships managed a landfall. Thanks to elite patronage and mercantile investment, Martin Frobisher and John Davis of England took the first substantive steps towards charting the Northwest Passage. Support for Frobisher came from the Cathay Company, founded by Michael Lok in 1575, but he also received encouragement from the Duke of Walsingham, Elizabeth I's chief intelligencer, and the queen herself bade him farewell in 1576 as his first expedition set out in the *Gabriel* and the *Michael*. Frobisher sailed past a large land mass he called Meta Incognita, soon determined to be Greenland, although England left it to the Danes to press their own claims there. Meanwhile, upon reaching the southern coast of Baffin Island, Frobisher entered the bay that now bears his name, convincing himself that it was a strait allowing eventual access to Asian waters. Returning in 1577, he convinced himself further that he had stumbled upon an astounding source of gold; he hauled back 200 tons of ore from Countess of Warwick Island (now Kodlunarn) and assembled a fleet of fifteen ships to extract even more in 1578. This third venture ended badly. Frobisher lost one of his ships and 40 men, and scandal drove the Cathay Company to bankruptcy when, upon closer examination, Frobisher's 'gold' proved to be a lustrous but worthless form of mica. Frobisher recovered his good name by serving in the battle of the Spanish Armada, earning a knighthood before his death in 1594. Of the Arctic natives he encountered, he remarked that 'they be like to Tartars', making him one of the first to speculate about the Asiatic origins of the Eskimo and Inuit peoples.

Even more accomplished than Frobisher was John Davis, another of Walsingham's protégés and a friend of Sir Walter Raleigh's. Voyaging three times between 1585 and 1587, Davis put Greenland's eastern and southwestern coasts back on European maps. He also charted the justly named Davis Strait – the waterway separating western Greenland from Baffin Island – up to 72°N, including Cumberland Sound. He did not find the Northwest Passage, but concluded that its existence was 'most probable, the execution easie'. He brought back reports of teeming stocks of cod, which his support vessels fished to offset the cost of his journeys, and also of bowhead whales. As opposed to Frobisher, who took Inuit hostages and cared little when they died in captivity, Davis dealt relatively amicably with northern natives. During his first voyage, he calmed the fears of one Greenland community by ordering his men to dance and play music. Although squabbles broke out occasionally when individual Inuit tried to take metal objects from his crew – communal sharing according to the native mindset, stealing as the Westerners saw it – Davis thought of them in general as 'tractable' and 'less rudely barbarous' than aboriginals he had met in South America and the Pacific. His *Seaman's Secrets*, published in 1594, remained a standard navigational handbook for many decades to come, and he went on to discover the Falkland Islands. He died near Singapore in 1605, during a skirmish with Japanese pirates.

Even larger portions of the northern map were uncovered in the early 1600s. With cooperation from England, Denmark–Norway launched three voyages to Greenland in 1605–7, setting ashore and trading with the natives for walrus hides, narwhal tusks and whalebone. But it seemed too much an effort to keep the Greenland route open, and the scurvy-racked winter passed in Canada in 1619–20 by Danish searchers for the Northwest Passage further convinced Copenhagen that ventures beyond Iceland, except for the purposes of whaling, were of little use. It is thought that Philip II of Spain, alarmed at his rivals' progress in settling North America, sent Juan de Agramonte to scout the shores of Newfoundland in 1611, but this is uncertain, and Spain's empire in the southern New World already took up enough of Madrid's attention.

The French, by contrast, committed themselves to colonizing Canada, with the explorer and administrator Samuel de Champlain transforming his country's New World foothold into *la Nouvelle France*. Port Royal in Acadia (present-day Nova Scotia) was founded in 1605, followed by Quebec City in 1608, and useful alliances were formed with natives like the Mikmaq, Innu and Huron. The Company of New France, chartered in 1627 by Cardinal Richelieu, and with Champlain as one of its investors, organized the colony's economic affairs. By Champlain's death in 1635, the French were firmly rooted along the St Lawrence Valley and in Quebec. They claimed Labrador, Newfoundland and Acadia, although the British contested their ownership of these places throughout the century.

In the meantime, more of Canada was being mapped by Henry Hudson and a succession of other Englishmen. Inspired by the cartographers Mercator and Ortelius in his belief that the North Pole was a huge formation of basalt, surrounded by warm waters beyond the pack ice, Hudson sailed for the top of the world in 1607, at first travelling up the east coast of Greenland as far as 73°N and continuing to Spitsbergen before turning back. Another northeast voyage took him as far as Novaya Zemlya in 1608, and he attempted to go farther via the same route in the spring of 1609, this time for the Dutch East India Company, with a crew half English and half Dutch, in the *Half Moon*. The ice here proved impenetrable, and Hudson, confronted by mutinous rumblings from his crew, set a westward course instead, finding himself off the coast of Newfoundland by July. After nosing around Acadia, Cape Cod and Chesapeake Bay, he sailed up the river now called after him, enabling the Dutch to claim present-day New York and the areas adjacent to it. Returning to England, Hudson passed a short time under house arrest, but was permitted to voyage again on condition that any lands he claimed in the future would be England's. In 1610, Hudson sailed to North America for the Virginia and British East India companies in the barque *Discovery*, and it was during this voyage that he entered the great embayment that marks the east Canadian land mass like the pawprint of a giant lynx impressed upon fresh snow. Hudson believed this to be a sea or strait leading to open water in the west and named the cape at its southern entrance 'Hopes Advance', but had little chance to test his supposition. The harsh winter spent by the *Discovery*'s crew on James Bay persuaded them that they risked starvation if they continued with their mission, and so they turned on their leader. Hudson, his son, and six men loyal to him or too ill to rebel were set adrift in an open boat, later to perish. The mutineers, after many tribulations of their own, returned to England in 1611, famished and frostbitten, claiming that those who had led the insurrection had been killed by natives. The survivors were tried for murder, not the more easily provable charge of mutiny, and all were acquitted.

The verdict stemmed from the fact that Hudson's men had expertise and knowledge to trade for their freedom, and a number of them returned to the North on England's behalf. Several voyages were dispatched to the Greenland shores and Labrador, and the *Discovery*, under new captains, returned to Canadian waters in 1612–13 and 1615–16. Thomas Button gathered evidence that 'Hudson's Sea' was in fact a bay, which he then lobbied unsuccessfully to have named after himself. Next to sail the *Discovery* was Robert Bylot, Hudson's former mate, pardoned by the English because of his usefulness. He and William Baffin, acting as pilot, surveyed the far shore of Hudson Bay, establishing beyond doubt that it was no gateway to Asia. In 1616, they took the *Discovery* up Davis Strait to Lancaster Sound, the eastern entrance to the Northwest Passage. This brought them to 77°45′N, a farthest north that went unsurpassed in the western hemisphere for another 200 years.

As the seventeenth century progressed, and with a number of routes to Asia well established, the exploration of the American north was motivated less by the search for the Passage and more by commerce. Tales of fish, seals and walruses in profusion, and of whales in the thousands, kept alive the interest of investors who cared more for profits than for expanding the bounds of geographical knowledge. With the bowhead population around Spitsbergen nearly annihilated by the late 1630s, European whalers moved first to the waters east of Greenland and then, in the later 1600s, to western Greenland and the east coast of North America. Meanwhile, fishing boats from many countries began to exploit the offshore banks of Newfoundland; by the mid-1600s, a full third of France's entire fleet consisted of ships fitted out for Canadian cod fishing. Adding to the continent's allure were furs. Beaver pelts were the mainstay of the North American fur trade, although marten, lynx and wolverine were valued as well. The French had harvested furs in Canada from the moment Cartier set foot in the St Lawrence valley, and others developed their own interest in this source of wealth.

Although half a dozen of Europe's powers vied to colonize the New World during the seventeenth century, France and England emerged as the primary competitors in the North. Under the patronage of Jean-Baptiste Colbert, Louis xiv's comptroller-general of finances and a tireless advocate of colonization, New France flourished after 1660. Its population rose from 3,000 to more than three times that in the next 40 years, and its territory expanded to include the Great Lakes, the vast Mississippi basin and the *pays d'en haut*, or large 'upper country' that lay to the west and northwest. The Compagnie de l'Occident, which succeeded the Company of New France in 1664, purchased furs from friendly Hurons and Algonquian-speakers. It relied as well on white woodsmen who, tutored by the natives, blazed trails into the forest and took their canoes everywhere the wilderness's web of waterways allowed. Defining the limits of legitimate trade proved difficult, for while non-native trappers were supposed to operate only under licence from the colony, many of these *coureurs des bois* ('runners of the woods') preferred to work independently, to the dismay of the Port Royal and Montreal merchants who lost money as a result. Over time, the famed *voyageurs* ('travellers'), who hewed more closely to colonial regulations, supplanted their free-spirited predecessors; until then, friction between the *coureurs* and the companies continued.

This ill-will caused far-reaching changes, starting with the north-ward sorties of veteran *coureur* Pierre Radisson and his brother-in-law, Médard Chouart des Groseilliers. In 1659, the pair set out for the still unfamiliar Hudson Bay coast, returning the following year with thousands of furs, only to find themselves under arrest, and their furs confiscated, for trapping without a permit. After their release, the disgruntled duo travelled to Boston and London, persuading the English to hire them as guides. In 1668–70 they accompanied a pair of ships provided by the king of England's cousin, Prince Rupert of the Rhine. The expedition entered Hudson Bay from the north, deftly sidestepping the French, and brought back to the court of Charles II staggering quantities of lynx, marten and beaver furs. This was a transformative moment, with Charles immediately agreeing to charter the Company of Adventurers of England Trading Into Hudson's Bay, known more simply as the Hudson's Bay Company (HBC). The new corporation was empowered to reap the riches of 'Rupert's Land', defined as the territory drained by all rivers flowing into Hudson Bay. Charles did not back it financially, proclaiming that 'it is for traders to traffic where they please, and I will furnish no men, ships, or money' – but the company extended England's colonial reach far into Canada.[5] Thanks to Radisson's and des Groseilliers' shifting loyalties, the French, already guarding against English threats to Newfoundland and Acadia, were now drawn into constant conflict with the HBC, as the two sides raided each other's outposts and interfered with each other's trapping. Radisson and des Groseilliers took part in these skirmishes, although in different ways: both re-entered French service in the mid-1670s, but Radisson switched sides again in the 1680s, working as an HBC agent and eventually retiring to England. Failure to dislodge the English from Hudson Bay compromised France's position in Canada, a situation made worse by the 1683 death of Colbert, the colony's most diligent caretaker, and Louis XIV's entanglement in pan-European conflicts. The 1713 Treaty of Utrecht, which ended Queen Anne's War, gave the English authority over Acadia, which became Nova Scotia, and Newfoundland, although fishing rights here were shared with the French. Britain's redcoats would advance even farther as the century progressed.

Anglo-French rivalry had multiple consequences for North America's northern territories. It anchored a foreign presence in Canada, with more than 10,000 French there by the 1690s, and English arriving in ever-growing numbers. Now in the east, but in time across the continent, First Nations and Inuit communities felt the newcomers' impact. Combat with the colonizers and exposure to their diseases, especially smallpox, took their toll. Black-robed Jesuits and other missionaries took up cudgels against the natives' shamanic traditions, and sexual intermingling brought into being a mixed-race population, the Métis, who, like creoles and mestizos throughout the Americas, suffered discrimination at the hands of whites and natives alike. Trade with the Europeans warped the natives' lifeways, as they turned more to trapping pelts to exchange for Western scrip or goods – or for liquor and tobacco – and less to the provision of food for themselves. It also sparked conflicts among native nations, whether over resources, as during the Huron–Iroquois Beaver Wars of the mid-1600s, or because natives who allied with the French or English had extra reason to war against those who allied with the other.

Affected just as much by the outsiders' presence was the northern wilderness, which the Europeans perceived as boundless, virginal, and theirs for the taking. The days of the worst overfishing and overwhaling were still in the future, but not far off, with larger fleets sailing out from Europe every year and the *upirnaaglit*, or 'men of springtime', as the Inuit called foreign whalers, an increasingly common sight. Sealing became lucrative business as well, but most noticeable was the appallingly rapid depletion of walruses and fur-bearing animals, especially the beaver and marten. During the 1600s, the hunger for ivory wiped out the walrus population of North America's east coast from the St Lawrence up to the Arctic. As for fur, the French alone, near the end of the century, were taking 550,000 beaver pelts out of North America every year. While they controlled the New Netherlands, the Dutch hunted the beaver no less assiduously, and the English, once they stepped into the market, outdid both their rivals easily. Beavers were all but eradicated along the Hudson River valley by the 1640s, and if furs of any kind were to be found in sufficient quantities to satisfy Europe's demand, it would have to be to the west and the north – and increasingly, as the years passed, towards the Arctic. The Europeans, their eyes dazzled by the seeming infinitude of the frontiers ahead, refused to acknowledge how 'their' new land, exploited more heavily than at any point before, groaned under the weight of their dominion, and would groan more grievously still with the passage of time.

The Scandinavian and Russian North, 1500–1700

'Twenty adieus, my frozen Muscovites!' exclaims the Princess of France in *Love's Labour's Lost*, as the King of Navarre and his court exit Act v, Scene 2 'disguised as Russians' – a stage direction that might as well have read 'dressed as dancing bears', calculated as it was by the Bard for exotic visual impact on an audience still newly aware of the wild, icebound lands lying to Europe's north and east.

More so than during the Middle Ages, the Arctic featured with prominence in Europe's imagination, although popular wisdom was informed by a mix of fear, ignorance and growing familiarity. Travellers to Muscovy recounted how 60 witches 'out of the North', from the White Sea coast, had foretold the death of Ivan the Terrible, and during the Thirty Years War, the battlefield triumphs of Sweden's Gustavus Adolphus were attributed to the storm-shaping magic worked by Lappish wizards on his behalf. In works of art and fiction, the Arctic continued to connote savagery and lifelessness, as well as metaphysical confusion. In Rabelais' *Fourth Book of Pantagruel*, the giant's quest to find the Oracle of the Holy Bottle takes him through 'the confines of the frozen sea', where words become ice the instant they are spoken and cannot be heard until thawed by the 'serenity and warmth' of milder climes: a vivid metaphor for incomprehensibility in the absence of wisdom. John Milton turns to Arctic imagery in *Paradise Lost* to convey the awful majesty of Sin and Death winging their way from the gates of Hell into the 'wide anarchie of Chaos': their flight is likened to the moment 'when two polar winds, blowing adverse . . . together drive mountains of ice'. In the 1677 canvas *Arctic Adventure*, the Dutchman Abraham Hondius stereotypes the far north as filled with doom. Here, dark clouds gather above a two-masted ship caught fast in the ice; with the help of dogs and muskets, the crew fights off the attack of a polar bear. They appear likely to win this encounter, but the dying of the sun behind them leaves the viewer in doubt about how well they, dwarfed by the surrounding emptiness, will cope with the perils yet to come.

Symbolism aside, the Arctic held out to Europe the possibility of tangible wealth. For Scandinavia and Russia, the far north, with its fisheries and its traffic in seals and whales, and as a source of furs, ivory and other goods, was a prize worth fighting for. The Kalmar alliance that had united Scandinavia's medieval monarchies shattered after 1520, following the 'Stockholm bloodbath' perpetrated by the king of Denmark and the resulting war of Swedish liberation. For the next three centuries, two kingdoms ruled in Scandinavia: Denmark–Norway and Sweden, which retained control over Finland. Throughout the 1500s and 1600s the two states feuded constantly over borders and trade routes. Overall, Denmark–Norway was stronger in the beginning, with Sweden ascendant after the early 1600s – but in the Arctic, the former gained permanent and decisive concessions in 1613, the fruits of victory in the Kalmar War. This conflict, which followed years of escalating tensions, began when Sweden's kings carved out portions of Norway's northern coast by erecting churches and forts between Lofoten and Nordkapp, and by taxing the Sami living there. When, in 1607, Karl ix of Sweden proclaimed himself King of the Lapps in the Norwegian county of Nordland, the Dano-Norwegians could tolerate no more and sent in their battalions. Soundly beaten, Sweden agreed in the Treaty of Knäred to give up large portions of Lapland and all claims to the northern shore, and to recognize Dano-Norwegian authority over Greenland, Iceland and the Faeroe Islands. Sweden exacted revenge on Denmark–Norway in future treaties, but never undid Knäred's major provisions, leaving its Norrland region forever cut off from the polar seas.

Russia, too, had a stake in these contests. It was no easy matter to settle on a Russian–Norwegian border, although one just west of the Kola Peninsula was negotiated in 1571 between Ivan the Terrible and Frederik ii, and both countries, each with a growing number of seasonal hunters on the Svalbard archipelago, felt entitled to squatter's rights over the islands – a dispute not resolved until the twentieth century. Sweden dealt even more aggressively with the tsars, owing to the longer boundary its Finnish and Karelian possessions shared with Muscovy. It happily joined the anti-Russian coalition during the Livonian Wars that Ivan the Terrible unwisely waged between 1558 and 1583; more happily yet, it invaded in the 1590s, and again in the early 1600s, during the 'time of troubles' that nearly tore Muscovy apart with dynastic crisis and civil war. Although Russia survived, it lost territory in the Baltic and spent the rest of the century fearing that Sweden might seize more of Karelia or parts of the Kola Peninsula and White Sea coast. Only in the 1700s would Russia break Swedish power and remove that threat for good.

Not for long were these the only states interested in Europe's high north. The same fervor that spurred the northwest search for a passage to Asia sped mariners to the northeast as well. Leading the way was an English expedition organized in 1553 by John Cabot's son Sebastian and commanded by Sir Hugh Willoughby. Three ships set out in May but separated in July. Two, including Willoughby's, came adrift on the Kola Peninsula, where all the crew and officers perished over the winter, but the *Edward Bonaventure*, captained by Richard Chancellor, beached itself near the St Nicholas-of-Karelia Monastery on the White Sea shore. Chancellor travelled to Moscow and negotiated terms of trade with Ivan the Terrible, made receptive by his desire to find new outlets for Russian commerce. Chancellor's success occasioned the founding of England's Muscovy Company, which, over the next half-century, sent a number of ships to the northeast, both to seek out wealth in the Arctic and to thread a way through its waters. In 1556, Stephen Burrough took the *Searchthrift* eastward along Russia's north coast, looking for the mouth of Siberia's Ob River. Although that goal eluded him, he traded with Nenets hunters for walrus tusks and polar bear skins, and became the first West European to enter the Kara Sea. Arthur Pet and Charles Jackman followed Burrough's route in 1580, but went no further along it than he had.

Subsidized by the burghers of Amsterdam, Dutch explorers ventured this way as well, none more celebrated than the pilot Willem Barentsz (anglicized on most maps as 'Barents'), who tried twice for the Northeast Passage in 1594 and 1595, only to be blocked by ice at the edge of the Kara Sea. The following summer saw him in the Arctic a third time, leading a two-ship squadron that stumbled upon the Svalbard archipelago, sighting Bear Island in mid-June and Spitsbergen later that month. Svalbard, the 'cold coast', had been known for several centuries to Fennoscandians and Russia's Pomors, but Barentsz fixed its position on European charts for good, recording in the process a farthest north of 79°49′N. Soon, however, he met with misfortune: although the ship accompanying his, fearing the approach of winter, returned to Holland, Barentsz pressed on to Novaya Zemlya, hoping to find an ice-free way through the Kara. Instead, he and his men were stranded on the island's frigid shore until June 1597, enduring the ravages of scurvy in the Behouden Huys, the shelter they constructed from the timbers of their ship. When the survivors took to the water in the lifeboats remaining to them, only twelve were left alive, and Barentsz was not among them; it fell to the ship's carpenter Gerrit de Veer, in his *True and Perfect Description of Three Voyages*, to tell the harrowing tale of their journey to the Kola Peninsula, where they were rescued by a Russian merchant ship.

In the person of Isaac Massa, their envoy to Russia, the Dutch gained an able booster of their Arctic trading interests, and when Henry Hudson was not charting northeast waters for the Muscovy Company, he did so in the pay of the Dutch. As we have seen, Hudson got no farther than Spitsbergen and Novaya Zemlya in his voyages of 1607–9, but his reports on the wildlife of these places are often credited with sparking the pan-European whaling craze that swept over the region soon afterwards. In fact, as much was done on this count by Jonas Poole – who led seal and walrus hunts to Bear Island for the Muscovy Company in 1604 and surveyed Spitsbergen in 1610 – and Nicholas Woodcock, who suggested using Muscovy Company ships to bring Basque whalers to the archipelago. Like bees seeking a new hive, Europeans swarmed to the White, Barents and Norwegian seas, where they pursued walrus, seals, polar bears and, as an extra source of ivory, the elusive narwhal. (Over many years and at great cost, the Danes assembled the frame of Rosenborg Castle's coronation throne entirely from narwhal tusks, finally completing it in 1671.) Above all, the outsiders came to hunt the bowhead and its *Eubalaena* cousin, the North Atlantic right whale, both dubbed 'right' for the copious quantities of whalebone and oil they yielded, and for the fact that, once slain, their corpses conveniently stayed afloat.

Chiefly competing for this bounty were the Muscovy Company and the Dutch Noordsche Compagnie, and although the two soon divided Svalbard into southern and northern spheres of influence, they still had Frenchmen, Dano-Norwegians and Basques to fend off, as well as Russians, Finns and Germans. Anchorages and bases were vital assets in these contests, the most famous being Smeerenburg, or Blubbertown, a Dutch outpost on Amsterdam Island, off the northwesternmost tip of Spitsbergen, so named for the great copper vats installed there to render blubber into oil. Tall tales have long circulated of Smeerenburg's size and prosperity, with otherwise sober chroniclers like Nansen and William Scoresby speaking of a boomtown receiving 10,000 visitors every summer, their needs attended to by shops and smithies, churches and bakeries, and even a casino and brothel. Since the 1970s, archaeological research has shown this polar Dodge City to have been a much humbler settlement than once thought, consisting of fewer than twenty buildings and hosting no more than 200 to 400 people at a time. This still made it a valuable holding, and the Dutch were compelled to defend it with a small fort and cannon. The northeast waters were no Spanish Main, but maritime skirmishes and raids on ports and island camps became commonplace. The French privateer Jean Vrolicq and the future Dutch admiral Michiel de Ruyter, a navigator for the Noordsche Compagnie in the 1630s, honed their seafaring skills in these melees before gaining greater fame elsewhere. As late as 1693, near Spitsbergen's Songfjorden, two of Louis xiv's frigates fell upon a fleet of Dutch whalers in what some consider the northernmost naval battle in history.

Between 1610 and 1640, the nations of Europe sent 500 to 600 ships per year to Spitsbergen and the Barents and White seas. The exact number of animals they took has never been tabulated – certain countries were less meticulous than others about inventorying their kills – but the scale of the slaughter was immense. Just on Bear Island, 20,000 walruses died at the hands of Muscovy Company hunters, with similar carnage wreaked throughout the 1600s on other shores and isles. The total of seals and lesser whales slain is beyond calculation, but worst off by far were the bowheads and right whales, reduced to pitifully small numbers around Spitsbergen and Novaya Zemlya by mid-century. Faced with this dearth, whalers relocated to the waters east of Greenland, with the newly discovered Jan Mayen Island becoming a key outpost. It took only till the mid-to-late 1600s to decimate the large whales here, and so the ships moved westward again, eventually reaching the American coast and, soon after 1700, proceeding into Davis Strait. The Dutch alone killed 500 or more bowheads annually, and while no country matched them on a one-to-one basis, other nations exacted an awful toll as well. The Europeans' success as sea-mammal hunters had predictable effects not just on the environment but on the Sami and other indigenes of Scandinavia and Arctic Russia. With the seal and walrus populations so depleted, and with outsiders intercepting the whales that had once migrated along the northern shores, aboriginal livelihoods underwent radical changes. Many natives were forced to abandon coastal economies and migrate into the interior, where they turned to hunting and reindeer herding. Sympathy for such hardships was conspicuously absent among outsiders: to the extent that Europeans paid any mind to Arctic natives in the 1600s, they tended to concur with Adam Olearius, the celebrated ambassador and traveller from the German duchy of Gottorp, that 'among them there is no understanding of higher things, no decorum, civility, or decency. They live like animals.'[6]

State consolidation meant greater control over natural resources, and over native and peripheral populations. Sweden, in 1621, granted a city charter to Luleå, a port on the Gulf of Bothnia at 65°N and a gateway into Lapland and the high north. With a will, the Dano-Norwegians exploited their northern waters and their new Crown monopolies over trade out of Iceland, the Faeroes and Finnmark, Norway's northernmost

Dutch whaling ships hunting bowhead whales off the coast of Jan Mayen Land.
The Beerenberg peak looms in the background.

county. Jurisdiction over Arctic seas meant added access to whales,
sea mammals, trade routes and some of the Atlantic's most desirable
herring- and cod-fishing grounds, fed all the way to the Lofoten Islands
by the warm waters of the Gulf Stream. Exports of cod, funnelled
through the port of Bergen, grew from 400,000 pounds per year in the
1500s to 14 million pounds per year by the mid-1600s. Land-based
wealth did not go ignored, either by Copenhagen or Stockholm, where
Sweden's chancellor, Axel Oxenstierna, compared Norrland to 'a new
India'. Furs were no longer to be had in large quantities this far west,
and farming, while possible, yielded a hardscrabble existence. But amber
could be found in the forests, tar from Finnish pines was indispensable
to shipbuilders throughout Europe, and Icelandic mines provided sulphur for the making of gunpowder. Since the 1300s, Sweden, a chief
exporter of metals, had been taking copper out of Falun in the Dalarna
province, at 60°N; it now aimed for the quantities of ore lying north of
the Arctic Circle. With help from Sami guides, Swedish prospectors
located huge deposits of iron around the Malmberget ('ore mountain') of
Gällivare and the nearby peaks of Kiirunavaara and Luossavaara. Not
for many years would large-scale mineral extraction be cost-effective
this far north, but, between 1634 and 1659, the Swedes sank a great
deal of effort into retrieving silver and lead from the Arctic mines of
Nasafjäll. Miners were brought up from the south, but the transfer of ore

to the smelting works, about 40 miles away, was accomplished by Sami sledders, recruited against their will and forced to work under armed guard. Nasafjäll was woefully unprofitable, yielding less than a ton of silver in 25 years, and it shut down after Dano-Norwegians crossed the border and burned it to the ground. The Swedes operated another northern silver mine at Jokkmokk between 1657 and 1702, during which time many of the region's Sami, wishing to avoid the fate of their Nasafjäll brethren, fled to Norway.

The Sami benefited the crowns of Denmark–Norway and Sweden more typically by paying tax in kind, whether they herded reindeer or lived a more settled life, fishing and sealing on the coastlines. The first schools for Sami, instruments of assimilation as well as of education, were built in the 1630s. Churches went up even faster, and Sami shamanism was attacked as forcefully by Scandinavia's new Lutheran churches as it had been by the Catholics. As late as the 1690s, *noiadi* could be punished by burning alive, and their drums fell silent in most villages and reindeer camps. Even where they did not, symbols of the new faith merged with those of the old: in his *Lapponia* of 1673, Johannes Schefferus reported seeing shamans' gear adorned with drawings of Christ and the Apostles intermixed with the images of pagan gods. Despite the dire penalties, shamanic practices survived long enough underground and deeply enough in folk memory that, even in the 1800s, it seemed the most natural thing for Hans Christian Andersen to include shaman-like characters – the Lappish and Finnish wise women who help Gerda rescue her playmate Kai from his wintry captivity – in his beloved retelling of *The Snow Queen*.

No country during this period engaged in more northern nation-building than Russia. Over the Arctic northwest – the Kola, the White Sea coast, the Dvina and parts of the Pechora basin – Muscovy already exerted firm authority, with Russian Pomors erecting ports, settlements and saltworks and Orthodox clergy ensconced in places like the Solo-vetsky and St Nicholas-of-Karelia monasteries. Sami living this far east, as well as their Komi neighbours, paid *yasak*, or tribute, to the tsar, and many were Christianized. Already by 1500, the Russians had gingerly stepped out farther to the east. On the mainland, they might still be hemmed in by the Ural Mountains and the Khanty and Mansi, known then as Ostyaks and Voguls. But along the Arctic coast, the Russians had sailed their single-masted, flat-bottomed *koches* through the Kara Gates to the Yamal Peninsula and the 600-mile-long gulf into which the Ob River empties. By the middle of the 1500s, they had inched their way to the mouth of the Yenisei.

It was Ivan IV, or the Terrible, best remembered for the ghoulish torments he inflicted upon his country, who advanced the cause of Arctic mastery beyond this point. He did so in two crucial ways. First, by acceding to Richard Chancellor's proposals in 1553 for trade between Russia and England, he made possible the creation of England's Muscovy Company and, in 1584, the building of Arkhangelsk on the North Dvina. Arkhangelsk quickly surpassed the Pomor town of Kholmogory as the region's chief centre, and it remains one of Arctic Russia's two most important ports – the other being Murmansk, founded centuries later on the Kola. Just as momentous was Ivan's opening up of the eastern frontier, starting with his conquest of the Tatar city-states of Kazan and Astrakhan in 1552 and 1556. With these enemies now removed, and with the Khanty and Mansi on the near side of the Urals pacified, the path to Asia now lay clear. Ivan did not invade directly but, in 1558, awarded a charter to the Stroganov clan to subdue the 'empty lands' beyond the Kama River. These magnates, who had gained their wealth manufacturing salt in the Pomor region, were eager to see what new riches they might earn from the still-mysterious border zone.

Over the next quarter-century, the Stroganovs established themselves in the Urals by building farms, iron and silver mines and fur-collection posts. With some of the eastern natives they traded peacefully, but when Kuchum, the Tatar khan of Sibir, refused to submit to the *yasak* and began raiding in reprisal, the Stroganovs hired mercenary cohorts to protect their investments. In 1581, the largest of these forces, under the Cossack adventurer Yermak Timofeyevich, struck at the source of the attacks by crossing the Urals and driving for Isker, Kuchum's capital on the Irtysh. Although Kuchum escaped, he was ousted in 1582; Russian muskets confounded the Tatars, and the invaders' steel helmets and mail hauberks made them near-impossible to wound with spears and arrows. Ironically, it was Yermak's own suit of armour – presented to him personally, some say, by Ivan the Terrible – that dragged him to death by drowning in 1585. Already by that time, the state had sent out military governors, or *voevody*, to build *ostrogi*, or fortified blockhouses, along rivers and portage routes in these new territories. Thus were founded the first Russian cities east of the Urals: Tiumen (1586) and Tobolsk (1587), not far from the broken ruins of Isker. More settlements would follow, and Giles Fletcher, England's ambassador to Russia, soon reported that 'the tsar hath divers castles and garrisons in Siberia, and sendeth many new supplies thither, to plant and inhabit as he winneth new ground.'[7]

Yermak and the freebooters who came after him, virtually unknown in the West, are Russia's answer to the New World's conquistadors, every bit as ruthless and with a similar impact on the course of world history. Already by 1620 they controlled enough of the west Siberian plain, 1.25 million square miles out to the Yenisei, that Moscow formally annexed it that year. Lines of outposts sprang up along the Ob and Yenisei, several of them on the serpentine Ob Gulf, between the Yamal and Gydan peninsulas. At the Ob's mouth, the Russians founded Obdorsk, or present-day Salekhard, in 1595. Half a decade later and not far to the northeast, Cossacks established the brief-lived Arctic oasis called Mangazeia, which stayed open to foreign trade until 1619 when the tsar, fearing the presence of outsiders so far east, forbade alien ships to sail east of the Yamal. Scouts, soldiers and *promyshlenniki* – independent trappers and traders with an entrepreneurial bent – pressed into the Siberian land mass.

East of the Yenisei, central Siberia's rugged highlands rise an average of 2,000 feet as they sprawl towards the majestic Lena, and eastern Siberia, colder and ridged with larch-covered mountain ranges, is even less accessible. Nonetheless, it took only twenty years for the Russians to carve their way through this wilderness and reach the Pacific, and only a few more after that to penetrate the far northeast. It was along the great rivers and their lateral tributaries, such as the Angara and the Tunguska's several branches, that they most easily progressed. The town of Yakutsk, the anchor point of Russian power in east-central Siberia, went up on the banks of the Lena in 1632, and several *ostrogi* were erected north of there, in and beyond the Verkhoyansk Mountains. From such strongholds, expeditions went out to gather *yasak* from the natives, and also to survey the Lena and other north-flowing rivers, including the Yana, Indigirka and Kolyma. In 1638, Ivan Moskvitin set forth in search of silver and the body of water the natives called 'the great sea-ocean'. He and his men reached the Sea of Okhotsk in the autumn of 1639, making him the Slavic Balboa: the first Russian to set foot on the Pacific shore. Movement into the far northeast, prompted largely by the search for walrus ivory, came next. In 1648, the tribute collector Semyon Dezhnev took a fleet of seven boats along the Kolyma to the Arctic Ocean. Losing four vessels along the way, he turned east, following the coast to the tip of Chukotka, then bore south. After an October landfall at the mouth of the Anadyr, Dezhnev built the fort of Anadyrsk in the spring of 1649. Although he was the first European to pass through the Bering Strait, most doubt that he knew he had rounded the continent's easternmost end. Either way, proof that the strait separated Asia from North America was not forthcoming until well into the eighteenth century.

Throughout the 1600s, the Russians, in expanding eastward, absorbed new territory equal in size to the British Isles every two and a half years. Early in the century, they imposed the obligation to pay *yasak* on the Khanty, Mansi and Nentsy of western Siberia, extending it to the Yakut (Sakha), Evenki and other central Siberians in the 1630s and 1640s, and to places beyond the Lena by the 1660s. They suffered a key setback in the south, where China's Qing emperors, by terms of the 1689 treaty of Nerchinsk, barred Russia for the next two centuries from the Amur basin, the most natural connection between Siberian towns like Irkutsk and reliably ice-free sections of the Pacific coast. Russia was forced instead to venture north into windswept Chukotka and, beyond that, Kamchatka, where Vladimir Atlasov led a contingent of Cossacks in 1697–9. The Russians' control over much of Siberia was notional, for their authority stretched over it less like a blanket and more like a net, and a frayed one at that. It required a full year to journey from Moscow to Yakutsk and another six months to continue to Anadyrsk, 1,800 miles to Yakutsk's northeast. Although it was easier to travel due east to the Pacific, almost 700 miles separated Yakutsk from the port of Okhotsk. Overland travel was difficult in the best of seasons, and only at certain times of the year could the all-important rivers be navigated.

Nor were the natives quiescent, even where the Russians had conquered. Nomadism made most of them difficult to administer, and some, including many Yakut and Yukagir, migrated northward to avoid paying *yasak*. In the heart of the Taimyr, the Dolgan likewise remained beyond the reach of Russian troops. Other groups resorted to armed rebellion. In the west, the Khanty and Mansi rose up on numerous occasions, and Nenets pressure on Mangazeia, which had survived as a gathering point for fur and ivory after the cessation of foreign trade, shut it down in 1672. Obdorsk withstood a frightening siege in 1679, and outposts on the eastern rivers, including Yakutsk, were repeatedly assaulted by the Yakut, Eveny and Evenki. Eventually, the Russians contained most native violence, but they failed conspicuously to do so in the far northeast. The Chukchi in particular proved doughty warriors, using their homeland's rugged remoteness to their advantage. The Russians abandoned many *ostrogi* in Chukotka during the 1690s, and their struggle to subjugate the region continued in vain through much of the eighteenth century. Entry into Kamchatka, where no suitable ports existed as yet, was possible only through a narrow, mountain-choked neck of land, restricting how much force the Russians could apply against the Koryak and Itelmen there.

Even with Russia's northern presence thus limited, its impact on the ecosystem and on native populations was heavy. Seals, whales and walruses were overhunted and indigenous economies damaged as prey became scarce or disappeared. Then came the insatiable lust for furs. Trappers, chartered and unchartered alike, pursued a variety of animals, but most of all they coveted the lordly sable (*Martes zibellina*), which had all but vanished from Fennoscandia after the 1400s and was exceedingly thin on the ground in European Russia by the 1570s. In an average year, the Russians took out of Siberia 22,000 red and blue fox pelts, 25,000 ermine, 20,000 sable and other furs besides, with this traffic accounting for a tenth to a third of the state's annual income. To keep up such numbers required constant movement to the east, for sable populations were trapped out with alarming speed, and peasants migrating to Siberia added to the problem by clearing forests for their farms. Sables were in short supply in western Siberia by 1650 and barely to be found along the Yenisei, or even the Lena, after 1670. The resulting shortages explain the urgency with which the Russians attempted to push into Chukotka and Kamchatka, and also the state's decision to assume monopolistic control over the fur trade in 1697. In the 1700s, Russian hunters encountered the sea otters and fur seals of the Pacific – the newest victims, before too long, of the fur trade's voracity.

As for the natives, most were brought to heel and put to work. The invaders utilized superior weaponry and tactics, and they adeptly pitted native groups against each other in order to divide and conquer. They also brought natives into contact with new and deadly infectious diseases. In the 1630s, smallpox ravaged many groups between the Ob and Yenisei, and it swept through the Tungus-speaking peoples of central and east Siberia in the 1660s. Most of all, Russia exacted tribute and labour by sheer brute force. *Yasak*, which was measured in sable pelts but could be paid in ivory or lesser furs at need, was levied on all able-bodied adult males; the Russians ensured that quotas were met by taking hostages or threatening military violence. Moreover, the Russians, like most effective empire-builders, created a comprador class of native elites, especially among the Yakut and their Tungus neighbours, who collected the *yasak* from their own people. Not only did natives work under duress as hunters and trappers, they were dragooned into clearing roads, catching fish, rowing or carting cargo and providing horses upon request.

Some were enslaved, many were pressed into military service against other natives, and large numbers of women were forced into concubinage. Certain Cossacks, such as Atlasov and Yerofei Khabarov, gained particular infamy for their treatment of natives, but they were merely the cruellest of a cruel lot. The Orthodox Church did little to ameliorate the situation, with even the archbishop of Siberia admitting in 1662 that most frontier clergy were 'drunkards and lechers'.[8] In 1697, Peter the Great reaffirmed the illegality of slavery, and state policy during the eighteenth century would oppose in principle the many abuses carried out by Russians in Siberia. But the capital was a quarter of the world away, and until the tsars developed the capacity to govern their remote holdings more efficiently, the will of local officers and officials, however corrupt or tyrannical, tended to prevail.

Colonial Transformations during the Eighteenth Century

An ever-expanding extent of far northern territory – Greenland and Alaska alone accounting for 1.5 million square miles – fell under Europe's colonial sway during the 1700s. At the same time, Europe's colonial methods, like its nation-states, modernized, which is to say that they became more ambitious, more grasping and more organized. One is less able to say that they grew more humane. As a purported 'age of reason', the eighteenth century is credited with bringing many enlightened tendencies to the fore. Few of them, however, were much in evidence on the Arctic frontiers.

In Canada, the standoff between the French and the ascendant British continued through the 1750s. The former were stalemated in the North, with Rupert's Land and Newfoundland now under British custodianship. Only in the west did the French have room to expand, and it was there that their *voyageurs* ventured, stringing a line of outposts across the prairies between the 1730s and 1750s, from the Great Lakes to the fork of the Saskatchewan River. This got them no farther north than the 55th parallel, but it allowed them to take out of the New World a yearly average of 300,000 beaver pelts and other furs. To outflank the French, the Hudson's Bay Company (HBC or the Bay), which had required natives to haul furs over long distances to its gathering points on the bay's shores, shook off its complacency and extended its own reach westward. Its outpost-building efforts remained modest until the last quarter of the century, but by the mid-1750s agents like Samuel Hearne had scouted routes almost out to the Rockies, forging ties along the way with First Nations trading partners. Farther to the north, HBC contacts with the Inuit remained limited. Not only were the Inuit less numerous and harder to reach, their ongoing feuds with First Nations bands forced the Bay to choose between trade with one or the other – and, for the moment, the Bay preferred the beaver pelts provided by the subarctic's First Nations to the ivory and sealskins that the Inuit had to offer. Unfortunately for the Inuit, this meant that their enemies enjoyed access to Western firearms much earlier, and in far greater quantities, than they did.

In Canada's northern waters, the scene was more cosmopolitan. France still controlled the Labrador coast and retained some of its Newfoundland fishing rights, and other nations' ships fished farther offshore or to the north. Driven to the lower Arctic by the Little Ice Age, bowheads and other whales teemed in the waters between Canada and Greenland, and it was here that Europe's whalers pursued them, having already butchered so many in the eastern Atlantic. Up Davis Strait they went, as far as the ice would allow, causing the same kind of carnage that their seventeenth-century predecessors had. In the North Atlantic as a whole, the grey whale became extinct during the 1700s. The British alone may have killed 38,000 bowheads in Davis Strait, and the Dutch, Germans and Basques sent a combined total of approximately 300 ships there every year during the early 1700s. White whalers often made landfall to trade with local Inuit and First Nations people, exchanging cloth, metal, tobacco and strong drink for ivory, baleen and whale oil. But they invariably offered swindler's terms, and they resorted often enough to extortion and physical abuse that, in 1723, the Dutch States-General felt compelled to pass laws against the 'robbery and murder' of aboriginal Americans. Another unwelcome consequence of these interchanges was the introduction of syphilis and gonorrhea to numerous native communities.

Canada's old political order disintegrated in the 1750s, leaving the colony wholly in British hands. In 1754, the French and Indian War broke out in North America and was quickly subsumed into the worldwide Seven Years War, which lasted until 1763. With fighting under way, the British began their infamous programme of expelling French Acadians – *le Grand Dérangement*, as its victims called it. A series of British victories in 1759, including the pivotal clash of arms on the Plains of Abraham, outside Quebec City, set the stage for the general surrender of New France in 1760. The Treaty of Paris signed in 1763 left France with nothing more of Canada than the tiny islands of Saint-Pierre and Miquelon, along with its Newfoundland fishing rights.

From this point on, contradiction characterized British policy in the Canadian north, for it was the product of two wills: that of the colonial government and that of the HBC. Both valued stability and profit, but the government felt obliged to tend somewhat to the interests of indigenous peoples, even if its definition of 'interests' was condescending, and its commitment to those interests inconsistent. The Indian Department, established in 1755, guaranteed natives all the 'protections and liberties' of English law. The most notable attempt to put benevolence into action came during the governorship of Newfoundland and Labrador by Sir Hugh Palliser between 1764 and 1768. A tireless protector of the region, Palliser combatted smuggling, illegal fishing by French and New England ships and oversettlement by English and Irish colonists. Mindful of the rough treatment afforded them by white whalers in previous decades, he sought also to prevent the region's natives, especially the Innu and the 3,000 or so Inuit of Labrador, from being overwhelmed by the seal-hunters and fishermen who streamed into the territory every year. To that end, Palliser allowed the Moravian Church, which had been active in Greenland since 1747 and in New England since 1735, to establish missions in Labrador, endowed with thousands of acres apiece. Such large holdings, Palliser reasoned, would give the gentle brethren the means to shelter the Inuit from foreign seamen and their unwholesome influence. Nain, the first of the Moravian settlements, opened in 1771, and others were soon founded in Quebec and the Northwest Territories. It was also during the Palliser years that James Cook, in the *Resolution*, began the most accurate survey to that date of the Newfoundland and Labrador coasts – a project completed by Michael Lane after Cook's 1768 transfer to Pacific service.

As before, expansion into the Canadian west and north resulted mainly from contests over fur. The French might be gone, but the HBC still faced rivals in the form of smaller corporations based in Montreal and the St Lawrence Valley, and of the seventeen trading posts that Canada had established in the northwest by the early 1770s only a handful belonged to the Bay. By 1804, when the number of posts had risen to 430, the HBC would have more than evened the balance. As competition heated up, the HBC, in 1769–72, commissioned the far-striding Samuel Hearne to survey a wide swath of the northwest. With the assistance of Chipewyan and Yellowknife Dene guides, he journeyed up the Coppermine River to Coronation Gulf on the Arctic Ocean, making him the first European to reach Canada's northern coast from the interior – and proving that, if a Northwest Passage existed, it did not run at a latitude lower than 67°N. Hearne also witnessed the Yellowknifes' ambush and massacre of two dozen Inuit, a 'horrid day' he could never recall afterwards 'without shedding tears'.[9] In turn, the Bay's St Lawrence competitors established a presence on Lake Athabasca, and both sides set up posts in the high northwest throughout the 1770s, on Great Slave Lake and along the Peace, Athabasca, and Slave rivers. In 1783–4, a number of the St Lawrence firms pooled their resources to create the North West Company (NWC), the Bay's most formidable opponent over the next three and a half decades. The NWC operated nimbly, relying on small groups and individual *voyageurs*; the Bay countered with larger teams who navigated the waters in their famed York boats, made of spruce and rowed by eight men. For both companies, opening the western frontier was like unlocking a newfound treasure chest. Between 1769 and 1868, the HBC sold a total of 1 million lynx pelts, 2.75 million mink and marten coats, 4.7 million beaver skins and 1.2 million furs from assorted other animals. In its prime, the NWC logged tallies no less impressive.

One of the NWC's more intrepid personnel was the Scottish explorer Alexander Mackenzie, who opened Fort Chipewyan on Lake Athabasca in 1788 and, the year following, began searching for a water route to Alaska and the Pacific. From Great Slave Lake, he canoed up the river that the Dene called Deh Cho, a major artery for native trade and travel, and followed it to the sea. This, however, took him not to the west, where he wished to go, but north to the shores of the Arctic Ocean. Despite the significance of his accomplishment – he had just navigated and mapped Canada's longest waterway – Mackenzie called the river Disappointment; it was later renamed in his honour. In times to come, the Mackenzie gave Europeans easier access to points in Canada's far north, including Great Bear Lake and the delta homeland of the Mackenzie Eskimo, or Inuvialuit. Both the HBC and NWC traded up the river during the 1790s.

Mackenzie eventually reached the Pacific, but along a more southerly axis, descending through the British Columbia interior in 1792–3. Since the mid-1700s, a quadrilateral competition over this Columbia District, or Oregon Country, as the Americans called it, had been shaping up among Britain, Spain, Russia and the young United States. Thanks to the massive coastal survey carried out between Oregon and southern Alaska by George Vancouver in the *Discovery* between 1791 and 1795, and to the exploration of the Columbia and Fraser river valleys by David Thompson and Simon Fraser in the early 1800s, British Canada was in a good position to argue for ownership of a sizable portion of this territory. But blocked by the southeastern arm of Alaska, Canada's presence on the Pacific never extended beyond 54°40′N.

In the European Arctic, the eighteenth century was bracketed by geopolitical shakeups. During the Great Northern War of 1700–21, Russia displaced Sweden as the leading power of northeastern Europe, gaining in the process a long-desired 'window on the west' with large acquisitions on the Gulf of Finland and in eastern Karelia. A century later, the Napoleonic wars rocked the region once again. Russia seized Finland from Sweden in 1808–9 and incorporated it into its own empire as a grand duchy until 1917. However, by joining the anti-French coalition after Napoleon's 1812 defeat in Russia, Sweden convinced the great powers to split the Dano-Norwegian kingdom – a Napoleonic ally – in two, and to place Norway's territory under the Swedish Crown for the next nine decades.

The years separating these upheavals witnessed hardship and modernization. Population grew in European Russia and in all parts of Scandinavia except Iceland, but this must be balanced against losses caused by epidemics, wars, crop failures and natural disasters. Finland began the century having lost a third of its people to famine in 1696–7, and it bore the burden of Russian occupation during the Great Northern War (the 'great wrath') and the Russo-Swedish War of 1741–3 (the 'lesser wrath'). Such travails drove northern Finnish migrants to Norway's north counties, where they formed the Kven minority. Smallpox and plague struck most of Scandinavia in the early 1700s, with the former killing roughly 30 per cent of Icelanders. Iceland also suffered periodic volcanic eruptions, including the devastating Laki blast of 1783, which killed 10,000 people and caused Copenhagen to contemplate resettling the entire colony back in Denmark. During the Napoleonic wars, all of Denmark–Norway, blockaded by Britain's navy, experienced hunger. The north had only tree bark and a little rye to grind into flour, and these years are still remembered there as the 'bark-bread times'.

Still, population expanded, and the North shared in this general growth. In Norway, Sweden and Finland, nature and the law limited how many people could be supported by farms in the south, or how far those farms could be subdivided among heirs, and so increasing numbers of homesteaders moved north to scratch out a living from the earth or to hunt and fish. In Russia, the relative freedom of life on the north-west frontier, where the system of serfdom had not been fully imposed, attracted a steady trickle of settlers. The Swedes mapped and surveyed the Norrland sites where iron ore was known to lie buried, although the Arctic deposits hidden under Malmberget and Kiirunavaara-Luossavaara remained little utilized for now. In Norway, cod exports doubled between the mid-seventeenth century and the late eighteenth, to 28 million pounds per year, due principally to more efficient fishing off the Lofoten Islands and the shores of Norway's Finnmark county. Denmark–Norway and Sweden took advantage of their northern forests to become major exporters of lumber.

With more southlanders came more civilization in the southern style. In Finnmark, Nordland, Troms and Sweden's Norrland, villages and harbours appeared in greater quantity; it was from one such community that Petter Dass, Norway's first modern poet, sprang. Although the Sami still outnumbered the settler population, further steps were taken to assimilate them. More churches and schools were built in their midst, most energetically by the Moravian Brethren and Lutheran Pietists. In Trondheim, the latter created the Seminarium Lapponicum, which trained young evangelists to minister to the Sami in their home territories. Not surprisingly, it was on the island colonies that life remained most primitive. Iceland's difficulties have already been noted. On the bleak Faeroes, only 7 per cent of the land was arable, and it took a mix of farming, fishing, sealing and puffin fowling, plus shipments from the homeland, to keep its tiny villages alive. The islands' economies, along with Finnmark's, were controlled by royal trade monopolies. These, in typically mercantilist fashion, took the best of what the colonists had to offer in exchange for substandard goods sold at exorbitant rates. Without them, though, settlements in these parts would probably have folded, and the system was reformed during the eighteenth and nineteenth centuries more to the colonists' advantage. The Finnmark monopoly was lifted in the 1780s, but those in Iceland and the Faeroes remained in effect until the mid-1800s.

The most striking change in the Scandinavian north was Denmark's re-establishment of the Greenland colony. The impetus was religious, provided by the renowned 'apostle of Greenland', the Lutheran pastor Hans Egede. Hoping to uncover traces of the Viking settlers and to preach the gospel to the island's natives, Egede sailed to Greenland with his wife and children in the summer of 1721, landing on the west coast in July and founding the settlement of Godthåb (present-day Nuuk, the capital). Egede explored the coast almost to the Arctic Circle and wrote much about the region's natural history – but most of all he denounced the native Greenlanders' 'blasphemous and bestial state' and applied his iron willpower to a long struggle against the influence of their *angakut*, or shamans.[10] Spiritual competitors arrived in the form of the Moravians, who opened their own mission houses in the 1730s, wooing converts away from the Lutherans with livelier services that included music.

Meanwhile, Egede convinced the Danish government that a viable colony could be rebuilt. In 1728, the king sent a fleet to oversee the fortification of Godthåb. Egede, appointed governor, overcame raids by Dutch ships and the setbacks suffered during the smallpox outbreak of 1733–5 – but while the colony remained in place, he did not. Having lost his wife to the smallpox, he returned to Copenhagen in 1736 with his younger children, leaving his son to govern in his place. In Denmark, he founded a seminary to prepare missionaries for work in Greenland, and he was named bishop of Greenland in 1741. Until his death in 1758, he toiled away on translations of the scriptures into Inuit dialects. Certain biblical concepts proved especially opaque. Because Greenland's natives were unfamiliar with bread, the 'body of Christ' given during the Eucharist resisted easy explanation, and Egede was obliged to include the line 'give us this day our daily seal meat' in the Lord's Prayer. The need for a day of rest on the Sabbath was not apparent to the Inuit, who likewise remained mystified as to why the Christian god was so testy about sex.

Like Denmark–Norway's other remote possessions, Greenland saw hard times during the Napoleonic wars and the British blockade, but under ordinary circumstances it was economically better off than Iceland or the Faeroes. The Royal Greenlandic Trading Company, awarded the monopoly in 1774, set prices more fairly than was the norm for the other island colonies. Native labour was not used without cynicism: one official boasted of how the Inuits' addiction to tobacco 'obliged them always to be more industrious'.[11] Still, natives and colonists alike kept five-sixths of whatever money they made from sales to the royal ships; the other sixth was put into a general fund that paid for poor relief and the delivery of mail. White settlers farmed and herded, while the Inuit fished and hunted seals and whales. The bowhead whale was by now so scarce as to be encountered only occasionally, and so humpbacks were taken in the summer and autumn, and beluga and narwhals whenever possible.

In Siberia, natives were shown less solicitude than in Greenland or in Canada. Russians now moved freely into the subcontinent, the non-native population rising from 70,000 in 1662 to 300,000 in 1700, and again to 900,000 in 1799. It was this sort of growth that fuelled Russia's colonial ambitions – many of which belonged to the titanic Peter I, who modernized Russia along European lines and raised up a new imperial capital, St Petersburg, from the Neva marshlands that his armies had wrested from Sweden during the Great Northern War. Peter's grand vision was of a country where order and rationality reigned, no matter how far away from the capital. In 1697, he established the state's monopoly on the trade in sable furs and outlawed the practice of enslaving native Siberians. He encouraged Pomors to hunt walruses on Spitsbergen, a trade they pursued until the 1840s, and he nurtured the metallurgical industries emerging in the Urals and western Siberia. As described later in this chapter, he initiated one of the most outstanding scientific undertakings in Arctic history, the Bering expeditions of 1725–8 and 1733–43. Throughout the century, the making of Siberian policy was sporadically infused with progressivist impulses, with humane measures occasionally passing, well-intentioned committees formed now and then to investigate wrongdoing, and efficient officials sometimes appointed.

But on the whole, the experience of ruling Siberia pointed out the limitations of eighteenth-century absolutism. Wayward *promyshlenniki* poached furs without licence, rogue Cossacks inflicted cruel punishments on the native populace, and usurious moneylenders placed indigenes and fellow Russians in debt bondage that was little better than slavery. The ranks of those who upheld the law were riddled with venality and incompetence. In 1721, Peter the Great was obliged to hang Siberia's first governor-general, Prince Matvei Gagarin, for selling offices and taking bribes. As for the Church, it was not always an effective promoter of good social order. Many of Siberia's religious were unlearned and prone to vices of their own, and even the best failed to restrain the roisterousness of Cossacks and frontier folk. Also, Orthodox clergy were less than gentle in their conversion of natives. Early in the century, the bishop of Tobolsk ordered the Khanty and Mansi to accept the cross or die, with the result that many retreated deep into the woods and tundra, beyond the Russians' authority. In 1745, Ivan Khotuntsevsky, sent to Kamchatka by Empress Elizabeth to preach to the natives, proved so vile in his chauvinism that he accomplished the previously unthinkable and superbly counterproductive feat of convincing the mutually hostile Chukchi, Koryak and Itelmen to put aside their differences and band together against the invading Russians.

For most native Siberians, the yoke of Russian overlordship grew heavier. They still had to meet their *yasak* obligations, although in the 1760s Catherine the Great abolished the practice of taking hostages to guarantee payment. In greater numbers than before, natives provided manual labour and food supplies, served as auxiliary troops and, in the case of the Yakut, gave up thousands of horses per year, requisitioned to haul carts and sleds. They continued to die of the colonizers' diseases: smallpox, new to the far northeast, killed half of the Koryak and Itelmen on Kamchatka in the late 1760s, while typhus, 30 years later, wiped out 30 per cent of those who remained. The Nganasan (Tavgi) of the Taimyr were hit badly enough by smallpox that they included it as a new demon in their pantheon of evil spirits – personified as a Russian. Above and beyond this, Siberia's natives found themselves on the receiving end of a deep-seated contempt: most Russians scorned indigenous ways and beliefs as barbaric. They were horrified by Khanty-Mansi scalp-taking, appalled by reports of infanticide and senilicide and shocked by what they saw as the libertine sexual customs of the Chukchi, Koryak and Yupik. They found shamanism, with its ecstatic trances and rituals of self-mutilation, to be outré and macabre. One can readily imagine what they thought of spells like the standard Chukchi incantation for calming the weather – in which the caster dropped his trousers and, clapping rhythmically, offered the winds a morsel of fat from his buttocks.

All of which justified the Russians in their minds as they brought violence to the northeast and beyond. Although Russian forces fought the Dolgans in the Taimyr, most of Siberia between the Urals and the Kolyma River was by now secure, leaving Chukotka and Kamchatka as main targets. In both places, the authorities discovered that it was easier to impose the *yasak* than to enforce it. Atlasov's foray into Kamchatka led to the opening of several useful *ostrogi*, including Bolsheretsk, the administrative centre, in the first decade of the 1700s. However, the overland route from Yakutsk to Kamchatka, nearly 2,000 miles long, was easily interdicted, and it took years to establish a reliable sea route between the mainland port of Okhotsk and Kamchatka's Avacha Bay. Meanwhile, between 1701 and 1715, uprisings flared up among the Chukchi, Yukagir and Koryak, with tribute collectors murdered and the all-important fur shipments intercepted, and with Masada-like mass suicides, rather than surrender, the rebels' typical response when the Russians deployed against them. After a temporary peace, the Koryaks rose again in the 1720s, followed by the Chukchi in 1729 and the Itelmen in 1731; the Yukagir by this time had been coerced into soldiering for the

Russian throne. Capable of speeding to the attack on skis, and of launching arrows and spears from dogsleds like ancient charioteers, the Koryak and Chukchi proved dangerous foes, all the more so once they obtained firearms of their own. In 1730, the Koryaks slew Afanasii Shestakov, one of the Cossacks' most skilled frontier fighters, and displayed his dried head as a trophy for years to come. Even the ships built in Kamchatka for Bering's voyages of discovery were used to bombard Itelmen villages.

In the 1740s, one of the Russians' key advantages – the bitter dislike of their enemies for each other – disappeared, as the Orthodox Church's heavy-handedness caused the Koryak, Itelmen and Chukchi to unite. The stakes by now had grown higher: while the government in the 1730s had been willing to make at least token inquiries into the root causes of native discontent, it called in 1741 for the 'total extirpation' of all natives who continued to resist. By the late 1750s, the Koryak and Itelmen had laid down their arms, but not so the Chukchi, who, in 1747, massacred the forces of the Cossack Dmitrii Pavlutsky, Little Bighorn-style, and continued after that to deny the Russians any safe foothold in Chukotka. In 1762, Catherine the Great, newly arisen to the throne, agreed to a truce that allowed the Chukchi to exist within the empire without paying tribute or having to tolerate a colonial presence among them. The Russian garrison pulled out of Anadyrsk, leaving it to operate as a humble trading post, and Chukotka remained independent in all but name for the next century and a half.

The Russians consoled themselves for this defeat with victories elsewhere in the North Pacific. Kamchatka, whose population of sables provided a steady supply of furs during the first half of the century, was theirs. The Bering expeditions, described below in detail, showed how well-positioned Russia was to carve out possessions in North America should it so desire. By the early 1740s, just as concerns surfaced about the sustainability of the Kamchatka sable trade, the Russians became aware of the teeming quantities of sea otters who lived on the islands of the Bering Sea. From Kamchatka's newly established port of Petropavlovsk, the Russians sailed south in search of otter pelts to Sakhalin and the Kuriles – and eastward to the Commander Islands, the 1,200-mile Aleutian chain and, by the early 1760s, Kodiak Island, a stepping-stone to mainland Alaska. In Sakhalin, starting in the 1780s, Russians raided Japanese outposts and intruded into the homelands of the Nivkhi, the Oroks and the bear-worshipping Ainu; across the Bering waters, they came to blows with the Koniag and Chugach Eskimos, the Tlingit and the Haida. The group with the greatest cause to regret the Russians' arrival were the Aleuts, or Unangan, about 25,000 of whom resided in large island villages.

Conflict marked Russo-Aleutian interactions from the outset. Ignoring repeated but feeble entreaties from St Petersburg to treat the Aleuts with decency, Russian trappers and scouts handled them with a brutality that would have shamed Attila. They slaughtered all men who resisted, raped women by the hundreds and took children as hostages to extort labour and military service from the able-bodied males they did not kill. Factoring in the impact of diseases and vodka addiction, the Aleuts suffered a death rate of nearly 90 per cent between the 1750s and 1790s, with only 2,500 or so left alive by 1800. For individual families, the shock was incalculable, with men transplanted hundreds of miles from home, sometimes permanently, to hunt otters and fox or fight other natives on the Russians' behalf.

The fur trade boomed for the Russians from the 1760s onwards, receiving an added boost in 1786, when the hunter Gerasim Pribiloff stumbled upon the rookeries of fur seals (*Callorhinus ursinus*) that live north of the Aleutians, on the islands now bearing his name. During the last quarter of the eighteenth century, the Russians took a minimum of 350,000 pelts per annum out of the North Pacific, the fur seal providing up to 70 per cent of the total by 1800. Other victims of this killing spree, which reached Alaska's shores in the 1780s, included sables, beaver, muskrat, lynx, wolverine, mink, fox, wolf and bear. As in the Atlantic, walruses were slain in enormous numbers for their ivory, and the Steller's sea cow, a docile creature which had the bad luck to be good to eat and easy to kill, was quickly hunted to extinction.

Leading the way east were the fur companies of Yakutsk and Irkutsk. In 1784, Grigorii Shelikhov, co-founder of the most enterprising of these firms, sailed to Kodiak Island. After firing a few cannonades to display his might, he bullied the Koniags into letting him build a fort, Three Saints Bay, on the island's southeast corner. Over the next decade, he and his wife Natalia, the first white woman to set foot in Alaska, established more outposts on the islands and mainland, giving them a logistical edge over their rivals. Catherine the Great allowed Shelikhov to build up Russia's presence in Alaska, but never granted his company the monopoly he so desperately wanted. He died in 1795 with that wish unfulfilled, but his widow and son-in-law, Nikolai Rezanov, kept the business going. After Catherine's death in 1796, the Emperor Paul, who hated his mother to the point of mania and reversed as many of her policies as he could, gave Rezanov the monopoly his predecessor had desired. Shelikhov's corporation was reformed in 1799 as the Russian-American Company (RAC) – which, in exchange for one-third of all profits, became lord and master of Alaska and the large territory that, for more than half a century, would constitute Russian America.

The Rise of Arctic Science

Exactly where science overlaps with exploration is an abstract and not entirely straightforward question. Do the navigational skills of travellers to remote regions or the fluency gained by traders in the tongues of newly encountered natives qualify as geographical or linguistic 'science' in the way scholars define such disciplines? The answer lies beyond the scope of this book, but there is no denying that Euro-American exploration took on a more recognizably scientific character during the later years of the early modern era. Although frontier zones like the Arctic were still studied with utilitarian aims in mind – to allow one to survive them better, to move through them more expeditiously, and to find and exploit their resources more efficiently – they were seen increasingly as worth knowing about for their own sake. Information was gathered and synthesized more systematically, and specialists from a broader array of sciences joined surveyors and mapmakers in delving into the secrets of the earth's most untamed places.

Navigation and cartography reigned as queens among the Arctic sciences during the 1500s and 1600s. Where the North was concerned, every drop of geographic knowledge was precious, and excepting the northeast Atlantic, the Arctic seas and waters remained a mystery to even the best-informed mapmakers. The *Carta marina*, completed by Sweden's Olaus Magnus in 1539, depicts Iceland, the Faeroes and Fennoscandia with laudable accuracy, but its rendering of 'Bjarmia', or northwestern Russia, is less successful. Even the famed Netherlanders Gerhard Mercator and Abraham Ortelius, in widely published maps from the late 1500s, mixed dubious elements with plausible ones in their images of the North. Leaving aside errors of scale that make tiny Iceland appear half the size of Greenland, both men place a huge boreal land mass around the North Pole, in the midst of what Ortelius labels the Mare Congelatum. 'Pygmies live here', they warn, and Mercator envisions the Pole as a magnetic rock, 'black and most high', rising out of an immense whirlpool fed by four rivers which flow from the seas below and quarter the polar continent.

Arctic knowledge through time, II: The North Pole as imagined by
the Flemish cartographer Gerhard Mercator in his *Septentrionalium
Terrarum Descriptio* ('Description of Northern Lands', 1595). Note the
existence of a Hyperborean continent and the representation of the
Pole as a pillar of black rock.

Other maps from the 1500s through the early 1700s confidently
transform waterways such as Frobisher Strait into open passages to
the northwest or include phantom sites like the 'Strait of Anian' and
'Juan de Gama Land', which turned out to exist only in rumour. Some
of this faulty mapmaking was the product of whim, fancy or false
tales, or the unwillingness of pilots to share their charts and logs, but
physical reasons contributed as well. The short navigational season
left little time for uninterrupted and consistent surveying, and the
glare off ice, snow and airborne ice crystals meant a higher incidence
of mirage. Shore ice concealed the contours of coastlines. Summer fogs
could hide the landmarks most useful for mapping. Compasses became
less reliable once one came too close to the Magnetic Pole. No matter
how much progress was made in the geographical sciences, it remained
impossible to chart the Arctic with complete precision until well into the
twentieth century.

As for the region's natural history and ethnography, no one who hunted or traded in the Arctic could remain ignorant of its plant and animal life, or of the indigenous peoples' ways and languages. Before 1700, though, comparatively few written works on these subjects existed, and much of their content was anecdotal, exaggerated or based on secondhand information, including native lore not always translated well into European languages. It was the eighteenth century, ushering in as it did a pan-European enthusiasm for rational inquiry, that put Arctic research and regional studies in general on a more systematically scientific footing. Throughout the century, governments and scientific societies conducted comprehensive surveys of northern territories, both for the sake of knowledge and to tally up whatever plant, animal and mineral wealth a country might possess. No less a figure than Carl Linnaeus, the botanist and pioneering taxonomist, undertook a half-year expedition to Lapland in 1732 with funding from the Swedish Royal Society. Leaving the University of Uppsala in the spring, he travelled 1,200 miles through Norrland and Norway's Scandinavian Mountains to points past 67°N, cataloguing mosses, lichens and other flora, including the twinflower, now named after him scientifically (*Linnaea borealis*). Fascinated by the Sami, Linnaeus spent as much time among them as possible, and one of the most famous images from his younger years is a portrait of him wearing Sami garb, holding a twinflower blossom in one hand and a shaman's drum in the other. In 1736, another of Sweden's scientific giants, the astronomer Anders Celsius, best known for devising the centigrade temperature scale, visited Lapland in the company of French mathematician Pierre Louis Maupertuis to measure the arc of a latitudinal degree in the North; by comparing the results with those recorded by another team working in Ecuador and Peru, Celsius and his colleagues confirmed Newton's belief that the earth was not perfectly spherical but slightly flatter at the poles. Not to be outdone by their neighbours, the Dano-Norwegians commissioned surveys of their own northern districts, and also of Iceland, resulting in the publication of Niels Horrebow's 1758 *Natural History of Iceland* and, in 1766, *Travels through Iceland*, by Eggert Olafsson and Bjarni Pálsson of the Royal Danish Society. In Greenland, Hans Egede, before dedicating himself fully to ecclesiastical efforts, compiled valuable information about the island's plant and animal life.

Nowhere was the impulse for all-encompassing study of the Arctic felt more keenly than in Russia. Peter the Great, a devoted admirer of the sciences, sponsored research in countless spheres. On his orders,

Ivan Yevreinov and Fyodor Luzhin of the newly created Naval Academy carried out the first proper survey of the Kamchatka Peninsula. Also in Peter's pay, the German naturalist Daniel Messerschmidt, from 1718 to 1728, completed a massive study of the flora, fauna and geology of western and central Siberia. And yet this was not enough for the endlessly inquisitive tsar, who dreamed of a Northeast Passage entirely in Russian hands. Peter hoped also to score a point or two on behalf of scholarship, as he confided to Fyodor Apraksin, head of the Russian Admiralty:

> Recently, I have been thinking over a matter which has been on my mind for many years, but other affairs have prevented me from carrying it out. I have reference to the finding of a passage to China and India through the Arctic Sea . . . In my last travels I discussed the subject with learned men and they were of the opinion that such a passage could be found. Now that the country is in no danger from enemies we should strive to win for her glory along the lines of Arts and Sciences. In seeking such a passage who knows but perhaps we may be more successful than the Dutch and English.[12]

In January 1725, Peter, gravely ill and with not much time left to live, dispatched Vitus Bering, a Danish officer in the Russian navy, on the First Kamchatka Expedition, with the principal task of determining whether open water separated Eurasia from North America. In all his northern travels, Bering's logistical skills were tested as sorely as his navigational expertise, and it says something about the state of transport in Siberia that it took him until October 1727, more than two and a half years, to reach Okhotsk with his men and equipment. From Okhotsk he sailed the small *Fortuna* to Kamchatka, where he built a double-masted, 60-foot ship, the *Archangel Gabriel*, armed with three cannon. With disturbances ongoing among the natives of the far northeast, Bering helped to enforce discipline among them, and he did not hesitate to act the martinet with the Yakut, whose horses he commandeered by the hundreds on the way to Okhotsk, or with the Koryaks and Itelmen, whose labour he conscripted once in Kamchatka.

The long months of effort yielded seven weeks of voyaging in the summer of 1728. With his two lieutenants, Martin Spanberg and the Naval Academy instructor Alexei Chirikov, who loathed each other and distrusted each other's judgment, Bering took the *Gabriel* north to Chukotka and, visiting St Lawrence Island (Sivuqaq') in the process, glided past its tip into the Chukchi Sea – reaching 67°24′N and seemingly accomplishing his mission. Only 'seemingly', because Bering and his crew were prevented by heavy mist from spying any trace of North America to the east, and although logic dictated that sailing so far north, then turning west, would place the *Gabriel* off Siberia's northern coast, this was surmise, not proof. On 16 August, when the ship reached its highest latitude, Bering convened a sea council with Spanberg and Chirikov to choose a course of action. Chirikov urged Bering to press on until they located the mouth of the Kolyma or some other point that was recognizably part of Siberia. Spanberg argued that one or two more days of travel would do. Bering, afraid of trapping his ship in the ice, overruled both and reversed course. He brought the *Gabriel* back to Kamchatka on 1 September. In March 1730, he reported on his deed to the authorities in St Petersburg.

Unfortunately, as Chirikov had feared, few considered Bering to have closed his case. To redeem himself, Bering spent the next two years in the capital, securing approval for a grander Second Kamchatka Expedition, better known as the Great Northern Expedition. Not only would this new enterprise settle the question of Asia's position relative to America's, it was intended to map Russia's north coast from the White Sea to Chukotka's East Cape, to establish sea routes from Kamchatka to North America and Japan, to verify whether the fabled Juan da Gama Land existed, to survey America's west coast as far south as possible and to augment Messerschmidt's findings from the 1720s by researching the natural history and ethnography of Siberia and, if possible, the Americas. Two eminent scholars headed the academic contingent: the naturalist Johann Georg Gmelin and the ethnographer Gerhard Friedrich Müller. Among the junior scientists was the amiably alcoholic astronomer Louis Deslisle de la Croyère, from a line of distinguished French scholars – although his pedigree proved more impressive than his capabilities. Empress Anna gave her blessing to Bering's proposals in early 1732, and the expedition began officially in April 1733, as the captain-commander set out from St Petersburg to Kamchatka, via Okhotsk and Yakutsk.

More than 900 individuals played direct or supporting roles in the Great Northern Expedition, although the range of their achievements tends to be overshadowed by the tragedy of Bering's own tale. Numerous parties tackled the charting of the northern coast, which was divided into five sectors: Arkhangelsk to the Ob River; the Ob to the Yenisei; the Yenisei to the humplike Taimyr Peninsula; the Taimyr to the Lena; and the Lena to East Cape, with a southward turn to the Gulf of Anadyr in the Pacific. Scurvy and cold claimed many lives during these surveys, which began in 1734, pitting flimsy sloops against ramparts of river and sea ice, and condemning dozens of men to the misery of long overland treks. One of the Taimyr explorers, Vasilii Prochishchev, brought his young bride with him to the 77th parallel, where both died of scurvy and remain buried to this day. These parts of the expedition were not completed until the autumn of 1743 – more than a year and a half after Bering's own death – when a weary Dmitrii Laptev, having journeyed from the mouth of the Lena and rounded the tip of Chukotka, wrapped up work in the easternmost sector by surveying the neck of Kamchatka and the Anadyr river. At sea, Martin Spanberg reconnoitred in the direction of Japan. In Kamchatka, he refitted the *Gabriel* and built a new ship, the *Archangel Michael*, to accompany it; although this flotilla went astray amid the Kurile Islands in 1738, Spanberg reached the Japanese home island of Honshu in 1739. To his annoyance, the Admiralty in St Petersburg refused to believe his report, insisting that his ships had landed in Korea instead. From 1741 to 1743, Mikhail Gvozdev charted the west and south coasts of the Sea of Okhotsk, and Sakhalin Island's eastern shore.

Bering himself, leading a cavalcade of hundreds, took over a year to get to Yakutsk, and nearly another three years passed before he reached Okhotsk, where he built two new ships: the 90-foot, 211-ton *St Peter* for himself, and its twin, the *St Paul*, to be commanded by Chirikov. During this interim, he heard the startling news that, in 1732, the geodesist Mikhail Gvozdev had sailed the *Gabriel* to within sight of Alaska's Cape Prince of Wales, at approximately 65°30′N, becoming the first European to chart the western coast of America this far north – and giving Bering a key reference point to work with as he planned his own voyage. Also at this time, Bering was confronted with a near-strike on the part of his scientific staff. Gmelin and Müller, not finding the rough life in outer Siberia to their taste, reneged on their agreement to join Bering's contingent in Kamchatka and instead ran their research out of better-appointed settlements like Irkutsk and Yakutsk. Gmelin deputized his assistant to go east in his place and, in 1739, sent a second substitute: a Wittenberg-educated physician and naturalist named Georg Wilhelm Steller. Steller had arrived in Russia in 1734, befriended Daniel Messerschmidt before his death, and married Messerschmidt's widow, thereby gaining access to the older scholar's Siberian notebooks. Hearing of the Northern Expedition, Steller wished feverishly to join it, and Gmelin, once acquainted with the young man, was only too happy to recommend him to Bering. Steller set out for the Pacific, riding into Okhotsk in the spring of 1740. To his sorrow, he and Bering proved a terrible match, his bookishness and piety – he had studied Lutheran theology along with medicine – clashing with the captain's hard-headed practicality and acerbic wit. For details of this relationship we have only Steller's diaries to go by, and so it may be that the image commonly held of Bering as 'a plodding man who had no love for science' is somewhat overdrawn.[13] Still, there is no doubt that, on this voyage at least, seamanship did not coexist easily with scholarship, and would pull rank on it at every turn.

With the construction of his new ships finished, Bering shifted to Kamchatka in the summer of 1740, first to Bolsheretsk and then to Avacha Bay, where he founded the Harbor of the Apostles Peter and Paul, the future port of Petropavlovsk. Steller crossed over in early 1741 and had his first serious quarrel with Bering, over treatment of the natives. In retaliation for the killing of Russian foremen by Koryak labourers, Bering led a punitive raid on Koryak villages, killing dozens, including women and children, with grenade blasts. Steller, who had opened a school for natives in Bolsheretsk and stood as godfather to an Itelmen boy, lambasted Bering for his 'unchristian and cruel' handling of the Koryaks. Not for the first or last time, the captain brushed off the scientist's concerns.

The time to sail came in June 1741. At an officer's council in May, Bering, Chirikov and their lieutenants decided to bear east by southeast to Spanish America, hopefully encountering Juan de Gama Land (indicated on their faulty maps but in fact nonexistent), and then turn up the coast, following it all the way north to the strait. De la Croyère was to serve as the St Paul's scientist, Steller as the St Peter's. Steller, more accepting of the stories told by Cossacks and natives of islands just off Chukotka (the Diomedes) and a 'big land' (the Seward Peninsula) to the east, thought it best to seek that nearer and narrower crossing – but he was excluded from the council, and already enough of a misfit that he would not have been heeded in any case. The St Peter and St Paul left Petropavlovsk on the 4th. A fierce storm separated them on the 20th, and the two ships would never meet again.

Not only did the storm split the expedition, it threw the captains completely off their bearings. Both let their vessels drift to the east, hoping to make landfall before water ran out or scurvy began to weaken the crew. In mid-July, Bering and Chirikov each stumbled upon the south coast of Alaska, although at points several hundred miles apart. The *St Paul* approached the Alexander Archipelago, where the Alaska panhandle begins, on 15 July, and Chirikov sent two parties ashore on the 18th. Both groups mysteriously vanished, either killed by the local Tlingit or drowned out of sight. Having lost both its smallboats, the *St Paul* no longer had any way to put men on shore, and its supply of water was dwindling. At the end of July, Chirikov began sailing back to Kamchatka, mapping what he could of the Aleutians on the way home. With six men dead or dying of scurvy – one of them the ship's scientist, de la Croyère, who numbed his suffering with brandy for a solid two weeks before expiring – the *St Paul* limped into Avacha Bay on 10 October.

The *St Peter* fared far worse. Its encounter with Alaska came just after the *St Paul*'s, on 16 July, when the majesty of Mount St Elias hove into view. Most impatient to set foot on dry land was Steller, who had whiled away the past six weeks fantasizing about lengthy excursions ashore and the numberless discoveries awaiting him. He was enraged, then, to find that Bering cared for nothing but making his maps and returning to port with as much haste as he could manage. One landfall would be authorized, and that only because the *St Peter* had used up two-thirds of its water. The site chosen was Kayak Island and, on 20 July, after arguing the point with Bering, Steller was given permission to join the shore party led by first mate Sofron Khitrovo. Steller made the most of this half-day on land, collecting 160 plant specimens, including salmonberry and skunk cabbage, and identifying a new species of bird, the Steller's jay. From the bird's resemblance to illustrations he had seen of blue jays from the Carolinas, he cleverly deduced that the *St Peter* had reached the New World. The natives kept themselves hidden, but Steller and the others came upon a cache of their food and tools, and 'traded' with them by leaving an iron kettle, some silk and a pipe with tobacco in exchange for some of the food. Back on board, Steller seethed at having been allowed so little time to savour what should have been the opportunity of a lifetime. 'Have we come only to carry American water to Asia?' he snapped at Bering, and in his diary, he noted angrily that 'The preparation for this ultimate purpose of sailing to America lasted ten years. Only twenty hours while the ship was at anchor were devoted to the matter itself.'[14]

Like Chirikov, but more slowly, Bering took his ship back to the west along the southern coasts of the Alaska Peninsula and the

Aleutian islands, narrowly missing Kodiak Island. Along the way, Steller took note of fur seals, otters and the sea lion that bears his name today; one evening, he became convinced that he had spotted in the moonlit water a creature he called a 'sea ape', but it has never been sighted since. In August, symptoms of scurvy appeared and, during the expedition's second and penultimate landfall, on the isle of Nagai in the Shumagin Islands, Steller temporarily staved off the threat by collecting heaps of anti-scorbutic herbs, such as spoonwort and crowberry. In September, off Bird Island, the *St Peter* met a group of Aleuts. Bering's Koryak interpreters could make no sense of the strangers' tongue, but the two groups exchanged goods – even though the Aleuts were visibly displeased by the smell of the Russians' tobacco and the taste of their vodka.

Scurvy returned in October, as Steller's store of herbs ran out. At the end of the month, the *St Peter*, which had sailed through snow and hail for several weeks, was caught in a winter tempest. Off course and with the ship badly damaged, Bering sought refuge in November on what he and his second-in-command, Sven Waxell, thought was the Kamchatkan coast but turned out to be one of the as-yet-unnamed Commander Islands – 400 miles from where they wished to be. The men endured the hardship and isolation of a winter encampment, pestered so badly by marauding Arctic foxes that they captured and tortured dozens of the animals to relieve their frustration and boredom. Bering passed away on 8 December, perhaps of scurvy, as has traditionally been thought, or perhaps of gas gangrene, as Steller concluded, or even of heart failure, which was the verdict of the Russo-Danish archaeological expedition that located Bering's burial site in 1991. Steller struggled to keep the sick alive and, when circumstances permitted, studied the local animals and plants, searching always for herbs to fight the effects of scurvy. Here he gathered the data that went into *De Bestiis Marinis*, his 1751 book on the Steller's sea lion, the sea otter, the 'sea bear' (as he called the fur seal) and the 30-foot-long Steller's sea cow, which grazed the kelp beds of the Commander Islands and delighted the *St Peter*'s castaways with its succulent taste.

In the spring of 1742, those who had survived the winter built a new boat from the *St Peter*'s remains, christening it the *Bering* in honour of their fallen leader; the island, too, they named after Bering. While they did this, Chirikov, in May, set out in the *St Paul* to search for them, but missed their camp altogether and decided to get some good out of this second trip by mapping more of the Aleutians. In a predictable irony, both the *St Paul* and the *Bering* sailed into Avacha Bay in August, within a few days of each other.

The ramifications of such a long and complex venture are not easily summarized, but they were many and profound. The maps based on the Northern Expedition's surveys, prepared with the assistance of Chirikov, gave Euro-Americans their clearest picture ever of the North Pacific and added immeasurably to Russia's understanding of its own northern coast. As for the scientific side of things, Gmelin produced an authoritative *Flora Sibirica*, while Müller filled 30 volumes with encyclopaedic descriptions of the indigenous Siberians and their lifeways, in addition to compiling the expedition's official history, released in 1756. Steller died in Tyumen, in 1746, on his way back to St Petersburg, and although some of his research became known quickly, most of it was published posthumously. Steller's work was of tremendous use to generations of scientists and explorers, but he inadvertently brought doom to the animals he studied: by alerting the wider world to the existence of sea otters and fur seals, he helped to precipitate the decades-long flood of hunters and trappers from many lands into the region. As species, the seals and otters survived the next century's slaughter, but only barely. The spectacled cormorants and sea cows that Steller had made known to science were used by hunters and trappers as a source of food – and driven into extinction as a consequence.

From the mid-century onwards it became standard practice for Arctic expeditions to make room for at least one working scientist, even if it was merely the doctor doing double duty. On his 1773 attempt to reach the North Pole via Greenland and Svalbard, England's Lord Mulgrave included an astronomer and a naturalist, with the latter performing the first scientific autopsies of the polar bear and ivory gull. He also brought along a Nigerian freedman named Olaudah Equino – the first African known to have entered the Arctic – and a fourteen-year-old midshipman destined for immortal fame: Horatio Nelson. Mulgrave's contemporary, James Cook, would no sooner have sailed without ship's scientists than without sextant or compass, and the same is true of George Vancouver after him. In 1785, when Louis xvi of France ordered Jean-François de la Pérouse to make a circumnavigation of the world – a trip that saw valuable survey work done off the shores of Alaska, Kamchatka and Sakhalin before shipwreck left all hands fatally marooned in the South Pacific – the captain brought along no fewer than ten scientists. (Among those who volunteered for this journey, but were rejected, was a sixteen-year-old Napoleon

Bonaparte, and the effect on history had he made the cut and perished with Pérouse can only be wondered at.)

Also in these years, royal societies, universities and informal scholarly networks began to back Arctic research more actively. In Russia, it was the country's best-known intellectual who spoke most fervently about the need to tame the North. This was Mikhail Lomonosov, a Slavic Ben Franklin, with his humble background – he grew up poor near Kholmogory, in the Pomor lands – and his polymathic versatility. A co-founder of Moscow University, Lomonosov wrote poetry and contributed worthily to fields as disparate as chemistry, lexicography, geology and astronomy. Advising two empresses, Elizabeth and Catherine the Great, that 'it is in Siberia and the Arctic seas that Russia's might will grow', he penned the following verse in honour of Bering's Northern Expedition:

> In vain does stern Nature
> Hide from us the entrance to the shores of evening in the East.
> I see with wise eyes
> A Russian Columbus speeding between the ice floes,
> Defying the mystery of the ages.[15]

It was thanks to Lomonosov's support, and his intercession with Catherine, that Vasilii Chichagov of the Russian navy attempted to lead a squadron through the Northeast Passage. In 1765, the year of his patron's death, Chichagov sailed to 80°N, but stalled in the vicinity of Spitsbergen. The outcome was dishearteningly identical when he tried again in 1766. Catherine's programme for the Arctic was never as ambitious as Peter the Great's, but she asked the Berlin zoologist Peter Simon Pallas to include Siberia in the huge natural history survey he carried out in the Russian provinces during the late 1760s and early 1770s. Alongside masterworks like his *Flora Rossica* and *Zoographica Rosso-Asiatica*, Pallas edited a two-volume comparative dictionary that included Siberian languages such as Yakut, and he arranged for the printing of those works by Steller that as yet remained unpublished. Ivan Lyakhov, in the 1770s, began the long effort to chart the New Siberian Islands, north of the Yana estuary. First visited by Cossack hunters in the 1710s, this wide-scattered archipelago would not be fully mapped until the twentieth century. In 1785, Catherine dispatched a ten-year expedition to the far northeast, led by the English commodore Joseph Billings, who had formerly served under James Cook, and including

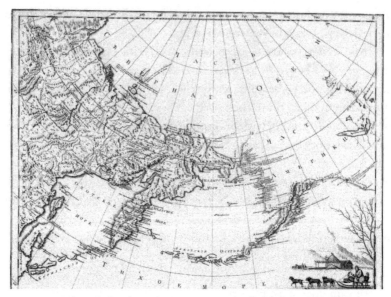

Arctic knowledge through time, III: A map of Irkutskaya Guberniya
produced in 1792, based on geographical discoveries made during Vitus Bering's
expeditions, carried out between 1724 and 1743.

Martin Sauer as secretary and Karl Henry Merck as linguist and
scientist. The Billings Expedition failed at one of its goals, which was
to traverse the Northeast Passage, but it drew up the most accurate
maps to date of Chukotka, the Aleutians, Kodiak Island and western
Alaska. It also sounded alarms – unfortunately unheeded – about the
abuse of native Siberians and Aleuts by Russian fur traders, and about
the catastrophic depletion of the sea otter population.

Other nations brought research agendas to the North, especially in
the Pacific, which attracted greater attention after the Bering expeditions,
and where Spain and England, like Russia, wished to assert territorial
interests. Both countries had claimed the New World's Pacific coast
long before: John Cabot, in 1497, asserted England's right to the 'New
Found Land' all the way to its opposite shore, wherever it might be.
Balboa, upon reaching Panama's Pacific shore in 1513, named Spain
the ruler of the ocean's entire eastern coastline. Francis Drake may have
visited British Columbia after declaring northern California to be 'New
Albion' in 1579, and in 1592 the Greco-Spanish sailor Juan de Fuca may
have reached the strait separating present-day Washington State from
Vancouver Island. But despite those possibilities, Europeans rarely
voyaged north of the San Francisco area until the 1770s, leaving moot
the question of who held jurisdiction there. Now, with the Russians

busying themselves in Alaska, and with Britain extending its reach westward through Canada, King Carlos III thought it advisable to secure, and even enlarge, Spain's position in California by sending explorers as far north as possible. Between 1774 and 1793, mariners like Juan Pérez, Juan Francisco de la Bodega y Quadra and Salvador Fidalgo sailed to Vancouver Island, the Queen Charlotte Islands and southeastern Alaska. In 1775, Bodega y Quadra claimed Spanish sovereignty over the Pacific coast up to 61°N.

The British were no less active. During the third and last of his great Pacific voyages, the incomparable James Cook, after discovering the Hawaiian islands in early 1778, crossed to present-day Oregon in the *Resolution* and *Discovery* and sailed up to Nootka Sound on Vancouver Island. From there, drawing on the skills in northern navigation he had honed in Newfoundland's waters during the 1760s, he began a prodigious coastal survey that took him to southern Alaska and the Aleutians, and then all the way around Alaska to the Arctic Ocean. Cook now aimed to find the Northwest Passage, but could force his ships no farther than Alaska's Icy Cape, at 70°N. He turned back to winter in Hawaii, little knowing that he would meet his death there the following February. He was the first to knock at the Passage's western gate, and it was he who, in a gesture of gallantry, bestowed the name 'Bering' on the strait running between Asia and America. Taking up Cook's mantle in the 1790s was George Vancouver, who had served the older explorer as a midshipman during the 1770s, and whose own North Pacific survey in 1791–5 accomplished much for science – not least because he brought to Alaska the shrewdly observant surgeon-naturalist Archibald Menzies, whose travelogue remains a valuable source for understanding northern North America as it was at the close of the eighteenth century.

Not just in the scientific sphere, but in all respects, the Arctic and near-arctic were by this point on the cusp of the modern age. To the extent that the great powers' political and economic rivalries affected the far north, seismic changes were on their way: the new United States, with all its hegemonic potential, had just been born, and the regime-changing convulsions of the French Revolution and Napoleonic wars were making themselves felt. Environmentally, the Little Ice Age that for several hundred years had preserved the Arctic's remoteness was left with only half a century to run, a change guaranteed to ease foreigners' penetration of the Arctic – just as said foreigners were accumulating the knowledge and expertise that would further facilitate the region's conquest. And in an era so thoroughly inflamed by the rising spirit of nationalism, the Euro-American desire to see that conquest consummated would burn with greater heat than ever before.

4

Crusades: 1800 to 1914

If his memoirs speak true, the Czech locksmith Jan Welzl left his homeland in the early 1890s to seek his fortune in the east, as one of the thousands of labourers laying track for Russia's mighty Trans-Siberian Railway. But after a short time at this work, he set out for the high north with a horse and cart, a chest of tools and no plan beyond performing kind deeds with larkish randomness: repairing broken objects for poor families, removing chains from the legs of Siberian prisoners and intervening when ruffian gold-miners tormented the Eskimos. Finally, he reached the Bering shore, from which he travelled to the New Siberian archipelago, St Lawrence Island and eventually Alaska, where, by his own account, he became a merchant with a reputation for dealing fairly with the natives. 'After years and years of dreadful suffering', Welzl boasts, 'I became a hunter of note and an established trader, proprietor of a splendid boat and the chief judge of New Siberia'; he claims also to have been named the leader of an Eskimo clan. To what degree he was a confabulator in the mould of Munchausen remains impossible to say, but the factual record shows that, in 1924, he was shipwrecked near San Francisco, where he had hoped to sell a large quantity of furs. Deported to Czechoslovakia, Welzl raised funds for a return to the New World by publishing *Thirty Years in the Golden North* and other reminiscences. His skills as a raconteur proved adequate to his purpose, and this Slavonic Jack London wound up in the Yukon town of Dawson, where one can still visit his tomb to this day.[1]

Tall or not – and Welzl's certainly were in places – tales like these resonated with their readership because they spoke to everything the public knew, or thought it knew, about the Arctic. This, by the turn of the nineteenth and twentieth centuries, was considerable, for the region had come to impinge on Western society's consciousness as never before. Blank spots on the Arctic map still existed, but its basic geographical contours had been sketched out by the late 1800s. While the Arctic remained a wild and remote space, the power of mass media had placed it well within the public's mental grasp, just as railways and steamers had placed its fringes – Iceland, Spitsbergen, coastal Alaska, the northern reaches of Hudson Bay – within the relatively easy physical reach of hunters, travellers and tourists. Over the course of the nineteenth century, Europeans and Americans came to associate the far north with a distinct, if internally inconsistent, set of concepts and images, fed by explorers' press reports and autobiographies, by greater familiarity with how Arctic goods enriched their lives, and by the various and many ways in which artists and authors employed northern leitmotifs in their creative work. It was seen by some as an adventure-filled frontier offering liberation, whether from political oppression or the stifling propriety of 'civilized' life, and the opportunity to win unimaginable riches, or as a place peopled by stalwart, morally unspoiled natives. To others, the Arctic was a land of despair, poverty and disorder – home only to the most debased of savages, the most unfortunate of exiles and the worst breed of outlaws. And in all quarters during this jingoistic age, how a given country chose to explore the polar world came widely to be seen as a reflection of its national character.

By the eve of the First World War, Americans and Europeans alike perceived themselves as having stormed and taken the Arctic, much like crusaders seizing a hoarfrosted citadel. They had reached the North Pole (or so they thought) and, not long after, the South Pole too. They had forced wide open the doors of the Arctic's treasury, hauling out riches by the fistful and devising ways to plunder more in time to come. They had probed its ecosystem's hidden workings: the patterns of its weather, the life cycles of its flora and fauna, the movement of its glaciers and seas. They believed as well that they had established dominion over its people and gained more perfect knowledge of them. And yet how complete the West's victory was, and how well it had come to understand the Arctic, is open to question. Many errors remained to be corrected in the following century, and many prejudices would take decades to shed, if they were shed at all. In conversation with the Danish zoologist Christian Vibe, the Inughuit Kutsikitsoq, a guide on the Van Hauen expedition of 1939–41, regarded with amusement all Euro-Americans who assumed that they could fully comprehend his people and environment. 'Don't write

too much about us', he advised. 'White men keep on running around with
notebook and pencil . . . and when they go home they feed their people
a lot of lies about us and [how they] themselves have been great heroes.
You will perhaps do the same and give us all something to laugh about,
when the priest tells us what you have written. Lend me your pencil, and
I will scratch it all out, for it is surely mostly lies.'[2] A more trenchant
comment on Western hubris, in the Arctic or elsewhere, would be difficult to find.

The Franklin Syndrome: Exploring the Arctic in the Early 1800s

Of all the ends pursued by foreigners in the nineteenth-century Arctic,
the one that most captivated the public imagination was the quest for
the North Pole, an effort that itself grew out of a renewed search by
Great Britain for the Northwest Passage.

In the English-speaking world, the father of modern polar exploration is traditionally considered to be Sir John Barrow, second secretary of
the Admiralty and initiator of the Passage- and Pole-seeking expeditions that ignited the era's enthusiasm for Arctic adventuring. With the
Napoleonic wars now ended, the Royal Navy lacked for missions, and
Barrow, upon hearing that whalers like William Scoresby were taking
advantage of warmer weather and thinner ice to hunt in Baffin Bay as far
north as 74 degrees, decided that his ships and officers could best be put
to use looking for the Passage. Barrow believed this to be a question not
just of prestige, but of economic benefit and national security: Spain, a rival
in the North Pacific in previous years, was losing its New World colonies
to wars of independence and was thus no longer a factor, but Britain's position in Canada was threatened by the young United States and especially
Russian Alaska. Allowing the Passage 'to be completed by a foreign
navy, after the doors of [its] two extremities had been thrown open by ships
of our own', Barrow believed, would have been 'an egregious piece of
national folly' and 'little short of an act of national suicide'.[3]

In 1818, to prevent such a grievous blow to Britannic pride, Barrow,
with support from the Royal Society, sent out twin expeditions to the far
north. David Buchan and Trafalgar veteran John Franklin, handling the
Dorothea and *Trent*, were ordered to approach Svalbard and traverse
the Northeast Passage, 'us[ing] your best endeavours to reach the North
Pole'. John Ross and William Parry, his lieutenant, were to take the
Isabella and *Alexander* to Baffin Bay, thread their way through the Northwest Passage, and meet Buchan and Franklin in the Pacific, the four

ships then returning to Britain in triumph. Neither squadron accomplished its mission, although Ross and Parry went up Davis Strait far enough to discover Melville Bay and Smith Sound. They returned with welcome reports of bowhead whales by the score in the so-called West Water, and they became the first Europeans to encounter the Inughuit, or Greenland's Polar Eskimos, since the days of the Vikings. 'What are you?' the baffled natives asked. 'Where do you come from? From the sun or the moon?' As to the Passage itself, Ross and Parry brought back conflicting impressions. Entering into Lancaster Sound, Ross, fooled by one of the tricks of light so common in northern waters, became convinced that the way west was barred by a mountain-capped land mass. Boldly contradicting his captain, Parry opined that no such obstacle existed. His confidence won greater favour with the Admiralty than did Ross's caution, and it was to him that the next eight years of Arctic voyaging were entrusted. Thus, it is said, began the Western world's nine-decade assault on the Pole.

A tidy narrative, and useful enough in its way, but it defines 'polar exploration' too narrowly and glosses over other noteworthy developments. Russia had its own counterpart to John Barrow, in the form of Count Nikolai Rumyantsev, imperial chancellor under Alexander I and the sponsor, privately and officially, of a number of Arctic ventures. One of the goals he set for Adam von Kruzenstern during Russia's first circumnavigation of the world (1803–6) was to test new routes for supplying the Russian-American Company's Alaskan holdings, and one of Kruzenstern's ships, the *Neva*, was briefly drawn into the RAC's wars against the Tlingit. Rumyantsev also funded silver-prospecting missions to Novaya Zemlya and surveys of northeast Siberia and Beringia. Between 1808 and 1811, Mathias von Hedenström and the hunter Yakov Sannikov mapped the Siberian coast between the Yana and Indigirka rivers, filling in some of the gaps left by Dmitrii Laptev during the Great Northern Expedition, exploring as well (and giving a name to) the still mysterious New Siberian Islands. Another of their tasks was to confirm the existence of two large islands thought to have been sighted recently – one by Stepan Andreyev, north of the Kolyma, and another by Sannikov himself. In neither case was there any chance of success; 'Sannikov Land' and 'Andreyev Land' are now known to have been figments of the imagination, even though hopes of finding them persisted into the twentieth century. Also on Rumyantsev's orders, Otto von Kotzebue took the brig *Rurik* through the Bering Strait in the summer of 1816, with the aim of completing the Northeast Passage from the Pacific side. This was to no avail, but Kotzebue mapped much of the Chukchi Sea and western Alaska, and returned to Alaskan waters in 1823–6. Between 1820 and 1824, joint expeditions under Pyotr Anzhu (Anjou) and Ferdinand von Wrangel covered much the same ground that Hedenström and Sannikov had. By observing the flight of birds and interviewing local natives, Wrangel deduced the existence of the island that today bears his name, but although he searched for it, he did not find it; it was charted in the 1860s and named in his honour. Anzhu, together with Hedenström, is credited with bringing to wider attention the phenomenon of polynyas, patches of the northern seas which remain ice-free the whole year round. Also during the 1820s, the Russian naval officer Fyodor Litke surveyed northern waters: first in a voyage to Novaya Zemlya and the White and Barents seas, and then as part of his 1826–9 world circumnavigation. During this second journey, he charted the Pribilof and Commander island groups, as well as Siberia's coastline between Petropavlovsk and the Bering Strait.

Alexander von Humboldt of Berlin, the most influential naturalist of the century save Darwin, conducted geological research in Siberia during his 9,600-mile journey through Russia in 1829, and neither was the Scandinavian north empty of scholars or voyagers during these years. Britain's Edward Sabine, the astronomer for Ross and Parry during their Arctic voyages of 1818 and 1819–20, and later a seminal figure in the early study of geomagnetism, spent much of the early 1820s in Svalbard and Greenland, measuring the extent to which Earth's sphere flattens in the polar regions. The Danes completed a large survey of Greenland's east coast in 1829 and an in-depth study of Iceland's Hekla volcano in 1845. Perhaps the most ambitious venture in this part of the Arctic was the La Recherche Expedition of 1838–40, led by the French naturalist and naval surgeon Joseph Paul Gaimard and arranged in partnership with the governments of Sweden and Norway. Accompanied by the painter François-Auguste Biard, scientists from several nations and the half-Sami, half-Swede botanist and folklorist Lars Levi Læstadius as a guide, Gaimard took the corvette *Recherche* to the Faeroes, Spitsbergen, the White Sea and Lapland. The mission proved a scholarly success, and Biard thrilled museumgoers with eye-catching canvases depicting polar bears in combat and Greenland kayakers pursuing walruses amid twisted spires of blue ice.

Still, as valuable as such undertakings were, they failed to rouse public and political passions to the same extent as the Anglo-American ones, and they contributed barely to the drama of the drive towards the Pole.

It was men like Franklin and Parry who advanced that plotline, and both, at the Navy's behest, went back to the Arctic in 1819. Franklin was now on foot and charged with leading a party to Great Slave Lake and repeating Samuel Hearne's trek up the Coppermine to the Arctic Ocean. There he was to chart as much of the coast as he could and rendezvous with the ships that Parry would hopefully be bringing through the Passage. Trouble plagued the expedition from the start, and Franklin, before retreating across the Barren Grounds in 1822 with only a fraction of his mapping work done, lost eight of his nineteen men and, with the other survivors, subsisted at the direst moments on maggot-ridden meat and scraps of boot leather. Praised for his fortitude, if not his skills, Franklin was given a second mission in 1825–7, when he marched up the Mackenzie and, enjoying better luck than before, surveyed hundreds of miles of Canada's and Alaska's Arctic shoreline. That appeared to be the last of his polar travels, for after service in the Mediterranean, he accepted the governorship of the penal colony in Van Diemen's Land, or Tasmania. But he would return, to the saddest possible end, in the 1840s. His compatriot Parry gained renown and a rear-admiralty out of his four return voyages to the Arctic (1819–20, 1821–3, 1824–5 and 1827), where he plowed more than halfway through the Northwest Passage, winning an Admiralty prize of £5,000 for crossing the 110th west meridian. On his final visit, Parry sailed to 82°45′N, a farthest north that stood unbroken for 49 years. Britain's next great Arctic voyage was paid for not by the navy, but by the gin merchant Felix Booth, who placed the small, steam-driven *Victory* at the disposal of John Ross and his nephew James Clark Ross, who had earlier sailed to the North with Parry. The Ross team set out in 1829, and while they failed to find the Passage, and in fact had to abandon not just the underpowered engine, but the *Victory* itself, they calculated the North Magnetic Pole, charted Boothia Peninsula and set a record for time spent consecutively in the Arctic. Only in 1833, after rowing their longboats out to Baffin Bay, did they return to Britain, having been rescued, ironically enough, by the *Isabella*, which the senior Ross had commanded fifteen years before. James later went on to become one of the celebrated explorers of the Antarctic shore.

The British are often criticized for having gone at the Arctic with bull-headed inflexibility, but their approaches, even during these early decades, were more diverse than is commonly thought. From the days of Samuel Hearne and before, the agents and trappers of the fur companies had a large store of experience and knowledge, much of it acquired from natives, to guide them on how to dress, how to transport themselves, and what kind of gear to use. Barrow, not least because he resented the Hudson's Bay Company's hold on Rupert's Land and disdained its men as rabble, rejected such rough-and-ready methods, insisting instead that discipline and gentlemanly virtue would carry Britain forwards in the North as they had elsewhere. For their part, the men of the Bay were not much impressed by Navy ways, as indicated in the scornful assessment of Franklin given by the HBC's George Simpson after the Coppermine expedition: 'he has not the physical powers required for the labour of moderate voyaging in this country; he must have three meals per diem, tea is indispensable, and with the utmost exertion he cannot walk above eight miles per day.'[4] The much-respected Scoresby took a similarly dim view of Barrow's fixation on hierarchy and moral qualities at the expense of experience, warning in his *Account of the Arctic Regions* about 'the want of experience in the navigation of icy seas . . . No judgment, however profound, no talent, however acute, can supersede the necessity of practice.'[5] Naval rigidity won out more often than it should have, and certain methods were employed in the face of all logic and long after their shortcomings had been exposed. Clothes and sleeping bags were made of wool, which retained too much moisture but not enough heat. Scurvy-preventing lime juice was stored in glass containers that shattered in low temperatures. Unlike Russian and Scandinavian explorers, who imitated the Sami and other natives in using reindeer sledges and dogsleds to travel overland, the British themselves hauled sleds made of wood and iron and loaded with hundreds of pounds of cargo – the polar equivalent of slaving at the oar of a galley – causing them to sweat dangerously and to burn too many calories as the cold sapped their strength.

Some things the British did well, and a few saw the wisdom of bowing before the Arctic's unique physical realities. Parry and the younger Ross befriended the Inuit, learning to eat the vitamin-rich food they ate and taking lessons in how to make and handle dogsleds. Indeed, the Ross expedition's success in lasting so many winters on the ice can be ascribed largely to the good relations James struck up with the neighbouring natives. Overwintering taught British explorers how to cope with the psychological debilitation caused by polar night, and Parry is noted for developing a repertoire of standard techniques to stave off depression and boredom during the long winters. He busied his men with the collection of scientific data, built a covered space for exercise, staged concerts and theatricals, and involved everyone in the 'publication' of a ship's newspaper, *The North Georgia Gazette and Winter Chronicle*. None of the crew complained when he authorized them to brew their own beer. Like the Russians, the British began to rely on canned provisions to make their stocks of food last longer – although improper canning, an alarmingly frequent problem, sickened or poisoned more than a few. Ship design improved as well. Ice was no friend to wooden hulls, and by about 1830, shipbuilders responded by thickening hulls with extra layers of wood or iron plate, and by cross-bracing the interior wherever space permitted. Sailing ships, unable to reverse course at will or to slow and speed up incrementally, were unable to manoeuvre through ice the way power-driven ones would do before the end of the century. But they made surprising progress with certain techniques: crashing through the edge with a full wind behind, towing the ship with smallboats, 'warping' (planting anchors in the ice ahead and winching forwards) and 'mill-dolling' (dropping a heavily loaded lifeboat from the bow).

By the second quarter of the century, the Arctic enterprise had fixed itself firmly in the culture as a matter of archetypal significance. The Pole was a centuries-old emblem of the ultimate in unattainability, and for humanity to besiege and capture it would symbolize, as few other achievements could, the limitless potentialities of Western civilization in the modern age. In London, and as far away as Prague and Dresden, a number of conventionally congratulatory paintings commemorated the early Arctic voyages, and Biard's paintings from the La Recherche Expedition created their own sensation after 1840. But as exemplified in two iconic works, a more complicated view of polar exploration – as quintessentially representative of human ambition at its most grasping – was taking shape. In the first and last chapters of Mary Shelley's *Frankenstein* (published in 1818, the year of the Ross-Parry and Buchan-Franklin voyages), we meet the idealistic Robert Walton, a former poet and young adventurer striking out for the North Pole from Arkhangelsk. Walton's thirst to reach the 'country of eternal light' and thereby win 'knowledge [and] dominion over the elemental foes of our race', is of a type with the unfulfilled Romantic yearnings that burn in Viktor Frankenstein, whom Walton encounters in the icy wastes of the high Arctic, where the doctor has pursued the monster he now hopes to destroy.[6] To conquer the Pole is presented as no less a Promethean feat than the creation of life – although Walton turns back before he, like Frankenstein, can be consumed by the fruits of his arrogance. More pessimistic yet was Caspar David Friedrich, the German Romantic artist best known for his metaphysical depictions of mountains and ruined churches. Possibly inspired by a reading of Parry's *Journal of a Voyage to Discover a North-West Passage*, Friedrich painted *The Sea of Ice*, a powerful and unsettling canvas, in 1823–4.[7] In it, the remains of a broken ship, which some believe represents Parry's *Griper* (even though the real-life *Griper* returned safely to port), are nearly hidden from sight by the cruel floes that, having crushed it to splinters, pile over it like a ziggurat assembled from jagged shards of glass and steel. This work is sometimes read as an expression of political disillusionment, in which the spirit of liberalism is snuffed out by the reactionary backlash that followed the Congress of Vienna. But as an early product of the darker outlook that later governed Friedrich's thinking, it also sounds a general warning about the fragility of human aspirations in a bleak and perilous universe.

If one believed in precognition, one could also see in *The Sea of Ice* a foretelling of the great tragedy that unfolded in Canada's north two decades later. Britain's search for the Northwest Passage had stalled during the 1830s, with voyages like George Back's in 1837 yielding few results, but Barrow successfully lobbied for a new expedition to be sent out in the mid-1840s, well-staffed and sumptuously supplied, and therefore sure to succeed. Navigationally, the task seemed simpler than it had half a century before: from the west, the entire coastline had been charted from Alaska to the Boothia Peninsula, not far from Hudson Bay, and it only remained to find a way west through Lancaster Sound, and then south to the mainland along the west side of Boothia, for the Passage to be completed. Asked to lead this final attack, James Clark Ross refused, and so the Admiralty turned to John Franklin as an old and reliable warhorse. In the *Erebus* and *Terror*, the iron-reinforced, steam-and-sail vessels that Ross had recently taken to Antarctica, Franklin sailed forth in May 1845, with 110 men and 24 officers. Passing through Lancaster Sound, Franklin wintered on Beechey Island, off the southwest corner of Devon Island, losing three of his crew. In 1846, he went north up Wellington Channel, circled Cornwallis Island, then headed south between Prince of Wales and Somerset islands till his ships reached the west coast of Boothia Peninsula. Had he continued to hug Boothia's shores, keeping east of King William Island, the *Terror* and *Erebus* would have made short work of the light ice in the James Ross, Rae, and Simpson straits. They could have then entered Queen Maud's Gulf, part of Canada's already charted coastline, without incident. Instead, Franklin swung wide to the west, around King William Island and into less-sheltered waters, and it was off the northwest tip of King

William that his ships were caught fast. It was also there that more than twenty members of the expedition perished, including Franklin himself, who died on 11 June 1847. The rest, under Francis Crozier, departed on foot, trying to cover the hundreds of miles separating them from Back's River, site of the nearest HBC outpost. None, however, survived. Traces of the expedition and clues as to the precise timing and nature of the various deaths were recovered only slowly, and debate over many details continues. Autopsies show clear signs of lead poisoning, but was this caused by the ship's filtration system or badly sealed tins of food? Was it the crucial factor in killing so many men, or did scurvy prove a more immediate danger? Were some of the men tempted to turn to 'the last resource', the delicate phrase used by British commentators to hint at the possibility of cannibalism?

By 1848, the only thing the wider world knew for certain was that an alarming amount of time had passed without any communication from the missing expedition. Franklin's disappearance shocked all of Europe and, more than any other event, transformed polar exploration into a half-century public obsession. One of England's most popular songs during the 1850s was 'Lady Franklin's Lament', with its haunting refrain:

> The fate of Franklin no tongue can tell,
> Lord Franklin alone with his sailors doth dwell.
> And now my burden, it gives me pain,
> For my long-lost Franklin I would cross the main.
> Ten thousand pounds I would freely give
> To know on earth that my Franklin doth live.[8]

More practically, dozens of missions were launched to save Franklin, or at least to determine what had become of him and his men. Not only did these ventures, over the course of eleven years, unravel many of the riddles surrounding the expedition, they revolutionized what was known about the Arctic and how it was explored. All but the remotest parts of the Canadian archipelago were charted. Expeditions became smaller and more nimble, and those on them were increasingly willing to adopt native clothing and native methods of hunting and transport. Contact between Euro-Americans and Inuit groups grew more frequent and more meaningful. Also, after Lady Franklin's stirring appeal to President Zachary Taylor in 1850, the U.S. became a major player not just in the Franklin saga, but in polar exploration more generally. Britain's first official searches were led by James Clark Ross, who took the *Enterprise* and *Investigator* to Canadian waters in 1848–9, and by Henry Kellett, who came up through Bering Strait in the *Herald*. Neither found anything useful.

The *Investigator* and *Enterprise* went out again in January 1850, the former under Robert McClure, Ross's lieutenant from the year before, the latter under Richard Collinson, the expedition's commander. Both approached from the east, through the Bering Strait, but became separated, and McClure, hungry for glory, seized this opportunity to run ahead of Collinson, who took till 1855 to complete his own journey. (Near Victoria Island, Collinson met Inuit who quite likely could have given him information about Franklin's demise, but the expedition's one interpreter was with McClure.) The *Investigator* reached the ice in the summer of 1850 and became trapped near Banks Island that autumn. Over the coming months, the ship progressed slowly and painfully to the east, and was finally abandoned in 1853. McClure and his men trekked to Melville Island, hoping to be rescued by Edward Belcher, whose squadron had been searching for Franklin since 1852. Belcher, however, had stranded four of his own vessels, including his flagship, *Resolute*, and not until 1854 did McClure and the others return to England. McClure faced a court-martial for losing the *Investigator* – which remained missing until its 2010 rediscovery by Canadian researchers – but the Admiralty acquitted him and even awarded him its long-posted prize of £10,000 for finding a way through the Passage.

By this point, a great many ships and overland travellers had set out after Franklin. Edward Inglefield, sailing in the *Isabel* in 1852, theorized that Franklin had sailed north against orders, a supposition that took him to Ellesmere Island, which he claimed as British territory. The Americans joined the search, thanks to the sympathy that Henry Grinnell, a shipping magnate and first president of the American Geographic Society, felt for Lady Franklin. Grinnell placed two privately purchased ships, the *Advance* and the *Rescue*, at the disposal of the U.S. Navy, on condition that it provide equipment, officers and crew. The Navy agreed, choosing Edwin De Haven to command this First Grinnell Expedition, which lasted from 1850 to 1851. Before he was forced home by adverse weather, DeHaven came across the remains of Franklin's Beechey Island winter camp, establishing his whereabouts as of early 1846. On land, the Irishman Francis McClintock, a master of the man-hauling technique (wisely, he used smaller and more agile sleds than his predecessors had), covered immense amounts of ground in 1852–4, but it was the HBC surgeon John Rae who, with a touch of serendipity, shed the first glimmers of light on the Franklin mystery. Surveying Boothia and King William Island for the Company in the spring of 1854, Rae heard stories from Inuit around Repulse Bay about the many white men who had died in the area a few years back. The Inuit showed Rae items that undoubtedly belonged to Franklin's men, and conveyed to him their opinion that some of the bodies had been mutilated in ways consistent with cannibalism. The response to Rae's report, written in July and published upon his return to England in October, was electric. Many took offense at even the slightest hint that cannibalism might have occurred, none more so than Charles Dickens, one of Franklin's most vocal admirers. In a December issue of *Household Words*, Dickens admitted that 'Dr Rae may be considered to have established, by the mute but solemn testimony of the relics he has brought home, that Sir John Franklin and his party are no more.' The charges of dishonorable behaviour, however, he answered angrily, and with more than a hint of racism:

> There is no reason whatever to believe that any of [them] prolonged their existence by the dreadful expedient of eating the bodies of their dead companions . . . The word of a savage is not to be taken for it; firstly because he is a liar; secondly, because he is a boaster; thirdly, because he often talks figuratively.[9]

Dickens went on to write the prologue for Wilkie Collins's dramatization of the Franklin story, *The Frozen Deep*, a play whose generous helpings of pathos reliably jerked tears from audiences for years after its 1856 premiere.

Lady Franklin conceded even less than Dickens, refusing to accept as definitive the evidence that her husband was dead, and protesting when the Admiralty declared the expedition lost. In 1857, with money raised through appeals to the public, she hired McClintock to continue the search in the *Fox*, a yacht specially refitted for polar voyaging. Unfortunately for her, the outcome was as Rae had suggested: in the spring of 1859, McClintock, now using dogsleds for overland journeying, came across the stone cairns in which Francis Crozier had left letters detailing Franklin's death and his own plans to lead the survivors to the southeast. He also recovered what was left of the expedition's log – a half-frozen lump of papers rendered unreadable by waterstains and ice damage.

Other expeditions of the 1850s, although nominally Franklin-related, were drifting from the original purpose: as clear a sign as any of how the search was reshaping national and institutional agendas in the Arctic. This shift in priorities became especially apparent during the Second Grinnell Expedition (1853–5), the event that drew America heart and soul into the new competition taking shape in the far north, in which a nation's polar prowess was seen as an index of its overall worth. Backed again by Grinnell, as well as by the Massachusetts philanthropist George Peabody, this venture was led by the naval surgeon Elisha Kent Kane, a veteran of the Mexican–American War and medical officer for the First Grinnell Expedition. Like Mercator and Hudson, and like a surprising number of his contemporaries, Kane believed that an open polar sea lay on the far side of the pack ice, and he feared that Britain would be the first to gain access to it. There were also the Danes to worry about, with the geographer Henrik Rink mapping northern Greenland and prospecting for coal there between 1848 and 1851. In May 1853, then, when Kane and his crew left New York in the *Advance*, he was thinking less of Franklin than of his own plans to outpace his country's potential rivals. By July, he had reached the west Greenland port of Upernavik, where he took on as a guide the resourceful Suersaq, better known as Hans Hendrik. Hendrik would accompany not just this mission, but three famed expeditions in the future. That autumn, to the alarm of his officers, Kane pushed the *Advance* past Etah and the 78th parallel, continuing north until 10 September, when stormy weather forced him to put into Rensselaer Bay. There, with its ship frozen fast in the ice, the expedition would remain for the next year and a half, the first Euro-Americans to overwinter so far north.

In many ways, Kane used this time productively, leading sled teams well above 80°N – man-hauled at first, switching later to dogsleds – to survey Smith Sound, Kane Basin and other parts of the gap between Ellesmere and northernmost Greenland. His men took astronomical readings and gathered other valuable data. To obtain food and to withstand the Arctic environment, Kane relied more than any polar explorer before him on native assistance and native skills, becoming, in his words, 'more than half Eskimaux'. Along with Rae of the HBC, Kane was among the first to promote a more flattering assessment of Eskimo-Inuit aptitudes and moral qualities – smacking of 'noble savage' romanticization, but still a more positive stereotype than that of primitive beastliness put forth by explorers like Ross and Parry. On the other hand, stress and isolation brought Kane's personal peculiarities to the fore. A physically frail but fanatically driven disciplinarian, he failed to command the confidence of his men. His first lieutenant, J. Wall Wilson, echoed the general consensus when he called him 'a peevish and sometimes insulting man', and Hendrik recalled how Kane, who on most occasions treated him like a foster son, grew so enraged at times that he threatened to flog him.[10] In August 1854, after a bitter fight about whether the expedition should risk a second winter of scurvy and short rations, Kane lost nearly half his contingent to mutiny, as eight men, including the surgeon Isaac Israel Hayes, decided to strike out on foot for Upernavik. The deserters returned in December, having gone 200 miles before realizing that they had no choice but to swallow their pride and go back. Kane readmitted them with frosty dignity.

The winter of 1854–5 was a time of desperation, as was the spring that followed. Insulating the living quarters as best they could with moss, Kane and his men dismantled much of the rest of the ship to burn for fuel. They supplemented their stores of food with stew made from rats, struggled mentally with the 'most depressing influence' of the polar night, and tended to those who fell sick with scurvy. With the arrival of spring, Hendrik, after bringing in one last load of meat to replenish his companions' supplies, accepted an invitation from the local natives to live among them. The rest of the men abandoned what was left of the *Advance* in mid-May, using their whaleboats as sail-sledges, which could be dragged across the ice and would take them across open water at need. After an odyssey lasting almost three months, the party returned to Upernavik on 8 August and was back in New York by mid-October. Although he contributed little to the Franklin search, Kane was now held up as a national hero and a paragon of unbreakable will. His record of the expedition, *Arctic Explorations: The Second Grinnell Expedition in Search of Sir John Franklin* (1856), became an immediate bestseller, and when his heart suddenly gave out in February 1857, his funeral procession – which went by steamboat from New Orleans to Cincinnati, and then by train to Philadelphia – was the best attended in u.s. history to that date and not exceeded in grandeur until that of Abraham Lincoln in 1865. Between them both, Franklin and Kane had brought polar exploration into the age of modern celebrity.

One retrograde fancy lived on into the second half of the century: faith in the existence of an open polar sea. Not only did the idea refuse to die, it had devoted and credible champions, among them Inglefield, Kane and a cluster of prominent scholars. From Europe came the voice of August Petermann, the most celebrated cartographer of his day, and founder of the yearbook *Petermanns Geographische Mitteilungen*, still published annually. In 1852, when Inglefield reported seeing ice-free water north of what would soon be called Kane Basin, Petermann was making his own case for the open sea theory, arguing moreover that a snout-like peninsula, which he called Transpolarland, protruded from the top of Greenland, thrusting across the Arctic Ocean to Russia's Wrangel Island. He would perpetuate these errors in the 1860s, both as a mapmaker and as the driving force behind Germany's first Arctic expeditions. On the other side of the Atlantic, Matthew Fontaine Maury, head of the u.s. Navy's Depot of Charts (the future Naval Observatory and Hydrographic Office) and one of the fathers of modern oceanography, discussed the strong possibility of open Arctic waters in his classic text from 1855, *The Physical Geography of the Sea*. Upon his return from the north, Kane did everything in his power to win acceptance of the thesis, focusing especially in his *Arctic Explorations* on how, in June 1854, his aide, William Morton, had supposedly sledded to 80°30′N on Greenland's northwest coast. As far as the eye could make out, Morton averred, 'the sea was open, a swell coming in from the northward and running cross-wise', and there was 'not a speck of ice'.[11] To drive the point home further, Kane's book supplied a beautifully idealized illustration of the moment, entitled 'The Open Polar Sea from Cape Jefferson'. Morton's claim to have travelled so far north was disputed in his own day, especially by Henrik Rink of Denmark, and is generally disbelieved now; the ice-free water he saw was most likely a polynya. But his tale seemed powerful proof at the time.

Carrying the mantle into the next decade was Kane's rebel angel, Isaac Israel Hayes, who, despite his differences with his former superior, remained true to the gospel of the open polar sea. It was to put this question to rest, ideally by finding a clear path to the Pole, that Hayes, in 1860–61, sailed to Greenland in the privately purchased *United States*. In the end, the most distinguished thing about Hayes's voyage was the artistic record he created of it. A friend of the Hudson River School landscapist Frederic Edwin Church, Hayes took up painting himself and came back from the expedition with a set of capably done watercolours – one of which provided Church with the model for his *Aurora Borealis* of 1865. (Church's other northern masterpiece, *The Icebergs*, from 1861, also had something of Hayes in it, for it was Church's acquaintance with the explorer that prompted his 1859 trip to Newfoundland, where he observed the silent southward drift of the ice.) Hayes also used the new calotype technique to take stunning photographs of the North, and these were assembled into a marvelous album in 1862. Beyond that, the venture brought Hayes little luck.

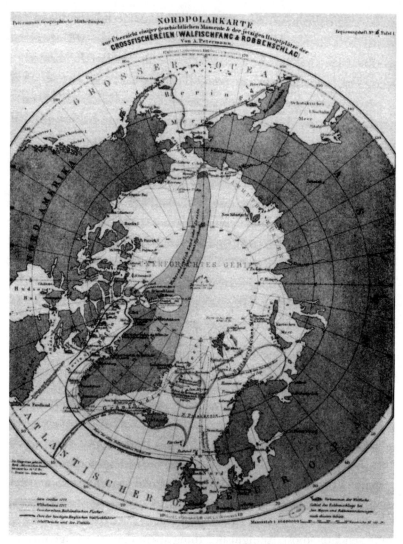

Arctic knowledge through time, IV: August Petermann's *Nordpolarkarte*
of 1869, illustrating his belief that northern Greenland extended
across the Arctic Ocean as far as Wrangel Island in a single land mass
called 'Transpolarland'.

Coming so soon after the Kane exploit, it was pure anticlimax, and all of
America was caught up in the Civil War when he returned. He proved
nothing about the polar waters, and though he tried to continue the
argument in his book *The Open Polar Sea*, his service obligations as a
military doctor delayed publication until 1867. Most damaging of all,
his proudest claim, to have sledded above the 82nd parallel, did not
stand up to scrutiny. His northernmost position was scaled back to 80°10′N,

and Hayes's error, for many years, cemented an international scepticism about the ability of u.s. explorers to record polar coordinates accurately.

In the later part of the century, the open polar sea theory would finally be put to rest. Other aspects of Arctic exploration would change as well. More countries became involved, and for a wider variety of reasons: scientific, economic, political and propagandistic. The technology and methods available to explorers improved, and respect among them for native expertise and lore – if not always for the natives themselves – increased. And as the world came to devote greater attention to their deeds, more of them began to fixate on the North Pole itself as the Arctic object most worthy of attainment.

Boreal Empires: Colonization and Exploitation in the Early Nineteenth Century

Sometime around 1850, the Inuit shaman Qitlaq, whose people lived in the northern parts of Baffin Island, professed to have had a vision in which the spirits urged him to guide as many as would follow to a new home in the northeast. Six families accompanied him when he set out, first for Ellesmere Island and then for the Siorapaluk region of northern Greenland. There the newcomers chanced upon a community of Inughuit and, for the better part of a decade, dwelled among them.

This, the last Inuit migration not caused by contact with Euro-Americans, was in several ways an epochal moment. The Inughuit, who had lost knowledge of the kayak, the bow and arrow and the fish-spear when the Little Ice Age disrupted old hunting and fishing patterns, learned from their guests how to make and use these crucial tools. The meeting confirmed the strength of cultural bonds over huge gulfs of time and distance, and for Westerners inclined to think of indigenous northerners as hermetically sealed in a bubble of timelessness before the arrival of foreigners, the episode serves to remind that the Inuit and groups like them fully experienced the ebb and flow of the historical process. Most of all, it demonstrates that, even this late in time, many Arctic natives were able to live as they liked and move where they pleased without regard for white governments or the lines scrawled on those governments' maps.

But not for much longer. Musing upon his time among the Netsilik Inuit in 1829–33, John Ross wondered, 'Is it not the fate of the savage and the uncivilized on this earth to give way to the more cunning and the better informed, to knowledge and civilization?' The confident reply he gave himself was typical of the time: 'It is the order of the world; and the right one.'[12] Right or not, this order was becoming the new reality in the Arctic, across all 360 degrees of longitude. With the exception of a few stubborn pockets where natural forces or human defiance prevailed, the habitable north was increasingly a realm governed and exploited from afar. European imperialism might arrive later in the highest Arctic than in India or the South Sea Islands, but it was already well-established in large parts of the North, and the nineteenth century would entrench it more firmly and more widely than ever.

In Canada, Britain's grip on the Arctic and subarctic was tightest in the east. The business here was whaling, sealing and fishing. After the Ross-Parry expedition of 1818, whaling vessels sprinted to Davis Strait and the North and West waters of Baffin Bay, killing perhaps 38,000 bowheads there over the course of the century; over 20,000 of these were slain by the British. The work was as perilous as it was lucrative. Until about 1830, when shipbuilders started stiffening the hulls of northbound vessels, hundreds of whalers lost their lives in the infamous 'breaking-up yard' of Melville and Baffin bays, or spent months marooned on the ice, praying, often in vain, for rescue. Other human victims included the Inuit who traded with the whalers and in the process contracted their diseases; in 1832 the Tununirmiut of Bylot Island were struck down almost to the last by smallpox and diphtheria. East and north of Newfoundland, the seal industry, which peaked every year with the late-winter and early spring visit of harp seals to the region, employed over 14,000 colonists by 1850 and accounted for one quarter of eastern Canada's total exports. Not only were pelts in demand, seals were valued for their oil, which provided lubricants and fuel for burning in the pre-petroleum era. Cod-fishing, the trade that had first drawn Europeans to these waters expanded, with shore-based salting and packing growing in importance with the actual catching. Mostly controlled by merchants in the west of England, the cod-fishing economy also attracted ships from other nations, especially France and America, which enjoyed access by right of treaty to several of the banks off Newfoundland.

All this enterprise, combined with English and Irish immigration and stepped-up missionary activity, led to sustained interaction between natives and non-natives. Newfoundland and Labrador, joined administratively in 1809, served as the primary contact zone between Europeans and the First Nations and Inuit to the north, although they mixed on the shores of Hudson Bay as well. The results were at times catastrophic. Apart from the danger of new diseases, violence was not uncommon. The most terrible case was that of Newfoundland's Beothuks, whose extirpation was hastened between 1818 and 1829 by white fishermen who viewed them as thieves and competitors – but who also lost population to epidemics and wars with the Innu, and were not, as was once commonly thought, hunted by whites purely for sport.

By contrast, the Moravians provided medical care, education and famine relief, expanding their presence in Labrador with new missions like Hebron and Zoar. With Catholics and Methodists also proselytizing in the region, and the Hudson's Bay Company moving in with new trading posts of their own by the 1830s, many Innu and some subarctic Inuit converted to Christianity and took up more settled lifestyles. As for the Inuit farther north who did not, European stereotypes about them were hardening into place: although whalers and explorers who dealt with them tended to think them more congenial than the 'savages' of other far-off seas, consensus had it that 'the Esqimaux' were, in the words of John Ross, 'disgusting brutes' and decidedly inferior.[13] The same men purported to be appalled by Inuit mores, and especially by what William Parry loftily condemned as their 'utter disregard for connubial fidelity' – although many of them, perhaps including Parry and his second-in-command, Joseph Lyon, managed to overcome this particular distaste, accepting or forcing sexual favours from, and occasionally fathering children with, Inuit women.[14]

In ways that translate easily to the histories of other Arctic natives, contact threw First Nations and Inuit lifestyles into disarray. Where old faiths were not swept away altogether, Christianity challenged the cosmological assumptions of shamanism. For communities that were more isolated, the out-of-nowhere appearance of such different-seeming outsiders caused tremendous cognitive dissonance. Some scholars now believe 'Arctic hysteria' to have been a psychological reaction to European contact – a striking instance, if true, of how the act of observation can change the object being observed. Although barter and trade were familiar concepts, land ownership, territorial boundaries and commerical exchange solely for the purpose of profit were not. Most crucially, trade with Euro-Americans altered how natives procured their own food and regulated their days, for satisfying the desires of an external market now came to seem as necessary as feeding one's own clan or hunting group. Native men spent more time harvesting furs or sealskins to sell to the whites, and native women devoted more of their labour to sewing garments and gear for them. In exchange, the natives obtained iron saws and knives, tin pots and pans, needles, bolts of canvas and other useful items; less helpfully, they were provided with tobacco and alcohol. All too often, harmful consequences followed. Certain food-gathering skills atrophied easily if ignored in favour of fur-hunting, but were not so easily relearned once the supply of furs dried up and the whites who wanted them departed. In addition, natives found themselves wholly reliant on white traders for an array of items that they had come to crave or to need.

To create such conditions of reliance was a matter of policy in Canada's west, where, at the start of the century, economic life still centred on fur, and where the Hudson's Bay Company exercised a sprawling custodianship over Rupert's Land, the amorphous North-Western Territory, and the recently defined Columbia District, or Oregon Country, which the British and Americans agreed between 1818 and the 1840s to occupy jointly. In 1821, the Bay absorbed the North West Company, its longtime rival in these parts, in a merger ordered by the British government. Immediately, George Simpson, head of the HBC's Northern Department and, after 1826, the Company's governor, used the leverage afforded by the new monopoly in all the predictable ways: he slashed payroll, fired staff and, with no NWC to bid against him, dramatically raised the prices of the goods sold to the natives in exchange for furs. He sought moreover to keep them in thrall to the Bay as the sole source of the material provisions they needed to survive, an aim he described to his deputy governor in 1822:

> I have made it my study to examine the nature and character of the Indians and however repugnant it may be to our feelings, I am convinced they must be ruled with a rod of iron, to bring and keep them in a proper state of subordination, and the most certain way to effect this is by letting them feel their dependence on us.[15]

It was precisely in the northern woods and the Barren Grounds, where food was hardest to come by, that this would be easiest, Simpson noted.

Colonial presence spread unevenly throughout Canada's west, but was strongest along the line of the 2,600-mile York Factory Express, or the 'Communication', which ran through Rupert's Land and linked the western shore of Hudson Bay to the HBC's Pacific headquarters in Fort Vancouver – now Vancouver, Washington, on the north bank of the Columbia River – via Lake Winnipeg, the North Saskatchewan River and Edmonton. Canadians also moved up the Pacific shore with relative ease, beyond Vancouver Island to the Queen Charlotte Islands and Fort Simpson, established near present-day Prince Rupert in 1831. Beyond that, at 54°40′N, the coast belonged to Russian Alaska, as determined by the Anglo-Russian Convention of 1825. American designs on this territory had to be countered until the Oregon Treaty of 1846 set a permanent U.S.–Canadian boundary at the 49th parallel. At times warring with them, at times trading with them, and in both cases reducing their numbers through the spread of disease – by 75 to 80 per cent, according to some estimates – the British brought coastal First Nations like the Nootka (Nuu'chah'nulth), Kwakiutl (Kwakwaka'wakw), Tsimshian and Haida under their authority. The Haida, with their strong fortresses and formidable war canoes, proved the fiercest foes.

During this half-century, the outsiders' hold was most tenuous in the enormous North-Western Territory that stretched from the Alaskan border, formed by the 141st meridian, to Boothia and Melville peninsulas. The colonial order's frailty here stemmed largely from geographical ignorance, and makes clear why the surveys carried out by Franklin, Rae and McClintock along the Mackenzie and Coppermine basins and in the Barren Grounds were so desperately needed. Roughly 100,000 First Nations people, mostly Athabaskan-speakers like the Tutchone, Han, Hare, Gwich'in, Dogrib (Tlicho), Tagish and Chipewyan, along with perhaps 10,000 Inuit, lived in this region. Those farther to the east or at lower latitudes were already integrated into the HBC's economic network; the peoples of the Yukon and the Mackenzie Basin were more on its fringes until the 1840s, when agents of the Bay (bringing mumps and scarlet fever with them) put up outposts like Fort Yukon in eastern Alaska's Gwich'in lands and Fort Selkirk in Tutchone territory, at the juncture of the Yukon and Pelly rivers. The Inuit of central Canada's tundra and coastlines had little to do with the HBC, aside from indirect commerce via First Nations bands who traded with the Bay. Most natives in these lands enjoyed de facto autonomy until near the end of the 1800s, and by repeated raiding, the Tutchone even forced the closure of Fort Selkirk in 1852.

By the mid-1800s, the very nature of colonial authority in Canada was on the brink of change. As an institution, the HBC had grown in size and sophistication. Economically and politically, it was an anachronism. The coastal fur trade fizzled out after the 1820s, with the depletion of the area's sea otters, and the land-based commerce in fur, while still a going concern, was not flourishing as before. Efforts to diversify the Bay's activities yielded mixed results. In the new age of steam, there was a future in shipping, but coal-mining, attempted in the 1840s on Vancouver Island and up British Columbia's coast to Prince Rupert, with Kwakiutl miners providing most of the labour, proved unrewarding. Beyond that, Her Majesty's government had less patience now for the Company's headstrong ways or its narrow-minded focus on cost-effectiveness at the expense of broader diplomatic and political priorities. Britain's decision to grant Crown colony status to Vancouver Island in 1849 and to British Columbia in 1858 can be seen as a blow against the HBC, even if the Bay received a ten-year lease to develop the former and was permitted in 1859 to formalize its authority over the North-Western Territory. In 1857, the House of Commons acceded in principle to Canada's 'just and reasonable wishes' to annex Rupert's Land. How long this would have taken to occur on its own is difficult to guess, but the discovery of gold in the Fraser and Thompson river valleys, in 1858 and 1862 respectively, accelerated the process by making clear the economic value of the west and stimulating massive growth there.

And then there was the birth of Canada itself: on 1 July 1867, the provinces of Ontario, Quebec, New Brunswick and Nova Scotia were confederated into a dominion that, while not independent, was to enjoy self-government within the framework of the British Empire. In 1869, this new entity took possession of Rupert's Land from the HBC and the North-Western Territory directly from Britain, combining the latter and northern parts of the former to form the giant Northwest Territories. Title to Britain's high-Arctic domains, including the islands, would not be granted till later, while Newfoundland and Labrador rejected confederation, remaining a British colony until 1907 and then a separate dominion until 1949. Still, already in the 1860s, Canada, both geographically and politically, was taking shape as the 'True North' that Tennyson would name it in the peroration to Queen Victoria that ends his *Idylls of the King*.

In Fennoscandia, the nineteenth century began with a thorough political realignment. The Napoleonic wars detached Finland from Sweden, transferring it to Russia in 1808–9, placed Norway under the jurisdiction of the Swedish Crown in 1814, and left an amputated Denmark to fend for itself as punishment for having sided with the defeated Napoleon. But once these shocks were over, the 1800s proved a pacific time for Scandinavia and, compared with the century just past, a relatively prosperous one. Despite high levels of emigration to North America, population here tripled over the course of the century, the legacy of peace and potatoes, as historians of the region like to quip. These were also years of heightened national consciousness. As in other parts of Europe, the Romantic movement in Scandinavia sparked a patriotic interest in folklore and cultural heritage, as demonstrated by the rapturous receptions that greeted new editions of the Norse and Icelandic sagas or Elias Lönnrot's reconstruction of Finland's medieval epic, the *Kalevala*. This new ethnocentrism enabled some northern minorities, notably the Icelanders and Faeroese, as well as the Karelians, to preserve a cultural distinctiveness that might otherwise have been lost. But by fostering as well a stronger sense of what it meant to be 'Norwegian', 'Swedish' and 'Finnish', it put greater pressure than before on other groups, such as the Sami, to conform to the majority's ways.

The Arctic reaches of mainland Fennoscandia were by this stage thoroughly charted and incorporated into Sweden–Norway's and Russia's administrative structures. There was still more to know about them ethnographically and scientifically, but the proper targets for exploration in the classic sense were now Greenland, Svalbard and other islands, whether partly known or as yet unrevealed. Population expanded in regions like Nordland, Troms, Finnmark and Norrland, even if not at the same rate as down south, and the trades practised here grew in scale. As always, fishing for cod and herring off the northern coast was paramount, but also important were sealing and whaling, the chopping and packing of ice, which was used everywhere in Europe for cooling perishables until the advent of modern refrigeration, and the harvesting of trees, both for timber and paper. Past 60°N, the scale of mining remained limited. Production at Falun, Sweden's 'copper mountain', was beginning to slow, and while iron ore veined the Arctic hills of Swedish Norrland, it was too high in expensive-to-remove phosphorus and too remotely sited to be retrieved profitably. Small quantities of ore were taken from here in the early 1800s, dug up in the summer and sledded out in the winter, but mining on a large scale came later. The same was true of the coal in Spitsbergen, where, for now, sealers scratched out just enough of the mineral to warm their shore-based camps. Industrialization began late in Scandinavia, and few signs of it appeared anywhere in the North until the second half of the century. The one exception was in forestry, especially in the Norrland provinces of Sweden, where steam-powered sawmills went into operation as early as the 1850s.

Social conditions varied as Scandinavia's north became more settled. Norway chartered its Arctic ports of Bodø and Tromsø as cities in 1838, and a greater quantity of villages, farmsteads and fishing ports appeared, although many of these were isolated pockets surrounded by wilderness. Famine was no longer the scourge it had been in the seventeenth and eighteenth centuries, but poverty and low levels of development were typical, and northern Norway and Sweden were plagued by a curiously high incidence of leprosy. The Finnish north was most backward of all, and many of its people continued to emigrate to Norway, enlarging the population of Kvens, or minority Finns, there.

Such prevailing bleakness may explain the special susceptibility of northern districts and Sami communities to the waves of charismatic religious evangelism that, much to the displeasure of the state-sponsored Lutheran churches, swept through Norway, Sweden and Finland in the early 1800s, starting with the ministry of the Norwegian Hans Hauge and continuing with those of Finland's Paavo Ruotsalainen and the internationally known half-Sami scholar Lars Levi Læstadius. In Lapland, Christianization of the Sami was all but total by the early 1800s, with shamanism practiced only in secret or in the most remote locales. More Sami adopted sedentary lifestyles, while some, still a minority, went south, assimilating and intermarrying into Swedish, Norwegian, or Finnish society. In all Scandinavian countries, Sami children attending school were forbidden to use their native tongues, although this policy was enforced most stringently in Norway. Sami who continued to herd reindeer in the far north often lived trans-nationally, paying heed to their animals' pasturing needs rather than to borderlines or checkpoints. Their passage between Norway and Sweden, or in and out of Russian Finland, often went unobstructed. Not always, though, and when it was blocked, trouble ensued, as in the Kautokeino revolt that broke out during the 1852 closure of the Finnish–Norwegian border. Two Norwegians were killed during this disturbance, and the Sami ringleaders were put on trial and beheaded.

The island colonies – Iceland, the Faeroes and Greenland – went to Denmark after the Dano-Norwegian dissolution. The first two trended towards the awakening of nationalist sentiment and greater political representation. A cadre of philologists saved the Faeroese language from extinction between the 1770s and the 1850s, and literary politics played an even more formative role in Iceland's public life. Poets like Bjarni Thorarensen, with his anthemic 'Ancient Iceland', stirred up national pride, while the scholar and activist Jón Sigurdsson used the journal *New Society* to issue open calls for autonomy. Iceland's general assembly, the Althing, which had been disbanded in 1799, was restored in 1843–4, and when Frederik VII granted Denmark its June Constitution in 1849, both the Faeroes and Iceland were allowed representation in the new Danish Parliament. Most restrictions on Icelandic and Faeroese trade were removed in the 1850s.

Denmark's relations with Greenland, where Europeans comprised only a sliver of the population, were more paternal, but its colonial method is widely regarded as the most enlightened in the circumpolar world. This was largely the doing of Henrik Rink, who surveyed North Greenland's Umanaq District between 1848 and 1851, and was asked in 1852 to serve on a royal commission charged with reforming Denmark's Greenland policy. The first half of the century had given cause for concern, with whalers and explorers from other countries molesting natives or violating the Crown monopoly on trade, especially in the northwest, and with famines breaking out in years when seal-hunting went poorly. Rink, who managed the Julianehåb and Godthåb districts and went on to become royal director of South Greenland, understood that only native skills and labour kept the colony economically viable. 'From a commercial point of view', he wrote, 'Greenland without Eskimo inhabitants would be a worthless possession.'[16] He also admired the natives and sympathized with how drastically the presence of outsiders had upended their way of life, an attitude evident in all of his publications, including his famous if dryly titled paper from 1862, 'Why Greenlanders and Similar People Who Live by Hunting Decline Materially through Contact with Europeans'. To prevent private traders from forcing unfair terms of exchange on the natives, or from overharvesting the fish, seals and whales on which they depended, Rink argued successfully for the continuation of the royal trade monopoly. Hand-in-hand with the Danish Ministry for Public Worship, and with help from Moravian missionaries, he set up schools. Above all, he strove to put native Greenlanders in as many positions of authority as possible. Municipal councils and Boards of Governors, established in 1862–3, conducted their business in the Inuit languages as well as in Danish, and representatives elected by the natives had a vote in how poor relief was distributed, how quarrels were resolved within the community and on which public improvements money was spent.

Russia's northerners were not so fortunate. Like his grandmother Catherine the Great, Alexander I came to the throne with reformist ambitions but hardened into a political conservative, and his brother and successor, Nicholas I, was a reactionary by nature. Alexander's most able administrator, Mikhail Speransky, served a turn as Siberia's governor-general and issued the well-intentioned 1822 Statute for the Governance of Non-Russian Peoples – hailed by some as a major humanization of native policy, but seen by most as disappointing in practice. Meant to safeguard the territory and folkways of native peoples, the Statute, as if classifying botanical specimens instead of human beings, tidily sorted all minority groups into one of three categories – 'settled', 'nomadic' (having a predictable route of migration) and 'wandering' (having no fixed pattern of movement) – with the majority of Siberia's 'small peoples' assigned to the third. Most northern and Siberian natives were exempted from the burden of military service, but, contrary to Speransky's original wishes, their *yasak* obligations rose steeply, and the few groups who fell into the 'settled' category, such as the Khanty and Mansi, had to pay the universally hated poll tax as well. 'Wanderers' were sometimes placed under the administrative authority of 'settled' neighbours, an idea that seemed innocent enough to office-bound bureaucrats, but the effect of which was often to leave weaker groups at the mercy of traditional enemies.

Such was the case with the Ob Nentsy, who now found themselves lorded over by the Khanty, with whom they had a long history of mutual detestation. Although the Nentsy proved unusually unlucky, their troubles illustrate the many ills that befell native Siberians in the early 1800s. Not only did the Nentsy rankle under their old foes' political authority, but they, like other reindeer-herders in the Urals and western Siberia, were economically marginalized by the Komi, who dominated the Russian market for reindeer meat and skins by moving from herding to large-scale reindeer farming. To add to the Nentsy's discontent, Orthodox missionaries descended on their most holy site, Vaigach Island, in the mid-1820s, burning or toppling more than 400 idols. Small wonder that many Nentsy joined the 1825 insurrection led by Vavlo Nenyang, who, in addition to fighting the Russians, stole reindeer from the wealthy and, in Robin Hood style, gave them to the poor. Although captured and briefly imprisoned, Nenyang fought on till 1839, when he was defeated for good and sentenced to hard labour in eastern Siberia. Native hardships were typically less dramatic than this, although no less serious. Racial prejudice ran rampant, and debt bondage became more common as natives took out high-interest loans to pay the *yasak* or their taxes. Influenza, leprosy and syphilis, imported by immigrants from the West, wielded the scythe that smallpox and typhus once had. Although Siberia's native population grew from 200,000 to 800,000 between 1700 and 1899, that growth overwhelmingly favoured a small set of peoples: the Chukchi, whose autonomy cut down their exposure to Russian diseases, the Yakut, and the Khanty and Mansi. Most northern groups were left with less impressive, if not negative, growth.

By contrast, the number of Europeans in Siberia rose from 900,000 in 1799 to just under 3 million in 1854, although much of this growth was concentrated in the south. The Great Siberian Tract, leading from Moscow to the Chinese border, was completed in the mid-1800s, bringing peasants, Cossacks and hunters to the frontier in unprecedented numbers. The discovery of gold in eastern Siberia, starting in the 1820s, encouraged more settlement; one of the country's richest goldfields opened in the Lena basin in the early 1860s, and the search for yet more gold gradually drew the Russians high into the Arctic northeast. The final reason for Siberia's population boom was the grimmest: the state's growing willingness to use the region as 'the bottom of the sack', as the foreign minister Karl von Nesselrode phrased it, for unwanted members of society. Criminals had been banished here since the mid-1600s, but it was under Catherine the Great and afterwards that this became a standard way to dispose of political opponents and dissident intellectuals. Enlightenment liberals who complained about Catherine's late-blooming conservatism, the Decembrist officers who rose against Nicholas I in 1825, the Polish rebels of the 1830s, and left-leaning university students, including a young Fyodor Dostoevsky: all these and others found themselves sent eastward, sometimes to perform hard labour at the side of common criminals. In the 1820s, approximately 2,000 souls per year were exiled to Siberia – an average that grew frightfully higher as the decades passed.

On the Pacific shores, the Russians steadily expanded their presence. Chukotka remained closed to them, except for trading posts in the Anadyr delta, but Petropavlovsk in Kamchatka, a vital link in the chain of communications between Yakutsk and Okhotsk on the mainland and Russia's New World colonies, gained town status in 1812 and continued to grow. Having encroached on Sakhalin since the 1780s, the Russians took it over in 1853, although they allowed the Japanese to occupy it jointly until the 1870s. As part of the same eastward thrust, Nikolai Muraviev, governor-general of Siberia, secured the annexation of the Amur basin, a strategically crucial territory to which Qing China had denied Russia access since the Nerchinsk agreement of 1689. The Sino-Russian Treaty of Aigun allowed Russia to build the new city of Khabarovsk in 1858, at the juncture of the Amur and Ussuri rivers, and the mighty Pacific port of Vladivostok in 1859.

Triumphs on the Alaskan side of the ocean proved more fleeting, although Russia left a heavy imprint there. As manager of the Russian-American Company, Alexander Baranov built solidly on the foundation that Shelikhov and Rezanov had laid during the 1780s and 1790s. He continued to harvest fur seals from the Pribilof Islands, where 2.5 million of the animals would be killed by 1820. From existing bases in the Aleutians and on Kodiak Island, he spread RAC authority into Alaska proper by building outposts near Glacier Bay and other points along the southern coast. Though it required a bloody struggle between 1802 and 1804 against the Tlingit, he founded a new capital, Novo-Arkhangelsk, atop the Tlingit settlement of Sitka in the Alexander Archipelago. It was also Baranov who sent expeditions south to stake claims on the Columbia River and in northern California, where he hoped not only to find sea otters and sea lions, but to build an agricultural base capable of supporting the Alaska colony. The Columbia District was too crowded already by agents of the HBC and John Jacob Astor's Pacific Fur Company, but Baranov had better luck in California, laying hold of the Farallon Islands and, in 1812, building Fort Ross, in what is now Sonoma County. Under Baranov's watch, the RAC brought in 30 million roubles' worth of profits. He retired in 1817, but died during the voyage home, just shy of his 72nd birthday. He was buried at sea in the Indian Ocean.

In 1818, the Russian government assumed direct control over the RAC. Baranov's successors, including the explorer Ferdinand Wrangel, emulated his methods, particularly the policy of forcing thousands of Aleuts to labour far from their homes and to fight the Tlingit, Haida, Tsimshian and Chugach. Wrangel oversaw the establishment of RAC enclaves up the Yukon River and on Alaska's west coast, particularly St Michael in Norton Sound, and he traded with the natives during periods of peace. Russification in another mode was carried out by the Orthodox Church, whose priests first arrived in the Aleutians and on Kodiak in the 1790s. As in Siberia, the quality and charitability of the clergy varied, but there were enough skilled doctors and winning teachers to establish the Church firmly in the New World. The most dynamic of these was Ivan Veniaminov, the 'Apostle of Alaska', who came to Unalaska in 1824 and completed an ethnographic study of the Aleuts, whom he converted with great success. Moving on to Sitka, he championed education and extended his ministry to the Tlingit; in 1840, he became the first Bishop of Kamchatka and Alaska, taking the name Innocent. Thanks to Veniaminov's influence and Wrangel's leadership, Sitka blossomed into what some called 'the Paris of the Pacific'. By the 1840s, the colony's population was about double what it had been under Baranov.

Translated into raw numbers, though, this was paltry growth: an increase from 500 Russians to a mere 1,000 or so, plus a handful of Swedish and Finnish employees. Such weakness left the Company on the horns of a dilemma. As its hunting and sealing grounds neared exhaustion, it lacked the wherewithal to bring new ones under its control. Tlingit uprisings kept Sitka under periodic states of siege. The Russians made little headway against the Haida to Sitka's north or the Tsimshian to its west, and only in a few places, primarily along the Yukon and Kuskokwim valleys, did they gain access to the mainland interior. The colony was grossly overextended – 1,200 miles separated Sitka from St Paul's Harbor in the Pribilofs, with another 3,000 miles stretching between St Paul's and Kamchatka – and it found itself in diplomatically awkward positions as well. Even after the Anglo-Russian Convention of 1825, HBC agents continued to cross the border illegally, and Russia's isolated California possessions were bound to be swallowed up by America or Canada eventually. In 1841, after long negotiations with George Simpson of the HBC to resolve boundary disagreements and ensure that the RAC could purchase food from the Bay in the future, Wrangel sold Fort Ross for $30,000. This, however, still left the RAC powerless to stop British, Canadian and especially U.S. mariners and merchants from bypassing it and conducting their own business in Alaska and the Bering waters. Drawn to the Bering and Beaufort seas in the 1840s by the prospect of whale-hunting, these foreigners became part of the trade network that moved goods to and fro among the natives of Yukon, Alaska, Chukotka and the islands.

Thus outflanked, and with support from St Petersburg dwindling, the RAC entered into decline during the 1850s and '60s. Native revolts and brushfire wars drained its resources. Having slaughtered 4 million fur seals on the Alaskan mainland since 1800, its hunters now strained to find enough furs to turn a profit. Finally, with Wrangel loudly protesting every step of the way, Russia made preparations to sell Alaska to the United States, which, thanks to lobbying by Secretary of State William Seward, was ready to buy it. The Alaska Purchase of March 1867 conferred ownership of Alaska itself to the United States for the price of $7.2 million, or roughly 2 cents an acre, while the assets of the RAC went to the San Francisco-based Hutchinson, Kohl & Company. The formal transfer of sovereignty took place in October, and with Canada having gained dominion status that summer, the North American Arctic had been altogether politically transformed.

Bonanzas and Blight: Territorialism in the Arctic from Mid-century to 1914

'Because men, groping in the Arctic darkness, had found a yellow metal', the opening lines of Jack London's *The Call of the Wild* tell us, 'thousands of men were rushing into the Northland'.[17] It was the Klondike gold rush London spoke of – but with only minor alteration, he could have been describing the bonanza fever that, in the late 1800s and early 1900s, brought multitudes of outsiders to many places in the far north: to Spitsbergen for coal, to Sweden's Kiruna mines for iron, to eastern Siberia for gold, and to the seas and shoals, where new technologies placed larger quantities of fish, seals and whales within easy reach. As they gained more knowledge of the Arctic and how to travel there, Europeans and Americans desired it all the more as an economic asset.

In this age of new imperialism and *Realpolitik*, they desired it for other reasons as well. Henri Lefebvre has proposed that a chief characteristic of modern states is their aspiration to centralize totally their control over geographic space; indeed, few in Europe or North America saw territorial self-aggrandizement as anything but an unquestioned good.[18] The strategic imperatives of great-power rivalry seemed to require it. Feelings of racial superiority, whether fed by the white-man's-burden impulse to 'civilize' the darker-skinned or by a harder-edged Social Darwinism, seemed to justify it. National pride stridently demanded it. In what were becoming today's Arctic nations, the compulsion to make the Arctic 'theirs' was felt more fervently than before.

By the end of the 1860s, the young Dominion of Canada found itself the legatee of huge Arctic estates, with Rupert's Land purchased from the Hudson's Bay Company and the North-Western Territory bequeathed to it by the British Crown. In 1880, Britain would hand over the rest of its high-Arctic holdings, which consisted of the islands and lengthy portions of Canada's northern coast. Also in the 1860s, the United States obtained its own Arctic domain in Alaska. The two countries coexisted civilly enough as northern neighbours, but not without tension, for the Alaska–Yukon and Alaska–British Columbia borders proved more difficult to settle than either government had supposed, and some Americans were of the opinion that the u.s. deserved as much control over the Arctic as it could lay hold of. Among these was the explorer Robert Peary, who brashly proclaimed that 'nothing can stop the ultimate destiny of this country to occupy that portion of the Western Hemisphere lying between the Panama Canal and the North Pole!'[19]

Luckily for Canadian–u.s. relations, only a few Americans, and none in a position of authority, shared quite the same vehemence as Peary. But it was true, as Canada would learn on several occasions, that sovereignty had to be asserted, not taken for granted, in such remote and poorly charted places.

In Canada's eastern Arctic – and in Newfoundland, which had opted out of confederation – fishing, sealing, walrus-hunting (which killed up to 60,000 walruses per year between 1865 and 1873) and whaling continued out of Labrador and Hudson Bay up to Davis Strait and the archipelago. After 1860, motor-driven and metal-hulled vessels, which manoeuvred more easily in the ice and better resisted its pressure, were gradually phased in. Beyond a certain latitude, the white presence was transient, but nonetheless influential: leaving aside the environmental impact of their hunting activities, whites took kills from the natives and, by whetting an appetite for their trade goods, eroded the natives' self-sufficiency as hunters. Among Inuit groups with the shortest histories of outside contact, Euro-American diseases still wreaked epidemic havoc. As late as 1902, the tiny Sadlermiut nation of Southampton Island, in north Hudson Bay, was snuffed out by a single case of what may have been influenza (although some say typhus or typhoid), contracted from the crew of a Scottish whaler. This era also saw the widespread appearance of measles, tuberculosis and polio. Administratively, Canada's First Nations people, both in the east and west, were subject to the Indian Act of 1876, placing them under parliamentary jurisdiction and obligating the Superintendent-General of Indian Affairs to see to their assimilation, protection and well-being. The Act's terms did not apply to the Inuit, and the government assumed no formal responsibility for them until the 1930s.

In the Canadian west, statebuilding in the 1870s and '80s focused principally on the lower latitudes, and most of all on the construction of a continental railroad, extended to the west coast by the new Canadian Pacific Railway. During the 1870s, Ottawa acquired ownership of the lands through which the railroad was to run by negotiating the first seven of Canada's 'numbered' treaties, which, in exchange for title, alloted reserves to the local First Nations, guaranteed traditional hunting and fishing rights, and promised to provide medical care, social services and education. It was in connection with this last assurance that the government, in 1883–4, began making school attendance compulsory for First Nations children in the west and in the territories – a policy extended in later years to the far north. Preoccupied with developing this southern corridor, the government spared little attention for the North and, in fact, deliberately shied away from entanglements with natives living above the 60th parallel. 'In that far northern country', the office of the Superintendent-General recommended, 'Indian Affairs should be administered as the needs of the case suggest', and not by treaty.[20] Neglect of the region was pronounced enough that a number of central Canada's Inuit groups remained unknown to southerners, or known to them only by rumour, until the 1890s – when the geologist Joseph Burr Tyrrell encountered the Ihalmiut, the Barren Grounds' 'people from beyond' – or the great ethnographic expeditions of the early 1900s. Whites in the Mackenzie or Yukon basins were more likely to be there for profit than for official reasons, although the North-West Mounted Police (NWMP), created in 1873–4 to patrol the prairie provinces, began to enforce Crown law on the northern frontier. Also, until proper surveys were completed in the 1880s, outsiders were as likely to be American as Canadian, with posts like Fort Reliance and Fort Eagle founded by the Alaska Commercial Company along the Yukon's east bank in the mid-1870s. Canada put up its own outposts in the 1880s. These included Forty Mile, home to one of the NWMP's first northern stations, and Rampart House on the Porcupine River, though the latter had to be moved 30 miles east in 1889–90 when improved maps revealed it to be on the wrong side of the Alaskan border.

For all the jokes they made about 'Seward's Folly', the Americans lost little time establishing themselves in Alaska. Outfits like the Alaska Commerical Company – the former Hutchinson, Kohl & Company, purchaser of the RAC's property in 1867 – led the way, as did sealers and whalers, many of them now using steamships or ships with sail and auxiliary steam. Sitka and St Michael on the west coast, along with Seward and the harbours of Kodiak Island, still served as Alaska's chief ports, with Juneau added to them in 1880. Four million fur seals were taken from Alaska and the Pribilofs between 1870 and 1911, when an international ban on hunting them went into effect – the first wildlife-protection treaty in world history. During the 1860s and '70s, an estimated 200,000 to 300,000 Pacific walruses were slaughtered in the Bering and Beaufort seas, and whalers, as in other waters at this time, operated on a new industrial scale. Americans predominated in the North Pacific, although they competed for kills with Canadians, Japanese and Norwegians. Russian vessels, more active in the Sea of Okhotsk near Japan, were underrepresented this far north. Some outsiders came to Alaska for reasons unrelated to commerce. Catholic and Protestant missionaries set up schools, provided medical care and tried to win the natives over from their shamanistic faiths or from Russian Orthodoxy. As part of the American contribution to the International Polar Year in 1882–3, the U.S. Signal Corps erected a weather station on the territory's northernmost tip, Point Barrow, an important site of interaction ever since between American scientific and naval personnel and the native Inupiat. In 1879, the environmentalist John Muir made the first of several trips to Glacier Bay and the Alexander Archipelago, which he pronounced 'the very paradise of the poets, the abode of the blessed'.[21] Muir's eloquent paeans to Alaska's natural beauty helped stimulate the later impulse to place large parts of it, beginning with Mount McKinley (Denali) and Glacier Bay, under the protection of the young National Parks Service.

Because the U.S. purchased Alaska outright and so late, its relationship with the indigenous population, which consisted of Eskimos, Aleuts and over a dozen Native American tribes, differed fundamentally from those that had evolved between Washington and the Native Americans of the Lower 48. There, several hundred treaties, however imperfectly they might be observed, confirmed U.S. authority over native groups, placed them onto reservations, and spelled out the obligations owed them by the Bureau of Indian Affairs (BIA). In Alaska, only with the Organic Act of 1884 did the federal government assume formal responsibility for indigenous Alaskans, including the obligation to educate their children, which it did by establishing English-only day schools, run directly by the BIA or by BIA-approved missionaries. Left unanswered for the time being were the questions of whether native Alaskans, who were not assigned to reservations, had any collective right to traditional lands, and whether any legal or administrative distinction should be made between 'Indians' and 'Eskimos', as was done in Canada.

Unofficially, America had already inserted itself into the pan-Bering economy that linked Chukchi, Koryak and Siberian Eskimos with the Aleuts, the natives of mainland Alaska and even the First Nations and Inuit of the Yukon and Mackenzie river basins. In an irony not much to the tsars' liking, the U.S. exercised more economic influence over northeast Siberia during this half-century than Russia did – to the point that St Petersburg, simply to profit in some way from land that otherwise did it no good, leased harbourage in the Commander Islands to the Americans and, from 1902 to 1912, granted them gold-, iron- and graphite-mining concessions in Chukotka. On both sides of the Bering, trade with the natives followed a predictable pattern, with the whites accepting fur, ivory and meat from whales, walruses and caribou in exchange for cloth, metal tools, firearms and indulgences like sugar, coffee, tobacco and alcohol. The natives themselves gathered annually for large summer trade fairs, the grandest of which were held at Sheshalik, on Kotzebue Sound; Kaktovik, located off the north coast on Barter Island; and Nigliq, in the western part of the Colville River delta. Fairs such as these were the occasion for inter-community dispute resolution, romantic courtship and athletic competitions.

For natives and newcomers both, it was the 1890s – the years of the Klondike gold rush – that revolutionized the structures of life in Alaska and northwest Canada. In the summer of 1896, the Tagish prospector Skookum Jim Mason struck it rich near the juncture of the Yukon and Klondike rivers, and by the following July, thousands of would-be miners were stampeding to the new boomtown of Dawson City, at the Klondike's mouth. They arrived one of three ways: via an all-Canadian route from Edmonton and up the Pelly River; by sea to St Michael, then 1,500 miles eastward along the Yukon; and, most commonly, by boat to Dyea or Skagway in southeastern Alaska, up from the tidewater through the rugged Chilkoot Pass, and finally to Dawson after almost 600 miles overland or by river raft. By 1898, the non-native population of the Klondike region had ballooned to 40,000, and the 'strange things done under the midnight sun' by these seekers 'who moiled for gold' were immortalized by Jack London and the English-born Robert Service, who, a clerk in the Whitehorse and Dawson branches of the Canadian Bank of Commerce, reinvented himself as the bard of the Yukon with poems like 'The Shooting of Dan McGrew' and 'The Cremation of Sam McGee'. No sooner did Dawson, with its bordellos and gambling halls, peak as a frontier entrepot than new bonanzas drew miners else-where. The 'three lucky Swedes' of Anvil Creek touched off western Alaska's Nome gold rush in 1898. Deposits were uncovered that same year in the Atlin region of northwest British Columbia, and in 1902 near present-day Fairbanks. In 1905, prospectors swarmed over the Kantishna Hills, near Mount McKinley. In all these places and others, the gold fever eventually passed, but large white populations were now in the North to stay.

The discovery of gold did not by itself Americanize Alaska or Canadianize the Northwest Territories, but it catalysed those processes. The effects on native life of such a sudden influx of outsiders includ-ed overcrowding, economic trespass and new outbreaks of measles, tuberculosis and smallpox. The Athabaskan Han, for example, had their grayling and salmon fishing grounds compromised by the expansion of the Forty Mile post and entered into a long demographic decline; their language is all but extinct today. Neither Nome nor Dawson became a polar Pittsburgh or Manchester, but the northern ecosystem still had to absorb the extra pressure of new trails, mines, towns and railways, starting in 1900 with the White Pass and Yukon line running out of Skagway and, in 1905, the Tanana Mines Railroad near Fairbanks, in the interior. In 1899, the Richardson Highway connected Fairbanks with the ice-free port of Valdez, on Prince William Sound at the foot of the Chugach Mountains. Most of all, the gold strikes persuaded Ottawa and Washington to shore up their countries' official presence in the North, and to revisit the question of boundaries. In 1898, Canada carved a new Yukon Territory out of the existing Northwest Territories. Even before that, it had strengthened its NWMP detachments and bulked up its military muscle with a 200-man Yukon Field Force. Both bodies curbed violence, protected property and discouraged the usual sorts of frontier mayhem. The police enforced customs regulations and denied entry into the Klondike to any party unable to prove that it was carrying at least six months' worth of food.

This was not just about upholding Canada's laws; it was to ensure that the territory itself remained Canadian. Both Canada and the U.S. observed the Alaskan–Canadian boundary as laid down by the Anglo-Russian convention of 1825, but the convention's language was vague in places, and the mapmaking from that day imprecise. Border squabbles in the 1870s and '80s were settled without too much ire as both neighbours agreed to commission new surveys and adjust their maps. The Klondike, however, was such a rich and emotion-stirring prize that disputes there could not be resolved so easily. After U.S. mobs forced the NWMP customhouse near Skagway to lower the Canadian flag, Ottawa feared a vigilante annexation that might never be reversed. Soon, both sides were fortifying high points along the Chilkoot and White passes, in some places with Gatling guns, and wrangling over every square inch of borderline. Cooler heads averted an actual shooting war, but it took from 1898 to 1903 for diplomats to agree on the exact placement of the boundary – and even then, resentful Canadians believed that Washington had gotten the better end of the deal because of Teddy Roosevelt's thinly veiled threats to resort to military force if the terms were not to his liking. This episode, combined with the alarmingly solid presence of foreign whalers and U.S. and Scandinavian explorers in the

Canadian archipelago, generated anxiety in Ottawa that, as Joseph Burr Tyrrell warned, 'through long continued acquiescence, these foreigners may be establishing rights [in the Canadian north] whilst ours are being allowed to lapse.'[22] In response, the government enlarged the NWMP presence in the western Arctic, particularly around Herschel Island (Qikiqtaruk) and Fort McPherson in the Mackenzie Valley. It purchased its first icebreakers, and it backed the 1903 voyage of the *Neptune* and the maritime patrols led by Joseph-Elzéar Bernier between 1906 and 1911. Described below, these had as their main objective the assertion of Canadian sovereignty over islands in the eastern Arctic, which Canada took care to claim officially and ostentatiously during these years. For its part, America bound Alaska more formally to the Union by granting it territorial status in 1912.

Scandinavia's states had their own sovereignty issues to iron out during the late 1800s. The liberalization of Danish policy towards Iceland and the Faeroes continued, with partial home rule extended to the former in 1874, followed by full home rule in 1903, and with both colonies sending representatives to the parliament in Copenhagen. Reykjavík became Iceland's chief city during this time, with the colony's first university founded there in 1911. Greenland remained under the protectionist regime set into place by the Danes during the 1850s and '60s, and for the most part did well under it – although the natives, for all their involvement in local government, were not afforded parliamentary representation. Finland, now a grand duchy under Russian rule, had no history as an independent nation to pine for. For most of the century, a majority of Finns remained quiescent, due to the high degree of autonomy afforded them by Russian authorities. In the later decades, as the arch-conservative Alexander III unleashed campaigns of Russification, Finnish nationalism gained in potency, emerging as a destabilizing force by the 1890s.

Even more friction arose between Sweden and Norway, with the latter chafing under the terms of the two countries' union. Starting in 1885, a series of constitutional crises, each accompanied by venomous quarreling, erupted over the question of whether Sweden, the union's dominant partner, was conducting foreign policy too unilaterally. By 1895, there was open talk in Norway of armed secession. In the end, the separation was engineered peacefully by means of the Karlstad Conventions of September 1905 and, in the person of Haakon VII, Norway crowned its first king since the 1300s. Lending a powerful voice to the cause of Norwegian independence, but also urging non-violence as a way of achieving it, was the most statesmanlike of polar explorers, Fridtjof Nansen, internationally respected by this point for his scholarly achievements and his monumental voyage in the *Fram*. Norway's territorial integrity was guaranteed by the international community in 1907, but it would be disappointed now and later by its inability to persuade the rest of the world of its right to the Iceland and Greenland colonies, which remained in Denmark's hands.

Growth and industry came to Scandinavia's northern provinces during these decades, but not full modernization. As late as the early 1900s, the region continued to be seen in the public mind as wild and underdeveloped – although opinion was split as to whether this was its virtue or its failing. In a neo-Romantic vein, numerous artists and authors idealized the northern landscape as transcendentally pristine or as embodying heroic qualities from the medieval or mythic past; one perceives strains of both in the music of Grieg and Sibelius, and in the canvases of painters like Finland's Akseli Gallen-Kallela. On the other hand, the playwright August Strindberg made no secret of the fact that he considered northern Sweden 'a prison of winter darkness', and the novelist Knut Hamsun unflinchingly depicted the squalor and poverty that prevailed in the lonely farmsteads and wind-blasted fishing villages of Norway's northern counties.[23]

Forestry, the first sector of the northern economy to have been industrialized, continued to mechanize, with Norway and Russian Finland labouring to catch up with Sweden. In fishing, sealing and especially whaling, Scandinavian fleets led the world in the transition to new technologies, rapidly adopting steam-powered vessels, then petroleum-driven ships and small motorboats. The harpoon gun, complete with explosive-tipped harpoons, was introduced in 1869–70 by Svend Foyn of Norway, exponentially magnifying the killing power of whaling vessels. The debut of the factory ship, with which the Norwegians experimented in the early 1910s, made the harvesting of whales, including the largest species, more brutally efficient. On Spitsbergen and Svalbard's other islands, Norwegian hunters developed their own embryonic industry, taking seals and trapping Arctic foxes in greater volume and, with tripwires specially designed to trigger gun blasts, killing large numbers of polar bears – an average of 400 per year by the 1890s.

The later 1800s also witnessed the expansion of mining throughout the Scandinavian north. Sweden led the way as always, still extracting copper from the Falun complex and now embarking on an ambitious effort to access the barely tapped reserves of iron ore above the Arctic

Circle, near Malmberget, Kiirunavaara and Luossavaara. Thanks to the Gilchrist-Thomas process, which, after 1878, allowed for the easy separation of phosphorus from iron ore, it no longer seemed unrealistic to expect profits from mining in Sweden's far north. In the 1880s, plans went into effect to link new excavations with a railroad that was to run from Luleå, on Sweden's Gulf of Bothnia coast, to a new port in western Norway: Narvik, which could be counted on to remain ice-free all year, despite sitting north of the 68th parallel. The project required almost two decades and the formation of LKAB, one of Sweden's most powerful corporations, to realize. Malmberget began operations in 1888, but the crowning achievements were the opening of Kiirunavaara's giant Kiruna mine in 1900 and the 1902 completion of the Luleå–Narvik line. Kiruna's labour force topped 7,400 by 1910, and more than a billion tons of iron ore would be excavated there over the next century. In Russian Finland, deposits of nickel were discovered near Pechenga, or Petsamo, on the Barents Sea. On Spitsbergen, the new treasure was coal, first mined commercially in 1899, by Norway's Søren Zachariassen. Others followed quickly, including a British firm and the Arctic Coal Company run by the American John Longyear, who arrived in 1901 and built the still-active Isfjorden harbour of Longyearbyen, at 78°N. Despite Norway's insistence on territorial sovereignty, other countries, including Sweden and Russia, took part in exploiting Spitsbergen economically after the First World War. Coal was available on Greenland as well, but not so plentifully. The Danes found more use for the island's graphite deposits, and even more for its cryolite, a rare substance that facilitates the processing of bauxite into aluminum and also served as a dyeing agent.

In Russia, two masterworks of landscape painting from the late 1800s evoke a pair of impressions, equally melancholy but deeply contrasting, popularly held about the country's northern frontier. Ivan Shishkin's *In the Wild North* (1891), celebrating the Mikhail Lermontov poem of the same name, presents a winter scene of ethereal but heartbreaking beauty. Against a dusky backdrop of slate-blue sky and dark forest, a snow-mantled pine stands on a high clifftop, eternally untroubled – but eternally alone. To those unfamiliar with its subject material, *The Vladimirka Road*, painted a year later by Isaak Levitan, seems completely unrelated to the North. It depicts instead a bare dirt path, stretching through grassy fields to the vanishing point under grey clouds overhead. To any Russian viewer, though, the title alone would have called to mind a more dreadful face of the North, for this was the route to Siberia, the Via Dolorosa leading recently sentenced exiles to the frozen Golgotha that awaited them.

During the tsarist era's last decades, Russia dominated Siberia as never before, flooding it with a non-native population of 8 million by 1911 and, between 1891 and 1903, building the planet's longest railway, the Trans-Siberian, to span it. Little of this energy, however, and few resources, were dedicated to exploring or developing Siberia's north, where the Russians became relatively inactive after their sale of Alaska to the United States. Expansion continued in Russia's northwest, along the White and Barents sea coasts. During the 1870s, several hundred Nentsy were transplanted from the mainland to Novaya Zemlya to shore up Russia's claims to sovereignty there. As for Arctic lands east of the Urals, the state let them remain much as they were, so long as order was maintained and taxes were collected. It was southern Siberia that cried out for the tsars' attention, with imperial wars in Central Asia to be supported from there, princely quantities of gold to be mined from sites like the Lena Goldfields, and positions in the Amur basin and along the Pacific to be secured. As one indication of the regime's complacency regarding the Siberian Arctic, of the 21.9 million roubles allocated to 'the construction of enterprises auxiliary to the Trans-Siberian Railroad', only 320,000 went towards maintaining or expanding infrastructure along the Northeast Passage.[24]

Not all agreed with the state's way of thinking, and a small but determined circle of polar enthusiasts emerged among Russia's scientific, naval and business communities. Key figures among them included the former explorer Count Fyodor Litke, now president of the Russian Geographical Society and the Russian Academy of Sciences; the financiers Alexander Sibiryakov and Mikhail Sidorov; scholars such as the marine biologist Nikolai Knipovich and the geologist-oceanographer Baron Eduard Toll; and naval officers like Stepan Makarov and Alexander Kolchak. Most outspoken of all was Dmitrii Mendeleyev, creator of the periodic table of elements, who used his scholarly prestige to lobby for the development of Russia's north. In a famous memorandum to Finance Minister Sergei Witte, the prime mover behind the Trans-Siberian's construction, Mendeleyev contended that 'our need to conquer the polar seas is absolute, both for Russia's and humankind's economic benefit, and for the triumph of knowledge.'[25] The chemist and his colleagues had little luck persuading the government to reassess its priorities in any meaningful way, but they succeeded in organizing a number of expeditions, described in the section below, and Makarov convinced the regime to begin assembling a fleet of icebreakers and ice-forcing ships. The first of these, the *Yermak*, completed its trial run, to 79°10′N in the waters of Svalbard, in 1899.

For the indigenes of Arctic Siberia, conditions improved neither politically nor materially. Many lived less under the authorities' thumb than those inhabiting lower latitudes, but all except the Chukchi – who, as one Siberian official complained, had at best 'a vague sense of belonging to the Russian Empire' – were subject to taxation and the strictures of Russian law, and few escaped the blandishments of the Orthodox Church, however hard they might resist.[26] In return, while comparative neglect might mean comparative freedom, it also meant that the 'small peoples' gained none of the structural improvements which, under some imperial regimes, serve as partial compensation for the woes of being colonized. Indigenous groups were burdened as well by those who came to Siberia on their own initiative. The rapidly expanding settler population placed indirect pressures on the natives economically and environmentally, while the *promyshlenniki* who hunted, trapped and prospected privately in the North competed with them directly, also bringing diseases and alcoholism in their wake. As noted above, the overall increase of Siberia's native population to about 800,000 by the year 1899 was not felt among most ethnicities in the far north. Although the Yakut and Chukchi experienced growth during this century, other groups suffered net losses, with outsiders' influence frequently to blame. In one drastic instance, the once-thriving Yukagir were reduced to a population of 1,600 by 1876.

Another demographic, whose enlargement no one rejoiced in, was the steadily rising number of prisoners banished to Siberia, whether for common crimes or for opposition to the regime. Except during a brief reformist heyday in the mid-1850s and 1860s, outbreaks of leftist agitation and political terrorism convulsed tsarist Russia, swelling the ranks of those sent to the east. Some poured out their sweat at tasks like clearing timber or mining for gold, others endured a simple political quarantine, allowed to live as they wished as long as they remained in their assigned place. During the early 1800s, the state had condemned roughly 2,000 people per year to Siberian exile; in the 1890s and early 1900s, that number spiked to 19,000 per year, 18 per cent of them women. As the new century approached, two-thirds of those living in Yakutsk province were prisoners or once had been, and the island of Sakhalin was converted into a gigantic penal colony after the 1870s. In 1900, exile was taken off the books as a punishment for ordinary criminals, but still handed out to those found guilty of political offenses. The ghastliness of Siberia's prisons and work camps was a secret to no one. Dostoevsky, returning from his own penal servitude in Omsk, gave a literary taste of it in his 1862 novel, *The House of the Dead*, while two authors from 30 years later, one American, the other Russian, penned exposés even more shocking. George Kennan (cousin twice removed to the future diplomat of the same name) visited Siberia in 1885 as an investigative reporter for *Century Magazine*. Expecting to find that rumours of Siberia's horrors had been exaggerated, he discovered instead that they were pale shadows of a more atrocious truth, which he described in his two-volume classic, *Siberia and the Exile System* (1891). In 1890, the playwright Anton Chekhov journeyed to Sakhalin, returning to tell similarly dire stories in *The Island* (1893–4).

Two ironies hover over the history of Siberian exile. One is that the Soviets, many of whose leaders experienced it early in their revolutionary careers, made it into something far more monstrous during their own time in power. The other is that many of the Russian scholars most knowledgeable about Siberia were themselves incarcerated there. The experts on this roster came from many disciplines, but the most important from the perspective of Arctic history were the ethnographers Lev Shternberg, Vladimir Bogoraz-Tan (Waldemar Bogoras) and Vladimir Jochelson. Jailed for their socialist activism, all three found themselves in a perversely ideal position to study their subjects of interest: the Nivkhi in Shternberg's case, the Chukchi and Siberian Eskimos in Bogoraz-Tan's, and the Koryak and Yukagir in Jochelson's. Each achieved lasting acclaim for his contributions to Franz Boas's Jesup North Pacific Expedition, one of the finest achievements in the history of anthropological research. As noted in chapter Five, Bogoraz-Tan went on to help shape early Soviet policy towards the native Siberians.

Sprints and Marathons: Racing to the Pole and Other Modes of Arctic Exploration

Reminiscing about his boyhood in the 1860s and '70s, the novelist Joseph Conrad, who in his own prose brought to vivid life some of the world's most exotic locales, confessed himself particularly moved as a youth by the 'stern romance' of Arctic adventuring.[27] He was far from the only one thus captivated, with Arctic exploration entering its golden age, and with the long endeavour to reach the Pole now viewed by the Western public as epitomizing courage, tenacity and ingenuity at their highest. When Conrad's fellow fictioneer, Jules Verne, proclaimed that 'among the martyrs of science, the most heroic are the navigators of the polar seas', he gave expression to the feelings of untold thousands.[28]

What thrilled those thousands, of course, were the races for the Pole and the passages. Throughout the history of exploration, the most undying fame goes rarely to those who journey most efficiently or most usefully. It goes instead to those who arrive first and to those who strive most dramatically or most tragically – a fact evinced in the Arctic's case by the outpouring of emotion over the Franklin saga and, to take another example, by the instant popularity of artworks like *Man Proposes, God Disposes*, a canvas of 1864 by England's Edwin Landseer. Here, two polar bears of malevolent visage pick over the spars and sails of a ship wrecked in the ice, gnawing at what are clearly human bones: a stark reminder of what could befall those who failed to carry away laurels in the sprints for the great Arctic prizes.

Too often, those sprints, with all the excitement attendant upon them, cause us to forget the wider range of motivations that brought Euro-Americans to the Arctic, and the debates they had at the time about why they ought to be there. Was the Pole a worthy aim in itself because, like Everest, albeit less solidly, it was there? Robert Peary thought so, arguing that to strive for the Pole was the best imaginable 'test of intelligence, persistence, endurance, and determined will' – in sharp contrast to the Inuit, who, seeing that the Pole offered nothing in the way of better hunting or more congenial dwelling places, dismissed it phlegmatically as 'white man's business'.[29] Were explorers to secure economic benefit for their countries, or strategic and territorial advantage, or should their mission be the advancement of the sciences, whether physical or human? Not that these goals were mutually exclusive: Fridtjof Nansen and Adolf Nordenskiöld, for instance, two scholars as serious about their research as anyone could wish, would have been overjoyed as well to be the first to reach the Pole. A few voices decried the record-setting craze as a foolhardy distraction from the real scientific work at hand. Among those sharing this austere sentiment was Sir Clements Markham of the Royal Geographical Society, who opined in 1894 that 'merely to reach the North Pole, or to attain a higher latitude than some one else', were 'objects unworthy of support'.[30] But this was decidedly a minority opinion.

Explorers entering the Arctic during the late 1860s and early 1870s favoured two lines of approach: Spitsbergen and eastern Greenland on one hand and, on the other, the Canadian archipelago, especially where it came nearest to converging with western Greenland. Greenland itself was increasingly an object of interest, both for the secrets it seemed to hold regarding the generation of icebergs and weather systems, and for the geographical riddles it posed. Was it an island or, as mapmakers like Petermann supposed, part of a transpolar land mass? And what lay in the interior, where the natives, who believed it to be the abode of evil spirits, dared not go?

A leading figure on the European side, and one of Arctic history's undeservedly underappreciated characters, was the mineralogist Nils Adolf Erik Nordenskiöld, a Finnish-born Swede and the eventual conqueror of the Northeast Passage. Undecorously vociferous about his desire to see Finland reunited with Sweden, Nordenskiöld ran afoul of the Russian authorities in 1857, and left his position at Helsinki's Imperial Alexander University for new ones at the University of Stockholm and Sweden's National Museum of Natural History. He began his Arctic career by participating in three of the four expeditions that Sweden sent to Spitsbergen between 1858 and 1868. In 1867–8, he attempted a North Pole voyage of his own and, in 1870, with funding from the industrialist Oskar Dickson, he paid the first of his two visits to Greenland. In 1871–2, he returned to Spitsbergen, where he staged an unsuccessful bid to reach the Pole via reindeer sled. During his Greenland travels, Nordenskiöld observed that the ice there was covered in many spots by a curious powdery substance that he named cryoconite when he wrote about it in the American journal *Science*. Lab analysis revealed the powder to contain iron, zinc and carbon; its dark hue absorbed the heat of the sun's rays, causing the ice underneath to form meltholes so numerous that 'it was impossible not to stumble into them at every moment.'[31] What Nordenskiöld had found was one of the earliest proofs of how far-reaching the environmental impact of industrial waste could be, for cryoconite turned out to be the residue of coal dust and other particulates belched into the sky by foundries and furnaces far to the south.

In 1870, Norwegian sealers charted and circumnavigated Novaya Zemlya. By then, newcomers were arriving in the Arctic, as the German-speaking states launched their own series of expeditions. In the case of rapidly unifying Germany, the motive force was provided by the geographer August Petermann, himself driven by Teutonic nationalism and the desire to prove his open polar sea hypothesis. 'What a triumph for Germany and the German navy', he wrote in 1865, 'if the seas and lands beyond 80°N received a *German* nomenclature, if a *German* mariner first advanced there, if a *German* keel first furrowed the floods of the North Pole!'[32] Petermann used his 'Polarpapa' status within the German scientific community to rally support, including from Chancellor Otto von Bismarck, for two Arctic voyages: an investigation of Spitsbergen and Greenland in 1868 and a more ambitious venture that sent the *Germania* and *Hansa* to Greenland and beyond in 1869–70. The Bremen navigator Karl Koldewey commanded both expeditions, and a key member of the second was Julius Payer, an officer in the Austro-Hungarian army. The *Germania* overwintered near Sabine Island, off the east Greenland coast, and Payer took the lead in gathering meteorological, hydrographical and botanical-zoological data. It sailed home without incident, unlike the *Hansa*, whose mission was to sail as far north as possible between Greenland and Novaya Zemlya. Trapped in the ice, the *Hansa* was crushed to bits in October 1869, leaving the crew adrift in their makeshift shelter, the *Hansa-Haus*, until the following May. The castaways returned safely, and the nation saluted their bravery, but German officialdom turned its back on polar exploration for the rest of the century. Curmudgeonly in his disillusionment, Petermann quarrelled with Koldewey, who made public his scepticism about the open polar sea. He fell into depression and committed suicide in 1878.

No sooner did the Germans surrender their place on the ice fields than it was taken by their Austro-Hungarian neighbours. Payer and the naval officer Karl Weyprecht voyaged to Novaya Zemlya in 1871 and sailed the *Admiral Tegetthoff* to uncharted waters in 1872–4. During this second journey, the duo discovered Franz Josef Land, the northernmost islands in the Eurasian Arctic – but lost the *Tegetthoff* and, because they were privately funded, had no authority to claim the new territory for Vienna. Payer retired to take up painting, whereas Weyprecht, impatient with the growing mania for record-breaking and farthest norths, made his mark as an advocate for international scholarly cooperation. In his paper of 1875, 'Fundamental Principles of Scientific Arctic Investigation', Weyprecht proposed the creation of a global network of Arctic research stations, an idea soon realized during the first International Polar Year.

In post-Civil War America, where the cartoonist Thomas Nast was beginning to fix in the national consciousness the association between Santa Claus's workshop and the North Pole (the reindeer motif having been provided four decades before by Clement Clarke Moore's 'The Night Before Christmas'), a number of parties drummed up interest in the actual Arctic. Isaac Hayes lectured widely, flogging his 1867 book on the open polar sea and calling for u.s. annexation of Ellesmere Island

The *Hansa-Haus*, the shelter constructed by castaways during the
Germania-Hansa expedition of 1869–70.

and northwest Greenland. Throughout the 1860s, the artist William
Bradford, like his Hudson River School colleague Frederic Church,
journeyed to Labrador to paint icebergs and northern landscapes, and
went even farther in 1869. That year, Bradford charted a Scottish vessel,
the *Panther*, to take him, Hayes and 40 others to Baffin Island and
Greenland's Melville Bay. His exhibitions, lecture tours and bestselling
album-memoir, *The Arctic Regions*, elevated him to the status of polar
expert on both sides of the Atlantic, and Queen Victoria purchased his
The 'Panther' off the Coast of Greenland in the Midnight Sun for the library
of Windsor Castle. And then there was Charles Francis Hall of Cincinnati,
accumulating fame of his own after a three-year immersion, from 1860
to 1863, among the Inuit of Baffin Island. No sooner had he published his
Arctic Researches and Life Amongst the Esquimaux than he was off again,
this time to Canada's central Arctic, between 1864 and 1869.

During both of his journeys, Hall collected artefacts left behind by
Franklin and Martin Frobisher, with most of these relics going to the
Smithsonian Institution. He covered hundreds of miles by dogsled,
charting large portions of the Gulf of Boothia and King William and
Melville islands. He became expert in Inuit dialects and ways of survival, and he befriended two Baffin Island Inuit, Tookoolito ('Hannah')
and Ebierbing ('Joe'), for life. But he also displayed flashes of the erratic
temperament that could make his company hard to bear. While he idealized the Inuit at first, his opinion of them soured – apparently the result

of learning that some Central Inuit had been aware of the Franklin
expedition's death throes on King William Island, but had done nothing to help. Even Tookoolito and Ebierbing were as much servants to
him, a Man and Woman Friday, as they were companions. Most unac-
countably, in the summer of 1868, he shot dead one of his expedition
members during an argument over which of them was better qualified
to converse with the natives.

Still, Hall was not without his charisma. Ingratiating himself with
Congress and President Ulysses Grant, he obtained funds and a ship – the
steamer *Polaris* – for an attempt on the Pole. In 1871, Hall sailed north
between Greenland and Ellesmere Island, accompanied by his crew and
eight Inuit: Tookoolito, Ebierbing, the guide Hans Hendrik, who had
adventured with Kane and Hayes in the 1850s and '60s, Hendrik's wife
Mergut, and the two couples' four children (a fifth, Charlie Polaris, was
born during the voyage). The expedition wintered at Thank God Harbor,
and it was here that Hall died, vomiting and raving deliriously, mere
days after drinking a cup of coffee that he believed had been poisoned.
An autopsy done in 1968–9 revealed sizable amounts of arsenic in Hall's
body, but arsenic was commonly ingested for medicinal purposes in the
nineteenth century, and Hall may have been dosing himself with it. If he
was in fact murdered, he had antagonized enough of the crew that there
is no lack of possible suspects, but Hall, while dying, accused the ship's
doctor, Emil Bessels of the Smithsonian. Several rejoiced openly to have
Hall gone. 'A stone off my heart', crowed the assistant navigator, Sidney
Buddington: 'The best thing that could happen for the expedition.'[33]
The death did not change things for the better. The *Polaris*, caught in the
ice, came nowhere near the Pole and, in a reprise of the *Hansa*'s recent
mishap, nineteen of the expedition's contingent were stranded on an ice
floe for almost seven months, after the sheet trapping the *Polaris* broke
apart. Those adrift were led by George Tyson, but owed their survival to
the hunting and kayaking skills of Hendrik and the other Inuit. The
Polaris was carried to the Greenland coast, near Etah, while the icebound
group was rescued by a Newfoundland sealing ship in April 1873.

Next to brave these waters was the British Arctic Expedition of
1875–6, captained by George Nares. Britain's longstanding interest in
the North had recently been stimulated further by paintings like
William Bradford's, and also by an Iceland fad among England's
authors and artists – the trend that led William Morris, for example, to
visit the island in 1871 and 1873 and, in his verse retellings of *Njál's Saga*,
to liken its sublimely stark landscape to a 'grey minster', an age-old

basilica carved into shape by wind and ice.[34] More officially, the Royal Navy, the Royal Geographical Society and the recently elected prime minister, Benjamin Disraeli, were stung into action by the possibility that other countries might overtake Britain's record of polar accomplishment. And so Nares, commanding 120 officers and crew aboard the *Discovery* and *Alert*, sailed out of Portsmouth in May 1875, with orders to carry out scientific and cartographic work and, if possible, to attain the Pole. Nares was one of the few servicemen still active who had taken part in the first Franklin searches, and his expedition hearkened back to earlier days, especially in its reversion to the use of man-hauled oaken sledges, weighing 1,500 pounds when fully loaded, for overland travel. Wintering on the north coast of Ellesmere, Nares's men surveyed both that island and northwest Greenland, with Hans Hendrik, fresh from the *Polaris* misadventure, as one of their guides. They took their sledges above the 83rd parallel, a new farthest north that placed them within 400 miles of the Pole. An unexpectedly high incidence of scurvy forced the expedition to return in 1876, earlier than planned, and some in the navy were disappointed by the results. Overall, though, Nares was judged to have done a creditable job. His new maps were useful, as were the meteorological readings and the wealth of information brought back about Greenland's glaciers. Most of all, Nares's observations went a long way towards disproving the open polar sea theory for good. With Britain only four years away from handing jurisdiction over the Canadian Arctic islands to Ottawa, this would be its last major exploration of the high north.

In the Eurasian Arctic, Nordenskiöld had spent the mid-1870s navigating the Barents and Kara seas, conducting hydrographical and marine biological research and venturing above the 81st parallel, a farthest north for the eastern hemisphere. In 1878, he felt ready to take on the entire Northeast Passage. That June, in the *Vega*, a three-masted sailing steamship commanded by Louis Palander, Nordenskiöld set out from the Swedish port of Karlskrona, rounding Scandinavia and heading east towards the Bering Strait. Although pack ice immobilized the *Vega* in September, stalling its progress for the next nine months, the ship by that point had traversed all but 120 miles of the passage and easily freed itself in the summer of 1879. Nordenskiöld and Palander reached Yokohama that autumn and were ennobled upon their return to Sweden in 1880.

During the *Vega*'s voyage, the less fortunate *Jeannette* expedition had begun making its way along Siberia's coast in the opposite direction.

Led by George Washington DeLong of the u.s. Navy and paid for by James Gordon Bennett, the *New York Herald* publisher who had recently hired Henry Stanley to track down David Livingstone in Africa, the *Jeannette* venture was intended to reach the North Pole via the Bering Strait. Setting forth from San Francisco in July 1879, the *Jeannette* entered the Chukchi Sea in August and found itself locked in the ice by September. For many months, this seemed no disaster, for the ship drifted northwest towards the Pole, allowing the crew to compile invaluable scientific data and to map the East Siberian Sea. DeLong confirmed that Wrangel was an island and not part of Petermann's 'Transpolarland', and discovered three islands – Bennett, Jeannette and Henrietta – classified by some geographers as part of the New Siberian Islands and by others as a separate chain. But in June 1881, the *Jeannette*'s hull collapsed, forcing everyone to take to the ship's three longboats and strike out for the Lena delta, 300 miles to the south. Of the expedition's 33 members, only thirteen returned alive. DeLong, resigned, as his journal tells us, to 'plodding to the southward, trusting in God [and] powerless to help ourselves', was not among them.[35] The decade ended, then, with one of the great Arctic challenges met – but with doubts also mounting as to whether the North Pole could be successfully assailed by sea.

Already by this juncture, calls were growing louder for alternative approaches to Arctic exploring that emphasized comprehensive under-standing and long-term presence. For example, while it was to find Franklin's lost diaries that the American Geographical Society sent u.s. Army officer Frederick Schwatka to the Canadian north in 1878–80, the expedition, which was guided by Charles Hall's former companion, Joe Ebierbing, stood out most for its decision to adopt native modes of subsistence as completely as possible. As Heinrich Klutschak, the group's Austrian naturalist, put it in the title of his 1881 memoir, Schwatka and his men lived 'as Eskimos among the Eskimo'. Doing so allowed them to dwell in the Arctic more safely and efficiently, a fact noted by later explorers like Peary. Schwatka applied similar techniques during his 1883 survey of the Yukon River, the longest rafting voyage ever made to that date.

In the meantime, Karl Weyprecht continued to denounce the race for the Pole as an 'international steeplechase' and repeated his plea for a multinational effort to establish an array of stations throughout the circumpolar north, 'with instruments precisely alike, governed by precisely the same instructions, and for a period of one year at least, to record a series of the utmost possible synchronous observations'.[36] Among those of like mind were Albert James Myer, founder of the U.S. Army Signal Corps and the U.S. Weather Bureau (today the National Oceanic and Atmospheric Administration); Georg von Neumayer, head of the German Marine Observatory in Hamburg; and the Swiss-born Heinrich Wild, of Russia's Main Physics Observatory. Starting in 1879, all three worked with Weyprecht to organize the first International Polar Year (IPY), set to run from August 1882 to September 1883.

Because Myer died in 1880 and Weyprecht in 1881, much of the IPY's implementation fell to Wild and Neumayer. Its centrepiece was the construction of twelve main Arctic stations, plus auxiliary posts, and the staffing of them by 700 meteorologists, oceanographers, geophysicists and other scholars from Austria–Hungary, Germany, France, the Netherlands, Norway, Sweden, Russia, Finland, Denmark, Canada, Great Britain and the United States. Key outposts and stations went up in places like Alaska's Point Barrow and Fort Rae on Great Slave Lake; Kingua Fjord on Baffin Island and Fort Conger on nearby Ellesmere; both of Greenland's coasts and Jan Mayen island; Bossekop in Norway's Finnmark county and Sodankylä in Finnish Lapland; Novaya Zemlya and Kap Thordsen in west Spitsbergen; and Yakutia's Sagastyr Island, in the Lena delta. Neumayer set up an ingenious data-gathering link between the Moravian missions in Labrador and his own observatory in Hamburg.

A miscellany of other expeditions supported or grew out of the IPY: the Second Dickson Expedition that took Nordenskiöld back to Greenland in 1883; Denmark's 1884 mapping of portions of the east Greenland coast; and the 1885–6 survey of the New Siberian Islands carried out for the Russian Academy of Sciences by geologist Eduard Toll. Useful work was done as a result of the International Polar Year, but not all the participant nations shared or integrated their research results in the platonically ideal fashion Weyprecht had envisioned. Furthermore, an unmitigated catastrophe on the American side left a blemish on the entire initiative. This was the Lady Franklin Bay Expedition of 1881–4, led by Adolphus Greely, an army lieutenant with no Arctic experience. Officially, Greely's mission was to sail north in the *Proteus* and erect an IPY base on Ellesmere Island's Lady Franklin Bay, but the lieutenant was equally determined to surpass the farthest north of 83°20′N attained by the Nares expedition half a decade before. As ordered, the party, 25 strong, set up their station, Fort Conger, and gathered meteorological and geophysical data. They explored widely, running up the Greenland coast past 83°23′N for a new farthest north. However, gross incompetence on the mainland kept the group from being resupplied in 1882 or retrieved in 1883 as per the original timetable, and pressure from the ice in Kane Basin cracked and sank the *Proteus*. In 1884, Greely relocated his starving men to Cape Sabine, hoping to find caches left over from Nares's venture. When rescue finally came, only six were still alive, and evidence of cannibalism was nigh incontrovertible. Greely eventually rose to the rank of major general and received the Congressional Medal of Honor, but his shrill insistence that '[I] did what I came to do – beat the best record' did not accord well with the stated goals of the IPY. In the Anglo-American and Scandinavian traditions, the Lady Franklin debacle marked the end for oversized, military-style Arctic expeditions that sought to bend the environment to their will rather than vice versa.

The Arctic became steadily more crowded with scholars and explorers over the next 30 years. Much of this traffic directed itself to Greenland, which many saw as the best avenue of approach to the North Pole, and where meteorologists and glaciologists yearned to learn more about the great ice cap – which, as late as Nordenskiöld's 1883 expedition, had been pierced only to a distance of 150 miles from Disko Bay on the west coast. Little surprise, for nearly 700 miles across at its widest point and rising to an elevation of more than 9,000 feet, Greenland's ice cap presents a most strenuous physical challenge. Among those squaring up to it during the 1880s were two colossi of modern exploration: Robert Peary and Fridtjof Nansen, longtime rivals who matched each other for stamina and ingenuity but differed in personality as much as two individuals can. The former, an engineer and officer in the U.S. Navy, pursued glory with Lucifer-like ruthlessness and singleminded fury. To his mother, who paid for his first Greenland journey, he declared that 'I *must* have fame and cannot reconcile myself to years of commonplace drudgery.'[37] In 1886, he set out to cross Greenland by foot, and although he went only 90 miles before turning back, he would return to the Arctic six more times. The cerebral and stoic Nansen, a doctoral student in zoology and future professor of oceanography, went on to serve his native Norway as an ambassador and public intellectual, and the global community as a humanitarian activist. It was he who triumphed in Greenland, taking advantage of his past as a competitive cross-country skier and inventing a light man-hauled sled inspired partly by Inuit design. Nansen began his trek in August 1888. While others had tried crossing from west to east, he chose to snowshoe from Angmagssalik (today Ammassalik) on the east coast to the high ground of the eastern interior, tackling the worst obstacle first and leaving him with a westward journey on skis that led downhill most of the way. He reached Godthåb Fjord on the western shore by late September.

Nansen's victory opened the door for more Greenland expeditions in the 1890s. The German geographer and future Antarctic explorer Erich von Drygalski came to study the glaciers in 1891–3. Peary, now working with the African-American explorer Matthew Henson and with his future adversary Frederick Cook, ventured to Greenland four more times between 1891 and 1902, crossing the ice cap twice and achieving a series of farthest norths as he tried to fight his way to the Pole. Peary's wife Josephine accompanied him on several of these journeys; pregnant in 1893, she gave birth to her daughter Marie – the 'snow baby', as an adoring press called her – while encamped in northwest Greenland. Denmark, understandably active in surveying the island, sent out Georg Carl Amdrup to head the Carlsberg (1898–1900) and East Greenland Coast (1900) expeditions, the second of which began the polar career of Ejnar Mikkelsen, a legendary figure in the exploration and governance of Greenland in the first half of the 1900s.

Elsewhere, there were too many Arctic journeys in the 1890s, and too many 'firsts' and new discoveries, to enumerate. Indeed, certain parts of the North were settled enough or sufficiently accessible that travel there bordered on tourism. Those with the money to spend on iceberg-viewing excursions or polar safaris had little trouble booking passage to the Baffin Island coast or Greenland's Disko Bay, or to islands like Kodiak and Novaya Zemlya. The North German Lloyd line began regular service to Spitsbergen by mid-decade and even operated a hotel there. The 1899 Harriman Alaska Expedition enabled the production of fourteen volumes' worth of research by two dozen geologists, geographers and naturalists, but was also a railroad tycoon's private hunting adventure, fitted out with the luxury of a pleasure cruise. Even in wilder country, polar research, while never without its risks, was in many places becoming a matter of routine. Against this backdrop of 'normalized' exploration, what stood out, aside from new records, were innovations in technique. One of these, too far ahead of its time, was Salomon Andrée of Sweden's fatal attempt in July 1897 to reach the North Pole in the hydrogen balloon *Eagle*, a venture backed by King Oskar II and Alfred Nobel. Andrée wondered before his forced landing near the 83rd parallel whether he would be 'thought mad or have successors'.[38] But while it was madness indeed to enter the Arctic skies in a conveyance whose direction could not be controlled, future pilots

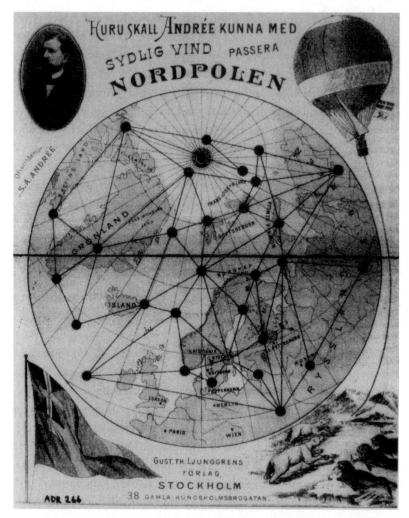

Advertisement for a board game sold to raise funds in Sweden for Salomon
Andrée's attempted balloon flight to the North Pole in 1897.

took heed of Andrée's example. Trials with steerable airships began in
the high north less than a decade later, and aeroplanes soon followed.

Ship design changed as well. Even in the age of steam, most vessels
used for polar voyaging had not been specially designed for it, but were
conventional ships adapted to the purpose. And for every success story
like the *Vega*'s, failures like the *Germania*'s, the *Jeannette*'s and the *Proteus*'s
demonstrated the inadequacy of simply reinforcing hulls or installing
steam engines on sailing ships. Russian admiral Stepan Makarov commissioned the world's first true icebreaker, the 8,730-ton *Yermak*, built
in Newcastle to his specifications between 1897 and 1899 and capable of

The polar explorer's foe – as seen by the public. During the nineteenth century, Caspar David Friedrich's painting *The Sea of Ice* (1823–4), along with a handful of other artistic and literary works, definitively shaped Western impressions of the Arctic wilderness.

cutting through ice six and a half feet thick. (In a rimy footnote to literary history, one of the naval engineers later stationed in Newcastle to oversee the construction of Russia's icebreakers there was Yevgeny Zamyatin, author in 1921 of the dystopian novel *We* – the direct inspiration for George Orwell's *1984*.) Also during the 1890s, Fridtjof Nansen, with money from Oskar Dickson and the Norwegian government, custom-designed a smaller but equally iceworthy schooner, the 128-foot *Fram*, whose name means 'forward'. Nansen intended that the *Fram*'s broad, 34-foot-wide beam and smoothly curved oaken hull would let it ride high in the ice and expose less of its surface area to crushing pressure.

For this unusual ship, Nansen had an unusual mission. Intrigued by the recent discovery of how flotsam from the unfortunate *Jeannette* had been carried all the way from the east Siberian coast to southwest Greenland, and aware as well of how the *Resolute*, abandoned in the 1850s during the search for Franklin, had been carried 1,200 miles from Melville Island to Davis Strait in two years, the young scientist wished to study the pattern of high-latitude ocean currents by setting himself deliberately adrift. With Otto Sverdrup as captain and ten others aboard, and provisioned with five years' worth of supplies, Nansen set out from Norway in the summer of 1893, following the Northeast Passage as far

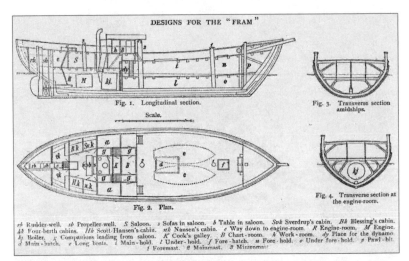

DESIGNS FOR THE "FRAM"

Fig. 1. Longitudinal section.
Scale.

Fig. 3. Transverse section amidships.

Fig. 2. Plan.

Fig. 4. Transverse section at the engine-room.

rh Rudder-well. *sb* Propeller-well. *S* Saloon. *s* Sofas in saloon. *b* Table in saloon. *Svk* Sverdrup's cabin. *Bk* Blessing's cabin. *4k* Four-berth cabins. *Hk* Scott-Hansen's cabin. *nk* Nansen's cabin. *e* Way down to engine-room. *R* Engine-room. *M* Engine. *h* Boiler. *g* Companions leading from saloon. *K* Cook's galley. *B* Chart-room. *h* Work-room. *dy* Place for the dynamo. *d* Main-hatch. *e* Long boats. *i* Main-hold. *f* Fore-hatch. *n* Fore-hold. *o* Under fore-hold. *p* Pawl-bit *1* Under-hold. *1* Foremast. *2* Mainmast. *3* Mizzenmast

Blueprints of the *Fram*, specially designed by Fridtjof Nansen in the 1890s for polar voyaging.

as the New Siberian Islands. At a point close to 78°N, he allowed the *Fram* to be borne along by the pack ice. He dispensed with hierarchy as much as possible, opening the common room to all – a touch of social democracy rare on most polar voyages – and the quality of the ship's construction allowed him, as he wrote in January 1894, to 'look out with a certain contempt at the horrible hurly-burly [that] nature is raising to no purpose'.[39]

As Nansen had anticipated, the *Fram* drifted to the northwest, but progress was slow, and it appeared by early 1895 that the ship would go no higher than 84°N. Pent-up and ready for action, Nansen, in mid-March, left the ship in Sverdrup's hands and selected Hjalmar Johansen to accompany him on a dogsled dash to the North Pole. The pair came within 225 miles of their destination, reaching a record latitude of 86°13′06″N in April 1896, but were forced to turn back as warmer weather broke up the ice. Hoping to kayak to Spitsbergen, they reached Franz Josef Land instead in June 1896. In a state of desperate exhaustion, they had the remarkably good luck to encounter the Jackson-Harmsworth Expedition (1894–7), there to survey Franz Josef for Britain's Royal Geographical Society. In the meantime, Sverdrup sailed the *Fram* safely into the Greenland Sea. Despite Nansen's failure to reach the Pole, his expedition proved an enormous success both popularly and scientifically. He became an instant celebrity and his *Farthest North* a huge bestseller, and the six volumes of scientific observations he published in 1906 contributed gigantically to the field of oceanography,

Scientist, athlete and future statesman: the Norwegian Fridtjof Nansen
at the time of his *Fram* expedition (1893–6).

a discipline he now pursued in preference to zoology. In addition to
his professorial duties, he headed the Norway-based International
Laboratory for North Sea Research and took part in establishing the
International Council for the Exploration of the Sea.

Another of the decade's innovations was the 'Peary system': Robert
Peary's fusion of Western logistics with Inuit methods of survival, tested

and continually improved during his journeys in northern Greenland and on Ellesmere Island. The protocol Peary perfected by the early 1900s was to plough as far north as a ship could take him, establish a base camp and, from there, send teams in advance to break ground and lay caches of food. Along such a well-prepared line of march, a small group would theoretically be able to speed to the Pole and back during the brief interval between the too-cold winter and the destabilizing thaw of the late spring. Only by travelling fast and light like the natives could Peary and his companions succeed, and so, while he was hardly the first Euro-American to wear fur clothing, sleep in igloos or use dogsleds for transport – he himself acknowledged Schwatka's influence from the 1870s and '80s – he staked more on their effectiveness than any predecessor had. He also relied more on native assistance. By the early 1900s, Peary would mobilize and relocate entire communities of Inughuit, whom he pridefully called 'Peary Eskimos' and 'my little brown children of the ice'. (In return, and behind his back, many of them called him 'the great tormentor'.[40]) The women hunted foxes, whose skins were sold in the States to offset Peary's expenses, and the men killed an inordinate number of musk oxen, walruses and caribou to supply the Americans' needs.

Not that Peary's many debts to the Inughuit caused him to regard them as anything like equals. And although his racial attitudes were more egregious than most, they nonetheless typify the complicated mix of condescension and admiration that informed much of the era's thinking about about indigenous peoples, northern or otherwise. For decades, Arctic explorers had come increasingly to depend upon, and even befriend, native guides and interpreters. Hans Hendrik and Joe Ebierbing spring readily to mind, as does Ootah (also known as Uutaaq and Odaq), who assisted Peary, Rasmussen and Mylius-Erichsen. The Scandinavians and Russians similarly employed and prized Sami, Yakuts and other aboriginals – most iconically Dersu Uzala, the Nanai hunter who guided the Russian surveyor Vladimir Arseniev through the Ussuri basin between 1902 and 1907 and is firmly linked in literature and film with Russia's north (despite not being technically from the Arctic). However, native hirelings were perceived by whites as hyperborean Sherpas and Gunga Dins: as praiseworthily loyal and useful, even nobly savage, but most definitely subordinate by virtue of status and blood. Not all of Peary's fellow explorers would have written, as he did, of his 'kindly and personal interest' in the natives, 'which any man must feel with regard to the members of any inferior race who had been accustomed to respect and depend on him' – but nor would all of them have disavowed the sentiment.[41] Peary also favoured openly the common but generally unspoken practice of entering into sexual relations with natives, justifying it eugenically and pragmatically. 'If colonization is to be a success in Polar regions,' he suggested, 'let white men take native wives . . . from that union may spring a race combining the hardiness of the mother with the intelligence and energy of the father.'[42] Besides, he continued, 'feminine companionship not only causes greater contentment but as a matter of both physical and mental health and the retention of the top notch of manhood it is a necessity'.[43] Peary took his own advice, as did Matthew Henson; both fathered children with Inuit women, and Josephine Peary, who came face-to-face with her husband's second family in 1900, bitterly resented this particular aspect of the 'Peary system'.

Paradoxically, a modern ethnographic sensibility was by now taking hold in Arctic studies. Euro-American understanding of circumpolar languages and lifestyles had been expanding throughout the 1800s. Among those adding to this pool of knowledge were Lars Levi Læstadius, Charles Francis Hall, Henrik Rink, George Kennan, author in 1870 of *Tent Life in Siberia: Adventures Among the Koryaks and Other Tribes of Kamchatka and Northern Asia*, and Heinrich Klutschak, whose observations during the Schwatka expedition dealt empathetically and judiciously with previously over-sensationalized aspects of Eskimo-Inuit life, including wife-sharing. During the IPY, the Germans on Baffin Island and the U.S. Signal Corps contingent at Point Barrow took special pains to study the local natives.

Still, anthropology and ethnography were in their infancies as academic disciplines. Even the most perceptive works to that date tended either to judge native groups, at least implicitly, by how they measured up against the yardstick of Western social development, or to over-idealize their 'cheerfulness, benevolence, and confidence' – the chief qualities attributed to the Inuit in Georg Hartwig's *The High North* of 1867.[44] It took a fundamental shift in the late 1800s and early 1900s for anthropologists to discard the notion that any culture could objectively be said to have evolved 'correctly' or 'primitively'. A resoundingly important figure in this transition was the German-American scholar Franz Boas, who, as a postdoctoral student in 1883–4, arrived in Cumberland Sound to study the Inuit of Baffin Island. Covering more than 3,000 miles on foot and by sled and boat, Boas gathered enough material for his first major monograph, *The Central Eskimo* (1888). While he moved on to research the Kwakiutl and other Native Americans of the Pacific

Northwest, it was the Baffin trip that implanted in him the lifelong habit of 'ask[ing] myself what advantages our 'good society' possesses over that of the 'savages'.' The answer, which he explained to his fiancée, Marie Krackowizer, never varied: '[I] find, the more I see of their customs, that we have no right to look down upon them.'[45]

In the mid-1890s, Boas returned to the Arctic sphere, courtesy of the American Museum of Natural History, whose president, Morris Jesup – an avid Peary supporter as well – handed him the opportunity to coordinate one of the largest anthropological field exercises ever attempted: the Jesup North Pacific Expedition, which began in 1897 and ran till 1902, with the publication of its multi-volume proceedings continuing till 1930. A North American contingent, which included Boas himself, studied the Kwakiutl, Salish, Haida and other peoples of Alaska and British Columbia. One of the expedition's purposes was to examine possible biological and cultural relationships between the natives of America and Asia, and so a sizable team worked in Siberia. There, the German-American ethnologist Berthold Laufer and Russia's Lev Shternberg, a socialist banished to Yakutia, conducted research among the peoples of Sakhalin and the Amur basin. Waldemar Jochelson, another Siberian exile, went among the Yukagirs, whose language he proved was not extinct, as most had thought, and also the Koryaks, Itelmen and Aleuts. Jochelson was joined by his wife Dina Brodskaya, who took photographs and compiled material for her own doctoral work. Waldemar Bogoras, or Vladimir Bogoraz-Tan, also serving a sentence in Siberia, studied the mythology and language of the Chukchi and the Siberian Eskimo, or Yupik. Like Jochelson, he worked alongside his wife Sofia. Some of the expedition's results have stood the test of time less well than others: gravest of all, Boas himself resisted the soon-to-be-proven theory that North America's Eskimos and Inuit originated in Asia. Still, the Jesup expedition set a new standard for ethnographical research in the North, and many volumes in its *Publications* series – Boas's work on the Kwakiutl, John Swanton's on the Haida, Jochelson's on the Koryak and, perhaps most enduring, Bogoras's *The Chukchee* – remain standard texts.

As the new century continued, ethnographic research grew in importance as a reason to explore the Arctic. In 1902–4, a young Knud Rasmussen, who grew up one-quarter Inuit in the west Greenland port of Jakobshavn (now Ilulissat), began his career as an ethnographer by accompanying Denmark's Ludvig Mylius-Erichsen and others on the Danish Literary Expedition. The purpose here was to study the Inughuit of Greenland's Cape York; one result was the publication of Rasmussen's *The People of the Polar North* (1908). Norway's Roald Amundsen conducted ethnographic studies during the long drift that took him through the Northwest Passage in 1902–6, and Vilhjalmur Stefansson of Canada got his start as an anthropologist among the Inuit of the Mackenzie Delta in 1906–7. Others active in the field at this time include France's Marcel Mauss, author of *Seasonal Variations of the Eskimo*, and Hans Steensby of Denmark.

Just as the Jesup expedition straddled two centuries, so too did a pair of other Arctic ventures, the contrast between them highlighting the schizophrenic divide in approaches to polar exploration. Both lasted from 1898 to 1902 and featured protagonists who loathed each other heartily. In one, Otto Sverdrup took the *Fram* once again to the Arctic on the orders of the Norwegian government, hoping to circumnavigate Greenland. The north coast defeated them, and so Sverdrup turned west instead, to Ellesmere Island. With quiet professionalism, the *Fram* contingent surveyed approximately 96,000 square miles of sea and land, including more than 1,700 miles of coastline, and discovered Prince Christian Island, Axel Heilberg Island and the Amund Ringnes and Ellef Ringnes islands. It was immensely useful work, but deemed utterly un-newsworthy by the press. *Popular Science* snorted dismissively that 'it can hardly be said that Capt. Sverdrup has fulfilled the expectations of his many admirers and friends.'[46] If one wanted drama, one turned to Peary, who had established a winter camp at Etah, in Greenland, and then settled into Greely's former Ellesmere post, Fort Conger, to prepare a run for the Pole. Not only was he on Ellesmere at the same time as Sverdrup, but Peary could not imagine that the Norwegian was not there to steal a march on him. In an oft-narrated encounter, Peary appeared unannounced in the *Fram*'s winter camp to inquire about Sverdrup's plans. Sverdrup offered him a cup of coffee and his assurance he had no interest in the Pole and wished only to chart the islands to the west. An unmollified Peary sledded away after a curt farewell, leaving the coffee undrunk.

What followed for Peary were four years of distress and discouragement, although with the adversity came lessons that later served him well. Frostbite in January 1899 cost him eight of his toes, ending any chance of reaching the Pole that year and consigning the party to a gloomy winter at Fort Conger. Henson suffered a bout of severe depression, which he drowned in rum and whiskey, while Peary is said by some biographers to have displayed his iron will by inscribing a Latin tag from

Seneca on the walls of the party's quarters: *inveniet viam, aut faciet* ('either find a way or make one'). Peary made a run at the Pole in April 1900, but encountered open water just south of the 84th parallel, and so he shifted east to survey Greenland's northern coast, discovering the island's northernmost tip – Cape Jesup, after Peary's principal backer – and leaving a stone cairn at 82°37′N to mark how far he had come down the northeast shore. In the meantime, his wife Josephine had come north in the *Windward* to search for him and, if necessary, resupply the party. The ship, however, was not sturdy enough for the ice and had to overwinter on Cape Sabine; it was at this time that Josephine experienced the emotional pain of meeting Alakahsingwah, Peary's Inuit wife. In 1901, Peary, his men, and his dogs were too fatigued for an attempt on the Pole. They waited instead until the spring of 1902, when they attained a latitude of 84°17′N: a farthest north for the western hemisphere, but well short of Nansen's record from 1896, which itself had just been surpassed by the Duke of Abruzzi Expedition, one of whose members, Umberto Cagni, had travelled from Franz Josef Land to 86°34′N in April 1900. Nansen responded to Cagni's achievement with characteristic aplomb, Peary with despair. Peary, however, did learn a great deal about how to manage caches and to prepare pathways ahead. Also, thanks to the *Windward*'s travails, he was, like Nansen before him, inspired to build a ship of his own, the doughty *Roosevelt*, specifically designed for polar voyaging.

Between 1902 and 1906, Roald Amundsen, a former medical student from Norway, became the first to sail through the Northwest Passage, in the sloop *Gjoa*. Along the way, he took meteorological readings, calculated the then-current location of the Magnetic North Pole, and spent two winters studying the Inuit of King William Island. In a short time, he eclipsed these achievements by narrowly beating Robert Falcon Scott in the race to reach the South Pole, and he became a noted pioneer in the field of Arctic aviation.

Amundsen and Peary loom large over the polar history of the earliest 1900s, but it is worth pausing to examine a sampling of other expeditions that, however overshadowed, unraveled secrets throughout the circumpolar north. During the Swedish–Russian Arc of Meridian Expedition, for example, geophysicists spent half a decade measuring spherical flattening over several degrees of latitude in the Svalbard archipelago. In Russia itself, the most energetic Arctic explorer of the 1890s was the geologist Eduard Toll, an expert on northern Yakutia's river basins and the New Siberian Islands. In 1899, Toll accompanied

Stepan Makarov to Spitsbergen, on the icebreaker *Yermak*'s first polar voyage. He was then authorized by the Russian Academy of Sciences to carry out the Russian Polar Expedition, a thorough survey of the New Siberian Islands and also a search for Sannikov Land, an uncharted land mass supposedly sighted north of the archipelago in the early 1800s. After the survey, Toll planned to sail east and complete the first traversal of the Northeast Passage since Nordenskiöld's voyage in the *Vega*. The expedition began in the summer of 1900, as Toll and nineteen others – including navy lieutenant Alexander Kolchak, the ship's hydrologist and, later, a contender for power during the Russian Civil War – sailed forth in the *Zarya*. The ship reached the New Siberian archipelago in 1901, after some months of survey work on the Taimyr Peninsula. The scientists split up into smaller parties to cover more ground, and it was on one of these excursions, to Bennett Island in the summer of 1902, that Toll, with the ship's astronomer and two Yakut guides, vanished. It was a terrible setback for the Russian polar community, and presaged several more to come in the next decade.

Denmark experienced its own tragedy in eastern Greenland, during the Danmark Expedition of 1906–8. The goal here was to survey the 400 miles of coast that stretched north from Cape Bismarck to the cairn left by Peary just above the 82nd parallel. Led by Ludvig Mylius-Erichsen, the expedition included Johan Peter Koch and the German geophysicist Alfred Wegener, the future originator of the continental drift theory. A party led by Koch headed north and located Peary's marker, while Mylius-Erichsen and two others went west to Independence Fjord to ascertain whether it opened into a larger 'Peary Channel', as the American had suggested. It did not, and when a warm spell melted the sea ice they had just crossed, the trio, left with no retreat, starved to death. One body was found, but not Mylius-Erichsen's or that of the other party member, prompting Ejnar Mikkelsen in 1909 to attempt the recovery of the missing remains and Mylius-Erichsen's notebooks. When Mikkelsen's ship, the *Alabama*, became trapped in the ice, he and Iver Iversen searched inland, only to be abandoned by their shipmates, who hitched a ride home with a passing whaler. The duo located the corpses and lost records, and held out in their 'Alabama cottage', built from the ship's wreckage, until rescue came in 1912.

Before plunging into the *Alabama* adventure, Mikkelsen had just returned from another expedition on the other side of the Arctic. This was the Anglo-American Expedition (1906–7) to the Beaufort Sea and Alaska's North Slope, co-organized by Mikkelsen and the u.s. geologist

Ernest de Koven Leffingwell. The two had become friends during the abortive Baldwin-Ziegler attempt to reach the North Pole from Franz Josef Land in 1900–02. Now, with funding from Leffingwell's family and John D. Rockefeller, they took the *Duchess of Bedford* to Flaxman Island, where they established a research base. They lost their ship to the ice, and Mikkelsen departed in 1907, but Leffingwell stayed on till 1914, travelling 4,500 miles through Arctic Alaska and mapping much of its north coast. He and Mikkelsen determined the dropoff point of the continental shelf off Alaska, and he was among the first to guess that the Beaufort region contained large reserves of oil.

Working in proximity to Leffingwell and Mikkelsen, but soon to gain greater fame, was Vilhjalmur Stefansson, a Canadian anthropologist of Icelandic descent. Stefansson researched the Mackenzie Delta Inuit in 1906–7 and received sponsorship from the American Museum of Natural History to continue his explorations in partnership with zoologist Rudolf Anderson. This Stefansson-Anderson expedition lasted from 1908 to 1912 and took the pair to multiple points between Alaska's Point Barrow and Canada's Coppermine River. Stefansson made his groundbreaking finds in the Dolphin and Union Strait that separates Coronation Gulf from Victoria Island. Here, he encountered bands of Copper Inuit who had never seen white men, an experience he likened in *My Life with the Eskimo* (1913) to waking up, like Mark Twain's Connecticut Yankee, in a past era, but 'into the country of the intellectual and cultural contemporaries of a far earlier age than King Arthur's . . . Their existence on the same continent with our populous cities was an anachronism of ten thousand years.'[47]

Arctic missions of another sort were commissioned at this time by the Canadian government. Angered by the results of the border dispute that followed the Klondike gold rush and distressed by annexationist rhetoric coming from parties in the u.s. and Scandinavia, Ottawa worried that the killing of caribou and musk oxen by foreign explorers on Canadian territory, or the taking of whales in Canadian waters, might legally constitute the kind of regular use that could support land claims by other countries. The fact that Peary, between 1898 and 1902, had transplanted Inughuit from Danish Greenland to Ellesmere Island complicated matters further. To reaffirm its sovereignty over the eastern Arctic, Canada sent out the Dominion Government Expedition of 1903–4, with the schooner *Neptune* carrying a team of scientists led by the geologist A. P. Low and a detachment of Northwest Mounted Police under J. D. Moodie. The *Neptune* sailed through the Canadian archipelago, informing foreign whalers and fishermen that they were subject to Canadian law and customs regulations, reminding the Inuit that the King of England was their rightful monarch and laying official claim to Ellesmere, Somerset and Southampton islands. For similar purposes, Ottawa deputized the Quebec mariner Joseph-Elzéar Bernier to patrol the northern waters in his newly acquired ship, the *Arctic*. Between 1906 and 1911, Bernier collected fees and duties, carried scientists on board to facilitate research, and visited as many islands as possible to demonstrate Canadian use and occupation. In July 1909, he placed a plaque on Melville Island, declaring the entire archipelago to be Canadian territory.

In later years, Ernest Leffingwell complained that he had become 'the forgotten man' of polar exploration.[48] But where popular memory is concerned, this was the fate of virtually everyone whose polar adventures coincided with the final laps of the races for the North and South poles. Peary returned to the Arctic in 1905–6, more desperate than ever to reach the Pole before someone beat him or before his backers – who included George Crocker of the Southern Pacific Railway and Morris Jesup of the American Museum of Natural History – lost faith in him. Convinced after the experiences of 1898–1902 that the bases he had operated out of earlier, such as Etah, were too far south, Peary designed for himself a ship strong enough to power all the way through Nares Strait to the Arctic Ocean itself, and large enough to serve as a winter headquarters. This was the steel-bowed, steam-powered, 1,476-ton *Roosevelt*, which Peary lovingly described as fighting the northern ice 'like a gladiator'. On this occasion, Peary made the best use yet of his relaying and caching system, supported by large numbers of Inughuit. His northward dash in April 1906 was enough to carry him to a new farthest north of 87°06′N, beating Cagni's record from 1900 by more than 30 miles. It was not the Pole, but an encouraging enough result that Peary was able to garner support for one more attempt in 1908–9. Largely ignored at the time, but attracting much scrutiny later, were Peary's claims to be covering ground that April at an astounding rate of 18 miles per day, and the paucity of navigational readings he took as he neared the Pole.

One last time, in the summer of 1908, Peary went north. Unbeknownst to him, although of overriding importance to him the following year, a former colleague, Dr Frederick Cook, the surgeon on Peary's 1891–2 Greenland expedition, had begun his own attempt on the Pole in 1907 – and if he spoke true, had already reached it on 21 April 1908.

Unaware of this, Peary sailed north in the *Roosevelt* to Cape Sheridan. There, he and 21 Americans, including Matthew Henson and Donald MacMillan, and more than 100 Inughuit men, women and children gathered supplies and prepared to haul them to Cape Columbia, on the north coast of Ellesmere. All was ready by the spring of 1909, when Peary, Henson and four Inughuit – Ootah, Seegloo, Egingwah and Ooqueah – selected 38 dogs and began the final march to the Pole. Whether by design or oversight, Peary was the only one in the group qualified to calculate latitude from the position of the sun; he was also the only one to keep a log, and his recordkeeping grew more erratic as he and his men progressed. Nonetheless, Peary's journal states that, on 6 April 1909, the party reached its destination: 'The Pole at last!!! The prize of 3 centuries. My dream and goal for 23 years MINE at last.'[49] Ooqueah snapped a photograph of the others standing with the flags of the United States, Peary's college fraternity, the Navy League, the Red Cross and the Daughters of the American Revolution, as well as a banner quilted from fragments of the flags Peary had placed at each of his previous farthest norths. The team sledded back to Cape Sheridan, where Peary put his journal in order, and the expedition returned to Etah that summer – only to receive the news of Frederick Cook's claim to have reached the Pole the year before.

The resulting controversy has never been resolved. Peary and his legion of supporters, which included the American Museum of Natural History and the National Geographic Society, heaped doubt and derision upon Cook. Deservedly, it seems, for while Cook still has his partisans, it is a matter of near-universal agreement that he lied not just about reaching the Pole, but about his other claim to fame, which was to have been the first to climb Alaska's Mount McKinley. Disgraced and later convicted of stock fraud, Cook spent most of the 1920s serving time at Fort Leavenworth. He died in 1940, still insisting on the rightness of his claim.

Deciding what to make of Peary's account is more difficult. The U.S. Congress and a host of other bodies credited him with conquering the Pole, and schoolbooks, general histories and popular memory still recognize him as having done so. But questions arose in Peary's own day, and they have continued to arise since. Nansen, Sverdrup and Greely flatly refused to believe him. Everyone agreed, as they do now, how unfortunate it was that no one else present could verify Peary's navigational readings (the same problem applied in Cook's case), and it has always been difficult to accept that he and his party walked and sledded an incredible 30 to 40 miles per day during the last approach and return – all

6 April 1909: the climax of Robert Peary's final attempt to reach the North Pole. Peary, Matthew Henson and the natives Ootah, Seegloo and Egingwah (photographed by Ooqueah) at what Peary maintained was the Pole. The validity of Peary's claim remains a matter of debate.

over terrain where, during a 1968 expedition, snowmobiles managed to cover only 11 miles daily. Then there is Peary's journal, which shows signs of tampering. The entry proclaiming his triumph is written on a loose sheet of paper, cleaner than the notebook's other pages, and naysayers maintain that Peary scribbled it and inserted it only after returning to Etah, hearing tidings of Cook, and panicking at the thought that he had used up his last chance to make his own case, true or not. It is entirely possible that neither man reached the Pole, making them both cheats, although Peary's story hangs together just well enough that it cannot be shaken apart as easily as Cook's. The only thing that has been conclusively proven is Barry Lopez's assessment of Peary as 'recklessly arrogant and despotic'.[50]

Whatever the merits of their cases, Peary's attack on Cook set a new low for vindictiveness, and he was churlish even to his allies. The Inughuit who accompanied him to the Pole remain all but nameless in his retellings of the adventure, and he bristled with rage when Henson tried to step out from backstage by publishing his own book, *A Negro Explorer at the North Pole*, in 1912. After retirement, Peary died in 1920 with all the public honours one could wish for – the rank of rear admiral, burial in Arlington National Cemetery – but is seen by many biographers as having lived his later years as a man not wholly content with his lot, or with himself.

The seeming attainment of the Pole did not bring an end to Arctic work. Much of the polar map had yet to be filled in, while the workings of Arctic weather, the gyring of the northern seas and the hiding places of the region's mineral wealth continued to defy scientific understanding. In 1910, Knud Rasmussen, with his friend Peter Freuchen, opened up the Thule (Uummannaq) trading post on northwest Greenland's Cape York. He did so partly to bring economic relief to Thule's impoverished natives, who lived beyond the reach of the Royal Greenland Trading Company and had long been offered unfair terms of exchange by foreigners like Peary. Thule also served as a base for Rasmussen's own geographical and anthropological research. Between the 1910s and the early 1930s, Rasmussen organized seven Thule expeditions; the first, in 1912, was a 600-mile dogsled journey across the northernmost ice to determine whether a channel separated Peary Land from the rest of Greenland. Other travellers crossed the Greenland ice cap in the early 1910s, including a Swiss group led by glaciologist Alfred de Quervain and the team of Johan Koch and Alfred Wegener, who, in 1912–13, became the first to overwinter on the Greenland ice by drilling into the cap's surface to create a camp.

In North America, Bernier, Leffingwell and others were still active, and their efforts were matched by Germans, Scandinavians and Russians in places like Spitsbergen, Franz Josef Land and Novaya Zemlya. Spitsbergen was especially busy: new geophysical stations and coal mines arose, and the orientalist Wilhelm Filchner used it as a practice site in 1910 before leading Germany's second Antarctic expedition in 1911–13. Spitsbergen also served as the proving ground for the first Arctic airship tests. In 1906–7 and 1909, the u.s. journalist Walter Wellman, who had attempted overland journeys to the Pole in the 1890s, launched three unsuccessful flights from nearby Danes Island. In 1910, Ferdinand von Zeppelin, the airship king, came to Spitsbergen in the company of Erich von Drygalski to conduct his own tests. A number of mechanical details, Zeppelin concluded, had yet to be worked out before lengthy polar flights were feasible, although he believed that airships had a future in the high north – as they did after the First World War.

Farther to the east, the Russians engaged in a burst of activity prior to the war. Three of their expeditions failed miserably between 1912 and 1914, deflating morale in polar circles; they were later seized upon by the Soviets as ammunition for their ideologically based criticisms of tsarist-era Arctic policy. In 1912, the geologist Vladimir Rusanov, an experienced explorer of Novaya Zemlya, led a government-commissioned expedition in the schooner *Hercules* to scout for coal deposits and conduct zoological surveys in the Svalbard archipelago. Instead of returning home, he attempted an unauthorized voyage through the Northeast Passage, but made it no farther than the Taimyr before perishing. Also braving the Passage that year was Lieutenant Georgii Brusilov in the *St Anna*, which progressed only to the Yamal Peninsula before the ice began dragging it north to the 83rd parallel. After more than a year of ensnarement, eleven members of the crew, including navigator Valerian Albanov, left the ship and began trudging in the direction of Franz Josef Land. The ordeal, recounted in Albanov's memoir, *In the Land of White Death*, killed nine of the travellers; Brusilov and the others who remained with the *St Anna* vanished without trace. In the meantime, Georgii Sedov, denied funding for a North Pole venture by the Russian Academy of Sciences, organized his own voyage in the *St Foka*. Sailing from Arkhangelsk in the summer of 1912, Sedov took till February 1914 to reach a position from which to strike out towards the Pole. Already weakened with scurvy, he died on the ice and was buried by his companions on Rudolf Island. It was the *St Foka*, returning home, that rescued Albanov and the other *St Anna* survivor, Alexander Konrad.

But the Russians enjoyed successes as well. In the summer of 1914, they became the first to fly aeroplanes above the Arctic Circle, as Jan Nagursky, in the MF.11 biplane *Pechora*, reached a latitude of 76 degrees. Additionally, the Russian Admiralty and Academy of Sciences cooperated on the massive Arctic Ocean Hydrographic Expedition of 1910–15, the planning for which began soon after the country's resounding military defeat at the hands of Japan in 1904–5 – a loss due largely to Russia's inability to move fleets quickly or reliably between the Atlantic and Pacific. The expedition starred the *Taimyr* and *Vaigach*, two new ice-forcing ships built between 1908 and 1910 in consultation with the naval officer Alexander Kolchak, who had returned to hydrological and cartographic research after service in the Russo-Japanese War. A complex operation captained by Boris Vilkitsky and chronicled assiduously by the *Taimyr*'s medical officer, Leonid Starokadomsky, the Hydrographic Expedition sailed out of Vladivostok and through the Bering

Strait to begin a detailed survey of Siberia's coast from the Bering Sea to the Yenisei River. Along the way, in 1913, Vilkitsky discovered Severnaya Zemlya, the last Arctic island chain to go uncharted. The *Taimyr* and *Vaigach* sailed into Arkhangelsk in 1915, completing the Northeast Passage for the first time since 1878–9.

They returned, as it happened, to a world at war. Unlike its sequel a quarter-century later, the First World War left the Arctic, except in a few areas, relatively untouched, and so the transition to global conflict after months of polar solitude jarred with particular dissonance. It was the same disorientation shared by other explorers who entered the North before the crisis of Sarajevo and reemerged into the midst of the clash of arms it had caused: Donald MacMillan with his Crocker Land Expedition of 1913–17, for example, or Stefansson, who led the Canadian Arctic Expedition between 1913 and 1918. But the grand bloodlettings to the south were only temporary interruptions in the Euro-American effort to master the Arctic. When the nations that had crusaded in the North during the nineteenth century turned their eyes back to it in the early twentieth, they looked upon it with territorialism, treaty-making and national development even more on their minds than before.

5
Subjugations:
1914 to 1945

In 1921, the Italian general Giulio Douhet, the father of modern air power theory, proclaimed aircraft to be the premier tool for conquest in the new twentieth century. 'Aeronautics', he asserted in the first lines of his classic *Il dominio dell'aria*, had 'opened up to men a new field of action, the field of the air'.[1] The entire blue, curving rim of the globe had become a new battleground.

Although Douhet had in mind a more literal form of warfare, aviation indeed added a third dimension to the modern world's effort to subjugate the Arctic. For the sake of adventure or science, or to discover wealth, pilots from many countries winged their way to the North during the early 1900s – sometimes over the Pole itself – fulfilling Promethean fantasies that combined the age-old dream of flight with equally captivating dreams of controlling the very top of the world. Of course, polar flying was only one component of the larger conquest, which was more comprehensive and went far beyond the symbolic. In steadily growing numbers, invaders from the south mastered the Arctic's skies and seas and gained suzerainty over more of its territory. Virtually all its land masses and waterways were now charted and politically claimed, although not always to everyone's agreement. Ever-larger measures of its wealth, particularly minerals and fossil fuels, were wrested from its bosom. Its ecosystem endured more human-caused devastation than ever before in its long existence – although more was yet to come in the century's later decades.

The subjugation was human as well. The imperial hold on Arctic peoples tightened. In the Soviet Union, the native Siberians who had so tenaciously resisted tsarist overlordship now had their shamans jailed and their reindeer expropriated by the same regime that exhorted them to love Stalin as the wisest of all chieftains and the sun-like provider of all bounty. In Canada the colonial grip, while not as steel-gauntleted as the USSR's, had grown firm enough that Inuit groups who, just a generation or two before, had barely known of the existence of whites were issued their own 'Eskimo books of knowledge', informing them that they were 'entitled to the privilege of regarding our king as your king' and comparing the Crown's lawgivers to 'wise men after the heart of King Solomon'.[2] Throughout the polar world, the legal and informal pressures placed on indigenous populations to assimilate and conform intensified. Coerced labour as a means of developing the North reached its apogee. Most tragically, the horrors of large-scale combat were visited upon the region during the Second World War – the worst bloodletting ever witnessed in the Arctic.

A Polar Mediterranean? Sovereignty and State-building in the Interwar Arctic

There was no lack of utopians among those drawn to Arctic development during the early twentieth century – individuals entranced by the idea of what might be made of the region by modern technology. Some dreamed of bringing medical care, electric power and book learning to the natives; others thrilled at the thought of bright cities and factory smokestacks rising up from the tundra, linked by new railways and canals, and by fleets of airships hovering serenely overhead. Fridtjof Nansen spoke of Siberia and other Arctic realms as 'lands of tomorrow'. Vilhjalmur Stefansson, borrowing Lord Kelvin's prediction of 1877 that the high north would soon become a 'polar Mediterranean', eagerly desired to bring 'the torch of science' there, to 'light the way to civilization and economic development'.[3] Others might not fantasize so fulsomely but, with the new century under way, many anticipated impressive growth in the Arctic.

Before any of that, however, the upheavals caused by the First World War and its aftermath had to be overcome. In a strictly military sense, most of the Arctic remained quiet during the war. Naval patrols and convoys ventured into the northern seas, and both sides operated high-latitude weather stations. But North America above the 60th parallel had little to do with the fighting, and Scandinavia, although affected economically by the belligerents' interdiction of each other's coasts, remained neutral – although Norway chartered the bulk of its merchant marine to the Allies. It was in Russia that the war most directly touched the North. With

Russian access to the Baltic Sea and the Mediterranean blocked by the Central Powers, the British and French, in order to aid and supply their beleaguered ally, were obliged to route ships through the North Atlantic and around Norway to Russia's Arctic shores. Arkhangelsk handled its share of this traffic, but a new port, more than 300 miles closer to Europe and ice-free all year due to warm ocean currents, went up in 1915 on the Kola Peninsula's north coast. This was Murmansk, a milestone construction in the history of Russian transport.

Affecting the Arctic most fundamentally were the political tremors set off during the war's final years. Russia suffered the severest shocks: there, the collapse of tsarism in early 1917, followed by the rise of Lenin's Bolsheviks that autumn and the Civil War of 1918–21, brought sweeping changes to the Eurasian north. One of these was the emergence of a new Arctic nation, as Finland won independence from revolution-weakened Russia in 1917–18. As for the rest of the Russian north, it gained a new master in the form of the Soviet regime, but only after a half-decade of violence and chaos. Murmansk and Arkhangelsk were occupied in the spring and summer of 1918 by French, British and American troops in tandem with the anti-communist White force led by Yevgeny Miller. Controlling west and central Siberia was an even larger White army commanded by the former polar explorer and naval officer Alexander Kolchak, who styled himself Supreme Ruler of All the Russias. East and north of Kolchak's domain, near-anarchy reigned, with miscellaneous White units battling the Red Army; Japanese and American soldiers garrisoning Vladivostok and parts of eastern Siberia; national minorities and indigenous peoples fighting for self-rule; and warlords and bandits pursuing their own agendas. In the northwest and centre, the Reds began to triumph in 1919: foreign interventionists pulled out of the conflict, Kolchak and Miller went down to defeat in early 1920, and the Ob and Yenisei basins came under Soviet power by 1921. Farther afield, victory took longer to achieve. White battalions and native insurgents remained active in Yakutia, the Taimyr, Chukotka and Kamchatka until 1923, while the Japanese held Vladivostok until 1922 and northern Sakhalin until 1925.

Meanwhile, with the world war over and the Paris Peace Conference having reordered boundaries across the globe, the international community turned more of its attention to adjudicating territorial claims in the Arctic. As the German geographer Richard Hennig noted in 1928, 'the division of the Arctic world, until now unruled because regarded as entirely worthless, is now in full swing.'[4] The peculiarities of Arctic geography, however, increased the difficulty of settling such questions, and whatever claims had prevailed in the past, much of the circumpolar north still fell into the legal category of *terra nullius*, or 'no-man's-land'. Many sites were too remote or inhospitable to allow would-be colonizers to demonstrate regular use. Maritime law left it unclear as to whether the Northern Sea Route, the Russian segment of the Northeast Passage, was a Russian waterway or a strait allowing international access, or whether the Northwest Passage belonged to Canada, whose islands it snakes through, or to all countries. Did Arctic waters in general, covered so thoroughly with ice, count as 'high seas'? What was the legal status of the ice itself, and did pack ice differ from the ice that forms seasonally on the edges of islands and coastlines? Most contentiously, how should jurisdiction over Arctic islands be assigned? Should they belong to the countries that discovered them? To those demonstrating effective occupation? Or to those claiming the most natural maritime proximity? And how did one judge what was 'most natural'? In the mid-1920s, Canada and Russia lodged claims to maritime boundaries which were drawn straight to the North Pole from the easternmost and westernmost points of their Arctic coastlines. This sector principle, as it became known, drew criticism from nations whose northern shores were less elongated. These countries favoured the equidistance, or median-line, principle, which in their opinion offered greater geographical precision. Here, the northward lines that extend from coastal endpoints do not run directly, but irregularly, along courses connecting the midpoints between Arctic land masses. Neither approach has won universal acceptance among experts on international maritime law or the governments of Arctic nations, and each still has its partisans today.

With varying degrees of cordiality, many of the Arctic's major sovereignty issues were resolved during the interwar period, or at least simmered without boiling over. Newfoundland and Labrador, which had attained dominion status under the British Crown in 1907, remained separate from Canada until 1949, but negotiated shipping, fishing and sealing rights smoothly enough. In 1918–19, Iceland changed the terms of its relationship with Denmark, exchanging home rule for the status of a sovereign nation within a common monarchy, and securing the right to declare itself independent in 25 years if it so desired. The 1920 Treaty of Tartu set the boundary line between Finland and Soviet Russia, with the latter retaining Karelia but ceding the port of Pechenga, or Petsamo, on the Barents Sea. Norway received Jan Mayen Island in 1920 and annexed it formally in 1930. Thanks to the 1920 Treaty of Svalbard, it won political custody over Spitsbergen and the rest of the archipelago, although the treaty's terms granted the right of economic exploitation to all signatories. In North America, the Aleutians were among the many islands that the United States agreed to leave unfortified in its naval limitations talks with Japan during the 1920s.

Some questions resisted arbitration more stubbornly. Throughout the 1920s and early '30s, Norway pursued an aggressive 'Arctic imperialism' campaign. On that basis, it opposed (albeit in vain) the USSR's declaration of sovereignty over Franz Josef Land in 1926. Until 1930, it angered Canada by pressing its own claim to the islands in the Canadian archipelago that Otto Sverdrup had discovered in 1898–1902. It clashed harder yet with Denmark in a complicated dispute over Greenland: although Norway pledged in its 1919 Ihlen Declaration to respect Danish sovereignty over the entire island, it had second thoughts once Copenhagen started exercising its right to restrict the movement there of foreigners, including Norwegian scientists, hunters and fishermen. With Norway openly harbouring designs on Greenland's eastern coast, Ejnar Mikkelsen strengthened Denmark's presence there by founding the colony of Scoresbysund (Ittoqqortoormiit), 80 persons strong, in 1925. Such measures, however, did not stop Norway from occupying Greenland's eastern shore between 71°30′N and 75°40′N in 1931, naming it Eric the Red Land. There the Norwegians hunkered down until 1933, when the Permanent Court of International Justice ordered them to withdraw. Less dramatic aggravations arose between Canada and Denmark, which refused for a long time to recognize Canada's sovereignty over the islands nearest to Greenland, such as Ellesmere and the Queen Elizabeths, and to this day continues to claim tiny Hans Island between Greenland and Ellesmere.

Soviet Russia, which took years to normalize its ties with other powers, contended with multiple contretemps in the Arctic. Not only did it fence with Norway over Franz Josef Land, it regarded the Svalbard Treaty as having prejudicially ignored Russia's historical presence on Spitsbergen and refused until 1934 to sign it. In their northeastern waters, the Soviets, like tsarist authorities before them, contested America's claim to Bennett, Jeannette and Henrietta islands. All of these had been discovered and proclaimed U.S. territory by George Washington DeLong in 1881, but every Russian government since has considered them part of the New Siberian archipelago; only in 1990 did the U.S. officially relinquish its claim. The Soviets were particularly vulnerable on Wrangel Island, where Canadian and American groups attempted several times during the 1920s to establish squatter's rights. Vilhjalmur Stefansson, obsessed with bringing Wrangel into Canada's orbit, organized the most tragically foolish of these ventures, settling four white amateurs and a female Inuit cook on the island in 1921, only to have all but the last die of cold and malnutrition. Other foreign parties were bodily removed from Wrangel by Soviet ships. Until the u.s. extended diplomatic recognition to the ussr in 1933, Moscow also feared encroachments on Chukotka from Alaska, both private and official, an anxiety that flared up anew during the Cold War.

On the domestic-policy side of things, all Arctic nations moved forwards with the internal development of their northern territories. For aesthetically minded souls who preferred their northern realms pristine, this was a sad occasion. The American printmaker and illustrator Rockwell Kent spent 1918–19 in Alaska's Kenai Peninsula and 1929 in Greenland, idealizing both lands as a 'Northern Paradise' whose ruggedness forced humans to live up to their best potential.[5] The Canadian painters A. Y. Jackson and Lawren Harris, both part of the famed Group of Seven, attached symbolic, even mystical, significance to the unspoiled beauty of the northern wilderness; Harris, a theosophist, saw the iceberg, which changed states from solid to liquid and eventually back to solid, as emblematic of reincarnation. One finds similarly anti-technologist sentiments among northern-influenced writers and artists from Scandinavia and Russia. Still, modernization marched on. In Canada, its most loquacious proponent was Stefansson, who promoted the concept of 'the friendly Arctic' in his 1921 book of the same name and as a policy advocate for years afterwards. As much as he admired the Inuit way of life, which he emulated with excellent results during his travels, Stefansson had a supremely positivistic faith in the concept of progress, and argued that the proper fate of the polar wilderness was to be exploited by the civilized societies of the south. No Muir or Thoreau, he longed to see oil wells, natural gas fields, deep-water ports and airstrips sprawling across the Arctic landscape, from Hudson Bay's northern shores to the mouth of the Mackenzie.

Reality could not match the grandiosity of Stefansson's vision, but changes came nonetheless. In Canada, the national police force – the Royal Canadian Mounted Police (rcmp) after 1920 – embodied state authority on the Arctic frontier and expanded its presence after the war. This involved a concerted effort during the 1920s and early '30s to establish new detachments throughout the Arctic and to patrol regularly the eastern parts of the archipelago, where foreigners were most tempted to question Canada's sovereignty. With assistance from Joseph-Elzéar

Bernier, who had escorted convoys through the Atlantic during the war and then returned to northern voyaging, the RCMP opened its Craig Harbour station on Ellesmere Island in 1922. Another Ellesmere outpost went up on the Bache Peninsula in 1926–7, followed by the Dundas Harbour station on Devon Island. From these sites, RCMP personnel paid visits to Melville, Axel Heilberg, Amund Ringnes, Elluf Ringnes and Prince Christian islands. The RCMP also experimented with recruiting natives as special constables, but never found as many volunteers for these positions as it would have liked. In 1924, the RCMP prosecuted Canada's first Arctic court case, trying two Inuvialuit for murder in the Bonehouse, a whalers' storage facility on Herschel Island's Pauline Cove. The jury, composed of local residents, found the defendants guilty, and both were hanged from a roof beam in the makeshift courtroom.

Infrastructure in the Canadian north developed unevenly. Well-established population centres – trading posts, mining towns, sea and river ports – were often well serviced by transport connections and sometimes offered surprisingly sophisticated amenities. Even before the First World War, electric power and the Yukon's finest movie house had come to Dawson City. In other places, often not far away, the emptiness was all but complete. Even with the obvious limitations placed on water transport during the winter months, rivers and sea coasts provided the most reliable means of moving passengers and freight around the Arctic, and this traffic steadily increased. The north's rail network eventually grew, but for now only a few lines operated there, including the White Pass and Yukon and, starting in 1929, the 'muskeg express' that ran to Churchill, newly constructed on the Manitoba shores of Hudson Bay as a transhipment point for grain grown in the prairie provinces. Paved roads were a rarity at best, and dogsleds still served as a common mode of ground transport.

Of most help in penetrating Canada's Arctic interior was the aeroplane, whose potential as a tool for northern settlement was tested by a new breed of aviator, the bush pilot, shortly after the war. Properly maintained for cold-weather flying and equipped with skis or pontoons to avoid the need for landing strips, aeroplanes assisted with prospecting for mineral deposits and the spotting of forest fires, and enabled pilots to map huge expanses with a fraction of the effort expended by a land- or ship-based explorer. By carrying cargo, passengers and mail, they knitted otherwise isolated communities into a larger social fabric. Between 1925 and the early 1930s, bush pilots surveyed Hudson Bay and the Boothia Peninsula. Outfits like Western Canadian Airways and the Northern Aerial Mining Expedition explored and serviced the

Yukon, the Mackenzie Basin, Quebec's Ungava Peninsula and similarly remote areas. The scale of bush flying expanded during the 1930s; in 1935 Canada developed its first home-grown model of bush aircraft, the Montreal-manufactured Noorduyn Norseman.

The interwar years also placed Arctic aboriginals more under Ottawa's influence. Certainly they were in the public spotlight, with the blockbuster release of *Nanook of the North* (1922), Robert Flaherty's depiction of 'life and love in the actual Arctic', to quote the movie's subtitle. Filmed among the Inuit of Inukjuak, on Hudson Bay, *Nanook* is considered the first full-length documentary in cinematic history, despite the many liberties taken to romanticize its subject. 'Nanook', which means 'polar bear', was a hunter named Allakariallak, and his 'wife' was in fact married to Flaherty. While the spear-hunting techniques 'Nanook' demonstrated against seals and walruses at Flaherty's request were authentic, Allakariallak preferred in real life to use his rifle. In Canada and America both, the film left a lasting, if over-idealized, imprint on popular perceptions of the Arctic and its peoples.

Not that this widespread fascination was of practical help to northern natives, whether First Nations or Inuit, in their dealings with the authorities. In the summer of 1921, the federal government, motivated by the discovery of oil in the Mackenzie Basin the year before, negotiated Treaty No. 11 with the local First Nations. This was the last of Canada's 'numbered' treaties and the only one that concerned Arctic territory. Almost two dozen Dene bands, assured by the authorities that they could continue to occupy their traditional homelands and that large game preserves would be set aside for their use alone, signed the agreement. Unfortunately, once it became clear that the region's oil could not be extracted profitably, the government backed away from many of its promises. In countless smaller ways, First Nations people throughout the Arctic and subarctic found that Canadian law regulated their existence more than it had the lives of their parents and grandparents. The same was true for the Inuit. During the 1930s, a series of legal decisions, culminating in the 1939 Supreme Court case *Re Eskimos*, caused the federal government to assume responsibility for the Inuit on terms similar to those of the Indian Act. Canadian authority thus weighed more heavily on how Arctic natives traded, travelled and worshipped. With Ottawa's blessing, the Hudson's Bay Company in the mid-1930s relocated a number of mainland Inuit, not entirely on a volunteer basis, to Dundas Harbour and Arctic Bay on Devon and Baffin islands, to hunt and trap for the outposts there.

Ottawa's most infamous impact on native life was felt in the sphere of education. During the 1920s and '30s, Canada's system of residential schools, established in the mid-1880s to provide mandatory education for all First Nations youth, neared the full extent of its growth. A number of these schools appeared in the northern reaches of the Yukon and Northwest territories, primarily taking in Athabaskan students, but with Inuit forced into attendance as well. The policy was well intentioned, if unapologetically assimiliationist, and many teachers had their pupils' best interests at heart. Still, the government ran the schools on the cheap, contracting many of them to Catholic and Protestant missions. Instructors and staff forbade the use of indigenous languages and held native religious beliefs up to ridicule, irreparably damaging the collective folk memory of many aboriginal groups. A large proportion of the children adjusted badly to the regimentation of school life; instances of corporal punishment and outright physical abuse were frequent, and sexual predation was not uncommon. Residential schools remained open in the North well into the post-Second World War period, inflicting cultural and psychological trauma on several generations of First Nations and Inuit students.

Alaska, recently promoted from colony to territory, had a growing number of towns and harbours around which to organize its transportational grid. Among the newest of these were Fairbanks, established in 1901 as a trading post in the Tanana Valley, and Anchorage, which sprang into being in 1914 as the landing site for railway-building supplies and is now Alaska's largest metropolis. The railway under construction was the Alaska Railroad, completed between 1915 and 1923 and designed to link the port of Seward on the south coast with Fairbanks, more than 300 miles to the north. As in earlier years, Alaskans took advantage of the mobility offered by such rivers as the Colville, Yukon and Kuskokwim, and they expanded their network of roads and railways. Building this sort of infrastructure required time – it took from 1921 to 1938 to finish the Mount McKinley Road – and dogsleds remained the most routinely used mode of ground transport throughout the 1920s and even the '30s. The most rapid developments took place in the air, as the Alaskans, no less than the Canadians, embraced bush flying. The undisputed king of Alaska's early pilots was Carl Ben Eielson, a Fairbanks science teacher who had learned to fly during the First World War and left the classroom for the chance to earn a living by delivering mail and passengers in Curtiss Jennys and de Havilland biplanes. By his death in 1929, Eielson had co-piloted the first trans-Arctic Ocean aeroplane flight and flown in the Antarctic.

Alaskan transport, though, was not without its challenges. Ports in the west and north, such as Nome and Barrow, froze up part of every year, sometimes for more than six months. Fog along the coast and in the Aleutians, along with unpredictable downdrafts called williwaws, grounded or wrecked aeroplanes. A full third of Alaska's air fleet met with destruction during the 1930s, and it was a long time before planes could fly reliably in the winter weather. One of the most storied episodes in Alaskan history shows the fragility of the territory's network under suboptimal circumstances. In January 1925, the 10,000 residents of Nome and its neighbouring settlements, the majority of them Native Americans or Eskimos with low resistance to foreign diseases, desperately needed a shipment of fresh antitoxin to stave off a diphtheria epidemic on the verge of breakout. The nearest supply was in Seward, more than 900 miles away, but no ship from there could hope to approach Nome through the iced-in Norton Sound. Carl Eielson had begun winter-flying trials only the year before and had never managed more than 250 miles at a time in winter conditions or in weather colder than -10°F. With snowstorms raging and temperatures dropping to -50°F, it was as impossible to approach Nome from the air as from the sea. The one remaining option was to move the medicine north by train to Nenana, near Fairbanks, and then convey it by dogsled for nearly 700 miles across the interior, linking up with the western end of the Iditarod Trail. Sledding between Nenana and Nome typically took three weeks or more, but in the Serum Run of 1925 twenty drivers, three-quarters of them Eskimo or Athabaskan Indian, and 150 dogs, including the celebrated Balto, relayed the shipment to Nome in an astonishing five and a half days – part of the mushing history commemorated each year by the Iditarod Trail Sled Dog Race.

Gold, which had fuelled Alaska's turn-of-the-century boom, still supported an active mining industry. Less glamorous but more lucrative by this stage were fishing and canning, with salmon having emerged as the territory's top-earning commodity since the 1890s and the Alaska Packers' Association now one of its key economic players. Sealing fell off after the 1911 moratorium on fur-seal hunting, but whaling continued without interruption – even though the decline of certain species, especially the grey whale, was apparent by the 1920s. Forestry generated respectable earnings, but those with hopes for Alaska's economic future were most excited about oil. Petroleum seepages had been spotted in many parts of the mainland during the 1800s, and wells were sunk on the Iniskin Peninsula as early as 1898. Not until 1911, however, with the opening of the Katalla field in Chugach country, did oil extraction become commercially viable. For now, returns remained modest, and when Katalla's refinery caught fire in 1933, the owners chose to shut down the wells rather than rebuild. Even so, hundreds of petroleum exploration permits were issued during these years and significant quantities of oil were located, including in the large North Slope section that President Warren Harding set aside in 1923 as Naval Petroleum Reserve No. 4 – today the 23.5-million-acre National Petroleum Reserve. The problem for the present was the high cost of production relative to places like Texas and Oklahoma, which pumped out floods of cheap oil during the 1920s and '30s. Only after the Second World War did Alaska become the petroleum powerhouse that interwar investors had hoped it would be.

With larger numbers of settlers flowing into Alaska, indigenous life changed substantially. Whether they were Eskimo, Aleut or Indian – and by the end of the First World War, the u.s. had elected to categorize them all equally as wards of the nation – few natives now lived or worked completely apart from whites. A majority accepted some form of services or aid from the government, with two-thirds of Alaska's native children attending schools run by the Bureau of Indian Affairs or churches on the BIA's behalf. By 1930, most rural natives had access to social welfare services, medical care and government-run cooperative stores, and the Bureau's Reindeer Service introduced the practice of caribou herding as a way to stimulate the native economy. Not all services were of uniformly high quality, though, and many BIA schools displayed the same assimilationist intolerance for native cultures and beliefs, and some of the abusive tendencies, associated with Canada's residential schools. Alaska was not the Jim Crow South, but anti-Indian and anti-Eskimo prejudice was pervasive, and segregation not unknown. This was particularly the case on military installations and in the educational sphere, where the Nelson Act of 1905 allowed the establishment of schools exclusively for 'white children and children of mixed blood leading a civilized life'.

Growing dependency on government assistance undermined native autonomy in Alaska, especially because self-advocacy remained limited until after the Second World War. During the interwar years, only one organization, the Alaska Native Brotherhood (and its affiliate, the Alaska Native Sisterhood), which had been founded in Sitka in 1912, existed to advance the social and political interests of the territory's Eskimos, Aleuts and Native Americans. Under the Franklin Roosevelt presidency, BIA Commissioner John Collier provided some remedy in the form of the 1936 Alaska Reorganization Act, a supplement to the Indian

Reorganization Act issued two years beforehand. Both acts, responding to the dismal picture of Native American living conditions painted nationwide by the 1928 Meriam Report, allowed for a higher degree of political and economic self-governance. The difference between the two was that, because Alaskan natives had never been placed on reservations and were considered less 'tribally oriented', the 1936 act offered them the choice of creating reservations for themselves or incorporating themselves on a 'village' basis – the option preferred in the end by most communities.

In mainland Scandinavia, northern development proceeded along many of the same lines as before the First World War. Forest industries still played a role in all three countries, and the emerging energy and fertilizer giant Norsk Hydro built some of its early plants in the North, but metallurgy was at the heart of Scandinavia's Arctic economies, at least on land. The Finns discovered nickel near Petsamo in 1921 and began mining it with the help of foreign investors in the mid-1930s. In Sweden, the extraction of iron ore continued to drive development along the rail corridor that connected Luleå, on the Bothnian coast, with the Norwegian port of Narvik. Halfway in between lay Sweden's mammoth Kiruna mine, whose working population rose from 7,400 in 1910 to over 13,000 by 1930. Production was supplemented by the Malmberget near Gällivare and the Luossavaara mine, which opened in 1921. Living and working conditions at Kiruna improved during the interwar years, largely as a result of several successful strikes.

Norway began taking zinc and aluminium out of mines north of the Arctic Circle, most notably around Glomfjord, and it enlarged its coal-mining operations on Spitsbergen. Here the Norwegians stood face to face with the Soviets, whose Arctic Coal Trust (Arktikugol) purchased the Barentsburg mine, approximately 30 miles from the port of Longyearbyen, in 1932. In 1917–18, the Swedes opened a sizable coaling operation of their own on Spitsbergen: the Sveagruva mine, above 77°N on the Van Mijenfjord. Fishing, sealing and whaling remained important both to Scandinavia and its island colonies, although with whales growing scarcer in Arctic waters, the Norwegians, having done so much to bring industrial whaling methods to a gory level of perfection, shifted their efforts more to the Antarctic during the 1920s and '30s.

With respect to indigenous rights, the Scandinavians' record was not spotless during these years. Comparatively benevolent as colonizing powers go, Denmark was still paternalistic in its handling of Inuit Greenlanders, and there arose among some on the island a desire for cultural and economic, if not political, autonomy. Debates about home rule became more common, as did open complaints about the royal monopoly on trade. For the time being, though, these remained minor rumblings, and most were convinced that the protection of the Crown, especially when it came to trade, was worth having.

It was the Sami who had it hardest in Scandinavia. Fewer than a quarter followed the reindeer-herding way of life after the First World War, but whether settled or nomadic, they faced the same assimilationist pressures that earlier generations had, and new ones besides. While Norway did so with the greatest fervency, all three countries, in their schools and in public life, did their best to stamp out the use of Sami dialects. The Sami suffered economic discrimination, as in the Norwegian law that stated until 1940 that, to buy or lease state-owned property in the northern counties, one had to demonstrate fluency in the Norwegian language and register under a Norwegian name. In Norway, Finland and most of all Sweden – with its National Institute for Race Biology, founded in 1922 and tinged with Aryanist and anti-Semitic tendencies – doctors and eugenicists laboured to prove 'scientifically' the purported inferiority of groups like the Sami. Large numbers of Sami graves were plundered to provide genetic material for such research, and Sami were disproportionately represented among the many women selected for forced sterilization throughout Scandinavia. A product of the eugenicist tide that swept Europe and North America during the interwar years, but continuing in some cases until the 1970s, the forced sterilization campaigns were intended to weed out disabilities that might burden Scandinavia's emerging welfare states, and also to purge the population of 'undesirable' elements. The Swedish programme, by far the largest, ran from 1934 to 1976 and claimed nearly 63,000 victims.

Ideological predilections, plus the pronounced underdevelopment of its northern territories, caused the USSR to adopt the most ambitious Arctic programme of the interwar era. Under Lenin and Stalin, Soviet policy in the North was driven by the twin desires to reap the region's riches and, for theoretically altruistic reasons, to bring socialist modernization to a barren, backward land. The western end of Russia's Northern Sea Route, around Murmansk and Arkhangelsk, was already infrastructurally well developed. Siberia's rivers were surveyed anew during the 1920s and their navigability improved, but top priority was assigned to the transformation of the entire Northern Sea Route into a regularly usable maritime artery. The Soviets tested their skills against the Kara Sea in 1920 during the Great Siberian Bread Expedition, which shipped grain to the famine-stricken Volga along the northern coast then south down Russia's rivers, and afterwards during the yearly Kara Expeditions, in which Soviet ships escorted foreign merchant vessels to the mouths of the Ob and Yenisei. The early Kara Expeditions were planned in consultation with the Norwegian Otto Sverdrup, Nansen's associate, and continued into the early 1930s. Throughout the decade, the Soviets accumulated the world's largest fleet of icebreakers and ice-forcing ships, using them to support the building of research stations and new ports on the Arctic islands and along the northern coast. The icebreakers *Malygin* and *Krasin* won renown for their roles in the search and rescue that followed the crash of the airship *Italia*. In 1932, in a mission that coincided with the Second International Polar Year, the ice-forcer *Sibiryakov* became the first vessel to traverse the Northern Sea Route in a single navigational season.

The architect of this voyage, the mathematician and physicist Otto Shmidt, used the *Sibiryakov*'s success to sell the Stalinist regime on the idea of centralizing all Arctic-related functions – transport, science, resource development and dealings with the natives – in the hands of a single multi-purpose agency. In 1932–3, Stalin agreed to the creation of the Main Administration of the Northern Sea Route (GUSMP, or Glavsevmorput) which, under the 'commissar of ice', as the press nicknamed Shmidt, enjoyed nearly complete control over the Arctic islands and all Soviet territory east of the Urals and north of the 62nd parallel. GUSMP had no authority over gold mining, the armed forces or the prison camps of the rapidly expanding Gulag system, although it frequently 'borrowed' Gulag labourers. It absorbed into itself the USSR's premier polar research agency, the All-Union Arctic Institute (VAI), superseded the organization previously in charge of native policy and coordinated the extraction of a variety of marine and land-based resources.

Most of all, GUSMP pushed ahead with its transport work, which involved both routine infrastructure building and some of the decade's most internationally admired polar exploits, such as the *Cheliuskin* airlift of 1934 and the SP-1 expedition to the North Pole in 1937, detailed at greater length below. Even more than the agencies preceding it, Glavsevmorput strove to realize aviation's potential as a tool for polar exploration and development. Throughout the 1920s and '30s, Soviet pilots performed aerial mapping surveys, flew ice-reconnaissance missions to aid shipping, researched the difficulties of navigating near to the magnetic North Pole and scouted new air routes across the breadth of the continent. In 1936, Vasilii Molokov became the first to fly the entire length of the Northern Sea Route. Such triumphs were glamorously fictional-ized in Veniamin Kaverin's beloved adventure novel *The Two Captains* (1938–44, with a film version in 1955), and the feature film *The Seven Bold Ones* (1936).

Immense economic prizes were at stake in Russia's north. Geologists such as Vladimir Obruchev and Alexander Fersman located a cornucopia of mineral wealth throughout the Soviet north. Salt, polymetals and coal – which the USSR's Arktikugol trust also mined in Spitsbergen – were there for the taking in places like Vorkuta, in the Pechora Basin; Norilsk, high up on the Yenisei; and Nordvik, east of the Taimyr, as long as the Soviets could overcome the elements to get at them. If the gold mines of the southern Lena had been Siberia's El Dorado in the nineteenth century, the astounding deposits of gold discovered in the late 1920s beneath the permafrost of the Aldan and Kolyma basins took their place. Although it was not exploited in any major way until after the Second World War, oil came to the notice of prospectors in the Pechora and Ob basins. Above ground, the new town of Igarka rose up from the empty banks of the Yenisei to serve as a new centre for Siberia's forest industry, and the Soviets eagerly cashed in on the returns from north-ern sealing, whaling, fishing and fur-harvesting.

More than any other Arctic power, the USSR stood out for the lengths it was willing to go to exploit its northern resources. Not only did Soviet agencies work to the breakneck tempo dictated by the First and Second Five-Year Plans (1928–32 and 1932–7) and under the conditions of para-noid distrust produced by terroristic witch-hunts and purges, but Arctic development was inextricably linked with the use of forced labour. As Aleksandr Solzhenitsyn notes in *The Gulag Archipelago*, 'it stank, too, even way up north, beneath the Arctic storms, at the polar stations so beloved in the legends of the thirties'.[6] The Soviet Union's first labour camp was the Solovetsky Monastery, on the Arctic islands of the White Sea, converted to that purpose on Lenin's orders in 1923. Although agen-cies like GUSMP were administratively distinct from the Gulag, some of their personnel worked for the latter as well, and they used prison labour or benefited from it. Between 1931 and 1933, the Northern Sea Route was joined to the Leningrad region by the White Sea-Baltic Canal, or Belomor, the first of the Stalinist megaprojects to be completed by means of inmate labour. Igarka, held up as a socialist 'forepost of culture', was the place of exile for thousands of peasants arrested during the Stalinist collectivization of agriculture. Mines and construction sites throughout the North depended wholly or partially on convict labour, including

Vorkuta, Nordvik, Norilsk and countless others. The country's first Arctic railway, built between 1935 and 1942 to connect Norilsk with the Yenisei port of Dudinka, was likewise a forced-labour project. Deadliest of all were the gold and tin mines operated on Chukotka by GUSMP's bureaucratic foe, the secret police's Main Administration for Far Northern Construction (Dalstroi), whose chief port, Magadan, was dubbed 'the moorage of Hades' by camp survivor Varlam Shalamov.[7] Brutally prodigal with its prisoners' lives, Dalstroi, enlarging itself at Glavsevmorput's expense, fashioned an empire of suffering that, after the 1930s, came to measure over 900,000 square miles and encompassed some 80 separate camps.

Soviet harshness also manifested itself in Moscow's policy towards northern natives, despite a promising start. Early nationalities policy in the Soviet Union followed a largely progressive line through most of the 1920s, based on the concept of 'indigenization' (*korenizatsiia*) and aiming to respect the dignity and traditions of minority populations. Some of the first measures pertaining to northern natives included the abolition of the *yasak* system and the cancellation of debts to moneylenders. Larger groups like the Yakut and Komi were seen as advanced enough to adapt well to the new order, but in 1924 a Committee for Assistance to the Small Peoples of the North (known informally as the Committee of the North) took charge of Sovietizing the rest. The Committee was staffed by some of the most eminent ethnographers of the day – including Vladimir Bogoraz-Tan, who also founded Leningrad's Institute of the Peoples of the North (INS) – and viewed its mission as one of uplift and fraternal solicitude rather than compulsion. Filled with starry-eyed expectations of grateful natives embracing a more modern way of life, Committee activists set up cultural bases and 'Red Tents' from which to dispense medicine, encourage personal hygiene and promote literacy. The INS devised a Latin-based script, the Unified Northern Alphabet, to suit the small peoples' languages, and prepared textbooks and primers in sixteen northern tongues. To 'denomadize' the small peoples' economic practices, the Committee erected trading posts called integral cooperatives, which exchanged store credits for furs, fish and other goods.

But much of this Marxian missionizing came to naught, with most natives dismissive or resentful of it. 'We have no use for the Red Tent', a Khanty hunter told one Committee official. 'Our fathers and grandfathers knew nothing about red tents, yet they lived better than we do.'[8] With time, the Kremlin's stance towards Arctic minorities hardened. In 1926, the regime outlawed 'relics of the tribal way of life', including blood feuds and the forcing of minors into marriage. Shamans were persecuted and arrested. The collectivization of native economies, which began in 1928, in parallel with Stalin's nationwide collectivization of agriculture, traumatized fishing, sea hunting and trapping, but caused even more damage to reindeer herding across the North, from the Pechora basin to the Chukchi peninsula. From an estimated 2.2 million in 1926, the USSR's population of domesticated reindeer fell to 1.6 million by the end of 1933 and to 1.4 million by 1937. Seeking purposefully to dismantle the traditional clan system, Soviet collectivizers compelled reindeer herders to work in brigades. Dissatisfied with the 'softness' shown by the Committee of the North, Stalin shut it down in 1935 and handed its economic duties over to GUSMP, which competed with natives for Arctic resources rather than nurturing their productive potential. Between 1936 and 1939, the government did away with the Unified Northern Alphabet in favour of the Cyrillic script and made Russian language instruction mandatory in all schools. It ended the native Siberians' traditional exemption from military service, and those living near Gulag facilities were pressed into providing them with food and drayage. Native resistance, which was considerable, occasionally turned violent but most often took the form of evasion. In the remotest places, such as the Taimyr and Chukotka – where Siberian Eskimos still fraternized freely with their Alaskan kith across the Bering – natives simply vanished into the tundra. Only one-tenth of non-coastal Chukchi, whose 'reindeer kings' refused to give up their private herds, were collectivized as late as 1939, and not until after the Second World War were the Dolgans and a few other diehards finally forced under the Soviet yoke.

The decade ended with Russia's Arctic in a muddle. Glavsevmorput had accomplished much, and its exploration and aviation exploits were universally acclaimed. But among polar workers on the ground (and out of the public eye), alcoholism and squalid living conditions were endemic. GUSMP's developmental efforts fell short of the quotas set for it, and the number of accidents it logged at sea and in the air spiked during the late 1930s. GUSMP owed these failures partly to the regime's unreasonable expectations and partly to the debilitating effects of Stalin's purges, but nature took a hand as well. The second half of 1937 proved unusually cold, leaving half of GUSMP's fleet, including eight of its nine precious icebreakers, frozen in the ice. Reprimanded for its shortcomings in the summer of 1938, GUSMP was stripped of all non-transport functions, with most of its assets transferred to its hated rival, Dalstroi. Otto Shmidt, lucky to escape arrest or worse, stepped down as Glavsevmorput's head in the spring of 1939. Only in 1940 did the last of the USSR's ice-trapped ships, the icebreaker *Sedov*, return to port. The eve of the Second World War found the Soviets scrambling to regularize traffic along the Northern Sea Route once more, and to get their Arctic house in order.

New Horizons: Science and Exploration
during the Interwar Years

As late as the twentieth century, ghost islands still haunted the Arctic. These were land masses whose existence had been sworn to by explorers and mariners from previous eras, but which turned out upon closer investigation to be mirages or the products of imagination.

Investigating more closely, however, was not always an easy thing, and during the first half of the 1900s it remained an open question as to whether places like Crocker Land and Bradley Land, supposedly spied by Peary and Cook respectively in the vicinity of Axel Heilberg, deserved places on the map. The same was true of Charles Francis Hall's President's Land; King Oscar's Land and Petermann Land, which the Austrians believed to lie near the Franz Josef archipelago; and Keenan Land, which Stefansson hunted for in vain in the Beaufort Sea. Among Russian scholars, theories long abounded about the possible locations of Andreyev Land and Sannikov Land off the Siberian coast. (For amusement's sake, Vladimir Obruchev, the doyen of Siberian geological studies and a science-fiction author in the vein of Jules Verne, used the latter as the setting for his novel *Sannikov Land* of 1926, in which a Russian expedition discovers the island to be heated by a volcano and inhabited by mammoths, Neanderthals and a lost tribe of Siberian Eskimos.) At this same time, confusion prevailed about another question that seemed similarly fundamental: the nature of permafrost and what it should be called. Despite its omnipresence in the North, and as engineers wrestled with the problem of how to build on it, scholars could not decide whether it was an object (frozen soil) or a process (the transformation of soil into a frozen substance), and neither could they settle on a name for it. Some preferred the older term 'pergelisol', others the descriptor 'cryolithozone', while the Russians, who opened their own Permafrost Institute in 1939, used the phrases 'perennially' or 'eternally frozen soil' (*mnogoletniaia* or *vechnaia merzlota*). The word 'permafrost' itself was coined only in 1943, in the United States, and is not universally accepted even today.

In other words, the state of geographical and scientific knowledge about the Arctic was far from complete, even after the First World War.

It was that deficit which private adventurers, national governments and academic institutions attempted to address during the 1920s and '30s, with a myriad of expeditions geared to study the region's weather, its ionospheric and magnetological mysteries, its glaciers and oceanic currents, its wildlife and geology, and its human inhabitants. These were the last decades of the 'golden' or 'romantic' era of Arctic exploration, an age prolonged, then ended, by the advent of polar flight. Introducing aircraft to the Arctic proved an adventure in itself, but flying there gradually became more commonplace – although never quite a matter of routine – and was seen by some to have drained the heroic glamour out of polar questing. So thought veteran trekkers like Matthew Henson, who, when interviewed by the *Polar Times* in 1937 about Arctic aviation, harrumphed that 'it was a damn sight harder the way we did it!'[9]

Exploration had not ceased during the First World War. Only in 1915 did Boris Vilkitsky close out the Russian Hydrographic Expedition by bringing the *Taimyr* and *Vaigach* through the Northeast Passage, and the war was not yet done when, in 1918, Norway's Roald Amundsen and the young scholar Harald Ulrik Sverdrup (third cousin to *Fram* captain Otto Sverdrup and the eventual director of the Scripps Institution of Oceanography) set out in the *Maud* in an attempt to drift to the Pole. Failing in that goal, Amundsen completed a west-to-east traversal of the Northeast Passage in 1920 and returned to the Arctic Ocean to gather scientific data until 1925.

During his Second Thule Expedition, Knud Rasmussen spent 1916–18 mapping part of Greenland's northern coast; marooned not far away was the American Donald MacMillan, trying to salvage what was left of his 1913 Crocker Land Expedition. MacMillan, who had taken part in Peary's last expedition only to be prevented by frostbite from accompanying him on the final run to the Pole, travelled some 30 times to the Arctic before retiring at the age of 82, but the Crocker Land venture was not one of his successes. The first ship he chartered ran up against rocks due to the captain's drunkenness. He pushed on so far towards the object of his search, in spite of being warned by the Inuit guide Piugaattoq that it did not exist, that he stranded himself and his companions. His engineer, Fitzhugh Green, shot Piugaattoq to death under highly dubious circumstances. Although some expedition members returned to safety on their own, MacMillan had to be rescued by the Newfoundland captain Robert Bartlett in 1917.

Bartlett himself, formerly the skipper of Peary's *Roosevelt*, was freshly returned from another wartime undertaking, Vilhjalmur Stefansson's

Canadian Arctic Expedition, which ran from 1913 to 1918 and produced some of the most wildly mixed results in the history of Arctic travel. A southern contingent led by Rudolf Anderson, Stefansson's expedition partner from 1908–12, carried out a multidisciplinary survey of the Mackenzie Basin and the coastal region between Cape Parry and Victoria Island, completing its task by the summer of 1916. Under Stefansson, the northern group was to explore the Beaufort Sea, but suffered a crippling blow at the outset when its flagship, Bartlett's *Karluk*, was carried westward by the ice into Russia's Chukchi Sea. In a decision for which he was later roundly castigated, the impatient Stefansson, claiming to be off on a ten-day hunt for caribou, set out on his own and left the ship to its fate. Before the *Karluk* broke apart and sank, Bartlett led everyone aboard on an 80-mile hike across the ice to Wrangel Island and then continued by himself to Siberia and Alaska to organize a rescue. Half the ship's complement perished before help arrived in September 1914, and Stefansson has never since shed his reputation for haphazard caprice. Yet he fared well enough himself, all afire with his 'friendly Arctic' rhetoric when he returned, and the expedition's scholarly results were undeniably excellent. He and his team of ethnographers, who included Diamond Jenness, added considerably to what was already his hefty contribution to the study of northern peoples. Stefansson depth-sounded much of the Beaufort's undersea bed and charted the last major Arctic land masses still unknown to Western science. Ever controversial, he served two times as the president of the Explorers Club and remained active until his death in 1962. He directed polar research at Dartmouth College, advised the u.s. Army's Cold Regions Research and Engineering Laboratory and busied himself with many other projects – including his well-publicized experiments with fish-and-red-meat diets, reported on during the 1920s and '30s in the *Journal of the American Medical Association* and *Harper's Monthly*.

The immediate postwar years saw activity in all sectors of the Arctic. Amundsen and Sverdrup were still voyaging in the *Maud*, and Stefansson moved on from the Canadian Arctic Expedition to his ill-conceived attempt to colonize Wrangel Island in defiance of the ussr. In 1921, MacMillan sailed the schooner *Bowdoin* to Baffin Island in order to test the feasibility of staying in touch with the south via radio. Don Mix, his radioman, broadcast to the States under the call sign 'Wireless North Pole'. The geologist Adolf Hoel, a full-throated supporter of Norway's 'Arctic imperialism', began his long career as a surveyor of eastern Greenland and the Svalbard archipelago. Between 1920 and 1923, the Danish Jubilee

Expedition, led by Lauge Koch, mapped Greenland's north coast between Cape York and Denmark Sound.

Koch's countryman, Knud Rasmussen, carried out three of his Thule expeditions in rapid succession after the war: the Third in 1919 to lay supply depots for Amundsen in the *Maud*, the Fourth in 1919–20 to perform ethnographic research in Greenland, and the Fifth, his finest accomplishment, in 1921–4. Starting in eastern Canada and proceeding to Nome, Rasmussen and his team, which included Therkel Mathiassen and Kaj Birket-Smith, carried out a comprehensive study of North America's Inuit and Eskimo peoples, combining the results with what they had already learned about native Greenlanders to buttress their argument – now the accepted wisdom – that the Eskimo-Inuit peoples had originated in Asia. During the expedition, Rasmussen, with two Inuit guides, became the first to travel the entire course of the Northwest Passage by dogsled, a journal chronicled in his book *Across Arctic America* (1927). He would have gone even farther, to Siberia, had the USSR seen fit to grant him a visa.

With their civil war over, the Soviets, in addition to running their yearly Kara Expeditions, sent survey teams under scholars like the geologist Georgii Ushakov to Novaya Zemlya in 1921, Franz Josef Land in 1923 and Wrangel in 1924, both to set up research stations and to shore up claims to territorial sovereignty. The Soviet Navy played a role in early Arctic hydrography, as did the Marine-Scientific Research Institute, but it was the All-Union Arctic Institute, founded in March 1920 and led by the affable, walrus-mustachioed geologist-geographer Rudolf Samoilovich, that came to dominate scientific work in the Soviet Arctic.

The mid-1920s witnessed the conquest of the North Pole from the air, both by dirigibles and aeroplanes. Each of these had advantages and disadvantages, and it remained uncertain until the 1930s which would prove more useful to Arctic aviation. Airships were sturdier than the aeroplanes of the day, had greater range and carrying capacity, and served better as platforms for cameras and scientific instruments. But despite the difficulties involved with building airfields in northern conditions, aeroplanes – which could be fitted with skis and floats if landing strips were not available – were far more effective at landing, taking off and delivering cargo in rough terrain. One of the dirigible's keenest advocates was Fridtjof Nansen, now a Nobel Peace Prize recipient for his work on famine relief and the handling of refugees displaced by the First World War. In 1924, Nansen became president of the International Society for the Exploration of the Arctic with Airships, or Aeroarctic, whose members included scientists and enthusiasts from twenty nations, although Germany and the Soviet Union, followed by the Scandinavian countries, were most heavily represented. Aeroarctic's fondest hope was to persuade Hugo Eckener, who had risen to head Germany's Zeppelin works after the death of Zeppelin himself, to provide it with the requisite airship, but it took a number of years to win the sceptical pilot over.

Other fliers acted in the meantime, using planes and dirigibles alike. Bush pilotry caught on throughout the Alaskan, Canadian and Soviet north (although the Russians did not use the term), and in 1925 came two expeditions aiming to fly aeroplanes to the North Pole. Operating out of Spitsbergen, Roald Amundsen and the American philanthropist Lincoln Ellsworth took two Dornier Wal flying boats almost to 88°N in May. Landing on the ice to switch over to reserve fuel tanks, they damaged one of the planes and were lucky to get all their team members back home in the second. A month later, the MacMillan-Byrd Expedition proceeded from Maine to Ellesmere and Axel Heilberg islands in the *Bowdoin* and the *Peary*. MacMillan hoped mainly to gather scientific data and to test further the usefulness of the radio in the Arctic, but because part of his funding came from the u.s. Navy, he was obliged to let Lieutenant Commander Richard Byrd practise Arctic flying in Greenland and, if the chance presented itself, attempt a flight to the Pole. The two men got along poorly, and although Byrd and his fellow officers carried out valuable mapping work, MacMillan remained unconvinced of the aeroplane's utility and ended the expedition before Byrd had a chance to try for the ultimate prize.

The following May brought Byrd back to the Arctic, this time to Spitsbergen, with the pilot Floyd Bennett and a Fokker triplane named the *Josephine Ford*. Also in Spitsbergen were Amundsen and Ellsworth, who had opted this year to fly in the airship *Norge*, designed and captained by the Italian pilot Umberto Nobile. Byrd and Bennett stole a march on their competitors, winging their way north on the night of 8 May. Overcome along the way by 'a flash of sympathy for the brave men who had in years past struggled northward over that cruel mass', the two men recorded in their journal that, as of 9 May, 9:02 a.m. GMT, they were the first ever to fly to the North Pole.[10] After they returned to Spitsbergen, Amundsen and his team extended their congratulations, then set off in the *Norge*, reaching the Pole on 13 May 1926, and continuing onwards to the Inupiat village of Teller, Alaska.

Byrd, the apparent victor in this contest, went on to a distinguished career as an Antarctic explorer, establishing the 'Little America' base on the Ross Ice Shelf and, in 1929, completing the first flight over the

Roald Amundsen and Lincoln Ellsworth's Dornier Wal flying boat on the ice during their attempt to fly to the North Pole, 1925.

South Pole. In the years since, though, a broad consensus has formed that Byrd and Bennett falsified their North Pole claim. Some, including the Norwegian-American aviator Bernt Balchen, one of Byrd's mechanics in 1926 and his co-pilot in 1929, doubted immediately that the *Josephine Ford* had been away from Spitsbergen long enough to have attained its goal. Byrd's log for 1926 contains multiple erasure marks and re-pencillings, and several witnesses have attested that both men admitted in private that they had come within sight of their target but fallen short of it. If true, this would make those aboard the *Norge* the first to fly above the Pole – and, if one disbelieves Cook's and Peary's claims from 1908 and 1909, the first to travel to the Pole by any means.

Also during the 1920s, research into the ethnography, folklore and archaeology of the North was pursued on a greater scale. Soviet ethnographers and archaeologists such as Lev Shternberg and Vladimir Bogoraz-Tan, as well as the generation trained by them, continued their research across the Arctic rim, from the Pomor lands to Chukotka – despite the ideological constraints that shackled their work. In North America and Greenland, Stefansson, Rasmussen and Rasmussen's colleague Therkel Mathiassen remained active among the Inuit peoples. Concurrently, the famed ethnolinguist Edward Sapir, a student of Franz Boas and chief anthropologist at the National Museum of Canada, studied the native populations of the Mackenzie Basin and subarctic British Columbia.

Alaska and Beringia attracted the attention of a bevy of social scientists during the 1920s and early '30s: the Smithsonian's Henry Collins; the Bavarian-born Otto Geist, nicknamed the 'white Eskimo'; and Frederica de Laguna, who conducted fieldwork among the Chugach Eskimos and the Athabaskans of the Tanana and Yukon valleys and later chaired the anthropology department at Bryn Mawr College. Laguna gained some of her early research experience with Denmark's Mathiassen, in Greenland, and collaborated in Alaska with Kaj Birket-Smith, a veteran of Rasmussen's Fifth Thule Expedition and an expert on the Caribou Inuit and Alaska's Eyak. One of the towering figures in the field during these years was the New Zealand-born Diamond Jenness, an alumnus of Stefansson's Canadian Arctic Expedition and Sapir's successor at the National Museum of Canada. A frequent adviser to the Canadian government on native affairs, Jenness published dozens of works, among them *The People of the Twilight* (1928), a classic about the Copper Inuit, and the standard reference *The Indians of Canada* (1932). As an archaeologist, his crowning achievement was the identification of the Dorset and Old Bering cultures in 1925 and 1926 respectively.

During the late 1920s and early '30s, the physical exploration of the Arctic proved highly eventful and claimed more than a few lives. Routine work often went well, as with MacMillan's 1926 search for traces of the Viking occupation in Labrador. In the *Effie A. Morrissey*, Robert Bartlett ferried Explorers Club and National Geographic Society expeditions to Canada's north, and RCMP officers like Albert Herbert Joy completed long patrols through the Canadian archipelago. Numerous Soviet voyages were made to Novaya Zemlya, Severnaya Zemlya (still not fully charted until 1932), the New Siberian Islands and Wrangel Island.

Other Arctic efforts took a wrong turn, occasionally with poignant contrasts between success and failure. In 1928, the Australian journalist and explorer Hubert Wilkins, who had surveyed parts of northwestern Canada for Stefansson during the Canadian Arctic Expedition, completed the world's first trans-Arctic aeroplane flight, from Alaska to Spitsbergen, with Carl Ben Eielson – a feat largely overshadowed by the calamity that befell the other marquee event in the Arctic skies that spring. On the morning of 24 May, Umberto Nobile's airship *Italia*, having flown over the North Pole on the third of five flights planned from King's Bay in Spitsbergen, crash-landed on the ice, killing one of its sixteen passengers and sweeping six others to their deaths with the balloon, which separated from the gondola. Despite serious injuries – Nobile himself broke an arm, a leg and some ribs – the survivors erected a camp, centred on the famous 'red tent', painted that colour for visibility, and began radioing their support ship, the *Città di Milano*, for help. Only on 3 June did a Soviet radio enthusiast pick up the s.o.s., and news of the wreck galvanized an international rescue operation. This mission killed Roald Amundsen, who, despite a frosty falling-out with Nobile after the *Norge* flight of 1926, took part in the air search for his onetime comrade; he and his crew vanished on June 18 between Tromsø and Svalbard, never to be seen again.

In the meantime, the *Italia* camp had split up, with Filippo Zappi, Adalberto Mariano and the badly hurt Swedish meteorologist Finn Malmgren setting out on foot towards Spitsbergen to seek help for the rest of the group. Malmgren died en route and the two others have since been dogged by suspicions that they fed on his remains. Nobile and the five men with him were spotted on 20 June, and Sweden's Einar Lundborg touched down three days later, but with room to evacuate only one person. To his everlasting regret, Nobile allowed himself to be cajoled into leaving first, opening himself to charges of cowardice and dereliction of duty for years to come. By 12 July, the Soviet icebreaker *Krasin*, in a search coordinated by Rudolf Samoilovich, had located and picked up both groups of survivors. Amundsen came away as a martyr, the Soviets as heroes and Nobile as 'a nervous jackass', in the words of fellow pilot Hugo Eckener.[11] Disowned by Mussolini's regime for not living up to Fascist standards of manliness, Nobile continued to design and fly airships, including for the Soviet Union, but lived with the taint of disgrace until his death in 1978. The disaster was commemorated on its 41st anniversary with the release of the Soviet–Italian film *The Red Tent* (1969), directed by Mikhail Kalatozov and starring Peter Finch as Nobile and Sean Connery as Amundsen.

Similarly contradistinct results played out during two expeditions to Greenland in 1930–31. Camping on the southeastern coast, Henry 'Gino' Watkins and the fourteen members of his British Arctic Air Route Expedition (BAARE) spent a year gathering meteorological data to assist in the planning of polar air routes between England and Canada. August Courtauld won special recognition for manning Icecap Station, over 100 miles inland and at an elevation of 8,600 feet, for five months by himself, and the BAARE group returned in triumph in 1931. During the same span of time, Germany lost one of its most distinguished scientists, Alfred Wegener, who had exchanged his pre-First World War Arctic adventures for almost two decades of university life, gaining repute along the way for elaborating the theory of continental drift. Wegener went back to Greenland on an expedition designed to establish a line of three meteorological stations along the 71st parallel: one on the west coast, one in the east and one in the interior called Eismitte, or Ice Central. To overcome the logistical difficulty of transporting enough gear and food to Eismitte before the winter set in, Wegener brought along two motorized sleds, 'Polar Bear' and 'Snow Sparrow'. Unfortunately, summer turned to autumn too quickly in 1930, and the sleds did not perform to Wegener's expectations. In September, communications from Eismitte led Wegener to believe that the three men stationed there needed one more shipment of supplies if they were to survive the winter. He led the relief mission in person, arriving in October to discover that the extra supplies had not been needed, and also that Eismitte had neither food nor living space to host him and his companion over the winter. During the return journey to the west, both men died, although with communication between the stations blacked out during the coldest months, no one knew about the deaths, or even that the pair was missing, until the spring of 1931. When the news of Wegener's demise reached Germany in May, it unleashed a wave of nationwide mourning.

A doleful irony for the German Greenland Expedition was that, as it wrapped up its work in the summer of 1931, Germany was preparing its finest Arctic venture ever. The previous year, in a loss to equal that of Wegener, Fridtjof Nansen had died of a heart attack. Taking his place as president of Aeroarctic was Hugo Eckener – reluctantly, for Eckener understood full well that to accept the position meant committing one of his beloved airships to a major Arctic flight. The result, a Soviet–German project in which the LZ-127 *Graf Zeppelin* carried Eckener and almost 50 others on a week-long journey between 24 July and 31 July, from Friedrichshafen to Leningrad, and then to the Russian Arctic and back, was one of the most competently run and scientifically useful endeavours in the history of polar exploration. On board with Eckener and the all-German crew were Lincoln Ellsworth, Walther Bruns of Aeroarctic and the author Arthur Koestler, covering the event for the Ullstein press syndicate. Rudolf Samoilovich represented the USSR, along with dirigible expert Fyodor Assberg, radioman Ernst Krenkel and the aerologist Pavel Molchanov. The terms of the insurance policy covering the *Zeppelin* forbade Eckener from flying north of the 82nd parallel, but even that restriction left room for an 8,250-mile circuit taking in Franz Josef Land, Severnaya Zemlya, the Taimyr Peninsula's forbidding Byrranga Mountains and Novaya Zemlya.

The *Zeppelin*'s trip was physically comfortable – 'polar exploration deluxe', quipped Ellsworth – even if relations between Eckener and the Soviets were noticeably chilly, a tension attributed by Koestler to the fact that 'German professors are never exactly a cozy lot.'[12] Using a balloon-mounted radiosonde designed by Molchanov, in addition to other instruments, the *Zeppelin*'s contingent recorded wind and weather conditions at a variety of altitudes. They observed geomagnetic phenomena, dropped sonic depth finders to chart the seabed and made stellar use of a Zeiss aerial surveying camera, likened by Koestler to 'an octopus with nine lenses', to map thousands of square miles of the sea and land below.[13] The one result that did not live up to expectations was the *Zeppelin*'s rendezvous with the icebreaker *Malygin* near Hooker Island on 27 July to exchange mail and cargo. The expedition had been paid for largely by an agreement to fly 75,000 letters bearing collectible 'Zeppelin North Pole' stamps to the Arctic and cancel them in mid-flight. Also, the manoeuvre itself was, in Samoilovich's words, an 'acid test' of whether airships would be able to interact effectively with infrastructural assets on the ground and at sea in remote areas. The interchange did not fail, but it was a messy, rushed affair, and a prime factor in the Soviets' decision to privilege aeroplanes over dirigibles in the expansion of their polar air fleet. Still, Samoilovich spoke sincerely when he exulted that 'we accomplished more in ninety hours than could have been accomplished in several years by a combined land-and-sea operation.'[14] In a busy season that included Rasmussen's Sixth Thule Expedition to East Greenland and Hubert Wilkins's abortive attempt to sail the submarine *Nautilus* to the North Pole and drill through the pack ice to the surface, the *Zeppelin* flight stood out as a triumph.

In commenting in 1930 on how 'real exploration' had 'ceased to be a blind and adventurous wandering into the unknown', the journal *Science* declared that 'the really big game of the polar hunt' was the body of 'scientific laws upon which the polar regions, and in some cases they alone, can shed light'.[15] In that spirit, over 40 nations took part in the Second International Polar Year of 1932–3, whose special research focus was the recently discovered jet stream. Although more attention was focused on Antarctica than during the first IPY, the second still led to the opening or expansion of many Arctic outposts, such as the Alaska Meteorological Station at Point Barrow. It also prompted numerous attempts to improve sea and air transport in the far north – the most singular being the *Sibiryakov*'s single-season crossing of the Northeast Passage, organized by the Soviet Union's Otto Shmidt.

Postage stamp commemorating the German–Soviet polar flight
of the airship *Graf Zeppelin*, 1931.

Denmark mourned the sudden death of Knud Rasmussen, a victim
of food poisoning in 1933, on the eve of his Seventh Thule Expedition,
but on the whole the Scandinavians invested heavily in Arctic research
of all types. Bernt Balchen scouted polar routes for Norwegian Air
Lines. In 1928, Harald Sverdrup and Adolf Hoel helped to establish
the Svalbard and Arctic Ocean Research Survey, which became the
Norwegian Polar Institute twenty years later. Sweden, Norway and
Finland built multiple stations in Lapland and Svalbard to study the
weather and observe the glaciers. The most influential scholar associated
with this research was the Stockholm geographer Hans Ahlmann, who
later earned the world-famous sobriquet 'Professor Ice'. Ahlmann and
Hoel were among the first to notice consciously the modern climatological trend towards global warming. Ahlmann began issuing warnings
about 'our hot hemisphere' in the 1930s, and would sound the alarm
even more loudly in the decades following the Second World War.

The mid-1930s brought a number of visitors, some professional, some
amateur, to the Arctic. Guided by Edward Shackleton, son of Ernest, the
Antarctic hero, the Oxford Exploration Club sponsored a trip to Ellesmere Island in 1934–5, and another in 1935 to Spitsbergen, accompanied
by the novelist Evelyn Waugh. August Courtauld, a Cambridge man, held
up his school's end of the university rivalry by participating in the first
ascent of the Arctic's highest peak, Greenland's Gunnbjørn, at over 12,000

feet above sea level. The poet W. H. Auden travelled to Iceland in 1936, ruminating the next year in his *Letters from Iceland* about the undying appeal of the ancient northern sagas. More ethnographers, including Paul-Émile Victor of France, made their way to the region as well.

The mid-to-late 1930s also featured a sensational series of Arctic spectacles staged by the USSR. In 1933, Otto Shmidt, head of the recently created Glavsevmorput, attempted to repeat his 1932 traversal of the Northern Sea Route, this time in a conventional vessel, to demonstrate how reliably navigable the Arctic waters had become under Soviet custodianship. The chosen ship, the *Cheliuskin*, set sail from Leningrad in July 1933, carrying Shmidt and over 100 crew and scientists, several bound for remote polar stations and accompanied by their spouses and children; a baby girl, named Karina after the Kara Sea, was born during the early stages of the voyage. The *Cheliuskin* crested the Taimyr Peninsula on 1 September, only to become trapped in the ice in October. On 13 February 1934, after months of drifting through the East Siberian and Chukchi seas, the ship sank off Chukotka's north coast, leaving 104 men, women and children trapped on the ice. Luckily, the castaways saved their radio and enough supplies to establish 'Camp Shmidt', where they awaited rescue. Public sympathy for the 'Cheliuskinites' reached tsunami-like proportions in the USSR, and ran almost as high elsewhere. In March and April, seven Soviet pilots, flying out of Alaska and Siberia, airlifted Shmidt and his companions before the spring ice became too unstable to support the camp. Returning home, the Cheliuskinites were feted as celebrities in America, Europe and the USSR. The seven aviators received a new award, the Hero of the Soviet Union, which became the country's highest honour until the regime's collapse in 1991.

And this was only the beginning. In 1935, Rudolf Samoilovich took the icebreaker *Sadko* on the first of three high-latitude drifts, emulating the *Fram* and the *Maud*, but with larger crews and a more sophisticated array of instruments to map the ocean floor and take hydrological and geophysical measurements. In July 1936, the test pilot Valerii Chkalov and his crew piloted a Tupolev ANT-25, an experimental long-range aeroplane, along the Arctic coast and through Yakutia from Moscow to Udd Island, near the mouth of the Amur, unofficially breaking the international record for non-stop distance flying. Chkalov then stunned the world in June 1937 by flying over the North Pole during a non-stop flight from Moscow to Vancouver, Washington. This set an official world record, although a briefly lived one, for a month later Mikhail Gromov followed the same route from Moscow over the Pole – but farther yet, to San Jacinto, California.

Grandest of all, and planned in coordination with Chkalov's and Gromov's flights, was the SP-1 (Severnyi Polius, or 'North Pole') Expedition, designed to land aircraft as close to the Pole as possible and to establish a research station which would drift southward and be retrieved the following year. In March 1937, the expedition, headed by Otto Shmidt and with *Cheliuskin* 'hero-pilot' Mikhail Vodopianov as its air commander, flew to Franz Josef Land to set up its forward base. From there, beginning on 21 May, a squadron of four converted Tupolev bombers landed within a short distance of the Pole. Once the SP-1 camp was erected, four of the party were left behind: station head Ivan Papanin, oceanographer Pyotr Shirshov, geophysicist Yevgeny Fyodorov and Ernst Krenkel, who had flown with the *Graf Zeppelin* in 1931 and served as radioman for the *Sibiryakov* and *Cheliuskin* voyages. The 'Papaninites' completed a battery of scientific tasks and provided radio guidance for Chkalov's and Gromov's transpolar flights, allowing themselves all the while to be carried by oceanic currents into the Greenland Sea. On 19 February 1938, they were extracted by the Soviet ships *Taimyr* and *Murman* and conveyed to Moscow for a gala homecoming, hosted by Stalin himself.

Already, though, the Soviets' polestar had been losing its lustre. As headline-grabbing as they were, the high-profile achievements could not conceal the rise of the Gulag or the thinning-out of the country's Arctic cadres by Stalin's purges. Samoilovich was arrested in 1937 upon returning from the *Sadko*'s third high-latitude drift, and later shot. Hundreds of polar workers and scientists spent time in the camps. GUSMP's attempt to stage a third transpolar flight, commanded by Sigismund Levanevsky and aiming to reach Los Angeles in August 1937, ended with the disappearance of Levanevsky's plane and the death of several aviators during the months-long search that followed. As described above, much of GUSMP's fleet was paralysed by an early freeze in 1937–8. Chkalov, who occupied the same place in Soviet hearts that Charles Lindbergh did among Americans, died during a test flight in December 1938. Vladimir Kokkinaki, whose Arctic flight from Moscow to America in April 1939 was meant to add extra prestige to the USSR's pavilion at the New York World's Fair, crash-landed in the Canadian countryside instead. Shmidt's own downfall came in the spring of 1939, although he suffered only a forced ousting from GUSMP at Papanin's hands, and not arrest.

By this juncture, there was little time left for Arctic exploration of any sort before the outbreak of the Second World War. David Haig-Thomas of England and America's Clifford MacGregor were active in Greenland and the Canadian archipelago in 1937 and 1938, while Adolf Hoel of Norway launched a major aerial survey of Svalbard. In 1939, August Courtauld sailed and mapped the length of the Norwegian coast by himself, and several expeditions departed for Greenland that summer, including one organized by St Andrews University, another to East Greenland under Hans Ahlmann, and the Danish Thule-Ellesmere Expedition led by James Van Hauen, which counted the young zoologist Christian Vibe among its members. Day-to-day research continued at weather posts and scientific stations throughout the north, and the Soviets hastened to resume navigation along the Northern Sea Route in the wake of the great freeze that had struck in 1937. In the summer of 1939, ten ships traversed the Route in its entirety. One of these was the USSR's newest icebreaker, the 10,000-ton *Stalin*, which passed through the Route both ways, the first such voyage in history – and the last record of note to be set before the war. In January 1940, the icebreaker *Sedov*, the last of the USSR's ships to have been ice-trapped in 1937, returned safely to port. In May 1941, the Soviet team of Ivan Cherevichnyi and navigator Valentin Akkuratov managed the first ever landing at the Pole of Relative Inaccessibility, some 450 miles from the geographic North Pole. A month after that, the USSR too was drawn into the global conflagration.

Frontlines Under the Midnight Sun: The Second World War in the Arctic

One of the near-forgotten gems of wartime cinema is the British propaganda film *49th Parallel* (1941), in which a German u-boat crew, hunting the icy waters of Hudson Bay, is forced ashore by the sinking of their submarine. Seeking to escape to the neutral United States, the captain and his men travel the length of the country, encountering various Canadian 'types' – a salty Scotsman, loyal Indians and Eskimos, a refined English gentleman, Hutterite pacifists – all driven by their love of Canada to spurn the Germans' attempts to threaten or suborn them. As a Quebec trapper, Laurence Olivier chews lines in an accent so outrageous, it makes the French knights from *Monty Python and the Holy Grail* sound like Voltaire. The villains, of course, are apprehended in the final act, but the movie's screenwriter, Emeric Pressburger, had no way of knowing until decades after the war that his fantasy had unwittingly anticipated a factual and successful German incursion into the Allied north. In September 1943, Germany's U-537 approached the northern tip of Labrador, where a shore party emplaced a Siemens-built unmanned weather station, whose existence remained a secret until the late 1970s. Nicknamed 'Weather Station Kurt' after the U-537's meteorologist, the machine now sits on display in the Canadian War Museum.

The Arctic was a vastly more active front in the Second World War than it had been during the First. More resources were at stake there. Key logistical questions, such as the continuation of Lend-Lease aid to the USSR and the preservation and interdiction of Allied shipping lanes across the North Atlantic, turned on the ability to move there effectively. A war of meteorology was fought in the Arctic, with the accurate reading of northern weather systems crucial to an array of military operations, from the smallest of air raids to the Normandy invasion in 1944. As a consequence, while there were no armed encounters in the Arctic on the scale of Stalingrad or Iwo Jima, a great deal of combat took place there – enough to put many tens of thousands of troops and sailors in harm's way under the borealis.

Most of the high north was only partially prepared for war when the fighting began. The Scandinavian nations still clung to the hope of remaining neutral. The USSR, facing threats from both Germany and Japan, and determined to use the Northern Sea Route as a secure maritime conduit between the west and the Pacific, rushed to equip its icebreakers and other ships with weapons, and to fortify its ports and island bases. But except in the northwest, on the Kola Peninsula and in the Barents and White seas, defences remained woefully thin until halfway through the war, to the dismay of GUSMP head Ivan Papanin and Arsenii Golovko, commander of the Soviet Navy's Northern Fleet. In an added paradox, the German Kriegsmarine, as part of the year-and-a-half rapprochement that followed the Nazi–Soviet Pact of August 1939, enjoyed full use of an Arctic harborage on USSR territory: Basis Nord on the shores of Zapadnaya Litsa Bay, between Murmansk and the Norwegian border.

In pre-war Alaska, where the westernmost Aleutians lay a mere 650 miles from the Japanese-controlled Kuriles, military planners dealt with deficiencies of their own. The lockers at tiny Chilkoot Barracks held First World War-vintage rifles, sleepy ports like Dutch Harbor cried out for upgrading and Army Air Force pilots navigated using Rand McNally tourist maps. The Aleutians remained unfortified until the last minute, and only in late 1939 were monies allocated for the construction of Elmendorf and Ladd airfields near Anchorage and Fairbanks.

During the final months before Pearl Harbor, the Alaska Defense Commander, Simon Bolivar Buckner Jr, complained that 'we're not even the second team up here – we're a sandlot club.'[16] For the moment, Americans forces resorted to animal rights activism as a way to thumb their noses at the Japanese threat. When Japan, in 1940, renounced the 1911 ban on the hunting of fur seals near Alaska's Pribilof Islands, the U.S. Coast Guard made it their business to escort the animals safely to the islands – a tradition that continued until the mid-1960s.

Once war broke out in earnest, Arctic territories were soon dragged into it. Among the first to see combat was Finland, in a conflict technically unrelated to the Second World War. This was the Winter War, forced on the Finns in November 1939 by the USSR, which, despite its momentary amicability with Germany, sought territorial concessions from Estonia and Finland to give Leningrad extra protection against the Nazi attack that Hitler and Stalin both knew would inevitably come. Five Soviet armies crossed the frontier, from Karelia in the south to the Kola Peninsula in the north, but with such overconfident bumbling that the Finns, led by Carl Mannerheim, held them off for many weeks, embarrassing them in the eyes of the world and teaching them more than a few lessons about cold-weather warfare. In December and early January, divisions of the Soviet Ninth Army, attempting to drive to the western port of Oulu and divide northern Finland from the south, were cut to ribbons by Finnish ski troops amid the frozen lakes and thick woods of Suomussalmi. In Finnish Lapland, other elements of the Ninth advanced to the Kemi River, only to be thrown back.

In the Arctic latitudes, the Soviet Fourteenth Army had better luck: open terrain allowed it to take full advantage of its superiority in air, tanks and sheer numbers, and exactly where the Finns were most shorthanded. The Fourteenth came out from Murmansk, capturing Petsamo with relative ease in January 1940 and moving as far west as Nautsi, near where the Paatsjoki River flows out of Lake Inari. Even here, Finnish troops used the cover of polar night to harass their enemy for weeks to come – but not indefinitely. After January, the stumbling giant regained its footing and directed its main strength against the south, where the so-far impregnable Mannerheim Line blocked the Red Army from crossing the Karelian isthmus into Finland proper. In a hurricane of blood, mainly their own, the Soviets battered down the Finns' defences in February, and the two countries signed the Treaty of Moscow in mid-March. Having taken over 300,000 casualties – compared to the 70,000 suffered by the Finns – the Soviets gained 11 per cent of Finnish territory, principally in

Karelia, but with a slice of Lapland as well. Stalin earned the enmity of the international community, and Hitler's high command, watching the USSR's appalling performance, persuaded itself that the Red Army would crumple like a set of tin soldiers when the Russian–German clash finally came.

For now, however, the Wehrmacht's next northern objective was Norway, the target along with Denmark of Operation Weserübung, the opening phase of Germany's *Sitzkrieg*-ending offensive against the West in the spring of 1940. Erich Raeder had impressed upon Hitler the danger to German naval operations of letting the British gain any presence on Norway's coast, and Germany needed access to the Arctic port of Narvik to guarantee a year-round supply of iron ore from neutral Sweden. Germany launched its attacks on 9 April, with Denmark capitulating in a day. Norway held out until June, by which point the next round of Hitler's offensive had opened up, on 10 May, against the Low Countries and France. Nickolaus von Falkenhorst's multiple landings and paratroop drops in April crippled most of Norway rapidly; the fighting lasted longest around Narvik, which fell to Eduard Dietl's feared *Gebirgsjäger* (mountain infantry) units in April but was retaken in late May by Allied units. Failure in Trondheim and elsewhere, though, plus the need to respond to the deteriorating situation in France, caused the Allies to pull out of Norway on 8 June. With Haakon VII and his family already evacuated to Britain, Vidkun Quisling set up his Nasjonal Samling regime, a Nazi puppet state. The Arctic scholar Adolf Hoel placed a permanent stain on his reputation by embracing the Quisling government and serving it as the wartime rector of the University of Oslo.

Consolidation in the North followed on both sides. More than 80 per cent of Norway's merchant marine escaped and served on the Allied side, as did fifteen of its warships and almost 14,000 sailors, soldiers and airmen. In Norway itself, a number of resistance organizations sprang into being in 1940 and 1941; the largest, the Militaer Organisasjon (MILORG), had 40,000 members by the war's end. In April and May 1940, the British occupied two of Denmark's possessions, the Faeroes and Iceland, although they left Greenland untouched at the United States' request. Germany moved quickly to ensure the shipment of iron ore from Sweden via the Luleå–Narvik railway, and also reached accords with Sweden and Finland allowing the transit of supplies and personnel through the high north. German air units moved into Arctic bases such as Bardufoss and Kirkenes, and naval forces began operating out of Tromsø, Narvik and Altenfjord, near Nordkapp. With these now available, Admiral Raeder abandoned the Basis Nord installation near

Murmansk that the Soviets had lent to the Kriegsmarine. In August–September 1940, the Germans, with Soviet cooperation, sent the cruiser *Komet* through the Northern Sea Route to raid Allied shipping in the Pacific. Disguised as the GUSMP icebreaker *Dezhnev* while in international waters, the *Komet* entered Soviet seas and rendezvoused with the icebreaker *Lenin* and later the *Stalin*. Its passage to the Bering Strait took only twenty-one days, a new record. The Germans used the voyage for a more covert purpose as well: prior to meeting the *Lenin*, the *Komet* placed reconnaissance teams on islands like Novaya Zemlya to update naval maps and to practise monitoring Soviet ship movements and radio transmissions.

As the combatants' Atlantic face-off escalated in late 1940 and early 1941, so too did the Arctic's importance to the war. To read the weather, an absolute necessity, the Allies relied on bases in Canada, Newfoundland, Greenland and Iceland. The Germans, handicapped by the tendency of northern systems to travel west to east – a disadvantage that their placement of Station 'Kurt' on the Labrador coast was meant to overcome – made do with outposts in the Svalbard archipelago and northeast Greenland, sometimes manned by pro-German Norwegians and Danes. U-boat activity forced maritime traffic between the British Isles and ports like Halifax to venture steadily farther to the north, into Icelandic and Greenlandic waters. In April 1941, the United States, still neutral but acting as much to assist the Allies as neutrality allowed, established the American Western Hemisphere Defense Zone, taking over from Britain the responsibility for occupying Iceland and obtaining permission from Denmark's ambassador-in-exile to garrison Greenland and provide for its defence while hostilities lasted. The long-term impact of the American occupation was to heighten the sense of detachment from Denmark that the war had already aroused among Icelanders and Greenlanders, with the former signalling in the summer of 1941 their intention to declare independence as soon as circumstances permitted.

In the shorter term, the Americans on Greenland began building their many 'Bluie' bases, first on the west coast at places like Narsarsuaq (Bluie West 1, near the southern tip) and Sondre Stromfjord (Bluie West 8, commanded by the Norwegian-American aviator Bernt Balchen), and later in the east around sites such as Angmagssalik. When Greenland Base Command formally opened in November 1941, there were over 700 Americans on Greenland, setting up airfields, harbours, a Coast Guard base and radar and weather stations. The U.S. also bankrolled and gave logistic support to the Northeast Greenland Sledge Patrol, a group of Danish, Norwegian and Inuit dogsledders who volunteered in the summer of 1941 to ferret out and report any clandestine German activity on the island. The American force on Greenland eventually grew to 10,000, while that on Iceland rose to 40,000, an indication of how crucial a bearing both places had on the ongoing Battle of the Atlantic. Aerial anti-submarine patrols flying out of Reykjavík and the Bluie airfields helped to close the 'Greenland gap' that had left Allied shipping without air cover once outside the range of aircraft based in Canada and Newfoundland or in Britain. Moreover, aeroplanes being transferred from North America to Britain now had places to stop and refuel, and could therefore be flown directly over the Atlantic rather than being disassembled and carried across the ocean in a ship's hold.

The Arctic war gained new dimensions in the second half of 1941. That June, Nazi Germany launched Operation Barbarossa, catching the Stalinist regime completely off guard and punching deep into Soviet territory on all fronts. Less famous than the Herculean struggles over Leningrad, Kiev and Moscow, the campaign in the high north was nevertheless of dire importance to Soviet transport and the USSR's prospects for economic survival. With Finnish troops under Mannerheim supporting his southern flank, Falkenhorst, commanding Axis forces in Norway, unleashed Operation Silver Fox. This was a three-part undertaking intended to secure the nickel mines of Petsamo (stage Reindeer) and then carry out twin assaults – one from Finnish Lapland against Kandalaksha, a port on the Kola Peninsula's southern shore and a key point on the Leningrad–Murmansk railway (stage Arctic Fox), and another from Petsamo, sending Falkenhorst's elite mountain infantry along the Arctic coast towards the main target, Murmansk (stage Platinum Fox).

The Germans roared into Petsamo with little effort, but the Soviet Fourteenth Army dug in hard enough to foil Arctic Fox and Platinum Fox. Had Murmansk fallen, it would have badly disrupted the Lend-Lease convoys begun by the U.S. and Great Britain in August. As it was, the front stabilized in December with the Germans stalled at the Litsa River, and with Murmansk and the railway leading south from it still in Soviet hands. For the next three years, during which 70,000 Germans would fight in this theatre, combat centred on the Murmansk–Petsamo–Kirkenes corridor; while they held Petsamo, the Germans used the nickel mined there to strengthen the armour plating for their panzers. The Finns, having recovered the territory lost to them in 1940, took a less active role in the fighting from this point on, although they continued to assist with the German blockade of Leningrad.

By this point, the Pearl Harbor attack had drawn the United States fully into the war. Not only did this accelerate the American build-up in Greenland and Iceland, it quickened the pace of events in Alaska. To the satisfaction of Alaska Defense Commander Simon Buckner, more troops and assets were placed at the disposal of his own ground troops, the navy's North Pacific Force and the 11th Army Air Force. More docks and airfields were built, many of the latter with Marsden steel matting, which had recently been put to good use in Greenland. Dutch Harbor eventually became capable of handling 400,000 tons of cargo per month.

This new infrastructure was created not just to increase Alaska's combat readiness, but to strengthen the Lend-Lease lifeline that the u.s. had extended to the ussr in the summer of 1941. When the programme first began, the Allies puzzled over the best way to ferry u.s. surplus aircraft to the Soviet Union. In July 1941, Mikhail Gromov, one of the recordbreaking transpolar pilots from the 1930s, visited Alaska to discuss the possibility of a Bering air bridge. This was the genesis of the Alaska–Siberia air route (ALSIB), by which 8,000 of the 15,000 u.s. aeroplanes eventually donated to the Soviet war effort were brought from Great Falls, Montana, to Fairbanks by airmen of the u.s. Air Transport command. From Fairbanks, they were flown to Nome and Krasnoyarsk by Soviet pilots of the First Ferry Aviation Division, whose commander was Ilya Mazuruk, one of the four sp-1 aviators who landed near the North Pole in 1937. Of the aeroplanes thus delivered, 5,000 were the p-39 Airacobra and p-63 Kingcobra fighters that Soviet pilots flew to famous effect on battlefields throughout the Eastern Front. Badly needed cargo was transported to the ussr via ALSIB as well.

United States involvement in the war expanded the continent's northern infrastructure in another and more enduring way, thanks to the construction in 1942 of the Alaska–Canada Highway (ALCAN). Since the 1920s, the Americans had been keen on such a project, with the engineer Donald MacDonald sketching out a viable route for it in 1928 and the outdoorsman Clyde 'Slim' Williams generating publicity for it by mushing the entire way by dogsled. For years, the Canadian government had demurred, citing the lopsidedness of the expense relative to the small number of Canadian citizens who would benefit from it, and leaving unspoken its concerns about American encroachments on Canada's northern sovereignty. Even in 1940 and 1941, when Washington argued how useful such a road would be for mobilizing against a common foe, the Canadians pointed out that it could just as well allow an enemy easy access to the continent from the north. But with America now under attack, the Roosevelt administration issued orders in February 1942 for construction to begin. The Mackenzie King government gave its consent in March, provided that the u.s. foot the project's $138 million cost and turn control of the road's Canadian sections over to Ottawa after the war. Work crews numbering 16,000 by the summer and proceeding from both directions at a blistering pace of 18 miles per day completed the road in November 1942, although it was not ready for general vehicular use until February 1943. At the time, it stretched almost 1,700 miles between Dawson Creek in British Columbia and Fairbanks, from which rail connections continued to Anchorage and other points throughout Alaska. The u.s. also flew aircraft through Canadian airspace and used airfields such as Fort Churchill in Manitoba.

The building of the ALCAN was merely one symptom among many of the growing militarization of the circumpolar north during 1942. Populations perceived as potentially disloyal were interned or deported, including Japanese-Americans and Japanese-Canadians from Alaska, the Yukon and British Columbia, and a number of Finns and Karelians from the Kola and White Sea coast. More of the war's burden fell on northern populations. Fishers, hunters and herders, from Faeroe Islanders to Alaskan Yupik and Soviet Khanty and Nentsy, supported their respective war efforts by contributing as much food as they could spare. Arctic natives also took part in combat. Sami, for whom the Second World War became literally a civil war, fought in Norwegian, Finnish and Soviet armies and resistance movements. As soldiers, they were prized as ski troops; as civilians under German occupation, they suffered atrocities, rapes and starvation caused by scorched-earth tactics. Having noticed during the Winter War the effectiveness of reindeer transport – one animal could carry 100 pounds of supplies, while a team of four could haul almost 650 pounds – the USSR mobilized over 1,000 Sami, Komi and Nenets herders, and more than 6,000 reindeer, for service on the Karelian and Kola fronts. The Red Army also conscripted large numbers of native Siberians, with many of them, particularly the Yakut, valued highly as marksmen. Greenland Inuit lent their skills to the Northeast Greenland Sledge Patrol and other anti-German efforts. In Alaska, the anthropologist Otto Geist assisted in organizing the Alaska Territorial Guard, nicknamed the 'Eskimo Scouts', although Aleuts, Athabaskan Indians and other natives served in it as well. By the same token, Alaskan natives turned out to be some of the most adept commandos in Lawrence Castner's Alaska Scouts, affectionately known as 'Castner's Cutthroats'. Until 1943, there was some armed forces discrimination against native troops in Alaska, a situation not ameliorated by General Buckner's less than enlightened views regarding race. But direct complaints to President Roosevelt from Alaska's governor, Ernest Gruening, brought an end to such segregationist practices.

Overall, military-related traffic and activity increased in every part of the Arctic throughout the year. The Norwegian resistance gained more recruits in 1942 and bloodied the Germans with their raids. Best remembered now for their attacks on heavy-water production facilities in the south, Norwegian irregulars of various political persuasions operated in the far north, gathering intelligence, liberating Allied prisoners held by the Germans and smuggling refugees into neutral Sweden. They carried out a major sabotage mission, Operation Musketoon, against the Norsk Hydro electric plant at Glomsfjord, which supported aluminum production, in 1942. Units in Troms and Finnmark counties observed and on occasion interfered with Axis naval movements along the Barents shoreline, and the Soviet-supported Finnmark Partisans reduced German pressure on the Red Army forces barring the way to Murmansk. Fighting above the treeline as they did, these Arctic guerrillas were particularly hindered by the lack of concealment offered by the terrain, a problem made doubly acute by the perpetual daylight that came with the summer months. The Germans struck back with two major countermeasures, Operations Tundra and Midnight Sun, and retaliated against the North's civilian population as well. A prison in the Arctic, not far from Kirkenes, awaited Norwegian partisans who fell into German hands.

The seasonal interplay of light and dark governed the realities of air and sea operations in the entire European Arctic. Throughout the war, 40 Allied convoys, starting with PQ-Zero (also known as Dervish) in August 1941 and eventually involving 800 ships, formed up in harbours like Reykjavík, Loch Ewe and Scapa Flow and braved the northern waters to carry a total of 4 million tons of arms and supplies to the Soviet ports of Murmansk and Arkhangelsk. During the relatively ice-free summer, Allied vessels could venture farther to the north, outside the range of land-based aircraft in Norway and Finland, but the longer daylight made them easier prey for U-boats. U-boats became less of a danger during the colder months, but the southward creep of the ice forced Allied ships back within reach of German planes. An air war of terrible ferocity raged in the skies over Kirkenes, Petsamo and Murmansk whenever the weather permitted, as German fliers tried not just to destroy Allied shipping, but to pulverize Murmansk. The German battleship *Tirpitz* and the cruisers *Lützow*, *Hipper* and *Scheer* were deployed here, and U-boats hunted these waters incessantly – never with greater success than in the summer of 1942. Early that July, they spent half a week laying waste to the 36 ships of the PQ-17 convoy, bound for Arkhangelsk but scattered and stripped of their escort in the waters west of Novaya Zemlya. Twenty-five of PQ-17's ships went to the bottom with their crews and cargo, calling into doubt the feasibility of this crucial component of the Lend-Lease system. Although a few independent flotillas sailed on their own, not until September did the Allies dare to send out the next official convoy, PQ-18, and even this lost thirteen of 40 ships.

In the interim, the Germans followed their PQ-17 success with Operation Wunderland, a deep eastward thrust into the Barents and Kara seas. During the course of the war, GUSMP managed to run 41 convoys through the Northern Sea Route, with 792 ships participating. The great hope in 1942 of Germany's Admiral of the Northern Waters, Hubert Schmundt, was to halt this traffic by catching a large concentration of Soviet vessels, especially icebreakers, at a choke point like the Vilkitsky Straits, between Severnaya Zemlya and the mainland. To that end, in August the cruiser *Scheer* sailed north of Novaya Zemlya into the Kara Sea, while U-boats diverted Soviet attention by torpedoing ships and shelling ports and weather stations on the southern half of Novaya Zemlya and around the Kara Gates. The *Scheer* got as far east as the Nordenskiöld and Mona islands, where it sank the steamer *Kuibyshev* and the venerable icebreaker *Sibiryakov*, but never encountered the sought-after GUSMP convoys. On the way back, it attacked the Soviet outpost on Dikson Island, at the mouth of the Yenisei, but to no great effect. GUSMP continued its own convoy work along the Soviet north coast, and up and down the Siberian rivers. The western Allies began a new and more effective series of Arctic voyages, the JW (USSR-bound) / RA (homebound) convoys, near the end of 1942. During the Battle of the Barents Sea, fought on 31 December, the cruisers *Sheffield* and *Jamaica* successfully defended the fifteen ships of JW51 against a force led by the *Hipper* and *Lützow*, bringing all their charges safely into Murmansk.

The summer of 1942 brought war to Alaska as well, for one component of Japan's elaborate plan for the attempted invasion of Midway was an assault on the Aleutian islands. On 3 June, planes launched from the carriers *Ryujo* and *Junyo*, under Vice-Admiral Boshiro Hosogaya, bombed Dutch Harbor, but heavy shrouds of mist kept damage to a minimum and prevented a takeover of the port. The Japanese had better luck on the 6th and 7th, when they landed on the islands of Kiska, their principal harbour for the rest of the campaign, and Attu. Before fighting ended in this 'theater of frustration', as naval historian Samuel Eliot Morison termed it, half a million troops would see duty there, including 200,000 Americans and more than 5,000 Canadians. In preparation for the retaking of Attu and Kiska, the Americans created more than a dozen new island airstrips along the Aleutian chain, including on Adak and Amchitka.

On all fronts, the strategic balance in the North shifted in the Allies' favour in 1943 and 1944. The u-boat threat diminished during the first half of 1943, and so the jw/ra convoys to Murmansk and Arkhangelsk proceeded in greater safety, even though they continued to be molested by German aircraft and surface vessels. With the aid of Free Norwegian forces, the British maintained better infrastructure in Arctic waters, including a weather station and refueling depot on Spitsbergen, although the Germans had their own secret airbase on Novaya Zemlya. In the Battle of the North Cape, which occurred in December 1943, the battleship *Scharnhorst* perished in vain during an attempt to intercept convoy jw55. In the autumn of 1944, Lancaster bombers sank the already damaged *Tirpitz*, one of the Kriegsmarine's few remaining capital ships, while it was moored near Tromsø. In Greenland, the Sledge Patrol grew more proficient at uncovering hidden German bases, and u.s. pilots lost no time in bombing these – as in May 1943, when Bernt Balchen deposited the payload of a b-17 Flying Fortress on the German radio and weather station at Eskimonaes, in the island's northeast quadrant. Germany's last Greenland outpost, Edelweiss ii, was rooted out in October 1944.

In Alaska, after months of frostbite, 'arctic malaria' (as lingering colds and flu were called), ceaseless fog and cold williwaw winds, the Aleutian campaign came to an end in 1943. That March, Japanese failure to press home the victory that should have been theirs at the naval battle of the Komandorski (Commander) Islands left the garrisons on Attu and Kiska without badly needed supplies. In Operation Landcrab, Castner's Cutthroats led the charge against Attu, which fell to the Allies during the second half of May. Kiska followed in August, brought down by Operation Cottage.

The last major deadlock to be broken in the North was the Kirkenes–Petsamo–Murmansk front. To aid with the conventional combat there, partisan groups in Norway stepped up their efforts in 1943 and 1944. America and Britain were eager to get as many pro-Western Norwegians into the theatre as possible, including elements of milorg. Sweden, under no illusion about the war's eventual outcome, secretly began to allow Britain, America and the Norwegian government in exile to insert such personnel, along with weapons, radios and supplies, into northernmost Norway via Swedish airspace and airfields.

The critical turnaround here came in the autumn of 1944. In September, the Soviets forced an end to the Finns' Continuation War against them and, by the terms of the Moscow Armistice, turned the Finns on the Germans in the seven-and-a-half-month Lapland War. Then, in October, Kirill Meretskov led the Soviet Fourteenth Army as it thundered west in the Petsamo–Kirkenes Offensive, the last of the 'Ten Great Stalinist Blows' dealt to the Axis by the Soviets that year. During his fighting withdrawal from Norway and Finland, Lothar Rendulic implemented Operation Northern Lights, a scorched-earth devastation of the region that involved not just the destruction of infra-structure and population centres – among them Bodø, Tromsø, Narvik, Hammerfest and Kirkenes – but also the burning of thousands of square miles of forest. The resulting impoverishment and dislocation made it necessary to enlarge the clandestine airlift efforts begun by the Allies earlier in 1944. Starting in December, Operation Where and When sent cargo planes to the north out of Kallax airfield near Sweden's Arctic port of Luleå. With the participation of Bernt Balchen, the Norwegian air ace Sven Heglund, and the zoologist and future explorer Thor Heyerdahl, later famous for his *Kon-Tiki* expedition, Where and When completed 572 missions between its inception and the summer of 1945, flying in 200 tons of supplies, including food and medicine for civilians and arms and ammunition for the partisans. The Germans were expelled from Norway by 23 April 1945. The last Finno-German battle, at Kilpisjarvi, in northwest Finnish Lapland, took place on 27 April, and VE Day followed a week and a half later.

The Second World War transformed the Arctic, albeit inconsis-tently. In mainland Scandinavia, much of the North lay in smoking, cratered ruins. By contrast, Russia's Northern Sea Route, damaged as it was, had become a far more useful infrastructural asset. Canada's Arctic, surveyed more precisely and patrolled more vigilantly during the war, was now more familiar to mariners and cartographers than ever before. Alaska, more integral to the United States and its interests, was only a decade and a half away from full statehood. Iceland seized inde-pendence, severing its colonial ties with Denmark in the summer of 1944. While Greenland remained under Danish rule, the Americans now assumed an equally dominant presence there. Finland lost a key piece of its Arctic territory, ceding Petsamo to the USSR and, with it, all access to the Arctic Ocean.

Beyond these developments, the most fundamental change of all was that the circumpolar north no longer stood apart as the remote periphery it once had been. The Arctic regions were now physically accessible. They were economically valuable. Moreover, with one global conflict ending and another about to begin, they were centrally important to the geopolitics of the postwar world.

6

Contaminations:
1945 to 1991

It is an enduring image of the Cold War, one to rank with snapshots of mushroom clouds, film footage of space flights and other visual artefacts of the last century's long superpower rivalry. On 17 March 1959, the u.s. nuclear submarine *Skate* became the second undersea vessel to reach the North Pole, and the first to break through the ice to the surface. The crew stayed at the Pole long enough to scatter the ashes of the Australian explorer Hubert Wilkins, who had dreamed of accomplishing this exact feat in the 1930s, and to capture the moment on film. Against the pristine white of the polar wilds, the dark sail of the *Skate* stands out ominously, like the dorsal fin of a cyborg orca. Equally striking is the photographic record of one of the ussr's many counter-strokes: in August 1977, the orange-painted bulk of the 23,400-ton nuclear icebreaker *Arktika* churned its way towards the Pole, becoming the first surface vessel to reach 90°N. Seen from above, the long ribbon of open water trailing the ship testifies to the strength of its 75,000-horse-power engine.

Every such triumph, however, came at a cost to the Arctic environment. Not only did the Cold War transform the region into an atomic-era battlefield, placing it under the perpetual threat of military annihilation, it caused astounding amounts of damage to the ecosystem, beyond anything the North had experienced in the past. It ushered in an age of contamination. Harmful emissions from the south increased exponentially, causing unprecedented volumes of carbon compounds, pcbs (polychlorinated biphenyls) and other impurities to drift into the far north. The amount of pollution generated *in* the Arctic reached levels that would have been inconceivable just a generation before: as the region's human population ballooned, so too did the quantities of fuel

The nuclear submarine uss *Skate* surfacing from the Arctic pack ice during
its pioneering voyage to the North Pole in 1959.

and electric power consumed there, the extent of infrastructure built, the
volume of sewage produced and the sheer mass of human-made objects
that appeared there. A landscape where trash had been unknown for
centuries now lay garishly strewn about in places with soda bottles, spent
batteries, gum wrappers, cigarette butts, scrap plastic and refuse of all
sorts. Managing such waste, and also the more insidious poisons released
into the wilderness by mining, oil recovery and other human activities,
has turned out to be an enormously costly and complicated affair – when
it can be accomplished at all. Nor were the postwar years kind to the
Arctic's wildlife, on land or at sea.

One happy counterbalance to this trend, especially during the era's
later decades, was a global rise in environmental awareness and activism,
which has curtailed some of the more flagrant abuses. In the sphere of
human relations, Arctic natives exhibited a powerful new willingness
to counter the hegemony of the nation-states governing them, and to
struggle for fairer treatment, ownership of their traditional lands and
greater autonomy. In some cases they proved victorious, although
hardships continued. One clear beneficiary of the Cold War era was
the scientific community, although whether it benefited from the Cold
War itself is a more difficult question to answer. The superpower rivalry
provided a new impetus for polar research, and a new set of patrons
for it, but it also conditioned the kind of science that could be pursued

in the Arctic, and by whom. Politics aside, the technology of the Cold War era enabled more extensive and more precise surveillance of the Arctic than at any time before in human history. Airships and aeroplanes, instruments borne on balloons and on undersea cables, and remotely operated cameras hugely magnified the power of the gaze that humans could direct at the high north. Satellite imagery, available in the most recent decades, expanded that range of vision even further.

Science, Security and Militarization: The Arctic as Cold War Battleground

In 1958, the notoriously hawkish physicist Edward Teller, a star player in the Manhattan Project and, after the war, an impassioned advocate of putting atomic detonations to 'peaceful' use, managed to bring the Atomic Energy Commission (AEC) on board for a highly idiosyncratic Arctic enterprise. His idea, codenamed Operation Chariot, proposed to create a man-made deepwater harbour on Cape Thompson, near northwest Alaska's Point Hope, by setting off a series of thermonuclear explosions. If all went according to plan, the blasts would carve out a mile-long channel suitable for large shipments of oil and coal, and also for naval action against the Soviets whom Teller so fiercely loathed. Enthusiasm dimmed, however, upon the realization that whatever port was created would be frozen in for two-thirds of the year, and even more when thought was given to the matter of radiation – which Teller dismissed as a trivial concern, but which most worried would harm local caribou herds and nearby Inupiat communities. With public indignation mounting, the AEC shut down the project. And yet during the Cold War, Chariot was only one of the many Strangelovean schemes hatched out of the intercourse between science and security concerns and implemented in the high north.

Although no single curtain, whether of iron or ice, could divide the Arctic the way the Cold War did Europe, new lines of conflict were drawn there after the Second World War's conclusion. As the Canadian diplomat Hugh Keenleyside remarked in 1949, 'what the Mediterranean was to the Roman world, what the Atlantic Ocean was to the expanding Europe of Renaissance days, the Arctic Ocean is becoming to the world of aircraft and atomic power.'[1] Less than 60 miles of sea separated the USSR from Alaska in the Bering Strait, and the shortest straight line between the Soviet and North American mainlands ran through the North Pole. As diplomatic and covert duelling commenced in the Arctic skies and waters, America held most of the early advantages. For one, it had more allies there. In signing the 1948 Friendship, Cooperation and Mutual Assistance Treaty with the USSR, Helsinki agreed not to cross the Soviets in matters of foreign policy, but this was a condition imposed by Moscow on a less than willing Finland in exchange for not forcing it to join the communist bloc. By contrast, Iceland's government, if not necessarily all its citizenry, leapt at the chance to join NATO in 1949, and was quickly followed by Norway and Denmark, whose membership placed Greenland's vast spaces at the alliance's disposal. Although sovereignty-related tensions continued to crop up between them, Canada and the U.S. entered into one of the closest military partnerships in world history. America also benefited from an initial lead in technological know-how. Aside from having developed the atomic bomb first, the U.S. had new heavy bombers capable of flying farther than anything the USSR could put in the air. The Soviet Northern Fleet, headquartered near Murmansk, had yet to develop true blue-water capability, and Soviet submarines during the 1930s and '40s had been small coast-huggers designed for defence. Soviet icebreakers were ageing, and half of them were underpowered by the standards of the day.

Whichever side held the better cards, a substantial part of all human activity in the postwar north was now military-related. Both sides began early on to adapt modern combat techniques and equipment to Arctic conditions. In 1946, Operations Frostbite and Nanook sent the U.S. aircraft carrier *Midway*, the sub *Atule* and other vessels into Davis Strait for exercises, some going as far north as Thule, Greenland. Alaska served admirably as a training ground and, in 1961, the U.S. Army established its Cold Regions Research and Engineering Laboratory in New Hampshire. Canada put ground troops through their polar paces in Operations Muskox (1946) and Sweetbriar (1950), and in 1947 created the Canadian Rangers, a reserve force popularly known as the Arctic Rangers and composed primarily (not wholly, as many believe) of Inuit and First Nations volunteers. It also deployed the carrier *Magnificent* on the 1948 Northern Voyage to show that it could guard its own Arctic waters from possible Soviet incursion. Norway, the NATO nation that abutted Soviet territory most directly, began in the 1950s to form special-forces units with expertise in high-latitude operations. In the USSR, the Red Army mustered native Siberian battalions specifically to take advantage of their aptitude for cold-weather combat.

Reconnaissance flights, started by the Americans over Chukotka and the Kola Peninsula in the late 1940s, became routine for both sides as the

Cold War escalated. The same was true of submarine probings: during the late 1940s and early '50s, the Soviets and Americans both experimented with under-ice navigation, each concluding that traditional diesel-electric subs, which could recharge their batteries only by running on the surface, would never suffice for operations in the ice-encrusted Arctic Ocean. Until the invention of nuclear submarines, however, conventional subs proved useful as a tool for coastal espionage. In 1948, the *Sea Dog* and *Blackfish* tested out radio-signal interception and ship identification off the USSR's Bering shores. During the ill-fated Operation Kayo, in 1949, the *Cochino* and *Tusk* spied on the Soviet Northern Fleet and monitored radio traffic between naval bases on the Kola Peninsula until the *Cochino* was lost to a shipboard fire. Throughout the Cold War, especially after the deployment of nuclear submarines – which entered U.S. service in 1954 and the USSR's in 1958 – the Arctic waters swarmed with subs of steadily increasing sophistication and deadliness, sparring in the undersea dark, gathering intelligence and mapping enemy coastlines. After the Polaris tests of 1960, subs comprised the third leg of the nuclear triad by carrying submarine-launched ballistic missiles (SLBMs). Canada assembled a fleet of small and short-range submarines, acquired mainly from Britain's Royal Navy.

The Arctic itself became a martial landscape. Where the adversaries were geographically closest, their shores bristled with submarine pens, dockyards, airstrips and radar and weather stations. Alaska, studded with bases and airfields from Gambell on St Lawrence Island and Adak in the Aleutians to Elmendorf on the mainland, faced off against the multitude of Soviet installations across the Bering and Okhotsk seas, at Magadan, on Kamchatka, and throughout Chukotka. Gone for good were the days when Chukchi, Koryaks and Siberian Eskimos had ignored political boundaries and mingled freely with trading partners and kindred across the Bering, for fortress-like security now clamped down on the region. Chukotka's non-native population mushroomed in size after the war, with many of the new arrivals staffing the air bases, missile platforms and tank units at sites near Anadyr and Provideniya.

In the west, at the interstice between Norway and Russia, the Kola Peninsula and the White Sea coast hosted the USSR's Northern Fleet and 70 per cent of all Soviet subs – transforming itself into a 'secret world' that combined the attributes of an armed camp and an overgrown factory complex.[2] Around the hubs of Murmansk and Arkhangelsk, numerous facilities sprang into being or grew larger, including the fleet harbour at Severomorsk, the sub pens at Poliarnyi, the airbase near Olenegorsk, and construction yards at Molotovsk (now Severodvinsk). Near Mirnyi in the Arkhangelsk region, the Plesetsk Cosmodrome, which has sent up more than 1,500 rockets and satellites since its establishment in 1966, was originally designed in 1957 as a launch site for intercontinental ballistic missiles (ICBMS). SLBMS were tested at Nenoksa, also near Arkhangelsk.

The entire ring of the Arctic, in fact, was strung by the Soviets and NATO alike with military facilities like a necklace beaded with pearls. Soviet Russia intensively developed the shipping capacity of its Northern Sea Route, assisted especially by the introduction of atomic icebreakers, beginning in 1957 with the *Lenin*, the world's first nuclear-powered surface vessel. Airbases capable of servicing strategic bombers, such as the Tupolev Tu-95 Bear, were added to the Soviet Arctic's existing air network. These included Rogachevo and Amderma-2 on Novaya Zemlya, Gofman Island in Franz Josef Land, Ledovyi and Arkticheskii on Severnaya Zemlya, and Tiksi, on the mouth of the Lena. As ICBMS came to dominate the arms race, more radar installations went up throughout the USSR's Arctic fringe. Those living in the region were reminded by the press that 'every denizen of the north must consider himself a potential defender of the motherland'.[3]

NATO's corresponding presence in the Arctic was a multinational effort, although spearheaded and coordinated by the United States. Airfields capable of supporting workhorse bombers like the 240-ton B-52 Stratofortress were at a premium in the high north, and included Eielson, Shemya and Elmendorf air force bases in Alaska, as well as Newfoundland's Ernst Harmon Air Force Base and Fort Churchill in Manitoba, placed at America's disposal courtesy of the Canadian government. In 1951, the U.S. secured permission from Iceland to use the large Keflavík airfield near Reykjavík, and Norway agreed in 1952 to allow American aeroplanes access to its Arctic airfields in the event of war. On Greenland, U.S. aircraft continued to fly into Second World War airfields like Sondre, and American submarines operated out of bases on the eastern coast, such as Station Nord and Daneborg. But the U.S. scored its biggest Greenland coup when Denmark permitted the construction of an American air base at Thule, in the northwest. Thule's 10,000-foot-long runway, which required a staff of 3,000 to maintain, opened in 1951–3 and decisively extended the range of U.S. air power. Its completion, however, required the forced relocation of several hundred local Inughuit who received no redress until almost half a

United States Air Force service patch, for duty at Thule Air Base in northwest Greenland. Rarely an airman's favourite posting.

century later. Greenland also hosted Camp Century, conceived in 1958 and built by the u.s. in 1959–60 as the first step in a larger plan called Iceworm, whose aim was to station as many as 600 nuclear missiles under the island's ice cap. Located 150 miles west of Thule, Century consisted of 21 tunnels carved deep into the ice's surface and sheltering a warren of prefabricated buildings, all powered by a modular nuclear power plant. Capable of supporting 200 people at a time, the camp operated for more than half a decade, but while useful research was done there – including pioneering work in the field of ice-core sampling – the ice sheet demonstrated a disturbing tendency to shift internally, ending all thoughts of housing nuclear weapons within it. Operation Iceworm was shelved, and Camp Century closed down in 1966. The u.s. bomber fleet gave Greenland a taste of near-Armageddon in January 1968, when a B-52 carrying four thermonuclear bombs crash-landed on the ice sheet near Thule. One bomb sank into the sea, and although no nuclear blast resulted, damage to the other weapons released enough radioactivity to contaminate 3 square miles of ice and, apparently, to elevate the incidence of cancer among the underequipped Danes who assisted u.s. Air Force personnel with the cleanup operation, codenamed Crested Ice.

Another u.s.-dominated initiative was the installation of the Distant Early Warning (DEW) Line, a continent-girdling chain of radar stations

Lockheed P-3 Orion patrol aircraft landing at the United States' Thule Air Base.

that stretched roughly along the 69th parallel between northwest Alaska and Canada's Baffin Island. An extension ran across the width of Greenland, and its functions were synchronized with those of air-defence facilities in Iceland and Britain. The stations, complete with hangars, airfields, barracks and power grids, plus the actual radar domes and antennae, were built at meteoric speed by the Western Electric Company, which worked through the bone-chilling blizzards of winter, between late 1954 and the spring of 1957.

Canada and the States administered the DEW Line jointly, form-ing the North American Aerospace Defense Command (NORAD) in 1958. Canada was the obvious junior partner in this relationship, and while it genuinely worried about possible Soviet threats, its partici-pation in NORAD also represented a pragmatic bowing to the inevitable. With America determined at any cost to monitor the continent's north-ern periphery, the best way for Canada to protect its sovereignty there was to assist with the monitoring, rather than fruitlessly standing on its rights. Unequal in the long run to the job of protecting against ICBMS, SLBMS and cruise missiles, DEW stations were phased out or automated over time, with surviving posts subsumed into NATO's North Warning System. This newer network put into place almost a hun-dred unmanned stations and microwave radars between 1985 and the early 1990s.

This militarization of the Arctic inflicted a tangle of scars on the polar environment, most of them described in the next section of this chapter. Arguably the most horrific, and the ones most relevant to the merging of war with science, were those left behind by the atomic tests conducted in the North by both superpowers. The site chosen by the u.s. was the tiny Aleutian island of Amchitka, which had served as an airstrip during the campaign against the Japanese and was selected as early as 1951 for possible testing. Three explosions were set off here over a six-year period. Long Shot, an 80-kiloton underground blast in October 1965, tested the aec's ability to measure the seismic aftershocks of nuclear detonations and released traces of tritium and krypton into the open. Milrow, in October 1969, yielded over one megaton, and the resulting public outcry prompted the creation of one of the world's best-known non-governmental organizations. Immediately after Milrow, meetings began in Vancouver, Canada, of the Don't Make a Wave Committee – so named because of its fear that the next test scheduled to take place on Amchitka, called Cannikin, would set off violent earth tremors and perhaps a tidal wave. Another opponent of the Cannikin test was the Committee for Nuclear Responsibility, which took legal action in an attempt to force its cancellation. The suit reached the Supreme Court, but failed on a 4-to-3 decision, and President Richard Nixon authorized Cannikin to go ahead in November 1971. The result was the largest underground A-test in American history, yielding approximately 5 megatons, causing an earthquake that registered 7.0 on the Richter scale, and killing as many as 2,000 sea otters in the Bering Sea. The Don't Make a Wave Committee, which had chartered a boat in the hope of sailing to Amchitka to protest, and perhaps prevent, Cannikin, failed to reach the island in time, but went on to reconstitute itself as the internationally famous Greenpeace. The aec vacated the site in 1973, and its environmental impact on Amchitka has been debated ever since. The Department of Energy and the University of Alaska Fairbanks claim minimal and containable radioactive contamination, while Greenpeace insists that the levels of plutonium and americum leakage are in fact much higher.

Even the worst projection of the damage done to Amchitka pales by comparison with what transpired on Novaya Zemlya, where Soviet physicists carried out 224 known atomic tests, many of them above ground, for a total blast force of 265 megatons. The programme began in 1954, with the evacuation of the islands' 300 Nenets residents and the construction of the first test site, Special Structure 700. The first

The 50-megaton blast released by the Soviet 'Tsar-Bomba' test over Novaya Zemlya, 1961 – the most powerful nuclear device ever detonated.

detonation took place in September 1955, at the archipelago's southern tip, and sites for other weapons tests were developed farther to the north. There was no containing the decades of fallout, which prevailing winds carried far to the east, irradiating much of Arctic Siberia. Mainland natives living within sight of the islands, who later recalled how 'the sky went red all day long', suffered the highest incidence of radiation-induced health complications, but because of the ease with which lichens – a prime source of food for reindeer – absorb airborne pollutants, herders who made their home far away from Novaya Zemlya found themselves adversely affected. The most fearsome weapon tested in the Soviet Arctic was the AN-602 hydrogen bomb, jokingly referred to as Tsar-Bomba. The largest nuclear device ever exploded in human history, this 'tsar bomb', theoretically capable of a 100-megaton blast, erupted on 30 October 1961, into a 50-megaton fireball that measured 5 miles in diameter and put one observer in mind of a planet 'powerful and arrogant, like Jupiter'.[4] Atomic testing continued on Novaya Zemlya until 1990, and the extent of the environmental devastation has yet to be fully documented.

For Arctic nations that happened not to be superpowers, life under atomic crosshairs became increasingly anxiety-ridden, especially in the

1970s and '80s, by which point nuclear weapons were deadlier and more numerous than ever before. Soviet submarines routinely trespassed into Scandinavian waters, and it was the state of heightened tensions in the Alaska–Chukotka–Kamchatka triangle that caused the South Korean passenger jet KAL 007 to be shot down over the North Pacific by Soviet Su-15 interceptors in 1983. Spitsbergen, where military presence of any kind had been forbidden by the 1920 Treaty of Svalbard, became the centre of potentially violent controversy in 1978, when the USSR upgraded the helipad at their Barentsburg mine to allow Mi-8 transport/gunship helicopters to land there. NATO responded in 1980 with a seven-nation military exercise code-named Anorak Express and involving more than 18,000 personnel. Olof Palme, the prime minister of neutral Sweden, decried the Cold War as 'entirely senseless', and even America's allies in the North began in the late 1970s and early '80s to place limits on how far they would stand with it.[5] Canada had already stated unequivocally that no nuclear weapons would be based on its soil, while Iceland and others started to ban all vessels carrying nuclear armaments from entering their territorial waters. Without consulting Denmark, the Greenland parliament proclaimed the island to be nuclear-free in perpetuity, regardless of whether a state of war existed. Throughout the 1980s, anti-nuclear sentiment developed into a politically potent force in Finland and the Nordic countries.

As for Arctic science, Cold War realities impinged on scholarly agendas with varying degrees of directness. Especially during the early years, logistical support and funding were far more readily available to scholars researching the physical sciences than to those working in the life or social sciences. Receiving highest priority were meteorology, geophysics, glaciology and permafrost studies, geology, oceanography and any discipline with practical military or national security application. Research that fed corporate and government interest in resource extraction met with equally generous treatment. Sadly, when the life sciences did receive military-industrial support, the results were not always benign. In 1956–7, in one of dozens of unethical radiation-effects experiments carried out nationwide by the Atomic Energy Commission and the U.S. armed forces, over 100 Inupiat and Athabaskans in northern Alaska were fed radioactive iodine tablets (deceptively offered as 'vitamins') so that the U.S. Army Aeromedical Laboratory could observe the effect on their thyroid glands.

This utilitarian tendency was not absolute, at least not in the West. For example, the U.S. Naval Arctic Research Laboratory (NARL), established in 1947 in Barrow, Alaska, tracked whale and bird migrations and counted the populations of polar bears and lemmings with nearly the same attention it devoted to ocean currents and weather patterns. NARL's interest in ethnography, which admittedly stemmed from a utilitarian curiosity about whether u.s. military personnel could learn Eskimo survival skills, led to the commissioning of Richard K. Nelson's well-regarded study from 1969, *Hunters of the Northern Ice*. Even the field of children's literature benefited from the work done at Barrow: it was a season spent among researchers there in 1970 that inspired Jean Craighead George to write the Newbery Award-winning *Julie and the Wolves*, a classic introduction to the Arctic for more than a generation of young readers. Cold War pressures did nothing to prevent Louis Giddings and Eigil Knuth from discovering in 1948 the link between Alaska's Denbigh Flint Complex and Greenland's Independence I culture, or Jørgen Meldgaard of Denmark's National Museum from pursuing archaeological fieldwork throughout Greenland and the American north. Nor did Cold War imperatives keep the French anthropologist Jean Malaurie, who travelled to northwest Greenland in the late 1940s, from speaking out vociferously in the 1950s against NATO's Thule Air Base, whose construction had such a disruptive effect on the lives of his Inughuit subjects.

Not surprisingly, research was more regimented in the USSR. Starting in 1946, GUSMP dispatched vessels on high-latitude drifts and cooperated with other agencies on hydrographical, bathymetric and meteorological surveys of the Kara, Laptev, East Siberian and Chukchi seas – all intended to boost the Northern Sea Route's strategic usefulness. The same was true of the annual air expeditions begun by GUSMP in 1948. These resulted in Alexander Kuznetsov's 1948 landing at the North Pole – the first time a human can be said without argument to have stood there – and tested the landing of large planes and helicopters on the Arctic pack ice. They also proved integral to the Soviets' most ambitious Arctic programme, the resumption of the SP series of drifting polar stations. In 1950–51, GUSMP oceanographer Mikhail Somov headed the sixteen-man SP-2 station, and Alexei Treshnikov followed with the even larger SP-3 expedition in 1954–5. Between that date and 1991, the USSR had at least one SP mission operating in the Arctic seas, and typically more, for as the expeditions grew more complex, many lasted more than a single year, and most involved several teams on separate floes.

The scientific data gathered by the SP stations proved immensely useful, and yet the outposts were yoked to the state's strategic priorities.

A key purpose of the sp-2 and sp-3 missions was to learn how to land heavy aircraft, including large bombers like the Tu-4, on the ice and lift them off again. Together, sp-2 and sp-3 received more than 200 aeroplane and helicopter flights, including the first pack-ice landing to take place during polar twilight, a feat accomplished by sp-1 veteran Mikhail Vodopianov in October 1950. These first stations were to act as small, mobile Greenlands, capable of lengthening the Red air fleet's operational radius. By the 1960s, the sp programme had shifted to anti-submarine detection and signals intelligence. The military stakes were spelled out with special bluntness to sp scientists, beginning with Somov, who was told by Stalin's secret police that if the floe carrying sp-2 should happen to drift into u.s. or Canadian waters, he would be responsible for destroying not just the station, but the crew and himself.

Although the u.s. never matched the Soviet effort, it launched its own ice stations, including t-3, which originated off Ellesmere Island in 1952 and remained afloat until 1974. These served as platforms for the same scientific and military/intelligence functions as their sp counterparts. In 1962, the Americans also seized a unique opportunity to parachute two cia operatives onto the drifting hulk of sp-8, abandoned by the Soviets when shifting ice cracked its landing strip. Operation Coldfeet, as the manoeuvre was named, successfully retrieved the landing party by means of the ingenious Skyhook surface-to-air recovery system and revealed much to American intelligence about Soviet sub-hunting techniques. The sp missions came to a temporary halt after the summer of 1991, when all the teams working as part of sp-31 returned home. The Putin government revived the programme in 2003 with the sp-32 expedition.

Hundreds of other projects, too numerous to profile individually, furthered understanding of the Arctic or lent themselves to the improvement of infrastructure there, or to the more efficient extraction of its resources. Even if the Cold War made them poorer cousins to the physical scientists, botanists and zoologists such as Christian Vibe of Denmark observed, classified and catalogued Arctic biota with a keen eye – and recorded the decline of all too many species as human presence in the region expanded. Ethnographers shed brighter light on the North's human dimensions, while archaeologists filled in more of the prehistoric picture.

Particularly striking among larger scientific ventures were the collaborative efforts undertaken by many countries in the Cold War north. While the International Geophysical Year of 1957–8 is best remembered for advances in Antarctic research and the Soviet Union's

Sputnik launch, many of the 67 participant nations devoted their scholarly energies to the Arctic as well. European nations frequently partnered in the north, sometimes as a way of bypassing the Cold War paradigm. Such enterprises included the EGIG I expedition of 1959, a study of the Greenland ice cap led by France's Paul-Émile Victor and drawing on the skills of French, Danish, Austrian, Swiss and German scholars, and the formation of the European Incoherent Scatter Scientific Association (EISCAT) in 1973–5. This involved the erection of three radar installations – one near Tromsø, one at the Sodankylä Geophysical Laboratory in Finland and one in the Svalbard archipelago – to study the ionosphere and magnetosphere. Still operating from the association's headquarters in Kiruna, Sweden, EISCAT is jointly funded by Norway, Finland, Sweden, Germany and Great Britain, as well as by Japan and China.

Although satellite photography began in 1959, it was in the early 1970s that the superpowers, and then other nations, gained access to advanced satellite imagery. NASA's (now NOAA's) Landsat programme, for instance, began in 1972. Satellite imagery came to be used widely during the later Cold War to map the Arctic more accurately and to model glaciological, oceanographic and meteorological changes more precisely. Another data-gathering method that grew in importance during the Cold War was deep ice-core sampling, a technique almost literally bestowing upon researchers the gift of time travel, allowing them to reconstruct weather patterns, plant distribution, pollutant types and other information from past eras. Greenland, with its especially thick ice, has always offered the best opportunities in the northern hemisphere for such research – as demonstrated by the massive Greenland Ice Sheet Project, conducted by scientists from the U.S., Denmark, Switzerland and elsewhere between 1971 and 1981, and the equally ambitious GISP 2. Ice-core research has occupied scholars elsewhere in the North as well.

Although much of the public is accustomed to think of it as a recently arisen issue, climate change became apparent to Arctic scientists early in the 1900s, and resoundingly so during the Cold War's later decades. Sounding the clarion in the late 1940s, as he had done during the 1930s, was Hans Ahlmann, Sweden's 'Professor Ice'. Ahlmann testified at public venues throughout Europe and America, including before the Pentagon, about receding glaciers and rising temperatures at Tarfala and other research stations in Finnmark, Swedish Lapland and Spitsbergen. Researchers who troubled to listen to native hunters and herders, whether in Scandinavia, Siberia or North America, learned about the altered migratory patterns of birds, fish and animals and about how the ice, more frequently every year, was hardening later and melting sooner. In 1972, the aviator Bernt Balchen, who spent the postwar years advising corporations such as General Dynamics and Phillips Petroleum on how to operate in Arctic conditions, observed in the *Christian Science Monitor* that 'a general warming trend over the North Pole is melting the polar ice cap and may produce an ice-free Arctic Ocean by the year 2000.'[6]

Balchen overpitched his case – although not, it appears, by terribly much – and the rate of change in the 1970s and '80s had not yet begun to avalanche the way it would in the 1990s and 2000s. Most, therefore, thought it perfectly reasonable to ignore or explain away the many warning signs already calling out for attention. James Hansen, head of NASA's Goddard Institute for Space Studies, discovered this to his frustration as he began in the 1980s to predict the opening-up of the Northwest Passage and other dire consequences of global warming. When Hansen, like a growing number of other scientists, urged policy-makers and the public to look to the shrinking polar ice caps as an indicator of the dramatic changes in worldwide weather patterns, he was ridiculed by officials in the Reagan and Bush Sr administrations as 'alarmist'. Hansen refused to be muzzled, and his testimony before the u.s. Senate in 1988 is widely considered a turning point in attuning the public at large to the problem of anthropogenic, or human-caused, climate change.

Finally, the Cold War witnessed a battery of Arctic 'firsts', some accomplished for scientific or political purposes, others for the sake of breaking records. The first air landing precisely at the North Pole, accomplished by the aforementioned Alexander Kuznetsov, came in 1948. The first submarine to reach the Pole was the uss *Nautilus* in 1958, a feat not matched by the Soviets until the polar voyage of the *Leninsky Komsomol* in 1962. By then, the uss *Skate* had already broken through the surface of the North Pole pack ice, and the crew of the uss *Seadragon* had played the world's first game of North Pole baseball. The Soviets, in turn, won the race to get a surface vessel to the Pole, with the atomic icebreaker *Arktika* bulldozing its way to 90°N in 1977.

The first verifiable overland journey to the Pole was completed by the American Ralph Plaisted and three others, including Canada's Jean-Luc Bombardier. Outfitted with Bombardier Ski-Doo snowmobiles and receiving supply support from the air, they reached their destination in

April 1968. Following on their heels were Wally Herbert and the rest of the British Trans-Arctic Expedition, which made the first surface crossing of the Arctic Ocean, a 1,500-mile trek from Barrow to Spitsbergen via the North Pole, in 1968–9.

What remained after Herbert's triumph was to add refinements or technical difficulties to the classic polar trek. Naomi Uemura of Japan travelled solo to the Pole in 1978, but, like Plaisted and Herbert, with outside logistical support. Between 1979 and 1982, British explorers Ranulph Fiennes and Charlie Burton completed the first circumnavigation of the earth that took in both the North and South Poles. To reach the North Pole overland and without external support, it fell to an American dogsled party led in 1986 by Will Steger and including the teacher Ann Bancroft, the first woman to reach the Pole on the surface. Steger's group left Ellesmere Island on 8 March and reached the Pole that May. Along with his dogsled crossing of Greenland from south to north two years later, also without external support, Steger's North Pole run proved to be the Cold War's last major feat of Arctic adventuring – although his and Bancroft's careers as environmental-awareness activists and educators have continued long afterwards.

Homes and Native Lands: Nation-building, Indigenous Rights and Environmental Concerns in the Postwar Arctic

Starting in the 1970s, a host of animal-rights organizations, reacting in particular to the annual spring killing of Canadian 'whitecoats', or young harp seals, launched an extraordinarily effective series of 'Save the Seals' publicity campaigns. By calling attention to shrinking seal populations and translating environmentalist passions into political action, 'Save the Seals' efforts played a meaningful role in passing many of the laws and sanctions that now regulate which species can be hunted and how heavily, the conditions under which they can be slain and where seal products can be sold. Less formally, they have created a widespread revulsion against seal-hunting, vastly reducing the global demand for seal furs and seal meat.

Similarly, in 1972, with extinction threatening more than a dozen large and mid-sized cetacean species, the United Nations' Conference on the Human Environment, held in Stockholm, proposed a ten-year halt to all commercial whaling; shortly afterwards, Greenpeace and other NGOs began their own anti-whaling crusades. Success on this front was even greater than with the seals, culminating in the worldwide moratorium on commercial whaling – technically a zero-catch quota – approved by the International Whaling Commission (IWC) in 1982 and put into effect in 1986. Restrictions were placed on the harvesting and sale of walrus and narwhal ivory, thanks to the United States' 1972 Marine Mammal Protection Act and the 1975 Convention on International Trade in Endangered Species of Wild Fauna and Flora (CITES). And in a 1976 agreement signed by Norway, Denmark, Canada, the United States and the USSR, the International Union for the Conservation of Nature and Natural Resources outlawed the hunting of polar bears.

There has been no doubting the environmental soundness of such policies, with once-endangered animal populations stabilizing and in some cases rebounding. Assessing their human impact, however, has proven more problematic. Leaving aside the complaints, discussed at the end of this chapter, of those industrialized states which claim sealing and whaling to be part of their national heritage, the generally negative reaction of indigenous northerners to restrictions on sea-mammal hunting raises an important but as yet unsettled question. To what degree should the protection of wildlife be considered an absolute good? Are the Arctic's large mammals, especially the whales, sufficiently at risk or of a high enough order of sentience that they should be shielded from harm under any circumstance, as organizations like Greenpeace and the World Wildlife Fund contend? Or, as the opponents of hunting bans maintain, is such conservationist zeal based on an unscientific anthropomorphization that blinds the public to the genuine needs of aboriginal peoples, or to the possibility that sea-mammal hunting, properly regulated, can satisfy human wants and still protect animal species adequately? Various exemptions have been granted to native populations and others, but debates over sea-mammal hunting regulations have never ended and are not likely to in any foreseeable future. Whichever position one takes, such questions throw into stark relief the core challenge that each Arctic nation faced during the Cold War era. As states continued to build their northern presence, an unceasing three-way tension placed their priorities, those of native peoples, and those of the environment at sharp odds with each other. Could those tensions be harmonized – and if so, exactly how?

The face of Alaska, which became America's 49th state in 1959, was changed above all by two things: military build-up and big oil. With airfields and DEW Line stations came highways, power grids and other amenities, especially in the cities and big bases. As in all parts of the Arctic, the introduction of radio during and after the Second World War improved communications hugely. In 1940, just over 72,000 people had been living in Alaska. By 1950, that figure had grown to more than 128,000, and it increased to 226,000 by 1960, just after statehood. It nearly doubled again over the next 30 years, reaching 550,000 by 1990.

Important as strategic imperatives were, this swelling of population had far more to do with resource extraction. Full-scale prospecting for Alaskan lead and zinc began in the 1950s, with large reserves discovered near Kotzebue during the late 1960s. The Red Dog Mine, developed there in the 1970s and opened in the '80s, quickly became the world's largest single producer of zinc, accounting for 10 per cent of the global supply. Thirty-two trillion cubic feet of natural gas had been located in Alaska by the mid-1980s, a fraction of what is now known to lie there. But the true monarch of Alaska's economy was and remains oil. The search for petroleum continued after the Second World War, although not until 1957 and 1959, with the opening of the Swanson River and Middle Ground Shoal fields on the Kenai Peninsula and the adjoining Cook Inlet, did major commercial production become viable. The most successful strike, and the one that most fundamentally transformed the state, came in early 1968, when the Atlantic Richfield Company, after a number of false starts, tapped into the deposits beneath Prudhoe Bay, on the North Slope. This turned out to be the largest oil field in North America, estimated at the time to contain 7 to 9 billion barrels of recoverable petroleum. That June, the state of Alaska auctioned off $900 million worth of North Slope drilling rights – all in a single day.

Exploiting this newfound wealth was no simple matter, and deciding how to do so refocused attention on long-unsettled debates about environmental policy and the relationship between indigenous and newcomer populations. First, a physical means had to be devised to move North Slope oil from the Arctic coast to the south. Thoughts of shipping it through the Northwest Passage were scuppered after the 1969 voyage of the *Manhattan*, a u.s. supertanker adapted for polar navigation and the first commercial vessel to successfully transit the Passage. Sent from New York to Prudhoe, the *Manhattan* loaded one barrel of Alaskan crude as a ceremonial gesture, then returned home. Although the ship, after being challenged by a party of Inuit kayakers, asked for and received permission to traverse Canadian waters, and was escorted by the Canadian Coast Guard icebreaker *John A. MacDonald*, its voyage provoked a howl of protest from a Canadian public concerned about northern sovereignty. Even more discouraging was the ice, which buffeted the *Manhattan* on at least 25 occasions with force deemed unsafe. Consequently, oil developers opted to build the costlier but more dependable Trans-Alaska Pipeline, stretching 800 miles from Prudhoe Bay to the terminus of Valdez on the coast of Prince William Sound, from which tankers could sail freely to the south.

Construction, however, was delayed until 1974, both by conservationists and native-rights groups. Pipeline proponents argued that a more than generous amount of Alaskan territory, including Mount McKinley, Glacier Bay, the Yukon delta and the Arctic National Wildlife Range (set aside by President Dwight Eisenhower in 1960), had already been protected from development. Environmentalists, however, whose fears about the impact of improperly regulated oil extraction have since been abundantly justified, persuaded the courts to impose such strict conditions on the pipeline's construction that its price tag ballooned to almost $10 billion, or roughly eight times the projected cost. The pipeline controversy also gave advocacy groups like the Alaska Federation of Natives maximum leverage to press land claims that had stalled or were going poorly. Key factors in the AFN's success were the willpower and negotiating skills of Inupiat activist Eben Hopson, who later went on to establish the North Slope Borough, seated at Barrow, and to serve as Barrow's mayor. The landmark result of this bargaining was the Alaska Native Claims Settlement Act (ANCSA), signed by Richard Nixon in December 1971 and supplemented with further legislation in later years. In exchange for renouncing all previous claims, Alaska's 85,000 natives received title to 44 million acres of land, roughly 12 per cent of the state's territory, and payments of almost $1 billion, which were distributed among twelve regional corporations and more than 200 village corporations. In twenty years' time, native communities would be free to sell their land at market value if they so decided.

Making way for the pipeline, though, was only one component of the larger social arrangement that grew out of these negotiations. Public contestation over the proper balance between development and environmental protection continued. In 1980, the federal government, despite tumultuous opposition from libertarian and pro-oil Alaskans, passed the Alaska National Interest Lands Conservation Act. This measure created or expanded eighteen national parks, preserves, and monuments. Much to the displeasure of the petroleum industry, the act doubled the size of the Arctic National Wildlife Range, which became the Arctic National Wildlife Refuge and currently abuts the Prudhoe oil field's eastern border.

Conversely, the Alaskan ecosystem sustained its most grievous blow to date on the early morning of 24 March 1989, when the tanker *Exxon Valdez* ran aground on Bligh Reef in Prince William Sound. Before sunrise, at least 11 million gallons of oil had poured out of the broken vessel, spreading a leprous black veil over 11,000 square miles of ocean surface and washing up onto 1,300 miles of shoreline. In spite of a mammoth volunteer cleanup effort, perhaps as many as a quarter of a million birds perished, as did 2,800 sea otters, 300 harbour seals and over a score of orcas. Untold numbers of herring and salmon died, and toxicity in these waters remains depressingly high more than two decades on. It is hard to know which is more frightening: the fact that the *Exxon Valdez* damage was so extensive even though only one-fifth of the oil aboard the ship leaked out, or the petroleum industry's continued and brazen confidence in the notion that it should be allowed to carry out recovery and transport operations in remote and dangerous locations on the cheap and under as little government oversight as possible. Pollution in more prosaic forms rose steadily throughout these years, thanks to the state's population explosion, and also to the hazardous waste and PCBs (polychlorinated biphenyls) generated by military bases and DEW Line stations. Cleanup of the latter continues to this day.

Also during the pipeline years, Alaska's natives endeavoured to win a less disadvantaged place for themselves in an increasingly American-ized landscape. As 'oil-age Eskimos' (and Indians), the phrase coined by anthropologist Joseph Jorgensen to connote the epochal change that the discovery of petroleum has wrought in their lives, native Alaskans had to cope with material conditions unlike anything experienced by their ancestors. No longer were they treated as cavalierly as during the 1950s and '60s, when projects like Operation Chariot or the above-mentioned iodine experiments were planned without their consent. DEW Line stations and facilities like NARL created jobs, brought creature comforts and opened windows onto a larger world. Official institu-tions, and more gradually the public, began to pay symbolic respect to native heritage by reverting to the use of aboriginal place names. A key step in this process came in the late 1970s, when the National Park Service began calling Mount McKinley by the traditional Koyukon name Denali, meaning 'High One'. With the 1977 formation of the Inuit Circum-polar Conference (now the Inuit Circumpolar Council, or ICC) – whose first meeting was called and hosted by Barrow's mayor, Eben Hopson – Alaska's Inupiat and Yupik found an international outlet for their cultural and political concerns. It was largely thanks to ICC lobbying, for example, that the International Whaling Commission allowed Eskimo and Inuit hunters to take limited quotas of bowheads and other whales every year.

And yet native Alaskans still had poverty and discrimination to overcome. Easing the way were regional and village native corporations, which strove to foster community and preserve old traditions while also using ANCSA money to pay for schools, medical services and other improvements. They sought to put fishing and hunting on a more profitable basis, and introduced new ways to make a living, such as caribou herding or tending to the small populations of musk oxen that Alaska transplanted from Canada.

Unfortunately, as with so many Arctic peoples, Alaska's natives were not served entirely well by partial adaptation to modern 'civilization'. More readily available than ever, alcohol became a true scourge. Increased intake of sugar and processed foods caused diabetes, heart disease and tooth decay so endemic that, in the 1980s, the World Health Organization, which had once ranked Eskimo and Inuit teeth the healthiest on the planet, rated them the world's worst. The most useful of their borrowed technologies, such as the rifle, snowmobile and motorboat, were double-edged in effect, encouraging the overhunting of deer and seals and causing traditional skills like dogsledding and kayaking to be lost. Radio and television made it more difficult to preserve knowledge of native languages, as did the emphasis in schools on improved English-language proficiency. Finally, a clash of world views often placed Alaska's natives on the wrong side of environmental protection regulations and game and fishing laws. As one anthropologist notes, 'non-compliance with resource management is a basic mechanism of resistance for local people' – a 'weapon of the weak', in James Scott's classic formulation – and the conservationist concerns of non-natives who dream of ethereally unspoiled wilderness while living comfortably hundreds of miles away tend to hold little meaning for the natives who actually inhabit the wilderness.[7] The Canadian scholar Hugh Brody has long said of Arctic peoples that 'what must be defended is not the traditional as opposed to the modern but, rather, the right of a free indigenous people to choose the components of their lives.'[8] But for Alaska's natives, hitting upon the most beneficial mix of traditional and modern has been a difficult problem to solve.

The same was true in postwar Canada, where Brody railed against the 'internal imperialism' that relegated Inuit and other indigenes to a secondary and impoverished status. Ottawa's growing concerns about

northern sovereignty caused it to assert its authority over these populations more forcefully than before; the 1949 entry of Newfoundland and
Labrador into Canadian confederation placed even more Arctic natives
under its direct jurisdiction. The most egregious of the government's
actions came in the early 1950s, when federal authorities resettled Inuit
communities far from their homes, not precisely by force, but neither
with their full agreement. In 1950, to relieve Ihalmiut groups from
starvation that had set in the year before, the government evacuated
them to Nuelten Lake, where they were to work for a recently established fishing outfit. But when the company folded in 1951, the Ihalmiut
were left stranded without assistance.

Graduating from clumsily well-meaning to straightforwardly self-
serving, federal officials decided in 1952 to transplant a number of Inuit
families from northern Quebec and Baffin Island to Ellesmere and
Cornwallis islands, in order to strengthen Canada's territorial claim
over the Arctic archipelago. The RCMP carried out this High Arctic
Relocation in 1953, moving the 'volunteers' hundreds of miles to
Grise Fiord and Resolute Bay, two of the world's northernmost points
of human habitation, where hunting conditions were completely different and the polar night longer and more forbidding. As Canadian
officials pointed out to the royal commission that looked into the
matter during the early 1990s, the Inuit were asked, not ordered, to
relocate, and were never threatened at any time. But readers must
judge for themselves how easy a marginalized people would have found
it to say 'no' to a law-enforcement agency armed and empowered by
its colonizer. Beyond that, the authorities refused to return the Inuit
to their homes, despite being begged to, and despite having promised
to do so upon request after a period of two years. Public scandal
erupted over the relocation in the late 1980s and was not quelled until
the mid-1990s.

Other policies aimed more simply for assimilation. Inuit received
the long-overdue right to vote in the 1950s. But their shamans, already
a rare breed, died out by the early 1960s. Better medical care included
much-needed vaccinations, but also tuberculosis screenings that, in the
mid-1950s, caused one in five Inuit families to lose at least one member to involuntary hospitalization in cities to the south. In assigning
them 'rational' family names for the purposes of better recordkeeping, the absurd initiative called Operation Surname perplexed Arctic
natives, and RCMP enforcement of dog-ownership laws better suited
to the south antagonized them. After a rogue sled dog killed an RCMP

constable's wife, Inuit were required to keep all dogs tethered and to certify that they had been vaccinated against rabies, or risk having them summarily shot. How many dogs were actually disposed of this way has never been determined. The RCMP maintains that only a few unquestionably dangerous animals were killed, while it is an article of faith among many – or the remote version of an urban myth? – that thousands were slaughtered, with the conspiracy-minded prone to believe that this was done deliberately to foster native dependency on snowmobiles and gasoline sold by whites. Be that as it may, the snow-mobile, which began to appear widely in the Canadian Arctic in the early 1960s, radically transformed Inuit hunting habits and lifeways, along with the introduction of rifles and motorized boats. As in Alaska, all three multiplied the mobility and killing power of native hunters, but increased as well their vulnerability to what ethnobotanist Wade Davis has called 'the seduction of modern trade goods'.[9]

Also during the postwar years, more Arctic natives were compelled to place their children in Canada's residential school system, which had spread further into the North. Publicly, this was presented as part of the nation's *mission civilisatrice*, and one can still view Canadian Broadcasting Corporation newsreels from the 1960s, featuring eager, apple-cheeked Inuit children filing into classrooms staffed by cheerfully maternal teachers. As before the Second World War, the reality in these schools was often grimly different, a fact hinted at in Michael Kusugak's 1998 short story 'Agatha Goes to School', whose protagonist has to force herself 'not to think bad thoughts' and to remember that 'there were some good things that happened in this awful place'.[10] The process of closing the residential schools began in 1969, but was not completed until 1996, and inquests into the many abuses committed in them continued into the 2000s. Writing in 1970 about the sum effect of such policies, Farley Mowat excoriated Ottawa for having reduced Canada's northern communities to 'debilitated, disorientated islands of human flotsam, nearly devoid of hope and of ambition, surviving on charity – when they survived at all'.[11] Less pungently, the historian Morris Zaslow speaks of 'well-meant but tragically inadequate efforts . . . to help [northern] peoples adapt as painlessly as possible to the requirements of the changing times'.[12] This plight was somewhat mitigated during the 1970s by a watershed series of land-claims disputes (discussed below), and also by the enshrinement of aboriginal rights in the Constitution Act of 1982.

Canada's postwar governments looked to the Arctic for new riches. Prime Minister John Diefenbaker articulated his famous 'northern vision' during the election campaign of 1958 and later avowed that 'the North is our ace in the hole. It is our economic future.'[13] Cod-fishing off the east coast and other forms of sea hunting continued, although returns here began to dwindle during the 1970s and '80s. The far northwest still yielded gold, but zinc was now more prominent, with Canada emerging as the world's largest producer of the metal. A number of zinc/lead mines turned profits in the Yukon and the Northwest Territories, including Nanisivik, which opened in 1976 near Baffin Island's Arctic Bay, and Polaris, which began operations on Little Cornwallis Island in 1981. Tourism generated earnings as well, especially where the boom-and-bust cycle common to extractive economies took one turn too many. Most unique was the example of Churchill, Manitoba, which fell on hard times in the late 1970s, as its usefulness to Cold War strategic deployment lessened. Taking advantage of the seasonal sojourn of polar bears into the town's environs, Churchill in the 1980s remade itself into one of North America's most popular ecotourism destinations.

As in Alaska, though, the biggest potential moneymakers for the Canadian north were natural gas and oil, especially beneath the surface of the Mackenzie River basin and the adjoining Beaufort Sea, where deposits of both had been found as early as the 1950s. In 1968, with excitement skyrocketing over Alaska's Prudhoe Bay strike, the Canadian government encouraged the formation of Panarctic Oils, a consortium that eventually operated over 100 wells in Canada's north. In 1969, Panarctic opened a lucrative gas field at Drake Point, on Melville Island, and it developed Canada's only high-Arctic oil field, Bent Horn on Cameron Island, between 1974 and 1996. However, the discoveries stimulating nationwide exhilaration were those between 1970 and 1972 of huge gas fields in numerous spots throughout the Mackenzie Basin. Quickly, plans were drafted for a Mackenzie Valley gas pipeline, running through the Northwest Territories to Alberta and touted as 'the biggest project in the history of free enterprise'.[14]

As with the Trans-Alaska Pipeline, the Mackenzie proposal met with opposition from environmentalists and native groups. The Inuit of the Mackenzie Delta created a Committee for Original Peoples' Entitlement (COPE), one of Canada's first native-advocacy organizations, and they and their First Nations neighbours used the pipeline debate to force larger discussions about native rights and land claims. Their timing was propitious, for high courts were already embroiled in a number of pivotal cases – the 1973 land claim brought before the

Supreme Court by the Nisga'a of British Columbia, the James Bay dispute between Hydro-Québec dam-builders and local Cree and Naskapi – that established a basis in law for aboriginal rights and created a favourable climate for the Mackenzie negotiations. These dragged on into the 1980s and early '90s; in the meantime, a national inquiry chaired by Justice Thomas Berger concluded that no construction could in good faith be allowed to proceed while title to the land was clouded. In 1977, on his recommendation, blueprints for the pipeline were shelved. Only in the twenty-first century would they again become relevant.

Questions of Arctic sovereignty preoccupied Ottawa during the Cold War. Most of these concerns were standard national-security ones: keeping the North safe from Soviet submarines and bombers, or staving off foreign, especially Danish and Norwegian, claims on the Canadian archipelago. The Northwest Passage remained a sore point, with Canada claiming control over it as an internal waterway, but the rest of the world viewing it as an international strait, freely accessible to all. Since 1970, Canada's stratagem for enforcing its will in these waters has been to do so on behalf of the ecosystem: the Arctic Waters Pollution Prevention Act, enacted in response to the tanker *Manhattan*'s 1969 double traverse of the Passage, authorizes Canada to ensure that all vessels sailing within 100 miles of its shores are in compliance with its environmental safety codes.

To a degree that many Americans find surprising, Canada's sovereignty anxieties were directed pointedly towards the United States. Although the two countries' alliance was a remarkable strategic partnership, it at times resembled a tussle between rival siblings. Canada's resentment of perceived American arrogance was near-constant – as when the uss *Nautilus* entered Canada's undersea depths without permission in 1957, or when concerns about possible u.s. unilateralism in the Arctic helped to motivate Canada's participation in the DEW Line programme. For its part, the u.s. continued to oppose Canada's claim over the Northwest Passage; when it sent the icebreaker *Polar Sea* through the Passage in 1985, it deliberately neglected to ask for clearance from its neighbour, on the grounds that, in Washington's eyes, no need for clearance existed. America and Canada likewise clashed over the still-unresolved ownership of 8,000 square miles of the Beaufort Sea extending from the Alaska–Yukon border.

Also related to sovereignty issues, but in an internal sense, were the land claims lodged by Canadian natives in the 1970s and afterwards.

Consider the text of the Dene Declaration, adopted by 300 First Nations delegates from throughout the Northwest Territories: 'We insist on the right to be regarded by ourselves and the world as a nation . . . we seek independence and self-determination within the country of Canada.'[15] Engaged as he was in a bitter struggle against Quebec separatism and believing as he did that all citizens should aim to enfold themselves within a single Canadian culture, Pierre Trudeau began his prime ministership with a less than sympathetic stance towards minority rights. He revised his views during the 1970s, both in response to court decisions and to the dilemmas raised by the cases themselves: fear of the environmental wreckage that might be caused by oil wells and gas pipelines, the drowning of caribou herds by hydroelectric companies flooding local rivers, and the disruption of fishing and whaling by the intrusion of supertankers into native-held waters. In a foundational way, the Constitution Act passed by Trudeau's government in 1982 guaranteed aboriginal rights.

In turn, those rights strengthened further land and hunting-rights claims made in the Canadian north. In the wake of the pipeline controversy, the Inuvialuit of the Mackenzie Delta settled their claims as early as 1984, although most of the First Nations and Métis of the Yukon and the western half of the Northwest Territories prolonged their negotiations until the 1990s, if they reached a conclusion at all. Most strikingly, Inuit in the east decided in a 1982 plebiscite to press for the creation of a homeland to be called Nunavut, or 'our land'. With the help of anthropologists such as Milton Freeman, the Inuit undertook an extensive self-study of their hunting practices; the findings, published in three volumes, assisted in making the case that, because traditional hunting methods required travel over vast distances, the Inuit were justified in claiming as their homeland more than 1.5 million square miles of land and sea. Ottawa agreed in principle to the Nunavut concept in 1988 and committed to it in 1993 – although not until 1999 did the new territory come into being. On the extranational level, Canada's Inuit have been major players in the Inuit Circumpolar Council since its establishment in 1977.

To judge by the landscapes of Iceland's Jóhannes Kjarval, with his evocative renderings of glaciers and lava fields, or by the haunting strains of Einojuhani Rautavaara's 1972 *Cantus Arcticus*, an orchestral work featuring birdsong recordings taken in the wetlands of northern Finland, the Scandinavian Arctic would seem never to have been touched by the storms and stresses of the late twentieth century. In reality, Finland and the nations of Scandinavia required a good deal of recovery after the Second World War, and their drive to develop their economies more fully in the postwar years jolted larger parts of their Arctic territories into the modern age.

During the late 1940s and early '50s, many of the region's northern denizens were pressured by state authorities to relocate. Military imperatives dictated the ouster of native Greenlanders from Thule to make room for the u.s. air base there, but the principal factor in most cases was infrastructural cost-effectiveness. Throughout the 1950s, Danish and Inuit Greenlanders alike were encouraged to cluster in population centres as much as possible; in the largest city, Godthåb, slums comprised of drab tenement apartments housed the influx of new residents. As part of its postwar settlement with the ussr, the Finnish government moved large numbers of Sami from the north coast into the interior, where they were forced to take up different forms of livelihood. Norway attempted its own programme of resettlement in the northern counties of Troms and Finnmark, both ravaged by retreating Germans during the Second World War. Hoping to lower rebuilding costs in this 30,000-square-mile territory, Oslo asked the independent coastal fishermen of the northern villages to move south and seek employment with large trawler fleets there. Here, stubbornness prevailed, and the village fishers stayed put, taking their small boats out to compete with the monster trawlers that prowled their shores. Rather than centralizing northern construction as it had hoped to do, Norway's government was obliged to thread a more attenuated network of roads, power lines and public services through dozens of tiny remote settlements.

Due to Cold War build-up, economic ambition, and the needs of growing populations – Iceland's, for example, rose from 70,000 in the 1950s to more than 200,000 by the 1980s – infrastructure rapidly expanded in the Scandinavian Arctic. The difference was especially noticeable on the islands, where airfields, highways and radios had been comparatively rare before the Second World War. Even the Faeroes now had their own airport, on the western isle of Vágar, a legacy of Britain's wartime occupation. Economic growth was for the most part steady, and many prominent firms operating in the north came to be fully or partially nationalized. These included long-standing giants such as Norsk Hydro and Sweden's lkab conglomerate, which operated the Kiruna mines in the Arctic, along with new arrivals like Norway's Statoil, founded in 1972, as the North Sea oil boom took hold, and Denmark's dong (Dansk Olie og Naturgas) Energy.

Uniquely structured among the region's corporations was the Scandinavian Airlines System (SAS), created in 1946 by the merger of a privately owned Swedish airline with the national carriers of Norway and Denmark. SAS took a leading role in developing Arctic aviation for commercial purposes and, in 1954, became the first airline to offer a regular transpolar passenger flight: Copenhagen to Los Angeles, with stops in Greenland and Winnipeg. Finland invested huge sums in naval engineering and emerged as the world's leading manufacturer of icebreakers. Not only did it capture much of the international market, it assembled a domestic fleet large enough to keep ports on the Gulf of Bothnia, such as Kemi and Oulu, open year-round. This considerably eased logistics for Finland's northern steel and paper industries.

A particular challenge for postwar Scandinavia was to diversify its northern economies. Iron mining continued in places like Kiruna, but no longer sustained Sweden's economy as it once had. The profitability of coal mining oscillated widely: Norway kept it up on Spitsbergen and even took over Sweden's Sveagruva facility there, but Denmark's Qullissat mine on Greenland vanished into ghost-town oblivion, its deposits exhausted by 1966. Roughly at the same time, Greenland's reserves of cryolite ran out. Cod fishing, which had thrived for Iceland, Norway and the Faeroes from the 1920s onwards, entered a difficult period in the 1960s, owing to shifts in the ocean currents, but as much to overfishing. Competition over ever-smaller catches grew urgent enough in 1958–61 and again in the 1970s to cause periodic 'cod wars' between Iceland and Britain, to the point that warships were dispatched to prevent fishing ships from ramming each other or exchanging gunfire. (Greenland, by contrast, benefited from the migration of cod stocks, as well as halibut, to its shores, and its Disko region enjoyed a shrimp boom in the 1970s and '80s.) Icelanders and Norwegians, as well as the Faeroese, were affected by the steep decline in northern whale populations, and by the stigmatization of whaling by environmental NGOs and the IWC ban. As noted below, anti-sealing activism had similar, but even more serious, ramifications for the Inuit of Greenland.

New sources of enrichment came from zinc, copper and gold in Sweden's Norrbotten district; aluminum in Iceland and Norway; and the development of hydroelectric and geothermal energy in Norway and Iceland, respectively. Tourism proved increasingly lucrative, with Longyearbyen recasting itself as a starting point for guided outdoor adventuring, and Iceland cashing in on the appeal of the ancient sagas and on the stark natural beauty that justifies its tourist catchphrase, 'land of fire and ice'. Norway received the most fantastic windfall of all in the 1960s, when massive quantities of oil and gas were discovered in the North and Norwegian seas. Most of the offshore deposits exploited by Norway during the Cold War years were subarctic rather than Arctic, but petrogeologists began nosing northward in the 1980s, discovering fields like Heidrun, west of Kristiansund at 65°N, and setting the stage for a push into the Arctic by oil developers in the 1990s and 2000s. During the 1980s, Norway and Sweden carried out exploratory gas and oil drilling throughout the Svalbard archipelago.

In the Fennoscandian north as elsewhere, natives and non-natives, as well as colonies and home countries, hammered out new relationships with each other. In 1953, Greenland ceased to be a colony and was designated a constituent part of the Danish kingdom. Public-relations campaigns during the 1960s spoke of the Greenlanders as 'northern Danes', and Copenhagen considered itself a generous patron to the island. Nonetheless, despite the comparatively good terms on which Danish colonizers and the Inuit majority managed to coexist, mutual incomprehensibility was never absent. As the half-Inuit narrator of Peter Høeg's bestselling *Miss Smilla's Feeling for Snow* comments, 'Not one day of my adult life has passed without amazement at how poorly the Danes and Greenlanders understand each other. It's worse for the Greenlanders, of course. It's unhealthy for the tightrope walker to be misunderstood by the person holding the line.'[16] Greenland natives played a crucial role in the indigenous-rights activism that brought the Inuit Circumpolar Council into being in 1977. Also during the 1970s, the home rule movement, under the leadership of Lutheran pastor Jonathan Motzfeldt and poet Moses Olsen, grew louder in its agitation. The Danes refused to transfer ownership of mineral rights, as Motzfeldt and Olsen requested, but agreed to home rule in 1979. With Queen Margrethe II proclaiming to all Greenlanders that 'you now hold the future in your own hands', Motzfeldt became the island's first prime minister.

By no means, though, did home rule cure all of Greenland's ills. Thanks to the 'Save the Seals' campaigns of the 1970s and the resulting boycotts imposed on seal products by the European Economic Community (EEC), Inuit seal-hunters, both in Canada and Greenland, saw their livelihoods wither; when the Inuit insisted that they ought not to be tarred with the same negative-publicity brush used to condemn industrial sealing or the clubbing to death of baby harp seals, their arguments fell on deaf ears. Poverty, overcrowding and pollution weighed down harder on Greenland. It could take ten years to obtain a housing permit in Nuuk, as the capital of Godthåb was now called, and Greenland's suicide rate rose during the 1980s to become the world's highest. The home rule government also made the highly controversial decision during the early 1980s to pull out of the European Economic Community. It took this step to protest the EEC's anti-sealing boycott and because European vessels were overfishing its waters, but also because the EEC's Euratom conventions obliged all members to allow the exploitation of any existing uranium deposits – which Greenland, with its passionately anti-nuke ethos, possessed in plenty – to the Community's benefit. After a nationwide referendum, Greenland withdrew from the EEC in February 1985, and it remains the only place to the date of this printing to take its leave of the EU or its predecessor organizations.

Compared to Greenland's Inuit, the Sami of Sweden, Finland and Norway enjoyed greater prosperity during the Cold War, but attained less autonomy. All three countries remained reluctant during this period to admit the existence of a Sami 'people', referring instead to a more loosely defined 'Sami-speaking population'. In 1956, the transnational Saami Council [sic] began advocating for the official recognition of Sami minority status, with appropriate rights and protections. The Sami also put forward claims to traditional homelands and herding grounds in those regions the Fennoscandian states referred to as 'Lapland', but which the Sami preferred to call Sapmi. Here, too, government officials stonewalled, arguing speciously that, as nomadic herders, the Sami had historically never owned land and were therefore not entitled to claim ownership in the present – conveniently ignoring the many coastal Sami who had lived settled lives and owned property in the past.

The Finns established a Sami Parliament in 1973, although it remained a minor affair until amendments to the Sami Parliament Act in 1995. It was in Norway that Sami politics led to high drama: an upsurge in Sami activism was sparked there by the state's announcement in 1970 that a large hydroelectric plant was to be built in the Alta–Kautokeino region. Like indigenous northerners in Siberia, Quebec and elsewhere, the Sami had already experienced unhappy collisions with hydroelectric projects, which caused pollution, disrupted hunting and herding activities, and often forced communities to relocate. In this case, Alta–Kautokeino required the removal of several Sami villages and threatened to wash out a vital reindeer-migration route. In a campaign of obstruction that absorbed the entire country's attention, Sami activists went on hunger strike, lay down in front of bulldozers and earth-movers and chained themselves to fences and equipment. They also brought legal action against the state. Although Norway's Supreme Court eventually ordered Alta–Kautokeino's construction to proceed, the Sami earned a great deal of sympathy during their long opposition to it.

Partly because of this, the Norwegian government agreed in 1987 to pass the Sami Act, which declared the Sami 'an indigenous people within the state'. In 1989, Norway's first Sami Parliament was elected. Sweden took until after the 1980s to make significant progress on the Sami issue, and even Finland's and Norway's concessions did not put all questions to rest. The powers of both parliaments, for instance, were (and remain) consultative and symbolic. Also, each Scandinavian polity has found it nettlesome to determine who is and is not Sami, given that only a tenth of contemporary Sami practise reindeer herding, and that many have little or no knowledge of the language. Norway, with the most inclusive definition, deems anyone Sami who speaks the language or has a Sami-speaking parent or grandparent, or who 'lives in accordance with the rules of Sami society', or who simply 'considers himself or herself a Sami'.[17] Such lack of specificity makes it difficult even to determine how many Sami reside in each country, although the best estimates from 1990 would place 30,000 to 40,000 in Norway, 15,000 to 17,000 in Sweden, and 5,000 to 6,000 in Finland.

In 1987, as part of his milestone 'Murmansk Initiatives' speech, Soviet leader Mikhail Gorbachev declared the Arctic a 'zone of peace'. At the same time, one of his advisers, Dmitrii Likhachev, promoted the concept of 'cultural ecology', whereby a society might achieve moral self-realization by tending faithfully to nature's needs. This was a dizzying about-face for a frequently ecocidal regime and one of the world's most reckless wielders of what the environmental historian Paul Josephson has called 'brute force technology'.[18] The rhetoric was also more noble in theory than in execution. The half-century of damage already done to Soviet ecosystems was too staggering to be so easily reversed, and the Gorbachev administration too weak to carry bold initiatives to their conclusion. Despite the valiant but Sisyphean efforts of Russian and native environmentalists, the Soviet legacy of widespread befoulment has ensured that the Russian north's road back to ecological health runs uphill, both steep and long.

Up through the 1960s, the relocation of Arctic populations was more sweeping in the postwar USSR than in other northern nations.

Novaya Zemlya was emptied of its Nentsy to clear the way for atomic tests. Komi, Sami and others on the Kola had to make way for the air and naval build-up in the northwest, while Khanty, Mansi and Nentsy were rousted out of oil- and gas-producing zones in the Urals and western Siberia. The most wrenching of these resettlements targeted the inhabitants of Chukotka, where hundreds of native settlements were brushed aside, especially in the 1950s, as military construction transformed the peninsula into a Cold War bastion.

While Stalin still lived, forced labour also remained a central component of Soviet northern policy. The Gulag reigned supreme over too many mines and camps to list, and thousands of prisoners toiled to build Arctic highways and railroads, such as the Dudinka–Norilsk line, completed in 1942, and a failed attempt between 1949 and 1953 to link Igarka and the Ob Gulf port of Salekhard by rail. In Siberia's northeast, the dread Dalstroi governed wherever the military did not. Already before the war, the free population of its chief city, Magadan, had reached 70,000, and its continued growth was attested to by the American diplomat Owen Lattimore, who paid a goodwill visit during the war with Vice-President Henry Wallace – and remained oblivious to the existence of the prison camps almost literally within sight. Magadan, Lattimore wrote,

> is the domain of a remarkable concern, the Dalstroi, which can be roughly compared to a combination of the Hudson's Bay Company and Tennessee Valley Authority. It constructs and operates ports, roads, and railroads, and operates gold mines and municipalities, including at Magadan, a first-class orchestra and a good light-opera company.[19]

One of the few heartening developments in the Cold War Soviet Arctic was the diminution of the prison-camp system after the death of Stalin in 1953 and the de-Stalinizing 'thaw' set into motion by Nikita Khrushchev in 1956. Mass amnesties emptied out most of the Gulag complexes, and Dalstroi was abolished in 1956–8. Instead of coercion, the Khrushchev and Brezhnev regimes turned to incentive as a means of mobilizing labour. The Soviet literary and propaganda machines conjured up the 'romance of the North', an influential trope that depicted Siberia and the Arctic as clean, open frontiers where socialism's destiny would be fulfilled most magnificently. Oleg Kuvaev's 1975 novel *Territory*, about a Soviet geologist who heroically boosts production in

Chukotka circa 1970, is typical of the genre. More effective as a recruit-ment tool were the material bonuses offered to those who worked in the remote north. These 'northern benefits' included higher pay (the 'long rouble'), larger living quarters, and access to luxury goods that, in Moscow or Leningrad, would be available only to the Party elite. The method succeeded brilliantly: thousands of Russians, Ukrainians and other non-natives cascaded into the north and east, in proportions that dwarfed indigenous populations.

Regarding the northern natives, Moscow went to great lengths to pose as their fraternal benefactor. It showered praise on native authors who hailed the Soviet regime's modernizing influence on their people and, in a phenomenon termed 'the return of Dersu Uzala' by one his-torian, portrayed Siberian and Arctic aboriginals not so much as noble savages, but as noble proto-communists.[20] Chief among these writers was the Chukchi Yuri Rytkheu, best known for the novel *A Dream in Polar Fog* (1968). Natives were appointed to positions of authority in numbers sufficient to maintain the desired image.

Of the facade thus erected, one leading specialist on Siberia has said cogently and succinctly, 'sadly, this is untrue.'[21] State control over native northerners tightened as never before. The Stalin regime carried out a new round of collectivization in the late 1940s and early '50s, this time corralling the Dolgan, Chukchi, Yamal Nenets and others who had remained economically un-Sovietized during the 1930s and the war years. Reindeer herders were subjected to even more 'sedentarization' than before the war, and the brigade system of reindeer farming became more deeply entrenched. Those who fished, sealed or whaled along the Arctic coasts were crowded out by Soviet factory ships. Abuse of vodka and *samogon*, or homebrew, became endemic.

In 1957, the Khrushchev government issued the decree 'On Measures for the Further Development of the Economy and Culture of the Peoples of the North', promising better medical care, veterinary assistance and other services. Such pledges, however, were fulfilled incompletely or not at all, and the modernizing benefits that did materialize often had pernicious side-effects. Rifles, motorboats and all-terrain vehicles ampli-fied the damage that indigenes could inflict on the environment, and reliance on them weakened their grip on the survival skills that their ancestors had mastered. Much as the government had intended, reindeer brigades, collective farms and state-run fishing and sea-hunting stations displaced kin-based clans as the basic unit of native social organization. Like Canada's residential schools, Soviet boarding schools – mandatory after about 1960 for native children between the ages of 5 and 15 – left Siberian and Arctic youth cut off from vital elements of their heritage, and at the same time failed to equip them for full acceptance into the Soviet mainstream. They also became breeding grounds for physical and emotional abuse, and the 'Aniko' tales of the Nenets storyteller Anna Nerkagi provide an excellent if dispiriting window into this aspect of the Soviet school experience. Russification caused fluency in native languages to decline. Aboriginal dances, feasts and holidays were stripped of their ritual significance and repackaged as examples of sec-ular folk art. The sanitization, if not outright erasure, of indigenous traditions in the Soviet north was so thorough by the 1980s that Yuri Rytkheu, once such a vocal champion of the regime, mourned publicly what had been lost, and openly reconsidered his previous support for the USSR's native policies.

With sledgehammer force, the Soviets pushed ahead with the full economic modernization of their northern rim. High-rises, radio trans-mitters and air-control facilities towered over the permafrost. The world's most northerly nuclear power plant, the Bilibino reactor, opened on the Chukotka Peninsula, well above the Arctic Circle, in 1976. GUSMP, with the world's biggest fleet of nuclear and conventional ice-breakers at its disposal, lengthened the navigational season along the Northern Sea Route and sent ever-larger quantities of freight through it each year. Place names such as Nikel (the nickel plant near Petsamo) and Apatity (the apatite deposits of the central Kola Peninsula) speak to the centrality of mining in the Soviet Arctic. Lenin himself would have wept tears of joy to see the tons of coal that were dug out of Vorkuta and Spitsbergen's Pyramiden and Barentsburg mines; the gold, tin and polymetals to come out of Norilsk and the Kolyma basin; and the diamonds unearthed in Yakutia. Timber, fishing, sealing, whal-ing, hydroelectricity, sable farming and uranium mining were all part of the expanding northern economy. Then, of course, there were the oil and gas reserves of western Siberia, exploited from the 1960s onwards without regard for any of the native rights or environmental issues that made the extraction of Arctic oil such a thorny affair in Alaska and Canada. Throughout the north Urals, the lower Ob basin and the Yamal Peninsula, wells were sunk and pipelines laid, and nothing could stop the state from moving the region's Khanty, Mansi, Nentsy and Komi out of the way. Tiny settlements like Nizhnevartovsk, which serviced the mammoth Samotlor oil field in the Urals at 61°N; Novyi Urengoi and Yamburg on the Yamal; and Surgut on the Ob experienced

Aerial view of the world's northernmost nuclear reactor, in Bilibino, Russia,
operational on the Chukchi Peninsula since 1976.

eye-popping rates of growth, with the population of the last rising
from under 10,000 in the mid-1960s to 280,000 by the late 1980s.

Impressive as this growth may have been from a quantitative point
of view, it resulted in a decades-long ravaging of the northern ecosystem.
Overfishing and overhunting became routine. Dam-building inundated hundreds of thousands of acres of taiga forest, while clear-cutting
took even more of a toll. Heavy metals, paper-mill refuse and mine
tailings poisoned lakes and rivers, large and small, throughout Siberia.
The Canadian prime minister Pierre Trudeau may have been sincere
when he called the sprawling complex of Norilsk the 'eighth wonder
of the world' – but he knew nothing of the ill effects caused by prolonged exposure to sulphur dioxide and other by-products of carelessly
regulated metallurgical production. An average of 3,000 pipeline breaks
per year bled untold gallons of oil and gas into the wetlands and tundra
of western Siberia, killing or driving away reindeer, wolverines, bears,
fox and wolves. Novaya Zemlya bore the radioactive scars of decades of
nuclear testing, and the soil in parts of Yakutia absorbed levels of plutonium comparable to those found in post-1986 Chernobyl. The incidence
of cancer in the industrialized zones of the Arctic was bone-chillingly
higher than normal. A dedicated but underpowered community of
conservationists persuaded the state to set aside some stretches of land
as *zapovedniki*, or nature preserves, and drew attention to the most dire

developments, such as the pollution of Lake Baikal, the jewel of eastern Siberia, or the shrinking of the polar bear population. But in the main, the environmental situation deteriorated to such an extent that, by the late 1980s, one Soviet commentator referred to human activity in the region as 'the AIDS of the north'.[22]

By this point, the Gorbachev reforms had begun, sparkling with promise, but soon to fester with frustration and disappointment, in the Arctic as throughout the rest of the country. Not only did Gorbachev hope to turn the Arctic into the aforementioned 'zone of peace', he intended it to be a zone of prosperity. Indeed, that year, the Northern Sea Route was enjoying a marvellous navigational season, with well over 300 ships voyaging through it. Gorbachev's Murmansk Initiative outlined plans for improvements in social, political and ethnic relations in the North, and promised to address the region's multiple environmental woes. A relevant component of *perestroika* was the privatization of reindeer ownership, with a limit of 40 animals set in 1988 and the ceiling removed altogether in 1990. Other such measures were to follow, but Gorbachev was by that point losing the confidence of his citizenry. The crumbling of the Soviet economy made it impossible to maintain the elaborate system of supply and transport that sustained Arctic communities, and among natives by the end of the 1980s, poverty, alcoholism and suicide had reduced life expectancy to 55 among women, and a pitiful 45 among men.

Also weakening Gorbachev's position was the rise of autonomist and separatist tendencies throughout the USSR, the North included. As Sami, Inuit and native Alaskans had done, the Arctic peoples of the USSR banded together for the advancement of native rights. They began attending meetings of the Inuit Circumpolar Council, previously forbidden to them, and they founded their own advocacy group at home in 1989–90: the Russian Association of Indigenous Peoples of the North (RAIPON), with the respected Nivkh author Vladimir Sangi serving as its first chair. More radically, Arctic regions began to separate administratively from the USSR. Yakutia, adopting its traditional name of Sakha, declared itself an independent republic in September 1990, while Chukotka broke away from the Magadan region that same month. Kamchatka and Sakhalin followed soon after. This was part of the larger regionalizing trend that, like a centrifuge, pulled the USSR apart in 1990 and 1991 – and within a matter of months, the Soviet regime no longer existed for the Arctic to be subject to. To its deep distress, however, the region would soon discover that it had exchanged authoritarianism for a solid decade of anarchy.

Skies and Seas: Transnational Spaces

With mounting frequency during the 1950s, pilots flying in the high north reported encounters with a novel but disturbing sight. Wafting through the otherwise clear polar skies, at an altitude of approximately 25,000 feet, was a rust-brown, vaporous discolouration that quickly came to be called 'arctic haze'. Chemical analysis of this mysterious fog revealed it to be a noisome, acidic mixture of hydrocarbons and other pollutants, carried northward by the wind, from distant places and from closer to home – and in both cases without respect for national boundaries.

Lines on a map of terra firma can be patrolled, monitored and otherwise translated into physical reality far more easily than those delimiting airspace or open water. The Arctic skies and seas are transnational spaces, unfettered by natural barriers and subdivided by human action only at great effort. They are each by nature fluid – literally in one case, figuratively in both – and it is this fluidity, their seeming formlessness and often uncertain status, that renders them capable of arousing profound political anxieties. They did so throughout the twentieth century and continue to do so in the twenty-first. How do states prevent nitric oxides or PCBs – or radiation – from travelling through the northern skies into their own airspace? By what right do nations determine who can or cannot kill Arctic animals, especially when they migrate through the territories of more than one country, or live beyond state borders? Such riddles abound in the Arctic skies and seas.

A prime cause for distress was the ease with which airborne and waterborne pollution could invade any nation's Arctic spaces. This problem had come to light as far back as the 1870s, when the explorer Nordenskiöld discovered traces of coal dust and burned metallic residue – his 'cryoconite' – on the remote Greenland ice cap. What startled onlookers during the Cold War was the new *extent* of the problem. Although they should not have, phenomena like Arctic haze came as a shock. So too did findings from the late 1970s which showed that, while the worst polluter of the Arctic was the USSR (no surprise to anyone), the second- and third-place contenders for this dubious honour were Great Britain and West Germany, both far from the region. Hair samples taken from Greenland Inuit in the early 1980s revealed that their bodies contained quantities of lead, copper, mercury and cadmium unknown to their ancestors. While some of these materials were of local origin, due to the island's postwar modernization, most had arrived from the south. The Arctic ports of all nations unavoidably generated waste and contaminated local waters. Farther from shore, ships navigating the northern oceans dumped litter and waste fuel, both in unclaimed seas and in other countries' territorial waters.

The uncontainability of such forms of pollution made the Soviet Union an especially hard neighbour to have in the North; much of the environmental damage it inflicted upon itself harmed the states around it as well. While Americans and Canadians contributed to the pollution of the Bering ecosystem, their transgressions paled by comparison to those of the Soviets. The ill treatment was even worse around the Kola Peninsula, in the vicinity of Arkhangelsk and Murmansk and farther to the west, nearer to Scandinavia. Here, the Soviet Navy unfastidiously disposed of hazardous materials, including radioactive waste. The effects of this carelessness spilled over into Scandinavian waters, to the particular dismay of Norway, which bore the brunt of it, and whose environmental watchdog group Bellona spent much of the late Cold War cataloguing such abuses.

The ussr's ground-based activities likewise tormented the Scandinavians. Only 80 miles from the Finnish border, the mines of Apatity coughed up 300 million tons of uncovered waste, and when northern winds blew, they whipped up toxic tornadoes that no boundary checkpoint could hope to control. Fallout from the Novaya Zemlya weapons tests irradiated the northern districts of Norway, Finland and Sweden, the greatest measure of it descending on Sami settlements. Most cataclysmic of all was the long reach of the Chernobyl disaster of 26 April 1986, when the explosion of one of the Ukrainian power plant's four nuclear reactors spewed clouds of strontium, plutonium and caesium more than half a mile into the sky and then far to the west. As with the Novaya Zemlya fallout, among those afflicted by Chernobyl were the Sami of Sweden, Norway and Finland – along with the region's reindeer, moose and Arctic char. Thanks to the proliferation of caesium-137, berries and lake fish from many parts of northern Scandinavia could not be eaten, and over 600,000 Swedish and Norwegian reindeer, having fed on contaminated lichen, had to be destroyed, their meat buried in special pits. Sami women expecting babies at the time worried for months about the outcomes of their pregnancies.

If no satisfactory means of safeguarding the cleanliness of the Arctic's skies and seas has yet emerged, neither has a completely effective mechanism for managing its oceanic resources. Anxieties about these escalated during the Cold War, especially its later years. Certain resources, long taken for granted, were becoming worrisomely scarce, while others, previously unknown or out of reach, now appeared tantalizingly accessible. Among the former were the great stocks of northern fish, once seemingly limitless, but now thinned out by relentless overharvesting. Shortfalls became apparent by the 1970s, sometimes glaringly so. Between then and the early 1990s, the worldwide catch of cod declined 70 per cent, a plunge felt especially keenly in northern waters. The Grand Banks off Newfoundland, to take the best-known example, was only a year away from being completely fished out, a turn of events that cost 30,000 jobs, when the Cold War ended. Similarly, the Bering Sea's plentiful supplies of salmon, crab, halibut and pollock began disappearing during the 1980s and early '90s. In turn, the depletion of Bering pollock set off a devastating chain reaction: the Steller's sea lions who fed on the fish died off or relocated, their numbers falling by 80 per cent. The orcas who normally preyed on the sea lions looked for sustenance to the sea otter population, which dropped by 90 per cent in those areas where pollock had been overfished. In retrospect, the cause of this collapse is plain. As a 2011 study in *Polar Biology* has shown, 'the amount of fish caught in the Arctic [was] dramatically underreported for decades.'[23] Of the 950,000 tons actually caught between 1950 and 2006 in Russian, Canadian and Alaskan waters, only 12,700 tons, or one fish in 75, were reported to the United Nations' Food and Agriculture Organization. Small wonder that a 'false sense of comfort' about remaining supplies prevailed for so long. When conflicts over fishing arose during these years, they were generally worked out by negotiation, but violence or near-violence threatened on occasion, as in the British–Icelandic 'cod wars'.

Also during the 1970s, concerns about sea mammal populations surfaced prominently. Protective meaures had been taken in the past, including the 1911 ban on fur-seal hunting and moratoriums in 1937 and 1946 on the killing of right and grey whales, but it was clear to many by the 1960s that such steps were not enough. In 1965, the IWC extended full protection to the blue whale, which was freefalling towards extinction. Still, the worries now arising, both scientific and popular, prompted an even stronger set of political and legal reactions.

Most nations willingly observed laws and agreements like the U.S. Marine Mammal Protection Act and the 1975 Convention on International Trade in Endangered Species. Even the nations where seal hunting continued (Canada, Norway, Greenland and Russia in the northern hemisphere) accepted quotas on how many of each species could be taken, along with rules regarding how and at what age they could be killed. Canada outlawed the hunting of harp seal pups in 1971 and has tended to be the most rigorous about enforcing quotas. As for whaling, the iwc began to set quotas for at-risk species other than the blue whale. Virtually all pelagic, or deep-sea, whaling was outlawed in 1979, and a number of countries, including the u.s. and Canada, gave up coastal whaling after the un's 1972 Conference on the Human Environment. Then came the iwc's 1986 moratorium on all commercial whaling, coastal or pelagic. Since its passage, the protectionist impulse has been firmly in the ascendant.

And yet compliance with such bans has never been perfect, with objections to them raised from the outset. Canada quit the iwc immediately after the moratorium was adopted, while Iceland left in 1992, returning only in 2002. The Soviets took several years to agree to the ban; Norway protested it, then began in the early 1990s to ignore it. Another opponent of the moratorium, Japan, persuaded the iwc to allow a small number of whales to be culled every year for scientific research – prompting the opportunistically nimble transformation of the Japan Joint Whaling Company into the more innocuous-sounding Institute of Cetacean Research.

Anti-protectionist arguments have been made on the basis of sovereign right and on the grounds that sealing and whaling are legitimately part of many national and ethnocultural traditions. Debate has also centred on the question of how total bans and boycotts ought to be. Not all seals or whales are equally at risk, sea-hunting proponents point out. What is the harm, they ask, in limited exploitation of marine mammals, so long as it is properly managed? Is it science or sentiment that drives anti-whaling forces to insist on granting identical protections to all cetacean species, regardless of whether they are endangered, like the blue and the humpback, or thriving, like the minke and arguably the grey? Is it conscience or squeamishness when countries that tolerate the factory farming of cattle and poultry complain about the supposed cruelty of seal-hunting? Environmentalist rejoinders include evidence of cetaceans' and pinnipeds' high intelligence and sociability, as well as the more pragmatic contention – based on ample proof from the past – that sea-mammal hunting, once permitted, is inevitably pursued to its maximum legal extent, and frequently beyond it. The issue of whose science can be trusted also comes into play, with pro-hunting and anti-hunting advocates rarely accepting each other's estimates of seal and whale populations.

Industrialized societies opposed to the IWC ban and other such measures have sincerely felt their rights and traditions to have been trampled on in ways they consider unfair and scientifically inconsistent. Whether their high dudgeon is warranted, or outweighs the tangible environmental risks that sea-mammal species continue to face in the Arctic, remains a matter of personal judgement. All can agree, though, that the groups placed in the greatest predicament by postwar management schemes have been the Arctic's indigenous populations – especially Eskimo and Inuit communities, who, from Chukotka to Greenland, still depended heavily on seal hunting and, to a lesser extent, walrus hunting and coastal whaling as sources of food and trade goods. Since the rise of anti-whaling regulations in the 1970s, Alaskan native and Inuit leaders, including Alaska's Eben Hopson, succeeded in winning exemptions for traditional native whaling, especially for the bowhead hunt so eagerly anticipated every year by the Inupiat and other denizens of the North Slope. These remain in place as exceptions to the IWC moratorium, and have been adjusted and expanded over time.

Environmentalist campaigns against sealing and the trade in walrus ivory have had more complicated results. While native populations are allowed to hunt seals and walruses in limited quantities and, in the language of the U.S. Marine Mammal Protection Act, 'non-wasteful' ways – meaning mainly for food – their ability to earn income from the sale of fur and ivory has been severely compromised. Public taste and the workings of the market are as much to blame as formal rules. Most regulations barring the sale of seal and walrus products contain exceptions for items harvested and handicrafted by aboriginal peoples. Even so, general bans have depressed overall demand not only by making the sale of animal products costlier and more complicated, but also by reshaping popular opinion about the ethicality of wearing fur or purchasing objects carved from ivory. Whatever the correct balance between animal rights and human rights may be in this case – to borrow the title of one anthropologist's work on the topic[24] – there is no doubting the vitiating impact on Arctic natives caused by the late-Cold War wave of environmentalism. Whatever exceptions were made for northern peoples at the time, and whatever regard was paid to them, it was not enough to stifle the resentment most felt at being told by outsiders how to conduct affairs that their ancestors had managed in their own way for centuries – or for the ruin visited on their fragile economies for ecological sins committed by faraway industrial societies.

If declining marine resources led to heightened tensions in the Arctic seas, abundance, paradoxically, raised the diplomatic temperature as well. As the Cold War neared its end, the northern ocean enlarged physically due to global warming, even if that fact was less discernable then than now. In 1979, the Arctic pack ice was roughly twice the size of the United States. It has become steadily smaller since, and although the rate of shrinkage was not yet so disturbing, the change was measurable throughout the 1980s. Might it be possible, many wondered, to make up for smaller catches in the usual fishing grounds by pushing farther to the north as more open water materialized above the Arctic Circle? With growing indications of how much natural gas and oil lay beneath the northern seas, might it become feasible to tap into this undersea bounty? Could the Northern Sea Route and the Northwest Passage, if not the Arctic Ocean basin itself, become more relevant to international shipping, and perhaps even transform it?

Whether or not it was becoming more navigable, the circumpolar north posed the same legal and diplomatic conundrums that it had for ages. A world away at the South Pole, the international community found it relatively easy, Cold War tensions notwithstanding, to negotiate the Antarctic Treaty of 1959 and to determine where on this ungoverned continent various countries would be allowed to establish a presence for the purposes of scientific research. Military and economic stakes were lower in Antarctica than in the Arctic, but the key reason for the difference was physical: it is simpler to adjudicate and fix boundaries on solid ground than in oceanic settings. According to the 1958 Geneva Convention on the Territorial Sea and the Contiguous Zone, it is easier to establish a claim on an island than on the waters around it or the seabed underneath. Maritime law has continued to grapple with the question of which Arctic waterways are national and which are international, and the sense of urgency surrounding this question has risen with the temperature of the hemisphere.

In the waning years of the Cold War, between 1973 and 1982, a new 'constitution of the ocean' was drawn up and signed to this date by over 160 states.[25] This was the United Nations Convention on the Law of the Sea (UNCLOS), which entered into force as a binding convention in 1994, having achieved the necessary threshold of 60 ratifying states. At the time of this printing, this roster does not include the United States. According to UNCLOS, coastal nations are allowed to exploit resources on and under the seabed up to a limit of 200 nautical miles from shore, and up to 150 nautical miles farther out where a natural prolongation of the continental shelf can be proven. States signing on to UNCLOS have been allowed ten years from the date of ratification to submit scientific evidence of the extent of their continental shelves to the Tribunal of the Law of the Sea in Hamburg, Germany.

The Tribunal's standards for determining whether an undersea formation or ridge in fact protrudes 'naturally' from a continental shelf are exacting, and an astounding array of new techniques and technologies has become available during these years to scientists engaged in undersea mapping and geological analysis. The process of ratification and submission, therefore, has been a lengthy one, and is still ongoing for a number of states. With riches of stunning magnitude at stake, countries with Arctic coastlines and island possessions in Arctic waters have assigned steadily higher priority to measuring their seabeds with care and precision. But while most signs during the transition from the Cold War to the present era have been encouraging, it remains to be seen how effective the UNCLOS protocol, or any instrument of dispute resolution based principally on science and diplomacy, will prove as a means for resolving questions of maritime territorialism in the twenty-first-century north.

7

Extinctions? 1991
to the Present

In 1889, Jules Verne penned a loosely connected sequel to his best-selling *From the Earth to the Moon*, called *Sans dessus dessous*, or 'upside down', but most often titled in English *The Purchase of the North Pole*. In it, the members of the Baltimore Gun Club, reappearing from the previous novel, hit upon a cunning but nefarious scheme to get rich in the Arctic. Acquiring the North Pole and its surrounding waters on behalf of the United States, the Gun Club plots to gain access to the enormous deposits of coal underneath by designing a supercannon with shells made from a new explosive called micro-meteorite. Fired from the top of Mount Kilimanjaro, the cannon's blast will tilt the world's axis by more than 20 degrees, melting the polar ice caps and allowing for easy mining of the coal. Much of Asia will be flooded, and millions will die or be driven from their homes, but Messrs Barbicane, Nicholl and Maston, the avaricious artillerists, will gain bounty beyond the dreams of kings. Despite the best efforts of government agents and other adversaries, the trio discharge their weapon as planned, but the explosion is too weak to have the intended effect. The earth spins on as before, and the Arctic retains its icy crown.

Where Barbicane and Co. failed, twenty-first-century civilization has been succeeding: inadvertently and with less drama, perhaps, but even more inimically than Verne's antiheroes could have wished. Even if one grants the generous hypothetical that climate change is not necessarily human-caused, there is no denying its tangible impact on the North. Arctic warming, already rapid during the Cold War, has accelerated frightfully and, in the opinion of some, irreversibly. Different parties have different views about the ultimate consequence of this transmutation. Developers and businessmen look forward to fatter profits, while foreign-policy analysts nervous about the head-turning effects of Mammon fret that competition over newfound Arctic wealth may touch off hot wars on the coldest horizon. Denizens of the North, both native and newcomer, are left to wonder whether warmer temperatures will mean an easier existence in the times to come or the destruction of their way of life.

Most gloom-ridden are the scientists, or the better part of them, who monitor the world's northernmost biomes and know all too well what an evil wind is blowing there. 'It is paradoxical', the president of Iceland tells us, 'that new opportunities are opening for our nations at the same time we understand that the threat of carbon emissions is imminent.'[1] True enough as a tepid recitation of fact, but grossly understated as an assessment of the problem. Hopefully, it is still too soon to bandy about the term 'arcticide', as this chapter will do. Unfortunately, the last two decades have made it clear that the Arctic we have known for centuries is already lost to us, very likely beyond recovery, and that even the altered Arctic of the present may be unrecognizable before too long. Whether the new northern space we will have created, or the climatological effects of the old Arctic's destruction, will be to our liking is a question worth asking ourselves before the fast-approaching point of irrevocability is reached.

Scrambling for the North? Resources and Sovereignty in Today's Arctic

The most salient fact about the Arctic since the end of the Cold War has been its disappearing act – or at least its changing state of matter, from solid to liquid. Temperatures there have risen twice as fast as elsewhere in the world for many years on end. In 1979, the Arctic pack ice was two times the size of the United States. By 2004, global warming had reduced its square mileage by an area equal to Georgia, New York and Texas put together. Glaciers have receded, permafrost has thawed. Everywhere in the North, the rate of melting has picked up speed like the rushing waters of a maelstrom as they near the vortex.

Although this change is likelier to prove bane than boon, corporations and governments are salivating at the prospect of an Arctic that may soon resemble the 'polar Mediterranean' spoken of a century ago by the physicist Lord Kelvin and the explorer Vilhjalmur Stefansson. This excitement stems from two possibilities. Will high northern waters become more freely navigable? And will Arctic resources prove recoverable on a more cost-effective basis? Should one or both come to pass, the Arctic will assume a greater economic and diplomatic importance than at any previous point in its history.

Examined casually, and with a blind eye to environmental ramifications, certain facts give cause for optimism. Over 6,000 vessels, half of them fishing craft, operated in Arctic waters in 2004. In the summer of 2011, the Arctic Ocean was traversed by boat in six and a half days, a new record. Yokohoma is 11,250 miles from Rotterdam if one uses the Suez Canal, but only 7,350 miles via Russia's Northern Sea Route. A Rotterdam-to-Vancouver voyage takes 8,920 miles if it runs through the Panama Canal, but can shave off 2,000 miles by travelling through the Arctic. Iron ore can be shipped from the Norwegian port of Narvik to Lianyungang in China in only twenty-one days by the Northern Sea Route, compared to 37 days via the Suez.

Resources have beckoned as well, none more seductively than oil and natural gas, the immensity of whose presence in the North was guessed at in the 1980s and '90s, but has only recently become widespread knowledge. The 'Circum-Arctic Resource Appraisal', conducted by the u.s. Geological Survey over four years and released in 2008, estimates that Arctic territories contain 90 billion barrels of undiscovered oil and 1.67 trillion cubic feet of natural gas. This amounts to 13 per cent and 30 per cent, respectively, of the world's untapped reserves, and is in addition to a possible 44 billion barrels of liquefied natural gas. Most of these deposits lie offshore, many of them in the vicinity of already-productive sites, such as the Beaufort Sea between Prudhoe Bay and the Mackenzie Delta, or the Russian coast north of West Siberia and the Urals. Others are more newly discovered, and in some cases still unexploited. These include reserves off Greenland's shores, new fields discovered by Norway, the offshore oil rig constructed by Russia near Varandei and Russia's yet-to-be developed Shtokman gas field, far out in the eastern Barents Sea.

If, as some have suggested, 'resource wars' are to emerge as a primary form of conflict in this new century, what is to stop the nations of the world from plunging into 'an armed mad dash' for the riches of the Arctic, as one author in the pages of *Foreign Affairs* has warned they might?[2] Should we be preparing for a pell-mell, internationally destabilizing scramble for the North, reminiscent of the reckless 'scramble for Africa' that set the powers of Europe on the road to the First World War? Disagreements about sovereignty are numerous in the North, and sabre-rattling rhetoric like the Russian government's comment in the daily

Rossiiskaia gazeta that 'the fight for the Arctic will be the spark for a new division of global power' would seem to portend an unhappily heated solution to at least some of them.[3]

Luckily, the dispute-resolution mechanisms that have come into being since the late Cold War, while structurally soft, have tended to function as intended. Ratification of the United Nations Convention on the Law of the Sea is near-universal among the coastal Arctic nations, and even the lone holdout, the United States, respects most of its articles as customary international law. Helping further to calm the waters is the Arctic Council, called into being by the Ottawa Declaration of 1996 and consisting of eight nations (Canada, the United States, Norway, Denmark, Sweden, Finland, Iceland and Russia) and representatives from six minority rights groups (the Inuit Circumpolar Council, the Saami [sic] Council, Russia's RAIPON, the Aleut International Association, the Arctic Athabaskan Council and the Gwich'in Council International). France, Germany, Poland, Spain, Great Britain and the Netherlands take part in the Council's deliberations as permanent observers, while China, Japan, Korea, Italy and the European Union have requested permission to do the same.

The Arctic Council has no powers of enforcement, and its members have chosen not to use it as a venue for discussing sensitive issues such as territorial questions or fishing rights. Friction has arisen on those occasions when the five coastal nations – Canada, Norway, Denmark, Russia and the United States – have met separately from the rest. Still, the Council serves as a useful forum for negotiation, communication and trust-building. Overall, the prognosis for non-violent outcomes seems good. Polar geopolitics will no doubt provoke harsh words and hard feelings in the years to come. But for every pundit who worries about open hostilities breaking out over the Arctic, there are others ready to remind us that 'anarchy does not reign at the top of the world'.[4] A headlong descent into conflict is not impossible in the North, but international law and the diplomatic process seem likelier to hold sway there.

It also remains to be seen how hard a struggle Arctic assets will be worth. On land, the value of mineral deposits must be high indeed to recoup the mind-boggling costs of setting up mines and the infrastructure to support them in the remote north. The pricetag, for example, of Agnico-Eagle's Meadowbank gold mine, near Baker Lake in Nunavut, had run to $1.5 billion by the autumn of 2011. This included road-building costs exceeding $340,000 per mile. Even the warming of the climate, which one might expect to simplify operations, complicates the construction of roadways and foundations by softening once-solid permafrost.

As for possible profits at sea, talk of truly open polar waters looks to be many years premature, even with the alarming loss of pack ice in recent decades. Russia's Northern Sea Route opened to international traffic in 1991 but grew sclerotic during the economically disastrous 1990s. It has rebounded somewhat in the 2000s, with two commercial ships passing through it in 2009, and eighteen in 2011. Traversing the Northwest Passage has become easier as well. The 'Arctic Bridge' voyage of October 2007 sent a cargo of fertilizer through the Arctic Ocean from Murmansk to the Hudson Bay port of Churchill in eight days, less than half the time it takes to travel between the two ports via the Atlantic. But at least for a generation or more, ice will remain sufficiently voluminous to make Arctic shipping slower, more hazardous and costlier than in warmer sealanes, and visions of supertanker argosies and container ships steering their way serenely through the polar seas from Barrow and Nuuk to Arkhangelsk, or between Narvik and the Mackenzie Delta, are likely to remain fantastical for some time to come.

In the meantime, the savings in time and canal fees theoretically realizable from Arctic voyaging must be weighed against the added expense of higher insurance, reinforced hulls and escort by icebreakers – which are not always available at one's convenience, and which have their own limitations. Helsinki's Arctic Research Center has projected the theoretical possibility of constructing icebreakers capable of ramming ice ridges many yards thick. Still, the doughtiest ships of the present, such as Russia's atomic-powered, 'Arktika'-class *50 Let Pobedy* ('Fifty Years of Victory'), commissioned in 2007, cannot plough through ice more than 9 feet thick. The largest non-Russian icebreakers, including Sweden's *Oden* and the u.s. Coast Guard's *Polar Sea*, are limited to about 6.5 feet, while Canada's most powerful icebreakers, the *Louis St Laurent* and the *Terry Fox*, are not only smaller, but can operate for only two seasons out of the year and must overwinter in subarctic ports. Russia plans to build three icebreakers capable of smashing through twenty to thirty feet of ice, but these will not enter service until 2020 at the earliest. Given all this, it will require catastrophic melting indeed, and for many years running, for safe and commercially viable shipping to become commonplace in the Arctic.

Nor are all, or even most, of today's Arctic prospects for oil, gas and other resources guaranteed to pan out. Because extraction costs in the region are so high, profit margins tend to be narrow and easily erased by even slight fluctuations in the market. Much of the oil and gas is placed most inconveniently: dauntingly deep, too far offshore, or both,

Agnico-Eagle's Meadowbank gold mine in the Baker Lake region of Nunavut, Canada.

as with Russia's Shtokman gas field, which has the potential to become the world's second-largest source of gas, but is located over 400 miles from land and at a depth of more than 1,000 feet. Even in the wake of the 2010 Deepwater oil-spill debacle in the Gulf of Mexico, corporations like BP, Rosneft and DONG continue to profess that they can safely and profitably develop Arctic reserves, no matter how remote the site or how unique the perils posed by drifting ice, the darkness of polar night and the foggy, frigid weather. Such breezy assurances fly not just in the face of experience, but of major feasibility studies which strongly indicate that, in oil-rich but ice-clogged seas like the Beaufort, Chukchi, Kara and Barents, the chances of successful emergency rescue or cleanup for rigs and drills beyond a certain distance or depth are virtually nil – and that, over time, the chances of a blowout or the ice-ramming of a rig or drilling ship are unacceptably high.[5]

Not that this has dissuaded governments and corporations from delving into the Arctic's geological mysteries and pressing claims wherever they are able. 'The future [for oil and gas] is on the shelf', proclaims the outspoken Russian explorer Artur Chilingarov. 'We've already pumped the land dry.'[6] He is seconded by the EU energy commissioner Andris Piebalgs, who plaintively moaned in 2008 that 'You can't say "this is a sanctuary", because it will not work. Otherwise where will we get our energy from?'[7] Energy-hungry China has sent its own Arctic research vessel, the *Xuelong*, or 'Snow Dragon', to prowl the polar waters, where it has been joined by Germany's *Polarstern* and other ships from nations with no natural ties to the region, but a yearning for what might be unearthed there.

Most active, of course, are the Arctic nations themselves. In Alaska, where decline appears to be in sight for existing North Slope production, discussion has centred on whether to extend offshore drilling further into the Beaufort and Chukchi seas. A more controversial option would be to heed the 'drill, baby, drill' mantra intoned so shrilly by Alaska's then-governor Sarah Palin during the 2008 presidential election, and to begin tapping into the billions of barrels lying beneath the so far untouched Arctic National Wildlife Refuge (ANWR). A few Beaufort leases granted to companies like Shell by the George W. Bush administration look set to go ahead in the near future, but federal regulators have so far blocked most other proposals on environmental grounds, and Alaskan native groups, both Gwich'in and Inupiat, oppose ANWR drilling. (So too does the ice-cream manufacturer Ben and Jerry's, which, in 2005, staged perhaps the most mouth-watering protest in U.S. history by joining with Greenpeace and the Alaska Wilderness League to serve out portions of a 900-pound baked Alaska on the Washington Mall.) Although it has not yet ratified UNCLOS, the United States is gathering data for possible claims to more of the polar seabed, and it has ongoing disagreements with Canada regarding the Northwest Passage and over a 4,600-square-mile wedge of the Beaufort Sea where eastern Alaska and the Yukon Territory meet. Nonetheless, both countries' Arctic scientists, as well as their coast guards and armed forces, cooperate closely as a rule; in 1994, the U.S. and Canadian coast guards dispatched an icebreaker team, the *Polar Sea* and the *Louis St Laurent*, to the North Pole. U.S. tensions with Russia over potentially conflicting territorial claims are not likely to be resolved as amicably.

Canada is due to submit its UNCLOS claim in 2013, and its scholars and coast guard are engaged in a flurry of undersea mapping and geological surveying. Its decades-long spat with Denmark over Hans Island continues, with each side paying occasional visits and ceremonially cacheing bottles of Canadian whiskey or *akvavit* as a way of marking ownership. Of greater concern are the underwater Lomonosov Ridge – much of which the Canadians, like the Russians, claim as an extension of their continental shelf – and the Northwest Passage, which Ottawa hopes will someday be internationally recognized as a Canadian waterway. Since 2006, Stephen Harper's Conservative government has made northern sovereignty a central plank in its policy platform, vowing to strengthen the mainly Inuit Canadian Rangers, to expand Canada's icebreaker and polar air fleets, and to construct a deep-water port at Nanisivik on Nunavut's Baffin Island and a military training facility at Resolute Bay. Little of this has been accomplished to date, although the government has boosted the enforcement capability of its coast guard icebreakers by arming them with deck-mounted guns. Since 2007, the Canadian Forces have carried out annual 'Nanook' air/land/sea exercises in the Arctic archipelago.

Developing the North economically has also preoccupied Canada. The OMNITRAX rail service purchased the port facilities of Churchill for the grand sum of CAD$7 in 1997, but has poured $50 million into them since, matched by $68 million from the Harper government, in the expectation that the town will become a major hub in a future polar shipping network. Zinc and diamonds, which Canada produces in prodigious quantities, have proven shaky bets in the North. Canada remains the world's number one source of zinc, and De Beers and BHP Billiton continue to take diamonds out of northern mines like Ekati and Diavik. However, the Arctic zinc mines of Nanisivik and Polaris shut down in 2002, and the Kitikmeot and Jericho diamond mines, which kindled high economic hopes in western Nunavut, closed in 2005 and 2008.

Fossil fuels are expected to generate the most dependable profits. Although Canada's one high-Arctic oil well, Panarctic's Bent Horn facility, ceased operations in 1996, other sites hold out promise – if certain obstacles can be overcome. As during the Cold War years, the most formidable of these have been environmental-safety regulations and oppositional pressure from native groups. Both were recently brought to bear against the Canadian government's proposals in 2010 to prospect for oil and gas in Lancaster Sound, the eastern entrance to the Northwest Passage and one of the Arctic's most famed sanctuaries for beluga whales and narwhals. The test itself, which would have subjected the seabed to seismic shocks, was cancelled on grounds that it was too potentially harmful to Lancaster's marine life and the folkways of the local Inuit. By contrast, plans for a Mackenzie Valley gas pipeline, first mooted in the early 1970s, received a long-delayed green light in 2009, when the National Energy Board approved the much-revised project as environmentally sound, and when the Dene and Inuvialuit who had blocked the pipeline a generation before changed their minds and decided to share in the profits by forming the Aboriginal Pipeline Group. A consortium led by Imperial Oil has begun construction on the 750-mile pipeline, which is expected to cost CAD$16.2 billion, making it the largest capital project in Canadian history. It is scheduled to come on line in 2013 or 2014.

In Scandinavia, each country is burdened by questions related to northern resources and northern boundaries: determining the legal extent of national versus international fishing grounds, coping with the transborder ecological impact of Russian pollution in the Arctic skies and waters, and figuring out how to keep core assets like Sweden's Kiruna iron mine and Norway's Spitsbergen facilities sustainable. With their high-Arctic coastal presence, Denmark and Norway are most acutely affected by such issues. The former is poised to become a bigger player in the international petroleum industry, thanks to the discovery in the 1990s of sizable oil reserves near Disko-Nuussuaq, off Greenland's west coast, and in the Kronprins Christian basin, in the east. (Iceland has similar cause for excitement, with oil present near Derki, on the Jan Mayen Ridge.) In other positive news for Denmark, western Greenland's Black Angel zinc mine, 250 miles north of the Arctic Circle and closed during much of the 1990s, resumed operations in 2005. Although it disputes various fisheries with other North Atlantic states, its most serious quarrel is with Canada, over Hans Island, in the narrow waters off northwest Greenland. Denmark will submit its case for the extension of Greenland's continental shelf to the UNCLOS tribunal in 2014.

Norway has been even more embroiled in conflicts over territorial waters, most frequently with Russia, although with Denmark and Iceland as well. Most of the points of contention date back to the Cold War or earlier. For decades, Norway has protested the passage of Russian submarines through Arctic waters that it considers its home seas – especially in the *gråsonen* ('grey zone') north of the Russo-Norwegian land border – and Russia's habit of dumping industrial and military waste in or near those waters. Norway claims fishing rights up to 200 miles out from the shores of Spitsbergen and the other Svalbard islands, and it lobbied for years to win control over several portions of the Barents Sea that Russia called its own, including the so-called Loophole north of the Kola Peninsula, the Banana Hole (also known as the Herring Loophole) and the Western Nansen Basin.

If there is an Arctic asset Norway cares about more than its fisheries, it is offshore oil and gas, on which the national economy, and with it the Norwegian welfare state, has become dependent since the 1960s discovery of North Sea oil. Already by the end of the 1980s, the search for additional sources of fuel had led Norwegian prospectors out of the subarctic and

Melkøya liquefied natural gas plant serving the Snøhvit field, off the far
northeastern coast of Norway.

into the high north, and gas/oil fields like Heidrun and Norne, just a few
miles south of the Arctic Circle, were brought on line during the 1990s.
Even larger and farther to the north, above the 70th parallel, are the
Goliat oil field, discovered in 2000 off the port of Hammerfest, and the
nearby Snøhvit gas field. Production at Goliat is not expected to start until
2013, but gas has been flowing out of Snøhvit since 2006–7. Extraction
at Snøhvit takes place entirely underwater, in seabed installations which
Statoil promises are impervious to the effects of ice movement or weather
on the surface. Snøhvit's gas is pipelined to the island processing plant
of Melkøya, 100 miles to the south.

Of the Arctic's five coastal nations, Norway was the first to put
together its UNCLOS case, which it placed before the tribunal in 2006. In
doing so, it deliberately renounced any claim to the top of the world. 'In
the discussion about who owns the North Pole,' Norway's foreign
minister said in 2007, 'it's definitely not us.'[8] Ruling in 2009, the UNCLOS
tribunal enlarged Norway's continental shelf to an area of over 90,700
square miles and adjusted its maritime boundaries with Iceland,
Greenland and the Faeroe Islands. Moreover, the UN has chosen to
support Oslo's claims over Russia's to the Western Nansen Basin and the
Barents 'loopholes'.

The most jarring transformations in the post-Cold War Arctic have
occurred in the Russian north. The breakdown of Russia's economy
during the late Gorbachev years and the shock-therapy bedlam of the
1990s demolished the elaborate system of supply and distribution that

had made possible such a large Soviet presence in the far north. The change threw native life into confusion as well, with state neglect and other factors causing a massive die-off of reindeer that reduced domesticated herds from 2.4 million to 1.2 million in the decade following the USSR's collapse. Non-natives who could get out did so in migrating swarms, and with Yeltsin-era officials tending towards incompetence or corruption, cities and towns fell into decay. The SP series of drifting polar research stations, uninterrupted since 1950, came to a halt after 1991, and the Northern Sea Route all but ceased to function. As the chair of Russia's 1995 Congress of the Union of the Far North and Polar Cities mournfully confessed, 'if this state of affairs continues, the Russian north will soon begin to die.'[9] A measure of prosperity has returned in the 2000s, under Vladimir Putin and the regional governors who were elected or appointed to office during his presidency in places like Evenkia, the Taimyr and Chukotka. Whether such improvements are due more to Putinesque leadership or to the post-9/11 spike in fuel prices that made Russian gas and oil worth many times what they had been in the 1990s is fodder for debate, but they have considerably stabilized conditions in the North.

They have also allowed explorers and developers to resume work there. In 2001, Russia sent the icebreaker *Yamal* to the North Pole in celebration of the new millennium, making it the twelfth surface vessel to reach 90°N. That same year, it presented its case to UNCLOS for the expansion of its Arctic continental shelf – although in 2002, the UNCLOS tribunal, without rejecting the claim, requested further scientific

The Russian nuclear-powered icebreaker *Yamal*, a 23,455-ton behemoth that entered service in 1992 and continues to voyage today.

verification, a process in which Russian scholars are still engaged. Russia rebooted its SP drifting station programme in 2003, with SP-32, and has continued the expeditions ever since. In addition to scientific research, the Russians have undertaken nostalgically oriented missions, such as the 2005–6 discovery of the *Cheliuskin*'s resting place on the seabed after its sinking in 1934, and searches for the remains of the doomed 1912 Brusilov Expedition. In an August 2007 expedition organized by Artur Chilingarov as part of the 2007–8 International Polar Year, the Russians scored their most dramatic coup, sending two miniature submarines, the *Mir-1* and *Mir-2*, to the floor of the Arctic Ocean, almost two and a half miles down. There, at the exact location of the North Pole, they placed a titanium case containing the flag of the Russian Federation.

Russia's rhetoric surrounding the seabed exploit, and international reaction to it, seemed at first to bode poorly for smooth relations in the Arctic. Chilingarov, a member of Russia's State Duma and President Putin's hand-picked special envoy for polar affairs, portrayed the expedition as confirmation of Russia's world-beating mastery of the Arctic and as a vindication of its territorial claims there. He crowingly declared that 'I don't give a damn what all these foreign politicians are saying, the Arctic has always been Russian', adding that 'we are going to be all over the Arctic – this is not just science, it is presence'.[10] Canada's foreign minister, Peter MacKay, countered such triumphalist bluster, noting that 'This isn't the 15th century. You can't go around the world and just plant flags and say "We're claiming this territory"', while Denmark's science minister, Helge Sander, dismissed the expedition itself as 'a joke'.[11] Enigmatically, Russia's official language on polar affairs has vacillated between bellicose posturing and moderated reasonableness, with generals speaking one moment of increasing the operational radius of the Northern Fleet's nuclear submarines or expanding special forces units trained for Arctic combat, and with officials like Chilingarov proclaiming the next that 'there should be only understanding and mutual assistance in the Arctic.'[12]

What is not at all ambiguous is Russia's determination to push forwards with the development of its Arctic oil and gas, with no hesitation on account of potential environmental or human impact. Plans are afoot to bring the giant Shtokman gas field on line by 2013 or 2014, and Russia hopes in 2012 to activate its first ice-resistant offshore oil platform, in the Prirazlomnoe field, south of Novaya Zemlya. Its most ambitious venture so far has been the August 2011 deal, inked between its state-owned petroleum company, Rosneft, and ExxonMobil, to invest U.S.$500 billion to explore and develop oil deposits in the Black and Kara seas. Preliminary drilling in the Kara is to begin in 2014.

With mainland wells in the Urals and Western Siberia beginning to run dry, and with Russia's global clout so dependent on its status as an energy superpower, these are all only first steps – as witnessed by the conversion of military shipyards outside Arkhangelsk to manufacture drilling platforms, and also by plans to deploy floating nuclear reactors, starting with the barge *Akademik Lomonosov* in 2013, to provide power to towns and facilities along the Arctic coastline. Russia can be relied upon as well to assert claims to a maximum amount of the Arctic seabed, and as forcefully as possible. Convinced that large portions of the undersea Lomonosov Ridge naturally project from its continental shelf, Russia considers the North Pole itself to lie within its rightful exclusive economic zone. It said so categorically in its 2001 claim to UNCLOS, and it will no doubt repeat the assertion when it finally updates that claim with its newly gathered scientific evidence.

The UNCLOS tribunal will cease to accept claims after 2014. While some calculate that the UN could take up to 35 years beyond that to decide all the cases before it, others expect a firm resolution of the Arctic's boundaries by around 2020. Inevitably, the UNCLOS decision, whatever form it takes, will disappoint at least some claimants, and it is entirely possible that the Pole will end up belonging to no one. At the 2008 International Geological Congress, scholars constructed a predictive model in which this was the case, and in which an unclaimable territorial 'hole' appeared on either side of the North Pole.

Will such rulings hold? Arctic nations continue to snarl at their neighbours over various questions as they emerge. Russia, while maintaining that 'we aren't going to wage a new Cold War in the Arctic', insists with a hint of menace that 'we will protect our interests', and the Norwegian ministry of defence has voiced concerns about the escalation of 'gunboat diplomacy' in northern waters like the Barents.[13] On the other hand, all Arctic nations have pledged repeatedly and publicly to seek peaceful solutions to Arctic disputes. With such an arsenal of advanced and precise underwater-mapping techniques now available – including robotic and mini-sub surveying, sonar scans, seismic and aerogravity probes and satellite surveillance – and with the risks of armed conflict so obviously outweighing any foreseeable benefit, there is good reason to hope that science will carry the day and that the Tribunal's judgements will be accepted by all, be it gracefully or grudgingly.

Nunangat: Indigenous Northerners in the Contemporary Era

In *Sermiligaaq 65°54′N, 36°22′W*, a 2008 documentary film recording the fieldwork of anthropologists Sophie Elixhauser and Anni Seitz in the southeast Greenland village of the same name, tradition and modernity coexist in every frame. Clapboard houses huddle on the rocky shores, sled dogs nap next to the snowmobiles parked outside, crucifixes and posters of Christian saints adorn the walls of Inuit homes. In one scene, an Inuit homemaker deftly butchers the carcass of a seal on the linoleum floor of her kitchen, conversing matter-of-factly with her interviewer while her husband and son put a Nintendo Wii through its paces in the next room over.

Of the 4 million people who inhabit the Arctic today, approximately 400,000 can be considered indigenous. For most, the years following the Cold War have been a time of increased political empowerment and somewhat greater prosperity, but have also offered choices with as much potential for confusion as for opportunity.

One area of particular success has been the quest for homeland – Sapmi in Sami, *nunaat* or *nunangat* in Inuktitut, with the latter term referring to the ice and water as well as the land. The most striking of these gains have been made in Canada and Greenland. In Canada, the long-awaited territory of Nunavut ('our land') was given parliamentary approval in 1993 – aided largely by the sympathy stirred up by official inquests into the High Arctic Relocation scandal from the 1950s – and came into being on 1 April 1999. Formed by splitting the sprawling Northwest Territories into two, Nunavut encompasses an area of 800,000 square miles, an expanse equal in size to Alaska and California combined, leaving a rump NWT measuring just under 520,000 square miles. Half of Canada's 50,500 Inuit reside in Nunavut, with the rest distributed throughout Nunavik (northern Quebec), Nunatsiavut (coastal Labrador), the NWT and the Yukon. With more modest results, Athabaskan groups and other First Nations of the Yukon and NWT have settled, or are near to settling, their own land claims with Ottawa. Greenland, or Kalaallit Nunaat, became a self-governing dependency in 2009, with its own elected parliament and control over finances, natural resources and domestic affairs. Denmark provides an annual subsidy and remains in charge of foreign policy and the armed forces, but many see the current arrangement as a penultimate step towards final independence.

Progress has been more limited in the rest of Fennoscandia and in Russia. In 1993, the Sami of Sweden, like their counterparts in Norway and Finland, won the right to form national-level parliaments. In all three cases, though, these bodies possess few substantive responsibilities. In contrast to Norway, which has settled the question most generously, arguments still rage in Sweden and Finland over who can be counted as Sami, with Helsinki and especially Stockholm insisting on restrictive litmus tests that involve meeting all or most of a list of language- and livelihood-based criteria, rather than one of a list, as in Norway. Moreover, the governments of all three states, anxious to limit the extent of potential land claims, are loath to acknowledge any more territory than they have to as ancestrally Sami. Sami historians and archaeologists have responded with a crusade to lay claim to as many ancient tombs, settlements and ritual sites as possible, with an eye to proving Sami presence in as large a space, and as far back in time, as they can.

In contemporary Russia, as during the Soviet era, native self-determination – theoretically embodied in the partition of territory into ethnically based autonomous regions and districts – remains more notional than substantial. In July 2000, the Russian federal government issued the well-intentioned 'General Principles for Establishing Communities of Indigenous Minority Peoples of the North, Siberia, and Far East', but has done little to follow through on them. What change there has been has tended to occur on the regional and local levels.

As in all postcolonial contexts, greater autonomy is only one desired end among Arctic peoples. Socioeconomic health is another, and one sorely lacking throughout the North, despite the steadily widening availability of modern technology and consumer goods. The most straightforward problems are poverty, limited access to services like education and medicine, and the sense of hopelessness brought on by stunted opportunities. Since the fall of the USSR, fully a third of all deaths among the 'small peoples' of Russia's north have been caused by alcohol, suicide, violent accident and murder. Readers are told in Peter Høeg's *Miss Smilla's Feeling for Snow* that when people say Greenlanders 'drink a lot', it is 'a totally absurd understatement', because Greenlanders in fact 'drink a colossal amount'.[14] Such ills may not operate on the same dire scale everywhere in the Arctic, but they wreak havoc in all too many places, from city neighbourhoods to nameless villages.

Squalor, however, is only one part of the native predicament. 'Materially, if not spiritually', one author notes, 'tens of thousands [of natives] are more secure than they have ever been. Survival is no longer a central issue.'[15] But even where material conditions are adequate, Arctic aboriginals are troubled by a more abstract and yet often crippling

social and cultural disorientation: they may have gained electricity gen-
erators and satellite TV, motorboats and Ski-doos, Gore-Tex and GPS,
but they have paid with centuries-old customs, mother tongues, traditional skills and lore, and much-missed community bonds. They of
course have no desire to live harder lives than anyone else, or to exist as
ethnographically 'authentic' artefacts in a gigantic open-air museum.
But their core dilemma is that modernity rarely serves itself up à la
carte, and indigenous peoples on the whole have found it hard to appropriate those aspects of it that they find desirable without being overwhelmed by its more harmful effects.

Further complications arise from the fact that indigenous peoples are
no likelier than any other to think with one mind or to speak with one
voice about such matters. Seldom, for instance, do they adopt totally
unified stances where development is concerned. In places like Russia,
the ability of citizens, native or otherwise, to affect such decisions is
minimal at best. Indigenous northerners with the bad luck to live near
deposits of natural resources, such as the Khanty, Mansi and Nentsy
who dwell in the Urals and West Siberian oil country, continue to be
treated like pawns by Russia's energy and mining conglomerates, which
are either state-owned or run by 'oligarch' billionaires who collaborate
closely with the state. Even so, while many among the 'small peoples'
want nothing more than to preserve their traditional reindeer-herding
economy, others eagerly await the expansion of the oil and gas industries,
in the hope that developers' promises of a 'silicon taiga', complete with
new and better-paying jobs, will materialize.[16]

And so it is elsewhere. Where land claims give Arctic aboriginals a
say in whether pipelines are laid or mines and gas and oil wells dug, they
are as likely to go along with such proposals – so long as they see some
return in the form of jobs, cash payment or capital improvements – as they
are to oppose them for the sake of old ways or ancestral land. One case
in point is the contrast between the willingness of natives to participate
in Canada's recently launched Mackenzie pipeline project and the stand
made by the Inuit of Lancaster Sound against fossil fuel prospecting.

Equally illustrative are the decisions of the Gwich'in and Inupiat living in oil-rich areas near Alaska's Arctic National Wildlife Refuge.
Since 1991, Alaskan native communities have been free to sell or otherwise dispose of the lands granted them by the 1971 Alaska Native Claims
Settlement Act. The Gwich'in who reside near the ANWR have decided
not to allow development of their land, forgoing oil money in favour of
their traditional caribou-hunting ways. Nearby, the Inupiat of Kaktovik,

a whaling village on the Beaufort coast, are split on the question of whether to allow oil exploration in the region, and under what conditions. In the summer of 2006, Kaktovik's village council formally denounced Shell Oil as 'a hostile and dangerous force' to be repulsed, but the Kaktovik Inupiat Corporation has expressed a greater willingness to open up selected portions of Inupiat land to development.[17] Likewise, Innu in northern Quebec have protested hydroelectric development along the lower Churchill River by throwing up roadblocks and organizing cross-border caribou hunts into Labrador. Such actions place them in direct opposition to their cousins in Labrador, who have supported big hydro in exchange for revenue and expanded hunting rights.

Native northerners have also moved in and out of step with Euro-American models of environmentalism. Allied at times against the most drastic intrusions into the polar landscape, native interests and Western greens have on other occasions diverged over the question of what constitutes proper stewardship over the land. The approach most favoured by non-native conservationists, the 'northern wilderness' paradigm, has assumed that 'arctic ecosystems be protected for the purpose of nature preservation, or as the nation's treasure, or for the sake of future generations'.[18] Park rangers and law-enforcement officials have correspondingly focused on ensuring that hunting and fishing do not take place beyond legal limits or out of season, and on banning the export or import of meat, skin or trophies taken from animals deemed worthy of protection by Western law. From the aboriginal perspective, this wilderness approach, with such heavy emphasis on safeguarding animal rights and the land, gives short shrift to the wilderness's human inhabitants. 'How can they love a seal more than a human being?' wonder Canadian and Greenland Inuit whose livelihoods are affected by the activism of NGOs like Greenpeace, the Humane Society International and the World Wildlife Fund.[19]

For most Arctic natives, fish and game laws rankle, and are often violated. The stigma placed by most of the Western world on sealing and whaling, irrespective of whether the species in question is endangered, remains an especially sore point. Much of the complaint is economic. Although most measures enacted for the protection of sea mammals, including the IWC moratorium and the EEC (now EU) embargo on seal products, have made a variety of exceptions for aboriginal peoples since the 1970s and '80s, they nevertheless decrease demand and make it harder for hunters to earn a living. More abstractly, the notion that outsiders' sensibilities ought to trump their needs and choices strikes many indigenes as neo-colonial paternalism. Some anthropologists, such as Canada's Milton Freeman, have gone so far as to accuse Western conservationist efforts of 'victimizing' native populations and violating their human rights.[20]

Native grievances, however, no matter how valid, must be balanced against two ecological facts. First, in the Arctic, it takes little to push even apparently thriving species to the point of endangerment. Second, when natives equip themselves with non-traditional gear to hunt traditional prey, they put non-traditional pressures on the environment. This impasse, by no means new, has been aptly summed up by Barry Lopez: the 'lack of discipline' shown by northern populations who flout Euro-American hunting regulations can cause unacceptable levels of damage. But those populations have also been 'routinely excluded' from the crafting of regulations and 'offered no help in devising a kind of hunting behavior more consistent with the power and reach of modern weapons'.[21] The clash between animal rights and the securing of social justice for Arctic natives may never be resolved completely, but better compromises between them must be reached, both for the good of the northern ecosystem and those who make their home there.

Happily, certain improvements have been forthcoming in the native north. Although many sociological indicators remain inauspicious, not all communities are in crisis. Respect for aboriginal heritage is on the rise, as reflected symbolically in the restoration of native place names to sites throughout the Arctic, and substantively by the creation of northern parks – even in Russia, where the native-rights record is comparatively weak – dedicated not just to wilderness, but to native culture. Environmentalist NGOs have engaged more helpfully in dialogue with indigenous northerners. Many national and regional governments, adopting strategies that have worked for other species pressured by poaching and overhunting, such as pandas, elephants and gorillas, have involved Arctic locals more meaningfully in wildlife and resource management, and in the now-lucrative industry of ecotourism. Cooperative management of caribou and musk ox herds has paid good dividends in Alaska and Canada, and the Russian government has assisted a number of Siberian communities by transplanting reindeer populations from places where they have fared well, such as the Yamal Peninsula, to areas where they have not, including Chukotka. Land-claim victories and other concessions continue to be won, in some places more speedily, in others more slowly.

None of this, however, is enough to settle the fundamental and still-unanswered question: when and how will a critical mass of the Arctic's native population be able to embrace modernity on their own terms? Will the structures of a fast-globalizing society permit it? And – a question of growing urgency in these recent years – how will the rapidly changing Arctic environment affect this process?

Arcticide? Towards a New Polar Ecosystem

As they have throughout the modern era, pollution, overhunting and human encroachment on animal habitats continue to inflict enormous stress on the northern environment. These days, though, the Arctic's most alarming problem is its shrinking albedo. For millennia, albedo, the coefficient that measures surface reflectivity, remained high in the far north, where the preponderance of ice and snow ensured that most of the sun's light and warmth were thrown back skyward.

Lately, however, with temperatures rising and the ice and snow less prevalent, the northern land and waters, rather than reflecting heat, have been absorbing much more of it. The ease with which this has spun into a vicious cycle is plain to see: the more heat the Arctic retains, the more ice and snow it loses for good, making it even more liable to retain heat. Put bluntly, the warmer the Arctic gets, the warmer it will keep becoming. Those who are blasé or sceptical about global warming shrug this off as part of the normal order of things, as merely one phase of a long-term climatological cycle. It seems far likelier, though, that we are witnessing, and surely abetting, a colossal act of what can fairly be called Arcticide. Of course, the Arctic in some form will exist for as long as the planet remains intact. But the Arctic as we know it now is dying – and if it does die, it will not have been of natural causes.

Discernible to specialists near the end of the Cold War and a matter of increasingly common knowledge during the 1990s, this trend now screams out from headlines on a regular basis. Even a small sampling of facts from such stories should disquiet any reader. In the summer of 2002, submarine-based surveys revealed that the Arctic Ocean pack ice, in addition to losing surface area, has shed an incredible amount of volume in the last decades, its thickness only half what it had been 50 years before. NASA satellite imagery indicates that even the ice of longest duration and greatest strength, the perennial ice closest to the North Pole, is fast disappearing, with over 965,000 square miles of it lost between early 2007 and early 2008. Recently, the Greenland ice cap has shrunk by approximately 50 cubic miles every year, and the island's glaciers, including those which empty into the majestic Ilulissat Icefjord, are melting at a worrisome pace. Off the coast of Canada's Ward Hunt Island, site of the Arctic's largest ice shelf, massive bergs have been breaking off and drifting south, in a prelude to what most anticipate will be the shelf's total disintegration. On land, up to 80 per cent of the top layer of permafrost in the northern hemisphere is expected to liquefy by the year 2100. In the polar Urals and throughout Arctic Siberia, larches and other conifers are appearing farther north than ever before, thoroughly redefining the Eurasian treeline.

Whether or where this will all end is a matter of conjecture, although a growing number of scientists are convinced that 'an ice-free state' is now 'inevitable' in the Arctic.[22] If this is so, what ramifications can be expected to follow? For the region's wildlife, they are sure to be extreme. Already, a number of the Arctic's resident species are hard-pressed by the effects of warming, while new arrivals have been attracted northward by the milder conditions. This has thrown the door wide open for almost anything to happen with respect to predator-prey relationships, and the Arctic's entire food web may find itself woven completely anew. What will it mean if puffins linger in the Arctic ecosystem longer than they currently do, or if blue mussels begin to spawn there in profusion? Will the harbour porpoises spotted lately off Spitsbergen deplete the stocks of fish in its waters? What will result if gigantic fin whales, which have started visiting the Arctic in larger numbers, end up devouring the North's plankton in quantities proportional to their size? Marine biologists wonder with anxiety whether, in time, oceanic species might be able to cross freely through the Arctic Ocean between the Atlantic and Pacific, a scenario with the potential to cause much ecological chaos.

Many scientists project that the ice-melt's profoundest effects will strike lower orders of life first, then work themselves up the food chain. Less ice cover means less ice algae, which feeds the crustaceans and krill that nourish a wide variety of avian and marine species, including baleen whales like the bowhead. Fish depend on the ice for shelter from birds. Larger creatures will face their own challenges. Most seals require access to thick floating ice for at least eight weeks during the spring and summer in order to breed and to feed themselves and their pups. Even the seemingly numberless population of the ringed seal could dip fast if enough ice is lost. Similar difficulties await the walrus, which cannot feed its bulky self during the warmer months merely by swimming out from shore; it must use ice floes as floating stations to hunt for meals far from the coast. Recent years have seen Pacific walruses badly overcrowded on Alaskan and Siberian beaches, competing over too-small supplies of food.

Narwhals, whose behaviour remained a scientific mystery until comparatively recently, because of their reluctance to range below 70°N, are confined to the region's northernmost waters by diet. One of the Arctic's most finicky eaters, narwhals subsist on fewer than half a dozen types of prey. All of these flourish under the ice, and if the ice vanishes, the narwhal is doomed. Less fussy than their tusked cousins, minke whales and beluga should be able to adapt their eating habits to the new climate. Unfortunately for them, the change will also bring them into more con-tact with their deadliest enemy: the orca, whose oversized dorsal fin, awkward for manoeuvring through ice floes, prevented it in the past from roaming too far, or for very long, in Arctic waters. Now less impeded by the ice, orcas have been penetrating Arctic seas earlier in the year than before and venturing noticeably farther to the north. The scaled-up pres-ence of such a powerful predator is certain to alter the polar seascape immeasurably.

The north's terrestrial animals are caught up in their own travails. In the summer of 2011, the International Boreal Conservation Panel declared Canada's woodland caribou to be 'on the road to extinction'.[23] Although not yet to the same degree, other reindeer subspecies in North America and Eurasia, as well as certain musk ox herds, are distressed by the compression of their foraging range, the disruption of their migra-tion routes, and the vagaries of the weather. Faltering most visibly is the polar bear, whose current population of 20,000–25,000 is predicted to dwindle by at least two-thirds before 2050, and perhaps completely after that. It is on the ice that the polar bear hunts for seals, and for all its prowess as a long-distance swimmer, it needs ice islands as resting spots as it wanders 20,000 square miles or more to ensure an adequate intake of food. Polar bears risk dying in the winter if they do not eat enough during the summer, and females who fail to feed sufficiently are less likely to become pregnant.

Already by the early 1990s, the loss of ice cover in Hudson Bay had raised the infertility rate among polar bears there to 28 per cent. That rate has climbed since, and zoologists calculate that the spring thaw would have to arrive only three or four weeks earlier to push it to 70 per cent or higher. No one with any knowledge in the field is optimistic about the polar bear's chances. A few zoologists have theorized that the species might survive after a fashion by migrating south and reverting over time to the form it once had before it diverged evolutionarily from its brown bear cousins. Most, however, consider this outcome improbable. Smart betting is on the orca to emerge as the new Arctic's next apex predator. The polar bear, along with the Pacific walrus and the narwhal, stands to be dealt permanently out of the game.

What of it?, some may ask, pointing out that Arctic species have gone extinct in the past, with new ones rising to take their place. Few today, after all, miss the great auk or Steller's sea cow. But even if one is unmoved by the plight of animals, human crises are waiting in the wings. Those residing in the far north will see more aspects of their lifestyle, not to mention sizable parts of their home territory, disappear. Hunters and fishers will find themselves flummoxed as animals shift their migratory patterns or die out altogether. The networks of ice roads, frozen lakes and snowmobile routes that provide northern communities with their sole means of ground transport for much of the year will spend more months out of commission. Not everyone faces frightful prospects. Localized water transport will become easier, and physical hardships will seem lighter – at least in the short term. Many Greenlanders jokingly refer to their increasingly temperate southwestern shoreline as the 'banana coast' and confess to a hope that global warming will bring them greater economic prosperity. They are not alone in such hopes. Overall, however, northern populations feel trepidation about the effects of warming. Since the late 1980s, the Russians have catalogued, and laboured to keep in repair, hundreds of structures and properties damaged by the softening of permafrost throughout Siberia. Yakuts and other northern natives have complained of entire villages being flooded out by the same phenomenon. Reflecting recently on the worldwide impact of global warming on Arctic aboriginals, an Inuit spokesman prognosticated morosely that 'we are becoming an endangered species'.[24]

Humanity as a whole may wind up in the same predicament, for the repercussions of Arctic climate change will assuredly be hemispheric, if not global. Not all scientists are agreed that the Arctic will continue to warm at its present pace, or that the ice will keep melting until none is left. The Arctic ecosystem has survived or adapted to warming trends in the past, and recent analysis of ancient driftwood by Denmark's Natural History Museum indicates that 5,000 years ago the Arctic lost up to 50 per cent of its ice cover without crossing the 'tipping point' beyond which the loss of the rest is supposed to become unavoidable.[25] Most climate-watchers, however, now believe that ice-free summers in the Arctic are a near-certainty sometime in the next twenty to 40 years. And even if the meltdown does not prove total, it can still have shattering consequences.

What might some of these be? Thanks to constant media coverage and the wide appeal of films such as Al Gore's documentary *An Inconvenient Truth* of 2006, public awareness is fixed on the possibility that melting ice will cause the world's oceans to rise to civilization-threatening levels. Should such a development come to pass, the Arctic pack ice is not expected to contribute as much to it as the frozen mass of Antarctica will, but the Greenland ice cap will more than make up for it. In 2010, Greenland's hottest year on record, four of the island's biggest glaciers surrendered more than 10 square miles of ice apiece, leading the Byrd Polar Research Center and the Woods Hole Oceanographic Institute to conclude that 'sea level projections for the future will again need to be revised upward.'[26] Whether the result will indeed be an apocalyptic engulfment of coastal communities ranging from Manhattan and Venice to Manila and Sydney remains to be seen, but as New Orleans's experience in the wake of Hurricane Katrina has shown, even a more modest flooding could prove highly traumatic.

Also in store is the release of unknown quantities of gases and toxins that, for decades, have been contained by the Arctic ice and permafrost, as if locked away in a freezer. Glaciers and sea ice throughout the North have accumulated large amounts of carbon dioxide and airborne contaminants that would be better left sealed up. Permafrost in Siberia is thought to be keeping an astronomical volume of methane – twenty times more powerful than CO_2 in its greenhouse effect – trapped underground. The impact on the course of global warming, and on atmospheric quality, should these evil djinni be freed from their bottles can only be guessed at, but is likely to be considerable. In the winter of 2010–11, a new cause for alarm surfaced, in the form of the first ever Arctic ozone hole, a northern counterpart to the more famous hole that opened up over Antarctica in the 1980s. As reported by NASA scientists, the Arctic hole is a delayed consequence of CFC (chlorofluorocarbon) emissions from the twentieth century: these chemicals are 'long-lived' and will take 'a few decades to be cleansed from the atmosphere'.[27] Lack of ozone, of course, is likely to mean faster warming.

Finally, we can expect changes in the Arctic to reshape the weather in more temperate zones, due to the role played by the northern climate in directing the global circulation of air and ocean currents. These effects will probably be as paradoxical as they are far-reaching, with hotter temperatures in the north causing cooling trends in the south. Oceanographers from Woods Hole and Germany's Alfred Wegener Institute have noted that, since the year 2000, the Arctic Ocean's uppermost layer has become 20 per cent less salty, due to the growing inrush of glacial meltwater. Aside from the potential harm this might cause Arctic marine species, the freshening of the water, if it spreads to the North Atlantic, could alter or negate the flow of the life-sustaining Gulf Stream – plunging the Norwegian coast, the British Isles and perhaps all of Western Europe into a deep freeze. The warming of Arctic air also appears to correlate to the recent prevalence of colder and more extreme weather at lower latitudes. First, the melting of polar ice saturates the skies faraway with more moisture, making it easier for even normal winter temperatures to trigger heavier-than-average snowfall. More fundamentally, the heating-up of the high north seems to be breaking down the 'arctic fence', the west-to-east pattern of wind movement that, in past years, has whirled the jet stream around in a tight spiral and confined the hemisphere's coldest air to the circumpolar margins.[28] With the 'fence' weakened, more of the North's frigid air is free to spill down to the south, bringing freakishly chilly winters to places like Atlanta and Lisbon – while Arctic communities experience unprecedented warm spells, as Nunavut's capital Iqaluit did in the winter of 2010–11, when unseasonably high temperatures forced the cancellation of the city's annual snowmobile parade. Seized upon by climate-change sceptics as 'evidence' that global warming is unproven pseudo-science, the aberrantly cold winters of the past half-decade are seen by a growing roster of scientists as a sure sign that global warming is in fact gaining momentum and that the ways in which it manifests itself will be frustratingly unpredictable.

Carbon emissions and other forms of human-caused climate change may not be solely responsible for the Arctic's rising fever, but they are undeniably a large part of it – 'empirically accounting' for up to 90 per cent of recent ice loss, according to the Norway Geophysical Institute.[29] All of which justifies a moment of dismayed head-shaking at the thought of developing the high north even more than it already has been. A more unhealthy synergy is difficult to imagine, especially when it comes to gas and oil. The profligate burning of fossil fuels has done more than anything else to reduce the Arctic to the state it is in today, and there is something perverse about exploiting this new vulnerability to plunder more fossil fuels, whose extraction and consumption will further undermine the region's ecological well-being. To begin with, the simplest level of safety cannot be taken for granted. Considering the record of industrial mishaps already racked up in the North, another *Exxon Valdez* or, worse yet, a polar version of the Deepwater disaster seems a statistical near-certainty. And does past experience really inspire trust in Russia's ability to construct 'ice-resistant' drilling platforms? Or to guarantee that the floating nuclear reactors it intends to station along the Arctic coast will not turn out to be the next Fukushimas? And even if the fuel industries prove able to work accident-free in the Arctic, they cannot do so without a crushing environmental impact, despite the soothing anodynes issued by Shell, Statoil and their ilk.

The Arctic can ill afford any such strains – it has yet to recover, after all, from the tortures inflicted on it during the last half of the previous century. Radiation wreaks its molecular malevolence on Novaya Zemlya and beneath the waves of the Barents and White seas; rust, metal tailings and noxious chemicals leach into the ground and waters in shipyards, mines and factories from Kiruna and Spitsbergen to the Black Angel and Red Dog mines in Greenland and Alaska. Oil is spilled and leaked from cracked pipelines, whether in Alaska or along the Ob and Taz deltas. Slowly decomposing garbage piles up in mounds outside airbases and radar stations. Hydroelectric projects flood the migratory routes of caribou in Canada and Norway, while whale songs are drowned out by fishermen's sonar systems and the churning of supertanker motors. If one could by wizardry cease all human activity in the Arctic from this moment forward, it would still require decades, if not longer, for all these injuries, and the many others not listed here, to heal.

Of course, any thought of total stasis is sheerest utopianism. The best that can be hoped for is to cauterize the damage done, and to limit what is surely yet to come. Some excellent steps have already been taken. Clean-up operations have scoured many areas blighted by past and present pollution, including DEW Line installations, the *Exxon Valdez* spill site, and mines and pipeline beds throughout the North. In Russia, post-Soviet oil firms have come to realize that leaks and spills blacken their reputation abroad and quite literally bleed profits into the ground. Environmental groups have become more attentive to the priorities of indigenous northerners and more respectful of their understanding of the Arctic ecosystem; more effective partnerships have arisen as a result. Parks, preserves and UNESCO heritage sites have been defended and created in greater numbers throughout the North. So far, Alaska's Arctic National Wildlife Refuge remains undeveloped, with NGOs and the local Gwich'in and Inupiat resisting corporate and political pressure to open up the so-called 'study area' on the coast to exploratory drilling. Canada's Lancaster sound is likewise safe from development – for the time being.

Even in Russia, the small but strong-willed green movement, which consists of scientists, native activists and NGOs such as Ecojuris, a Moscow-based organization of environmental lawyers, has succeeded in expanding the system of *zapovedniki*, or protected zones, that came into being during the late Soviet years. Successes in the post-Soviet north have included the creation of a chain of nature parks on the Yamal Peninsula and in Khanty-Mansi territory, the restoration and preservation of pagan and Christian religious monuments on Vaigach Island and the Solovetsky archipelago, and the formation of large preserves in Chukotka and on the Taimyr Peninsula. The latter is home to Russia's largest *zapovednik*, the Great Arctic, which, since 1993, has provided safe haven to polar bears, walruses, beluga whales and reindeer herds.

Nonetheless, much remains to be done, and there is much to guard against. Too many northern species are at risk, too many northern forests and glaciers are dying. What will become of the ice and the tundra, and the fauna that depend on both, is anyone's guess. Although shipping firms and oil and gas companies are lining up to surge into the region, nothing has changed the core reality that, in the words of the World Wildlife Fund, 'the Arctic offers the highest levels of ecological sensitivity' to development – 'and the lowest level of capacity to clean up after an accident'.[30] As desirable as a complete ban on Arctic development might be, nothing of the sort is legally or diplomatically feasible. But is a partial moratorium possible? Calls for such arrangements have been made, among them an intriguing 2009 proposal by experts affiliated with the Council on Foreign Relations and the Rule of Law Committee for the Oceans to cordon off the highest north.[31] All waters above the 88th parallel, or within a 120-mile radius of the North Pole, would be set aside as a giant marine park, administered and studied jointly by an 'international cooperative' consisting of the United States, Canada, Russia, Denmark, Norway and any other nation interested in Arctic science. The concept flows from the same logic underlying the Antarctic Treaty, and it touches only on the least accessible part of the Arctic – the part of least concern to governments and corporate interests. But will this suffice to win wider acceptance for it, or for any scheme like it? Given the temper of the times and the potential wealth to be had in even the remotest sectors of the North, chances are that it will not.

In the end, then, the Arctic's ecological fate would appear to depend principally on the restraint and self-discipline of individual states and businesses. This is not a comforting thought, looking back over the history of the developed world's interactions with the polar north. If consolation is to be had, it rests in the fact that the states in question are ultimately answerable to their citizens, and the businesses to their share-holders and consumers. In other times and places, public activism and advocacy have forced an end to the manufacture of toxic substances like DDT, brought endangered species back from the brink of extinction and safeguarded countless square miles of wilderness. Can popular mobili-zation exercise the same sort of influence in the Arctic? And can it be roused soon enough for it to matter? One must hope that it will. This is no simple choice between economic prosperity on one hand and, on the other, abstract sentimentality about wild places, or about animal species that most people will never encounter outside zoos or aquariums. If even a fraction of what scientists predict about unchecked Arctic warming turns out to be correct, the choice may well come down to one of survival: not necessarily of humanity itself, but of the favourable climatological conditions that human populations in the middle latitudes have enjoyed for many centuries. Out-of-control development in the circumpolar north – in a word, Arcticide – will not just kill off polar bears, walruses and narwhals, or destroy some of the planet's most awe-inspiring glaciers, or fatally disorient reindeer herds and migrating whale pods. It will in all likelihood rebound on southerners in the form of flooding and heavier snowfalls along the coasts. Continental interiors may experience prolonged periods of drought, if not desertification. If ocean currents and jet streams go topsy-turvy, as many expect them to do, extreme and capricious weather are in store for all of us.

Such are the possibilities that biologist and journalist Alun Anderson had in mind when he spoke of 'the Arctic's Revenge' in 2009. 'Did we really think', asked Anderson, 'that we could make so many changes to the far-off Arctic and strip it of its ice, without the Arctic biting back? If we ever did, we were foolish.'[32] The history of the last half-millennium points out the long succession of environmental follies that humankind has committed in the far north. The present is making clear the consequences of those follies, although not everyone seems inclined to pay attention. The future will witness what form those consequences will take and how severe they will be – and whether we have the will and the wits to undo them before it is too late.

Finding Our Bearings: An Epilogue

Conducting fieldwork among the coastal communities of northern Norway, anthropologist Anita Maurstad recorded a telling anecdote which illustrates, among other things, the various ways that people create mental maps of the Arctic and of their own place in it. At the heart of the vignette is a veteran fisherman unenthused about GPS technology and content to sail without it. One evening, returning to port with his catch, the fisherman switched on his radio to join in the general conversation about where his fellow mariners had fished that day and where they were bound. It took only a few minutes, though, for him to grow audibly irritated by his comrades' insistence on referring to locations solely by their GPS coordinates, rather than their names or physical descriptions. Frustrated at being hedged all about by newfangled gimmickry, the fisherman shouted into his receiver, 'Give me a break! Use the names of the places. I don't know where 69.48.389N and 017.40.211E is!'[33]

The old sailor's practical confusion is readily understood, and there is a tidy parable here about the clash between technological modernization and traditional ways of knowing. But a more existential disorientation is at work as well, for today's Arctic teems with contradictions. Houses in Inuit villages boast hallmarks of the twenty-first century – Internet-equipped computers, microwave ovens and larders stuffed with TV dinners and bottles of Coca-Cola – while just beyond their limits, like totemic spirits conjured up from ages past, whales glide past frozen shores and Arctic wolves stalk caribou in the elemental vastness of the tundra. For security purposes, Russia has categorized all foreign icebreakers as ships of war, and yet has recently agreed to lease its own largest icebreakers, the *Yamal* and the *50 Let Pobedy*, as assets to adventure-tour companies hoping to convey paying passengers to the North Pole. A scant 35 miles apart on Spitsbergen are the port of Longyearbyen, which the Norwegians have built into a thriving centre for eco-voyaging, and the decaying hulk of Pyramiden, a Russian mining community where 800 families lived and worked until the 1991 collapse of the USSR consigned it to its present delapidation. Iceland sells itself as a land of primordial volcanism and Viking heritage, and at the same time, thanks to performers like Björk and Sigur Rós, it rules Europe's airwaves and night clubs as the queen of avant-garde coolness. Similar incongruities abound.

It is therefore no surprise that, like a compass needle in flux as it approaches the Magnetic North Pole, modern society is in a state of confusion when it comes to the Arctic. Apart from uncertainty regarding the progress of climate change in the North, perhaps the greatest source of befuddlement is our proverbial desire to have our cake there and to eat it too. On one hand, we want the Arctic to remain a nature preserve, an untamed wonderland of natural beauty that we can occasionally visit vicariously via the Discovery Channel or the pages of *National Geographic*. We would like to sustain pleasant fantasies about it as the mythical abode of Santa Claus and his charmingly magical reindeer. On the other hand, we demand of the Arctic the right to trespass there and to take from it as we please: to harvest its mineral and animal wealth, to deploy machines of war in its skies and waters, and to blanket it from east to west with poisons and pollutants. It is difficult to imagine any person actively desiring the demise of the polar bear or the narwhal. But every day, millions of individuals unknowingly bring these and other harmful eventualities closer to consummation, simply by paying no heed to the carbon emissions they are responsible for, or by pursuing lifestyles so completely dependent on an endless supply of cheap petroleum. For many, the mere realization that hard choices have to be made about the Arctic triggers a serious shock – and an equally serious loss of bearing. And yet never before has a clear sense of direction been necessary in the high north. The best first step that can be taken at this juncture is for states and citizens to rid themselves of the illusion that the Arctic can be controlled without coming to grievous harm and, in its pain, turning that hurt back on its brutalizers.

Speaking in St Petersburg, Russia, during a 2003 tour of northern nations, Canada's governor-general at the time, Adrienne Clarkson, observed that 'our countries have had to overcome the idea that we were going to dominate and tame the North'.[34] Clarkson's comment was correct in every respect save one: the tense of her verbs, for there has been little in the years since she spoke these words to indicate that the lesson contained within them has been learned. We cannot send the Arctic back in time to the crystalline state in which it existed before the appearance of humankind, or even the arrival of Euro-Americans. But there is perhaps yet time for us to halt, and conceivably even reverse, the scarifying abuse that we have inflicted on the Arctic throughout the industrial era. If we fail, we may end up punishing ourselves as badly as we have punished the polar regions these many centuries. I myself confess to dark expectations about whether we will set our course correctly and respond adequately or in time. I hope for nothing more than to be proven wrong.

REFERENCES

I
Origins: Introduction and Environmental Overview

1 Fridtjof Nansen, *Farthest North* (London, 1897), p. 318.

2 Ibid., p. 440.

3 Elisha Kent Kane, *Arctic Explorations*, vol. II (Philadelphia, PA, 1856), p. 57; and Farley Mowat, *People of the Deer* [1951] (New York, 1971), p. 17.

4 Barry Lopez, *Arctic Dreams* (New York, 1986), p. xxii.

5 The North Magnetic Pole marks the actual point in the northern hemisphere where the earth's magnetic field 'dips' toward the surface at a 90-degree angle. Its shifts are due not just to fluctuations in the magnetic field itself, but also to the slow but constant motion of the molten iron deep within the earth's surface. The North Geomagnetic Pole is the northern axis of the theoretical dipole formed by where the North and South Magnetic poles *should* be mathematically. The Pole of Relative Inaccessibility lies at about 84°N 175°W, or just over 400 miles from the Geographic North Pole.

6 See David Damas, ed., *Arctic: Handbook of North American Indians*, vol. V (Washington, DC, 1984); and Pamela R. Stern, *The A to Z of the Inuit* (Lanham, MD, 2009), pp. 50–51. As for the origin of 'Eskimo', many linguists now believe that it derives from the Montagnais (Innu) phrase for 'stringer of snowshoes'.

7 Until 2009, when the International Union of Geological Sciences readjusted the date to 2.55 million years ago, the Pleistocene, the first epoch of the Quaternary period, was considered to have started approximately 1.8 million years ago.

8 Once known as oxygen isotope stages, marine isotope stages measure the ratio of light to heavy oxygen (^{16}o to ^{18}o) in the world's oceans at a given point in history; during glacial periods, the proportion of light oxygen lessens, and the isotopic record is preserved in ice cores and in the fossilized shells of marine molluscs, which are recoverable from datable deep-sea cores. Research done by Nicholas Shackleton and Neil Opdyke in the 1970s demonstrated that such measurements are globally consistent. Not only do marine isotope stages distinguish between glacial and interglacial/interstadial periods, but the oscillation can be plotted on a graph to show *how* warm or cold a given period was. The Quaternary is divided into approximately 100 such stages.

9 Jack London, *The Call of the Wild and Selected Stories* (New York, 1960), p. 162.

10 The 'conveyor belt' image grew out of work done by Henry Stommel in the 1950s. Although oceanographers popularized it, they understood it from the outset to be an oversimplification of how the 'overturning' of the world's

waters occurs. Since the 1990s, its viability even as a metaphor has been called into question by a number of scholars who believe that oceanic circulation is influenced by a more complicated mix of factors than previously thought.

11 Lopez, *Arctic Dreams*, p. 173.

12 Maxwell J. Dunbar, 'Stability and Fragility in Arctic Ecosystems', *Arctic*, XXVI/3 (1973), pp. 179–86.

2
Encounters: Prehistory and Early History to 1500 CE

1 Ted Goebel et al., 'The Late Pleistocene Dispersal of Modern Humans in the Americas', *Science*, 319 (14 March 2008), pp. 1497–1502, notes that, by identifying several lines of descent among Native Americans, early genetic studies from the 1990s seemed to lend weight to the possibility of multiple crossings; later studies have indicated that those lines branched off from each other quite recently and that 'modern Native Americans descended from a single source population.' In the 1980s and 1990s, physical anthropology and linguistics appeared to deliver a one-two punch in support of multiple-crossing scenarios. In 1986, Joseph Greenberg sorted Native American languages into three groups – Eskimo-Aleut, Na-Dene and Amerind (the last a controversial category of Greenberg's own devising) – each corresponding to a separate migration. In 1994, the 'sinodonty' thesis, based on Christy Turner's examination of 15,000 dental samples, likewise envisioned three crossings. Turner's work continues to hold interest, but Greenberg's classificatory system has fallen into disrepute, with critics of his method using its principles to 'prove', for example, that Finnish belongs to the Amerind family. Taking a different tack, linguists like Johanna Nichols have since the 1990s proclaimed it 'absolutely unambiguous' that the sheer diversity of languages in the New World would require it to have been inhabited for at least 35,000 years. This assumes a constant rate of linguistic evolution, as if such changes could be carbon-dated, and opponents have countered that rapid dispersion into a large land mass with multifarious ecosystems would be more than enough to cause rapid and considerable linguistic drift.

2 Tim Ingold, *Herders, Pastoralists and Ranchers* (Cambridge, 1980), p. 80; and, for the 'guerrilla warfare' metaphor, Stephen Mithin, *After the Ice: A Global Human History, 20,000–5,000 BC* (London, 2003), pp. 246–57, 385–6. Also see John F. Hoffecker and Scott Elias, *Human Ecology of Beringia* (New York, 2007), pp. 72–5; Igor Krupnik, *Arctic Adaptations: Native Whalers and Reindeer Herders of Northern Eurasia* (Hanover, NH, 1993), pp. 79–80, 124–5, 216–49; and Clive Ponting, *A Green History of the World* (New York, 1991), pp. 34–5.

3 Terms that define stages of cultural and technological development are difficult to apply across different regions. Based on conventions common among those who study northern Europe, I have assigned the following dates to the standard prehistoric eras: Paleolithic (prior to 8000 BCE), Mesolithic (*c.* 8000–4000 BCE), Neolithic (*c.* 4000–1800 BCE), Bronze Age (*c.* 1800–1000 BCE), and Iron Age (*c.* 1000 BCE–800 CE) – although some prefer a date of 500 BCE as the dividing point between the Bronze and Iron Ages.

4 N. K. Rerikh [Roerich], 'Drevneishie finskie khramy' ['The Most Ancient Temples of Finland'], *Starye gody*, 2 (February 1908), pp. 75–86.

5 Cited in Ingegerd Holand, 'Managing the Sámi Cultural Heritage in Norway: The Legal Landscape', in *Northern Ethnographic Landscapes: Perspectives from Circumpolar Nations*, ed. Igor Krupnik, Rachel Mason and Tonia W. Horton (Washington, DC, 2004), p. 95.

6 Adapted from M. G. Levin, *Ethnic Origins of the Peoples of Northern Asia* [Russian, 1958] (Toronto, 1963), pp. 3–7. Also see A. P. Okladnikov, *Ancient Population of Siberia and Its Cultures* (Cambridge, MA, 1959); and Krupnik, *Arctic Adaptations*, pp. 8–11.

7 Okladnikov, *Ancient Population*, p. 33.

8 'Lost Visions, Forgotten Dreams' exhibition held at the Canadian Museum of Civilization from 17 October 1996 until 19 May 1997, see www.civilization.ca, accessed 25 January 2012.

9 '5,000 Years of Inuit History and Heritage', available at Inuit Tapiriit Kanatami, www.itk.ca, accessed 25 January 2012.

10 Although familial ties between the Paleoeskimos and the modern Eskimo-Inuit were once assumed, they are no longer taken as certain, and are considered unlikely by some. Also, scholars differ as to which peoples should be included in the categories 'Paleoeskimo' or ASTt; some apply these terms to the Dorset, while others do not.

11 Farley Mowat, *People of the Deer* [1951] (New York, 1971), p. 211.

12 Interview with Netsilik Inuit living west of Hudson Bay, conducted in 1923 by the Fifth Thule Expedition. Cited in 'Lost Visions, Forgotten Dreams', Canadian Museum of Civilization.

13 Henrik Rink, *Danish Greenland* [1877] (Montreal, 1974), p. 136.

14 *Eskimo Songs and Stories Collected by Knud Rasmussen on the Fifth Thule Expedition* (New York, 1973), pp. 46–8; also see Pamela R. Stern, *The A to Z of the Inuit* (Lanham, MD, 2009), pp. 136–7.

15 Knud Rasmussen, *Intellectual Culture of the Iglulik Eskimo*, vol. II [1929] (New York, 1976), p. 54.

16 Fridtjof Nansen, *In Northern Mists: Arctic Exploration in Early Years* (London, 1911), p. 314.

3

Incursions: 1500 to 1800

1 George E. Tyson, *Arctic Experiences* (London, 1874), p. 209.

2 McClure and Boas cited in Barry Lopez, *Arctic Dreams* (New York, 1986), pp. 286–92.

3 Henrik Rink, *Danish Greenland* [1877] (Montreal, 1974), p. 137.

4 Clive Ponting, *A Green History of the World* (New York, 1991), pp. 32–3; see also Igor Krupnik, *Arctic Adaptations: Native Whalers and Reindeer Herders of Northern Eurasia* (Hanover, NH, 1993), pp. 75–80, 230–49.

5 Cited in Fred Bruemmer and William E. Taylor, Jr, *The Arctic World* (New York, 1989), p. 119.

6 Cited in Karen Oslund, *Imagining Iceland* (Seattle, WA, 2011), p. 92.

7 Giles Fletcher, *Of the Russe Commonwealth* [1591], cited in Richard Hakluyt, *The Principal Navigations, Voyages, Traffiques and Discoveries of the English Nation* (Glasgow, 1903), vol. III, p. 389.

8 Cited in Benson Bobrick, *East of the Sun: The Epic Conquest and Tragic History of Siberia* (New York, 1993), p. 109.

9 Samuel Hearne, *A Journey from Prince of Wales' Fort in Hudson's Bay, to the Northern Ocean* [1771] (Toronto, 1911), p. 180.

10 Cited in Bruemmer and Taylor, *Arctic World*, p. 125.

11 Cited in Sam Hall, *The Fourth World: The Heritage of the Arctic and Its Destruction* (New York, 1987), p. 98.

12 Cited in W. H. Dall, 'A Critical Review of Bering's First Expedition, 1725–1730', *National Geographic*, 11 (1890), pp. 135–43.

13 Bruemmer's assessment in *The Arctic World*, p. 116.

14 Steller's journal cited in Orcott Frost, *Bering* (New Haven, CT, 2003), p. 162.

15 Cited in John McCannon, *Red Arctic* (New York, 1998), pp. 93, 115.

4
Crusades: 1800 to 1914

1 An English-language version of *Třicet let na zlatém severu* ('Thirty Years in the Golden North'), introduced by Karel Čapek, was published by Macmillan in 1932. Also see Rudolf Krejčí, *Pravda a fikce o životě Jana Welzla*, or 'Truth and Fiction about the Life of Jan Welzl' (Prague, 1997). More recently, the acclaimed children's author and illustrator Peter Sis has used the Welzl tale as the inspiration for *A Small Tall Tale from the Far Far North* (New York, 1993).

2 Cited in Lyle Dick, *Muskox Land: Ellesmere Island in the Age of Contact* (Calgary, 2001), p. 485.

3 John Barrow, *Voyages of Discovery and Research within the Arctic Regions, from the Year 1818 to the Present Time* (London, 1846), pp. 16–17.

4 Simpson's journal cited by Clive Holland, 'Sir John Franklin', in *Dictionary of Canadian Biography Online*, at www.biographi.ca, accessed 25 January 2012.

5 Cited in Barry Lopez, *Arctic Dreams* (New York, 1986), p. 343.

6 Mary Shelley, *Frankenstein* (New York, 1983), p. 15.

7 In 1822, Friedrich painted a similar scene, *Wrecked Ship off the Coast of Greenland under a New Moon*, featuring a vessel called *The Hope*. *The Sea of Ice* is often confused with this work and sometimes given the erroneous subtitle or alternative title *Wreck of the Hope*. See Russell A. Potter, *Arctic Spectacles* (Seattle, WA, 2007), pp. 57–9.

8 Indexed by George Malcolm Laws in 1852. Available at 'The Traditional Ballad Index', at www.csufresno.edu, accessed 25 January 2012.

9 Charles Dickens, 'The Lost Polar Voyagers', *Household Words*, 245 (2 December 1854).

10 Wilson cited in Jean Malaurie, *Ultima Thule: Explorers and Natives of the Polar North* (New York, 2003), p. 78.

11 Cited in Charles Officer and Jake Page, *A Fabulous Kingdom: The Exploration of the Arctic* (New York, 2001), pp. 103–4.

12 John Ross, *Narrative of a Second Voyage in Search of a North-West Passage* (London, 1835), p. 257.

13 Ross cited in Russell A. Potter, *Arctic Spectacles: The Frozen North in Visual Culture, 1818–1875* (Seattle, WA, 2007), pp. 63–4.

14 Parry cited in Officer and Page, *A Fabulous Kingdom*, pp. 76–7.

15 Cited in Margaret Conrad and Alvin Finkel, *History of the Canadian Peoples* (Toronto, 2006), pp. 306–7.

16 Henrik Rink, *Danish Greenland* [1877] (Montreal, 1974), p. 296.

17 Jack London, *The Call of the Wild and Selected Stories* (New York, 1960), p. 13.

18 Henri Lefebvre, *The Production of Space* (Oxford, 1991).

19 Cited in Dick, *Muskox Land*, p. 267.

20 Cited in Kenneth S. Coates and William R. Morrison, 'Treaty Research Report: Treaty No. 11 (1921)', *Indian and Northern Affairs Canada*, available at www.ainc-inac.gc.ca, accessed 25 January 2012.

21 John Muir, *Travels in Alaska* (Boston, MA, 1915), p. 14.

22 Cited by W. Gillies Ross, 'Canadian Sovereignty in the Arctic: The *Neptune* Expedition of 1903–04', *Arctic*, XXIX/2 (1976), pp. 87–105.

23 Strindberg's sentiments as paraphrased in Peter Davidson, *The Idea of North* (London, 2004), p. 11.

24 Constantine Krypton, *The Northern Sea Route: Its Place in Russian Economic History before 1917* (New York, 1953), p. 81.

25 D. I. Mendeleev, cited in *Sovetskaia Arktika* (June 1937), pp. 53–6, 71–6.

26 Unterberger's comment serves as the title for Andrei Znamenski's '"Vague Sense of Belonging to the Russian Empire": The Reindeer Chukchi's Status in Nineteenth Century Northeastern Siberia', *Arctic Anthropology*, XXXVI/1–2 (1999), pp. 19–36.

27 Joseph Conrad, 'Geography and Some Explorers', *National Geographic*, XLV/3 (March 1924), p. 253.

28 Jules Verne, foreword to 'Un Hivernage dans les Glaces' ['Winter Quarters'], in *Musée des Familles* (March 1855), p. 161, cited in Herbert R. Lottman, *Jules Verne: An Exploratory Biography* (New York, 1996), p. 62.

29 Robert E. Peary, 'Moving on the North Pole', *McClure's* (March 1899), p. 418; Pualuna, brother of the famed Inughuit scout Ootah, interviewed by Jean Malaurie in 1950–51, cited in Jean Malaurie, *The Last Kings of Thule* (Chicago, IL, 1982), p. 52.

30 Clements Markham, 'The Promotion of Further Discovery in the Arctic and in the Antarctic Regions', *The Geographical Journal*, IV/1 (1894), p. 7.

31 A. E. Nordenskiöld, 'Nordenskiöld on the Inland Ice of Greenland', *Science*, II/44 (1883), pp. 732–8.

32 Cited in David Thomas Murphy, *German Exploration of the Polar World* (Lincoln, NE, 2002), p. 20. Emphasis in the original.

33 Cited in Bruce Henderson, *Fatal North: Adventure and Survival aboard USS 'Polaris'* (New York, 2001), p. 89.

34 William Morris, 'Gunnar's Howe Above the House at Lithend', the 29th poem in the cycle *Poems by the Way* (London, 1891).

35 George Washington DeLong, *The Voyage of the 'Jeannette'* (Boston, MA, 1884), vol. II, p. 782.

36 Karl Weyprecht, 'Scientific Work of the Second Austro-Hungarian Polar Expedition, 1872–4', *Journal of the Royal Geographical Society of London*, XLV (1875), pp. 32–3 ('steeplechase'); Weyprecht cited in 'The First International Polar Year, 1881–1884', National Oceanic and Atmospheric Administration, available at www.arctic.noaa.gov, accessed 25 January 2012 ('with instruments').

37 Cited in Officer and Page, *A Fabulous Kingdom*, pp. 132–3.

38 Salomon Andrée, *The Andrée Diaries* (London, 1931), p. 86.

39 Fridtjof Nansen, *Farthest North* (London, 1897), p. 384.

40 Sam Hall, *The Fourth World: The Heritage of the Arctic and Its Destruction* (New York, 1987), p. 91.

41 Robert E. Peary, *The North Pole* (New York, 1910), p. 333.

42 Cited in John Edward Weems, *Race for the Pole* (New York, 1960), p. 27.

43 Cited in Dick, *Muskox Land*, p. 382.

44 As translated by Murphy, *German Exploration of the Polar World*, 167.

45 Franz Boas, journal entry of 23 December 1883, in Douglas Cole, 'Franz Boas' Baffin Island Letter-Diary, 1883–1884', in *Observers Observed: Essays on Ethnographical Fieldwork*, vol. 1, ed. George W. Stocking (Madison, WI, 1983), p. 33.

46 *Popular Science Monthly* (November 1902), p. 64.

47 Vilhjalmur Stefansson, *My Life with the Eskimo* (London, 1913), pp. 173–4.

48 'Ernest de Koven Leffingwell', www.explorenorth.com/library/bios/leffingwell .html, accessed 25 January 2012.

49 As cited in Pierre Berton, *The Arctic Grail* (Toronto, 1988), p. 581. Emphasis in the original.

50 Lopez, *Arctic Dreams*, p. 389.

5
Subjugations: 1914 to 1945

1 Giulio Douhet, *The Command of the Air* [1921] (Washington, DC, 1983), p. 3.

2 *The Eskimo Book of Knowledge* (London, 1931), pp. 16, 62.

3 Lord Kelvin used the phrase 'polar Mediterranean' in an 1877 address to the Geological Society of Glasgow; see W. T. Kelvin, *Popular Lectures and Addresses* (Cambridge, 2011), p. 282. The 'torch' comment appears in Vilhjalmur Stefansson, *My Life with the Eskimo* (New York, 1913), p. 15. Nansen cited in John McCannon, *Red Arctic: Polar Exploration and the Myth of the North in the Soviet Union, 1932–1939* (Oxford, 1998), p. 89.

4 Cited in David Thomas Murphy, *German Exploration of the Polar World* (Lincoln, NE, 2002), p. 110.

5 Rockwell Kent, *Wilderness: A Journal of Quiet Adventure in Alaska* (New York, 1920), p. 1.

6 Aleksandr I. Solzhenitsyn, *The Gulag Archipelago Two* (New York, 1975), p. 644.

7 Cited in Leona Toker, 'Varlam Shalamov's Kolyma', in *Between Heaven and Hell: The Myth of Siberia in Russian Culture*, ed. Galya Diment and Yuri Slezkine (New York, 1993), p. 151.

8 *Sovetskii Sever*, 3 (April 1932), p. 94.

9 *Polar Times*, 5 (October 1937), p. 2.

10 Cited in Carroll V. Glines, *Polar Aviation* (New York, 1964), p. 41.

11 Hugo Eckener, *My Zeppelins* (New York, 1980), p. 129.

12 J. M. Scott, *The Private Life of Polar Exploration* (Edinburgh, 1982), p. 80, for Ellsworth; and Arthur Koestler, *Arrow in the Blue* (New York, 1952), pp. 337–8.

13 Koestler, *Arrow in the Blue*, p. 341.

14 'Malygin and Graf Zeppelin Meet in Arctic', *Soviet Union Review*, IX/9–10 (1931), p. 190.

15 Isaiah Bowman, 'Polar Exploration', *Science*, LXXII/1870 (1930), p. 441.

16 Cited in Brian Garfield, *The Thousand-Mile War: World War II in Alaska and the Aleutians* (Fairbanks, AK, 1995), p. 14.

6

Contaminations: 1945 to 1991

1 Cited in Elizabeth E. Elliot-Meisel, 'Arctic Focus: The Royal Canadian Navy in Arctic Waters, 1946–1949', *Northern Mariner*, IX/2 (1999), pp. 23–39.

2 Sam Hall, *The Fourth World: The Heritage of the Arctic and Its Destruction* (New York, 1987), p. 204.

3 Niobe Thompson, *Settlers on the Edge* (Vancouver, 2008), p. 42, in slightly modified form.

4 An observer quoted in Viktor Adamsky and Yuri Smirnov, 'Moscow's Biggest Bomb', *Cold War International History Project*, 4 (Fall 1994), pp. 3, 19–21. The 'sky went red' comment comes from here as well.

5 Cited in Hall, *The Fourth World*, pp. 212–13.

6 Bernt Balchen, 'Ice-Free Arctic Ocean Near?' *Christian Science Monitor* (8 June 1972).

7 Donald G. Callaway, 'Landscapes of Tradition, Landscapes of Resistance', in *Northern Ethnographic Landscapes*, ed. Igor Krupnik, Rachel Mason and Tonia W. Horton (Washington, DC, 2004), p. 198. Also see James C. Scott, *Weapons of the Weak: Everyday Forms of Peasant Resistance* (New Haven, CT, 1985).

8 Cited in Gretel Ehrlich, *In the Empire of Ice* (Washington, DC, 2010), p. 201.

9 Wade Davis, *The Clouded Leopard* (Vancouver, 1998), p. 43.

10 Michael Kusugak, *Arctic Stories* (Toronto, 1998), pp. 28–40.

11 Farley Mowat, *The Siberians* [1970] (Toronto, 1982), p. 68.

12 Cited in 'General Resources: Resources', Northern Resources Portal, University of Saskatchewan, available at http://scaa.usask.ca/gallery/northern, accessed 25 January 2012.

13 John G. Diefenbaker, 'The Role the North Should Play in Canadian Development', notes for a lecture given at Carleton University, Ottawa, 25 September 1968.

14 'Mackenzie Valley Pipeline: 37 Years of Negotiation', CBC News, 11 January 2011, available at www.cbc.ca, accessed 25 January 2012.

15 Cited in Hall, *The Fourth World*, pp. 160–61.

16 Peter Høeg, *Smilla's Sense of Snow* (Toronto, 1997), p. 95. The book was published in the UK as *Miss Smilla's Feeling for Snow*.

17 Ingegerd Holand, 'Managing the Sámi Cultural Heritage in Norway: The Legal Landscape', in *Northern Ethnographic Landscapes*, ed. Krupnik et al., pp. 90–91.

18 Paul R. Josephson, *Industrialized Nature: Brute Force Technology and the Transformation of the Natural World* (Washington, DC, 2002). Also see his 'War on Nature as Part of the Cold War: The Strategic and Ideological Roots of Environmental Degradation in the Soviet Union', in *Environmental Histories of the Cold War*, ed. J. R. McNeill and Corinna R. Unger (Cambridge, 2010).

19 Owen Lattimore, 'New Road to Asia', *National Geographic*, LXXXVI (1944), p. 657.

20 Yuri Slezkine, *Arctic Mirrors: Russia and the Small Peoples of the North* (Ithaca, NY, 1994), p. 352.

21 James Forsyth, *A History of the Peoples of Siberia* (Cambridge, 1992), p. 397.

22 Cited in ibid., p. 395.

23 'Researchers Warn Arctic Fishing Under-Reported', Reuters.com (4 February 2011), based on Dirk Zeller et al., 'Arctic Fisheries Catches in Russia, USA, and Canada', *Polar Biology*, XXXIV/7 (2011), pp. 955–73.

24 George W. Wenzel, *Animal Rights, Human Rights: Ecology, Economy, and Ideology in the Canadian Arctic* (Toronto, 1991). See also Milton M. R. Freeman, *Endangered Peoples of the Arctic* (Westport, CT, 2000); and Finn Lynge, *Arctic Wars: Animal Rights, Endangered Peoples* (Hanover, NH, 1992).

25 Description coined by Roger Howard, *The Arctic Gold Rush* (London, 2009), p. 3.

7

Extinctions? 1991 to the Present

1 Andrew E. Kramer and Clifford Krauss, 'Russia Embraces Risky Offshore Arctic Drilling', *New York Times* (15 February 2011). Also see Will Englund and Brad Plummer, 'ExxonMobil Signs Russian Oil Pact', *Washington Post* (30 August 2011).

2 Scott G. Borgerson, 'Arctic Meltdown: The Economic and Security Implications of Global Warming', *Foreign Affairs*, LXXXVII/2 (2008), pp. 63–77. See also Michael T. Klare, *Resource Wars: The New Landscape of Global Conflict* (New York, 2002).

3 Cited in Matthias Schepp and Gerald Traufetter, 'Riches at the North Pole: Russia Unveils Aggressive Arctic Plans', *Spiegel Online International*, 29 January 2009.

4 Lawson W. Brigham, 'The Arctic', *Foreign Policy* (September–October 2010), pp. 70–74.

5 *Science Daily*, 31 January 2008; 'The Arctic After the Gulf', *New York Times* (25 May 2010); Kramer and Krauss, 'Russia Embraces Risky Offshore Arctic Drilling'; and Debra Black, 'Why a Gulf-Style Oil Spill Would Be Even More Devastating in Canada', *Toronto Star* (8 June 2010).

6 Kramer and Krauss, 'Russia Embraces Risky Offshore Arctic Drilling'.

7 Roger Howard, *The Arctic Gold Rush* (London, 2009), pp. 68–9.

8 'Limits of Norway's Arctic Seabed Agreed', BarentsObserver.com (16 April 2009).

9 *Open Media Reseach Institute Daily Digest* (19 October 1995).

10 Cited in John McCannon, 'The Drive for the Arctic', *Ottawa Citizen* (10 August 2007); and Howard, *The Arctic Gold Rush*, p. 205, respectively.

11 'The 15th century' in *Montreal Gazette* (2 August 2007); and 'a joke' on Bloomberg.com (30 May 2008).

12 'Russia Hopes to Promote Arctic Dialogue', *Moscow News* (21 September 2010).

13 'New Cold War', *Atlanta Journal-Constitution* (13 February 2009); Tom Robertsen, 'Making New Ambitions Work: The Transformation of Norwegian Special Operations Forces', *Defence and Security Studies*, 1 (2007), p. 67 ('gunboat diplomacy').

14 Peter Høeg, *Smilla's Sense of Snow* (Toronto, 1997), p. 24.

15 Sam Hall, *The Fourth World: The Heritage of the Arctic and Its Destruction* (New York, 1987), p. 217.

16 Paul Starobin, 'Send Me to Siberia: Oil Transforms a Russian Outpost', *National Geographic*, CCXVI (June 2009), pp. 69–85.

17 *Siku News* (10 June 2006).

18 Igor Krupnik, Rachel Mason and Tonia W. Horton, eds, *Northern Ethnographic Landscapes: Perspectives from Circumpolar Nations* (Washington, DC, 2004), p. 5.

19 Wade Davis, *The Clouded Leopard* (Vancouver, 1998), p. 42.

20 Richard Cairney, 'End Whaling Moratorium, Researcher Says', *University of Alberta ExpressNews* (19 December 2002).

21 Barry Lopez, *Arctic Dreams* (New York, 1986), pp. 148–9.

22 Ron Lindsay of the University of Washington, cited in Alun Anderson, *After the Ice: Life, Death, and Geopolitics in the New Arctic* (Washington, DC, 2009), p. 99.

23 Randy Boswell, 'Scientists Warn Caribou on "Road to Extinction"', *National Post* (13 July 2011).

24 Cited in Howard, *The Arctic Gold Rush*, p. 32.

25 Matt McGrath, 'Arctic "Tipping Point" May Not Be Reached', BBC News online (4 August 2011).

26 Deborah Zabarenko, 'Warmer Arctic Probably Permanent, Scientists Say', Reuters (21 October 2010).

27 Gloria L. Manney et al., 'Unprecedented Arctic Ozone Loss in 2011', *Nature*, CLXXVIII (27 October 2011), pp. 469–75.

28 Justin Gillis, 'Cold Jumps Arctic "Fence", Stoking Winter's Fury', *New York Times* (24 January 2011); and Zabarenko, 'Warmer Arctic'. On other matters discussed in this section, see 'Arctic Ocean Has Become Less Salty, More Unstable', *Montreal Gazette* (29 March 2011); Deborah Zabarenko, 'Polar Bears and Walruses at Risk as Arctic Ice Melts', Reuters (9 February 2011); Margaret Munro, 'Cut Greenhouse Gas Emissions or Polar Bears Doomed, Report Says', *Vancouver Sun* (15 December 2010); Thomas Homer-Dixon, 'Disaster at the Top of the World', *New York Times* (23 August 2010).

29 Ola M. Johannessen, 'Decreasing Arctic Sea Ice Mirrors Increasing CO_2 on Decadal Time Scale', *Atmospheric and Oceanic Letters*, I/1 (2008), pp. 51–6.

30 *Science Daily* (31 January 2008).

31 Scott G. Borgerson and Caitlyn Antrim, 'An Arctic Circle of Friends', *New York Times* (28 March 2009).

32 Anderson, *After the Ice*, p. 10.

33 Anita Maurstad, 'Cultural Seascapes: Preserving Local Fishermen's Knowledge in Northern Norway', in *Northern Ethnographic Landscapes*, ed. Krupnik et al., pp. 282.

34 *The Globe and Mail* (1 October 2003).

BIBLIOGRAPHY

Reference Works

Damas, David, ed., *Arctic: Handbook of North American Indians* (Washington, DC, 1984)

Hayes, Derek, *Historical Atlas of the Arctic* (Vancouver, 2003)

Helms, June, ed., *Subarctic: Handbook of North American Indians* (Washington, DC, 1981)

Mills, William James, and David Clammer, *Exploring Polar Frontiers: A Historical Encyclopedia*, 2 vols (Santa Barbara, CA, 2003)

Nuttall, Mark, ed., *Encyclopaedia of the Arctic*, 3 vols (London, 2005)

Stern, Pamela R., *The A to Z of the Inuit* (Lanham, MD, 2009)

General

Anderson, Alun, *After the Ice: Life, Death, and Geopolitics in the New Arctic* (Washington, DC, 2009)

Armstrong, Terence, et al., eds, *The Circumpolar North: A Political and Economic Geography of the Arctic and Sub-Arctic* (London, 1978)

Baird, P. D., *The Polar World* (New York, 1965)

Berton, Pierre, *The Arctic Grail* (Toronto, 1988)

Borgerson, Scott G., 'Arctic Meltdown: The Economic and Security Implications of Global Warming', *Foreign Affairs*, LXXXVII/2 (2008), pp. 63–77

Brigham, Lawson W. 'Think Again: The Arctic', *Foreign Policy* (September–October 2010), pp. 70–74

Bruemmer, Fred, and William E. Taylor, Jr, *The Arctic World* (New York, 1989)

Byers, Michael, *Who Owns the Arctic? Understanding Sovereignty Disputes in the North* (Vancouver, 2010)

Collis, Dirmid R. F., *Arctic Languages: An Awakening* (Paris, 1990)

Cosgrove, Denis, and Veronica della Dora, eds, *High Places: Cultural Geographies of Mountains, Ice, and Science* (London, 2009)

Davidson, Peter, *The Idea of North* (London, 2004)

Dodds, Klaus, 'A Polar Mediterranean? Accessibility, Resources and Sovereignty in the Arctic Ocean', *Global Policy*, I/3 (2010), pp. 303–11

Ehrlich, Gretel, *In the Empire of Ice: Encounters in a Changing Landscape* (Washington, DC, 2010)

Emmerson, Charles, *The Future History of the Arctic* (New York, 2010)

Fogelson, Nancy, *Arctic Exploration and International Relations, 1900–1952* (Fairbanks, AK, 1992)

Franckx, Erik, *Maritime Claims in the Arctic* (Dordrecht, 1993)

Freeman, Milton M. R., *Endangered Peoples of the Arctic* (Westport, CT, 2000)

Glines, Carroll V., *Polar Aviation* (New York, 1964)

Hall, Sam, *The Fourth World: The Heritage of the Arctic and Its Destruction* (New York, 1987)

Hoffecker, John F., *A Prehistory of the North* (New Brunswick, NJ, 2005)

Howard, Roger, *The Arctic Gold Rush: The New Race for Tomorrow's Natural Resources* (London, 2009)

Ingold, Tim, *Herders, Pastoralists and Ranchers: Reindeer Economies and Their Transformations* (Cambridge, 1980)

Jackson, L. J., and P. T. Thatcher, eds, *Caribou and Reindeer Herders of the Northern Hemisphere* (Aldershot, 1997)

Kirwan, L. P., *A History of Polar Exploration* (New York, 1959)

Krupnik, Igor, Rachel Mason and Tonia W. Horton, eds, *Northern Ethnographic Landscapes: Perspectives from Circumpolar Nations* (Washington, DC, 2004)

Lewis, Jon E., ed., *The Mammoth Book of Polar Journeys* (New York, 2007)

Lopez, Barry, *Arctic Dreams* (New York, 1986)

McGhee, Robert, *The Last Imaginary Place: A Human History of the Arctic* (Oxford, 2005)

Malaurie, Jean, *Ultima Thule: Explorers and Natives of the Polar North* (New York, 2003)

Mirsky, Jeanette, *To the Arctic! The Story of Northern Exploration from Earliest Times to the Present* (Chicago, IL, 1970)

Officer, Charles, and Jake Page, *A Fabulous Kingdom: The Exploration of the Arctic* (New York, 2001)

Osherenko, Gail, and Oran R. Young, eds, *The Age of the Arctic: Hot Conflicts and Cold Realities* (Cambridge, 2005)

Polar Peoples (London, 1994)

Potter, Russell A., *Arctic Spectacles: The Frozen North in Visual Culture, 1818–1875* (Seattle, WA, 2007)

Price, Neil S., ed., *The Archaeology of Shamanism* (London, 2001)

Riffenburgh, Beau, *The Myth of the Explorer: The Press, Sensationalism, and Geographical Discovery* (Cambridge, 1993)

Scott, J. M., *The Private Life of Polar Exploration* (Edinburgh, 1982)

Vaughan, Richard, *The Arctic: A History* (Phoenix Mill, Stroud, 1994)

Wheeler, Sara, *Magnetic North: Notes from the Arctic Circle* (New York, 2011)

North America and Beringia

Bandi, H. G., *Eskimo Prehistory* (Fairbanks, AK, 1969)

Barnhardt, Carol, 'A History of Schooling for Alaska Native People', *Journal of American Indian Education*, XL/1 (2001)

Barrow, John, *Voyages of Discovery and Research within the Arctic Regions, from the Year 1818 to the Present Time* (London, 1846)

Bloom, Lisa, *Gender on Ice: American Ideologies of Polar Expeditions* (Minneapolis, MN, 1993)

Boas, Franz, *The Central Eskimo* (Washington, DC, 1888)

Bockstoce, John R., *Furs and Frontiers in the Far North: The Contest among Native and Foreign Nations for the Bering Strait Fur Trade* (New Haven, CT, 2009)

—, *Whales, Ice, and Men: The History of Whaling in the Western Arctic* (Seattle, WA, 1995)

Brody, Hugh, *Living Arctic: Hunters of the Canadian North* (London, 1987)

—, *The People's Land: Inuit, Whites and the Eastern Arctic* (Toronto, 1975)

Bryce, Robert M., *Cook and Peary: The Polar Controversy, Resolved* (Mechanicsburg, PA, 1996)

Burch, Ernest S., Jr, *The Iñupiaq Eskimo Nations of Northwestern Alaska* (Fairbanks, AK, 1998)

Chance, Norman, *The Iñupiat and Arctic Alaska: An Ethnography of Development* (San Francisco, CA, 1990)

Cole, Douglas, 'Franz Boas' Baffin Island Letter-Diary, 1883–1884', in *Observers Observed: Essays on Ethnographical Fieldwork*, vol. 1, ed. George W. Stocking (Madison, WI, 1983)

Colombo, John Robert, ed., *Poems of the Inuit* (Toronto, 1981)

Conrad, Margaret, and Alvin Finkel, *History of the Canadian Peoples* (Toronto, 2006)

Cruikshank, Julie, *Do Glaciers Listen? Local Knowledge, Colonial Encounters, and Social Imagination* (Vancouver, 2005)

Dall, W. H., 'A Critical Review of Bering's First Expedition, 1725–1730', *National Geographic*, II (1890), pp. 135–43

David, Robert G., *The Arctic in the British Imagination, 1818–1914* (Manchester, 2000)

Davies, T. D., 'New Evidence Places Peary at the Pole', *National Geographic*, CLXXVII/I (1990), pp. 44–61

Dick, Lyle, *Muskox Land: Ellesmere Island in the Age of Contact* (Calgary, 2001)

Dickason, Olive Patricia, and David T. McNab, *Canada's First Nations: A History of Founding Peoples from Earliest Times* (New York, 2009)

Dumond, Don, *The Eskimos and the Aleuts* (London, 1987)

Elliot-Meisel, Elizabeth B., *Arctic Diplomacy: Canada and the United States in the Northwest Passage* (Frankfurt, 1998)

—, 'Arctic Focus: The Royal Canadian Navy in Arctic Waters, 1946–1949', *Northern Mariner*, IX/2 (1999), pp. 23–39

The Eskimo Book of Knowledge (London, 1931)

Eskimo Poems from Canada and Greenland (Pittsburgh, PA, 1973)

Eskimo Songs and Stories Collected by Knud Rasmussen on the Fifth Thule Expedition (New York, 1973)

Fagan, Brian M., *Ancient North America* (London, 2005)

Fitzhugh, William, and Aron Cowell, eds, *Crossroads of Continents: Culture of Siberia and Alaska* (Washington, DC, 1988)

Fleming, Fergus, *Ninety Degrees North* (London, 2001)

Fossett, Renée, *In Order to Live Untroubled: Inuit of the Central Arctic, 1550 to 1940* (Winnipeg, 2001)

Frost, Orcutt, *Bering: The Russian Discovery of America* (New Haven, CT, 2003)

Garfield, Brian, *The Thousand-Mile War: World War II in Alaska and the Aleutians* (Fairbanks, AK, 1995)

Giddings, James Louis, *Ancient Man of the Arctic* (New York, 1967)

Goebel, Ted, et al., 'The Late Pleistocene Dispersal of Modern Humans in the Americas', *Science*, CCCXIX (14 March 2008), pp. 1497–1502

Grant, Shelagh D., *Polar Imperative: A History of Arctic Sovereignty in North America* (Vancouver, 2010)

Griffiths, Franklyn, ed., *Politics of the Northwest Passage* (Montreal, 1987)

Hearne, Samuel, *A Journey from Prince of Wales' Fort in Hudson's Bay, to the Northern Ocean* [1791] (Toronto, 1911)

Henderson, Bruce, *Fatal North: Adventure and Survival aboard USS 'Polaris'* (New York, 2001)

—, *True North: Peary, Cook, and the Race to the Pole* (New York, 2005)

Herbert, Wally, 'Did Peary Reach the Pole?' *National Geographic*, CLXXIV/3 (1988), pp. 414–24

Hopkins, David M., *The Bering Land Bridge* (Stanford, CA, 1967)

Jorgensen, Joseph G., *Oil Age Eskimos* (Berkeley, CA, 1990)

Kane, Elisha Kent, *Arctic Explorations* (Philadelphia, PA, 1856)

Karamaski, Theodore, *Fur Trade and Exploration: Opening the Far Northwest, 1821–1852* (Vancouver, 1983)

Kent, Rockwell, *Wilderness: A Journal of Quiet Adventure in Alaska* (New York, 1920)

Knuth, Eigil, *Archaeology of the Musk-Ox Way* (Paris, 1967)

Lackenbauer, P. Whitney, and Matthew Farish, 'The Cold War on Canadian Soil: Militarizing a Northern Environment', *Environmental History*, XII/4 (2007), pp. 920–50

Laguna, Frederica de, ed., *Tales from the Dena: Indian Stories from the Tanana, Koyukuk, and Yukon Rivers* (Seattle, WA, 1995)

Levere, Trevor, *Science and the Canadian Arctic: A Century of Exploration, 1818–1918* (New York, 1993)

Loomis, Chauncey, *Weird and Tragic Shores: The Story of Charles Francis Hall, Explorer* (New York, 1971)

Loukacheva, Natalia, *The Arctic Promise: Legal and Political Autonomy of Greenland and Nunavut* (Toronto, 2007)

McGhee, Robert, *Ancient People of the Arctic* (Vancouver, 1996)

—, *Canadian Arctic Prehistory* (Toronto, 1978)

Marston, M. R., *Men of the Tundra: Alaska Eskimos at War* (New York, 1969)

Mowat, Farley, *People of the Deer* [1951] (New York, 1971)

Muir, John, *Travels in Alaska* (Boston, MA, 1915)

Neatby, L. H., *In Quest of the Northwest Passage* (New York, 1958)

Nelson, Richard K., *Hunters of the Northern Forest* (Chicago, IL, 1973)

—, *Hunters of the Northern Ice* (Chicago, IL, 1969)

Norman, Howard, ed., *Northern Tales* (New York, 1990)

Paine, Robert, *The White Arctic* (St John's, NL, 1977)

Pálsson, Gisli, *Travelling Passions: The Hidden Life of Vilhjalmur Stefansson* (Winnipeg, 2009)

Peary, Robert E., *The North Pole* (New York, 1910)

Pullum, Geoffrey K., *The Great Eskimo Vocabulary Hoax* (Chicago, 1991)

Rasmussen, Knud, *Intellectual Culture of the Copper Eskimos* (Gyldendal, 1932)

—, *Intellectual Culture of the Iglulik Eskimo* [1929] (New York, 1976)

Rawlins, Dennis, *Peary at the North Pole: Fact or Fiction* (Washington, DC, 1973)

Ray, Dorothy Jean, *Eskimo Art* (Seattle, WA, 1977)

Robinson, Michael F., *The Coldest Crucible: Arctic Exploration and American Culture* (Chicago, IL, 2006)

Ross, John, *Narrative of a Second Voyage in Search of a North-West Passage* (London, 1835)

Ross, W. Gillies, 'Canadian Sovereignty in the Arctic: The *Neptune* Expedition of 1903–04', *Arctic*, XXIX/2 (1976), pp. 87–105

Schledermann, Peter, *Crossroads to Greenland* (Calgary, 1990)

Stefansson, Vilhjalmur, *The Friendly Arctic* (New York, 1921)

—, *My Life with the Eskimo* (New York, 1913)

Weems, John Edward, *Peary: The Explorer and the Man* (Boston, 1967)

Wenzel, George W., *Animal Rights, Human Rights: Ecology, Economy, and Ideology in the Canadian Arctic* (Toronto, 1991)

West, Frederick H., *The Archaeology of Beringia* (New York, 1981)

Zaslow, Morris, *The Opening of the Canadian North, 1870–1914* (Toronto, 1971)

Eurasia and Greenland

Albanov, Valerian, *In the Land of White Death* (New York, 2000)

Anderson, David G., *Identity and Ecology in Arctic Siberia: The Number One Reindeer Brigade* (Oxford, 2000)

Andrée, Salomon, *The Andrée Diaries* (London, 1931)

Armstrong, Terence, *The Russians in the Arctic* (Westport, CA, 1958)

—, *Russian Settlement of the North* (Cambridge, 1965)

Baev, Pavel K., *Russia's Arctic Policy: Geopolitics, Mercantilism and Identity-Building* (Helsinki, 2010)

Balzer, Marjorie M., ed., *Shamanic Worlds: Rituals and Lore of Siberia and Central Asia* (Armonk, NY, 1996)

Baron, Nick, *Soviet Karelia: Politics, Planning, and Terror in Stalin's Russia, 1920–1939* (London, 2007)

Barr, William, 'Baron von Toll's Last Expedition', *Arctic*, XXXIV/3 (1980), pp. 201–24

Bartels, Dennis A., and Alice L. Bartels, *When the North Was Red: Aboriginal Education in Soviet Siberia* (Montreal, 1995)

Bloch, Alexia, *Red Ties and Residential Schools: Indigenous Siberians in a Post-Soviet State* (Philadelphia, PA, 2004)

Bobrick, Benson, *East of the Sun: The Epic Conquest and Tragic History of Siberia* (New York, 1993)

Bogoras, Waldemar [Vladimir Bogoraz-Tan], *Chukchee Mythology* (Leiden, 1910)

Chernetsov, V. N., and W. Moszyńska, *Prehistory of Western Siberia* (Montreal, 1974)

Clark, Grahame, *The Earlier Stone Age Settlement of Scandinavia* (Cambridge, 1975)

Conquest, Robert, *Kolyma: The Arctic Death Camps* (Oxford, 1979)

DeLong, George Washington, *The Voyage of the 'Jeannette'* (Boston, MA, 1884)

Derry, T. K., *A History of Scandinavia* (Minneapolis, MN, 1979)

Diment, Galya, and Yuri Slezkine, *Between Heaven and Hell: The Myth of Siberia in Russian Culture* (New York, 1993)

Drivenes, Einar-Arne, 'Adolf Hoel – Polar Ideologue and Imperialist of the Polar Sea', *Acta Borealia*, XI/1 (1994), pp. 63–72

Fisher, R. H., *The Russian Fur Trade, 1550–1700* (Berkeley, CA, 1943)

Fletcher, Giles, *Of the Russe Commonwealth* [1591] (Cambridge, MA, 1966)

Forsyth, James, *A History of the Peoples of Siberia: Russia's North Asian Colony, 1581–1990* (Cambridge, 1992)

Friedman, Robert Marc, *The Expeditions of Harald Ulrik Sverdrup* (San Diego, CA, 1994)

Golovnev, A. B., and Gail Osherenko, *Siberian Survival: The Nenets and Their Story* (Ithaca, NY, 1999)

Grant, Bruce, *In the Soviet House of Culture: A Century of Perestroikas* (Princeton, NJ, 1995)

Gray, Patty A., *The Predicament of Chukotka's Indigenous Movement* (Cambridge, 2004)

Haüsler, Alexander, 'Burial Customs of the Ancient Hunters and Fishers of Northern Europe', *Arctic Archaeology*, V/I (1968), pp. 62–7

Hill, Alexander, ed., 'Russian and Soviet Naval Power in the Arctic', *Journal of Slavic Military Studies* special issue, XX/3 (2007)

Hilson, Mary, *The Nordic Model: Scandinavia Since 1945* (London, 2008)

Horensma, Pier, *The Soviet Arctic* (London, 1991)

Humphrey, Caroline, 'Theories of North Asian Shamanism', in *Soviet and Western Anthropology*, ed. Ernest Gellner (London, 1980)

Huntford, Roland, *Nansen* (London, 1997)

Hutton, Ronald, *Shamans: Siberian Spirituality and the Western Imagination* (London, 2001)

Jacobs, Ken, 'Returning to Oleni'ostrov', *Journal of Archaeological Anthropology*, XIV (December 1995), pp. 359–403

Jochelson, Waldemar [Iokhel'son, V.]. *The Koryak* (New York, 1905–8)

Jones, Gwyn, *A History of the Vikings* (Oxford, 1973)

Jones, R. H., *The Road to Russia: United States Lend-Lease Aid to the Soviet Union* (Norman, OK, 1969)

Jordan, B. B., and T. G. Jordan-Bychkov, *Siberian Village: Land and Life in the Sakha Republic* (Minneapolis, MN, 2001)

Kerttula, A. M., *Antler on the Sea: The Yupik and Chukchi of the Russian Far East* (Ithaca, NY, 2000)

Krupnik, Igor, *Arctic Adaptations: Native Whalers and Reindeer Herders of Northern Eurasia* (Hanover, NH, 1993)

Krypton, Constantine, *The Northern Sea Route: Its Place in Russian Economic History before 1917* (New York, 1953)

Kuzmin, Y. V., and S. V. Krivonogov, 'More about Diring Yuriak', *Geoarchaeology*, XIV/4 (1999), pp. 351–9

Levin, Maksim G., *Ethnic Origins of the Peoples of Northern Asia* [Russian ed., 1958] (Toronto, 1963)

Lincoln, W. Bruce, *The Conquest of a Continent: Siberia and the Russians* (New York, 1993)

McCannon, John, *Red Arctic: Polar Exploration and the Myth of the North in the Soviet Union, 1932–1939* (Oxford, 1998)

McDougall, Walter A., *Let the Sea Make a Noise: Four Hundred Years of Cataclysm, Conquest, War and Folly in the North Pacific* (New York, 1993)

Magnússon, Sigurdur, *Wasteland with Words: A Social History of Iceland* (London, 2010)

Malaurie, Jean, *The Last Kings of Thule: A Year Among the Polar Eskimos of Greenland* (Boston, MA, 1956)

Mann, Chris, and Christer Jörgensen, *Hitler's Arctic War* (New York, 2003)

Martin, Janet, *Treasure of the Land of Darkness: The Fur Trade and Its Significance for Medieval Russia* (Cambridge, 1986)

Michael, H. N., ed., *Studies in Siberian Ethnogenesis* (Toronto, 1962)

Mowat, Farley, *The Siberians* (London, 1970)

Murphy, David T., *German Exploration of the Polar World: A History, 1870–1940* (Lincoln, NE, 2002)

Nansen, Fridtjof, *Farthest North* (London, 1897)

—, *In Northern Mists: Arctic Exploration in Early Years* (London, 1911)

—, *Through Siberia: The Land of the Future* (London, 1914)

Nordenskiöld, A. E., 'Nordenskiöld on the Inland Ice of Greenland', *Science*, II/44 (1883), pp. 732–8

—, *The Voyage of the Vega Round Asia and Europe* (London, 1881)

Nordlander, David J., 'Origins of a Gulag Capital: Magadan and Stalinist Control in the Early 1930s', *Slavic Review*, LVII/4 (1998), pp. 791–812

Nordstrom, Byron J., *Scandinavia since 1500* (Minneapolis, MN, 2000)

Okladnikov, A. P., *Ancient Population of Siberia and Its Cultures* [Russian ed., 1956] (Cambridge, MA, 1959)

Oslund, Karen, *Imagining Iceland* (Seattle, WA, 2011)

Paine, Robert, *Herds of the Tundra: A Portrait of Saami Reindeer Pastoralism* (Washington, DC, 1994)

Pavlov, Pavel, et al., 'Human Presence in the European Arctic Nearly 40,000 Years Ago', *Nature*, CDXIII (6 September 2001), pp. 64–7

Pitulko, V. V., et al., 'The Yana RHS Site', *Science*, CCCIII (6 January 2004), pp. 52–6

Rethmann, Petra, *Tundra Passages: History and Gender in the Russian Far East* (University Park, PA, 2001)

Rink, Henrik, *Danish Greenland* [1877] (Montreal, 1974)

Riordan, James, *The Sun Maiden and the Crescent Moon: Siberian Folktales* (New York, 1989)

Rowe, Elana W., ed., *Russia and the North* (Ottawa, 2009)

Slezkine, Yuri, *Arctic Mirrors: Russia and the Small Peoples of the North* (Ithaca, NY, 1994)

Slobodin, Sergei, 'Western Beringia at the End of the Ice Age', *Arctic Anthropology*, XXXVIII/2 (2001), pp. 31–47

Ssorin-Chaikov, Nikolai V., *The Social Life of the State in Subarctic Siberia* (Stanford, CA, 2003)

Starobin, Paul, 'Send Me to Siberia: Oil Transforms a Russian Outpost', *National Geographic* (June 2008), pp. 60–85

Starokadomski, L. M., *Charting the Russian Northern Sea Route* (New York, 1976)

Stephen, John, *The Russian Far East: A History* (Stanford, CA, 1994)

Stoliar, Abram D., 'Milestones of Spiritual Evolution in Prehistoric Karelia', *Folklore*, 18–19 (Tartu, 2001), pp. 80–126

Sulimirski, Tadeusz, *Prehistoric Russia* (London, 1970)

Taracouzio, T. A., *Soviets in the Arctic* (New York, 1938)

Thompson, Niobe, *Settlers on the Edge: Identity and Modernization on Russia's Arctic Frontier* (Vancouver, 2008)

Treadgold, Donald W., *The Great Siberian Migration* (Princeton, NJ, 1957)

Van Deusen, Kira, *Raven and the Rock: Storytelling in Chukotka* (Seattle, WA, 1999)

Vasil'ev, Sergey A., 'The Final Paleolithic in Northern North Asia', *Arctic Anthropology*, XXXVIII/2 (2001), pp. 3–30

Vitebsky, Piers, *Reindeer People: Living with Animals and Spirits in Siberia* (Boston, MA, 2006)

Weiner, Douglas R., *A Little Corner of Freedom: Russian Nature Protection from Stalin to Gorbachev* (Berkeley, CA, 2002)

Welzl, Jan, *Thirty Years in the Golden North* (New York, 1932)

Wråkberg, Urban, 'Nature Conservationism and the Arctic Commons of Spitsbergen, 1900–1920', *Acta Borealia*, XXIII/1 (2006), pp. 1–23

Ziker, John Peter, *Peoples of the Tundra: Northern Peoples in the Post-Soviet Transition* (Prospect Heights, IL, 2002)

Znamenski, Andrei, '"Vague Sense of Belonging to the Russian Empire": The Reindeer Chukchi's Status in Nineteenth Century Northeastern Siberia', *Arctic Anthropology*, XXXVI/1–2 (1999), pp. 19–36

Science and the Environment

Adamsky, Viktor, and Yuri Smirnov, 'Moscow's Biggest Bomb', *Cold War International History Project*, 4 (Fall 1994), pp. 3, 19–21

Althoff, William F., *Drift Stations: Arctic Outposts of Superpower Science* (Dulles, VA, 2007)

Arctic Dinosaurs (NOVA/Big Island Pictures, 2008)

Barr, Susan, and Cornelia Lüdecke, *The History of the International Polar Years* (Berlin, 2010)

Barr, William, *The Expeditions of the First International Year* (Calgary, 1985)

Bocking, Stephen, 'A Disciplined Geography: Aviation, Science, and the Cold War in Northern Canada, 1945–1960', *Technology and Culture*, L/2 (2009), pp. 265–90

—, 'Science and Spaces in the Northern Environment', *Environmental History*, XII/4 (2007), pp. 867–94

Bravo, Michael, and Sverker Sörlin, *Narrating the Arctic: A Cultural History of Nordic Scientific Practices* (Canton, MA, 2002)

Doel, Ronald E., 'Quelle place pour les sciences de l'environnement physique dans l'histoire environnementale?' *Revue d'histoire modern et contemporaine*, LVI/4 (2009), pp. 137–64

Dunbar, Maxwell J., *Ecological Development in Polar Regions* (Englewood Cliffs, NJ, 1968)

—, 'Stability and Fragility in Arctic Ecosystems', *Arctic*, XXVI/3 (1973), pp. 179–86

Friedman, Robert Marc, 'Making the Aurora Norwegian: Science and Image in the Making of a Tradition', *Interdisciplinary Science Reviews*, XXXV/1 (2010), pp. 51–68

Hoffecker, John F., and Scott Elias, *Human Ecology of Beringia* (New York, 2007)

Irving, Laurence, *Arctic Life of Birds and Mammals* (New York, 1972)

Josephson, Paul, *Industrialized Nature: Brute Force Technology and the Transformation of the Natural World* (Washington, DC, 2002)

—, 'War on Nature as Part of the Cold War: The Strategic and Ideological Roots of Environmental Degradation in the Soviet Union', in *Environmental Histories of the Cold War*, ed. J. R. McNeill and Corinna R. Unger (Cambridge, 2010)

Kohlhoff, Dean, *Amchitka and the Bomb: Nuclear Testing in Alaska* (Seattle, WA, 2002)

Krupnik, Igor, Michael A. Long and Scott E. Miller, eds, *Smithsonian at the Poles* (Washington, DC, 2009)

Launius, Roger D., James Roger Fleming and David H. DeVorkin, eds, *Globalizing Polar Science: Reconsidering the International Polar and Geophysical Years* (Washington, DC, 2010)

Linden, Eugene, *The Ragged Edge of the World: Encounters at the Frontier Where Modernity, Wildlands, and Indigenous Peoples Meet* (New York, 2011)

Lynge, Finn, *Arctic Wars: Animal Rights, Endangered Peoples* (Hanover, NH, 1992)

McKibben, Bill, *Eaarth: Making Life on a Tough New Planet* (New York, 2011)

Mithen, Steven, *After the Ice: A Global Human History, 20,000–5,000 BC* (London, 2003)

Piper, Liza, ed., 'History of Circumpolar Science and Technology', *Scientia Canadensis: Canadian Journal of the History of Science, Technology and Medicine* special issue, XXXIII/2 (2010)

Ponting, Clive, *A Green History of the World* (New York, 1991)

Radkau, Joachim, *Nature and Power: A Global History of the Environment* (Cambridge, 2008)

Remmert, Hermann, *Arctic Animal Ecology* (New York, 1980)

Shadian, Jessica M., and Monica Tennberg, eds, *Legacies and Change in Polar Sciences* (Farnham, Surrey, 2009)

Stephens, Sharon, 'Lapp Life after Chernobyl', *Natural History*, XCVI/12 (1997), pp. 32–42

Stoett, Peter, *The International Politics of Whaling* (Vancouver, 1997)

Vibe, Christian, *Arctic Animals in Relation to Climate Fluctuation* (Copenhagen, 1967)

Young, Oran, and Gail Osherenko, eds, *Polar Politics: Creating International Environmental Regimes* (Ithaca, NY, 1993)

Websites

ALFRED WEGENER INSTITUTE FOR POLAR AND MARINE RESEARCH
www.awi.de

ARCTIC COUNCIL
arctic-council.org

ARCTIC INSTITUTE OF NORTH AMERICA
www.arctic.ucalgary.ca

ARCTIC STUDIES CENTER OF THE NATIONAL MUSEUM OF NATURAL HISTORY
(SMITHSONIAN INSTITUTION)
www.mnh.si.edu/arctic

BARENTS REGION PORTAL
www.barentsinfo.org

BELLONA FOUNDATION
www.bellona.org

CANADIAN MUSEUM OF CIVILIZATION
www.civilization.ca

CIRCUMPOLAR CIVILIZATIONS (UNESCO)
www.arcticmuseum.com/en

EUROPEAN POLAR BOARD (EUROPEAN SCIENCE FOUNDATION)
www.esf.org/research-areas/polar-sciences

'GEOPOLITICS IN THE HIGH NORTH' RESEARCH PROGRAMME
www.geopoliticsnorth.org

INUIT CIRCUMPOLAR COUNCIL
www.inuitcircumpolar.com

NATIONAL OCEANIC AND ATMOSPHERIC ADMINISTRATION, ARCTIC THEME PAGE
www.arctic.noaa.gov

PEARY-MACMILLAN ARCTIC MUSEUM AND ARCTIC STUDIES CENTER (BOWDOIN UNIVERSITY)
www.bowdoin.edu/arctic-museum

POLARFLIGHT
polarflight.tripod.com

RUSSIAN STATE MUSEUM OF THE ARCTIC AND ANTARCTIC
www.polarmuseum.ru

SAAMI BLOG
saamiblog.blogspot.com

SCOTT POLAR RESEARCH INSTITUTE
www.spri.cam.ac.uk

SVALBARD MUSEUM
www.svalbardmuseum.no

UNIVERSITY OF THE ARCTIC
www.uarctic.org

ACKNOWLEDGEMENTS

The intellectual journey that led to the completion of this book began long ago, with the research I did on Soviet polar exploration for *Red Arctic*, my dissertation and first book. It seems fitting that I should begin with a renewed thanks to those who assisted me with that project, especially my main PhD advisers, Sheila Fitzpatrick and the late Richard Hellie, as well as my graduate-student cohort at the University of Chicago.

Since then, numerous scholars have generously involved me in conferences and research projects which sustained my interest in the Arctic and broadened my knowledge of it. Among these are the individuals who organized and participated in the Russian Academy of Sciences' 1999 Global Conference on Science and Politics in Oceanography and Arctic Exploration; the University of Toronto's Seventh International Conference on German–Soviet Medical and Scientific Relations between the Wars; the Horning Lecture Series on Science and Politics at Oregon State University; the 2002 International Conference on Conflict and Cooperation in the Arctic, in Kirkenes, Norway; and the 'Exploring Ice and Snow in the Cold War' Conference hosted in 2011 by the Rachel Carson Center for Environment and Society in Munich, Germany. These and other gatherings introduced me to a wonderful community of polar specialists, and much of what I learned from that community has found its way into this volume.

I also thank Alexander Hill and the *Journal of Slavic Military Studies* for asking me to contribute to its 'Russian and Soviet Naval Power in the Arctic' special issue in 2007, and Liza Piper of *Scientia Canadensis* for involving me in its special issue of 2010 on the history of circumpolar science and technology. Colby College in Maine was kind enough to name me a Goldfarb Center Visiting Fellow during its 2012 seminar on Historical and Environmental Aspects of Arctic Resource Development Policy for the 21st Century. During the years I have studied Siberia, the Arctic, and questions related to science and the environment, I have received advice and encouragement from too many people to list, but I particularly wish to acknowledge the goodwill of Daniel Alexandrov, Jim Andrews, Mark Bassin, Ron Doel, Paul Josephson, David Murphy, James Nolan and Douglas Weiner.

I am grateful to Michael Leaman at Reaktion Books for inviting me to write this book, and I have appreciated his patient guidance at every step of the process. Also at Reaktion, I am indebted to Harry Gilonis, Aimee Selby, John O'Donovan and Maria Kilcoyne for turning a raw manuscript into such an appealing product. Above all, I owe an iceberg-sized 'thank you' to my wife, Pamela Jordan. It is no exaggeration to say that this book owes its very existence to the sturdiness of her support and the sharpness of her editorial eye. In addition, my daughter Miranda, with her sprightly curiosity about polar bears, beluga whales and the Northern Lights, made writing polar history much more fun than it would have been otherwise. It is to Pam and Miranda that I dedicate this book.

PHOTO ACKNOWLEDGEMENTS

The author and publishers wish to express their thanks to the following sources of illustrative material and/or permission to reproduce it (some locations are also given below for reasons of brevity):

Photos author: pp. 220, 242; photo Dean Biggins/U.S. Fish and Wildlife Service: p. 19; from Waldemar Bogoras [Vladimir Bogoraz], *Publications of the Jessup North Pacific Expedition (Memoirs of the American Museum of Natural History)*, vol. VII: *The Chukchee* (Leiden and New York, 1904–9): p. 54; from *Fridtjof Nansen's "Farthest North": Being the record of a voyage of exploration of the ship 'Fram', 1893–96, and of a fifteen months' sleigh journey by Dr. Nansen and Lieut. Johansen . . .* (London, 1897): p. 178; from Emil Hanselmann, *Naturgeschichte des Tierreichs* (Stuttgart, 1868): p. 20; from Karl Koldeway, *Die zweite Deutsche Nordpolarfahrt in den Jahren 1869 und 1870 unter Führung des Kapitän Karl Koldeway*, 2 vols (Leipzig, 1873–4): p. 169; Kunsthalle, Hamburg: p. 177; from Knud Leem, *Knud Leems Beskrivelse over Finmarkens Lapper, deres Tungemaal, Levemaade og forrige Afgudsdyrkelse, oplyst ved mange Kaabberstykker . . .* (Kiæbenhavn [Copenhagen], 1767): p. 48; photo Eilev Leren/Statoil: p. 288; Library of Congress, Washington, DC: pp. 63 (Prints and Photographs Division – Edward S. Curtis Collection), 122 (Geography and Map Division), 179 (Prints and Photographs Division – George Grantham Bain Collection); from *Mittheilungen aus Justus Perthes Geographischer Anstalt über wichtige neue Erforschungen auf dem Gesamtgebiet der Geographie von Dr. A. Petermann*, 26 (1869): p. 140; Nasjonalbiblioteket, Oslo: p. 215; photo National Aeronautics and Space Administration (www.nasa.gov): p. 243; photo National Archives, USA (National Archives Gift Collection of Materials Relating to Polar Regions): p. 189; photo Jennith Peart (bog.araska.org): p. 284; courtesy of the Perry-Castañeda Library Map Collection, University of Texas: pp. 6, 8, 9; photo Pink floyd88 a: p. 289; from Henry [Henrik] Rink, *Danish Greenland its People and its Products* (London, 1877): p. 79; photo United States Geological Survey: p. 270; photo U.S. Navy Arctic Submarine Laboratory, reproduced courtesy of U.S. Navy: p. 237; photo © 2007, Alan D. Wilson: p. 21.

INDEX